The World Bank is dedicated to the promotion of sustainable economic development and to poverty reduction throughout the developing world. It faces new challenges as capital shortages are replaced by large but volatile capital flows. The contributors to this volume argue that the Bank's greatest asset is its accumulated knowledge and experience of the development process, and propose that it organise itself around the concept of a 'Knowledge Bank'. They propose a shift in priority, away from lending with conditionality imposed on borrowing governments, towards assistance to governments in devising good development strategies. Part One examines the existing structure of the Bank and considers the World Bank as an institution. In Part Two the effectiveness of World Bank assistance is evaluated. This book provides essential reading for politicians, civil servants, workers in the non-official sector, and academics and students involved or interested in the development process.

Christopher L. Gilbert is Full Professor in the Department of Finance and Financial Sector Management at the Vrije Universiteit, Amsterdam. He is also a Visiting Professor of Economics at Queen Mary and Westfield College, University of London.

David Vines is Fellow in Economics at Balliol College, Oxford. He is the Director of the Research Programme on Global Economic Institutions of the UK Economic and Social Research Council. He is also an Adjunct Professor of Economics at the Australian National University.

The World Bank
Structure and Policies

The World Bank

Structure and Policies

edited by

Christopher L. Gilbert and David Vines

CAMBRIDGE UNIVERSITY PRESS

PUBLISHED BY THE PRESS SYNDICATE OF THE UNIVERSITY OF CAMBRIDGE
The Pitt Building, Trumpington Street, Cambridge, United Kingdom

CAMBRIDGE UNIVERSITY PRESS
The Edinburgh Building, Cambridge CB2 2RU, UK   http://www.cup.cam.ac.uk
40 West 20th Street, New York, NY 10011-4211, USA   http://www.cup.org
10 Stamford Road, Oakleigh, Melbourne 3166, Australia
Ruiz de Alarcón 13, 28014 Madrid, Spain

First published 2000

Transferred to digital printing 2001

Printed in Great Britain by Biddles Short Run Books, King's Lynn

Typeface: Times 9/11pt *System*: [3B2] KW

A catalogue record for this book is available from the British Library

ISBN 0 521 79095 6   hardback

Global Economic Institutions

This is the third of a series of books produced under the auspices of the Global Economic Institutions Research programme of the UK Economic and Social Research Council. The first two titles have been about Europe, East Asia and regionalism, and about the IMF and international financial crises. There will also be an overview book on global architecture and the reform of global economic institutions, and further volumes may follow.

Oxford Policy Institute

The Oxford Policy Institute (OPI) is an educational charity which brings international research and policy experience to bear on improving public sector policies and performance. It concentrates on areas of economic activity in which the state has a substantial role:

- the provision or financing of health services and education,
- the regulation of economic activity,
- the redistribution of income (including tax policy, social security and international aid).

OPI is concerned both with the role that governments should play at all levels – local, regional, national and international – and with improving the effectiveness and accountability of all kinds of organisations in the public sector.

Oxford Policy Institute
21 St Giles
Oxford OX1 3LA
Tel. +44 1865 250233
admin@opi.org.uk

Centre for Economic Policy Research

The Centre for Economic Policy Research is a network of over 500 Research Fellows and Affiliates, based primarily in European Universities. The Centre coordinates the research activities of its Fellows and Affiliates and communicates the results to the public and private sectors. CEPR is an entrepreneur, developing research initiatives with the producers, consumers and sponsors of research. Established in 1983, CEPR is a European economics research organisation with uniquely wide-ranging scope and activities.

CEPR is a registered educational charity. Institutional (core) finance for the Centre is provided by major grants from the Economic and Social Research Council, under which an ESRC Resource Centre operates within CEPR; the Esmée Fairburn Charitable Trust and the Bank of England. The Centre is also supported by the European Central Bank; the Bank for International Settlements; 22 national central banks and 45 companies. None of these organisations gives prior review to the Centre's publications, nor do they necessarily endorse the views expressed therein.

The Centre is pluralist and non-partisan, bringing economic research to bear on the analysis of medium- and long-run policy questions. CEPR research may include views on policy, but the Executive Committee of the Centre does not give prior review to its publications, and the Centre takes no institutional policy positions. The opinions expressed in this book are those of the authors and not those of the Centre for Economic Policy Research.

Centre for Economic Policy Research
90–98 Goswell Road
London, EC1V 7RR
UK
Tel: (44 20 7878) 2900   Fax: (44 20 7878) 2999
Email: cepr@cepr.org   Website: http://www.cepr.org

January 2000

Contents

Part Two: The Effectiveness of World Bank Assistance

Figures

Tables

Contributors

Christopher L. Gilbert is Research Professor of Finance in the Faculteit der Economische Wetenschappen en Econometrie, Vrije Universiteit, Amsterdam. He is Visiting Professor of Economics at Queen Mary and Westfield College, London, a Research Fellow of the Centre for Economic Policy Research in London and a Fellow of the Tinbergen Institute. He has worked with the World Bank over a number of years.

David Vines is Fellow in Economics at Balliol College, Oxford. He is the Director of the Research Programme on Global Economic Institutions of the UK Economic and Social Research Council, and is also an Adjunct Professor of Economics at the Australian National University. He is a Research Fellow of the Centre for Economic Policy Research in London.

Craig Burnside is an economist in the Development Economics Research Group of the World Bank. He was formerly Assistant Professor of Economics at Queen's University (Canada) and also at the University of Pittsburgh, and is a former National Fellow of the Hoover Institution.

Paul Collier is Director of the Development Research Group of the World Bank. He is on leave from the University of Oxford where he is Professor of Economics and Director of the Centre for the Study of African Economies. He is a Research Fellow of the Centre for Economic Policy Research in London.

Shantayanan Devarajan is Research Manager for Public Economics in the World Bank's Development Research Group. He is also the Editor of the *World Bank Research Observer*.

David Dollar is Head of the Macroeconomics and Growth team in the Development Research Group of the World Bank. He is the co-author (with Lant Pritchett) of the World Bank's 1999 report, 'Assessing Aid'.

Francisco Ferreira is currently on leave from the World Bank's Poverty Reduction and Economic Management group and is a Professor in the Departamento de Economia at Pontifíca Universidade Catòlica do Rio de Janeiro. He was formerly a researcher at STICERD at the London School of Economics.

Raul Hopkins is Lecturer in International Finance and Development Economics, Queen Mary and Westfield College, London. He is Research Associate of STICERD at the London School of Economics and a member of the Instituto de Estudios Peruanos, Lima.

Jonathan Isham is an Assistant Professor in the Department of Economics and the Program in Environmental Studies, Middlebury College. His current research focuses on the social foundations of micro-economic performance and economic growth.

Stephen Jones manages the Economic Policy Programme at Oxford Policy Management. He has worked on economic reform and aid policy in Africa, Asia and the former Soviet Union.

Ravi Kanbur is T. H. Lee Professor of World Affairs and Professor of Economics at Cornell University. From 1989 to 1997 he was on the staff of the World Bank, serving successively as Economic Advisor, Senior Economic Advisor, Resident Representative in Ghana, Chief Economist of the African Region of the World Bank and Principal Advisor to the Chief Economist of the World Bank. Prior to joining the World Bank, he was Professor of Economics and Director of the Development Economics Research Centre at the University of Warwick, UK, having previously taught at the Universities of Oxford, Cambridge, Essex and Princeton. Mr Kanbur is the Director of the World Bank's *World Development Report on Poverty and Development* (September 2000).

Daniel Kaufmann is a Senior Manager at the World Bank Institute, heading the Governance, Finance and Regulatory Reform Group. Previously, he was a Lead Economist in the Development Economics Group. During the early 1990s he was the first Chief of Mission of the Bank in Ukraine. He was a Visiting Scholar at Harvard University in the mid-1990s, where he provided policy advice on a range of economic and institutional issues to governments in emerging economies and in transition.

Louise Keely is a Research Fellow in Economics at New College, Oxford. She is a Research Associate at the Centre of Economic Performance at the London School of Econmics.

Andrew Powell is Chief Economist of the Central Bank of Argentina. Previously, he held academic positions at the University of Warwick and Queen Mary and Westfield College, University of London.

Amlan Roy is Vice-President in the Global Emerging Markets Strategy Group of Credit Suisse First Boston in London. Mr Roy is also a Research Associate of LSE's Financial Markets Group. He was previously a lecturer at Queen Mary and Westfield College, University of London.

Lyn Squire has just completed a three-year assignment to the World Bank as Director of Development Policy in the Office of the Bank's Chief Economist, Joseph Stiglitz. He is now Director of the Global Development Network, an emerging association of research and policy institutes whose goal is to generate and share knowledge related to development.

Joseph E. Stiglitz was, at the time of writing, serving an appointment to the World Bank as Senior Vice President for Development Economics and Chief Economist. Previously, he served as Chairman of the US Council of Economic Advisers from June 1995, and was a member of the Council and an active member of President Clinton's economic team from 1993. Mr Stiglitz is on leave from Stanford University, where he is a Professor of Economics. He was previously a professor of economics at Princeton, Yale and Oxford. In 1979, the American Economic Association awarded him its biennial John Bates Clark Award, given to the economist under forty who has made the most significant contribution to economics. His work has also been recognised through his election as a fellow to the National Academy of Sciences, the American Academy of Arts and Sciences and the Econometric Society.

Vinya Swaroop, a Principal Economist, holds a joint appointment with the Development Research Group and the Public Sector Group of the Poverty Reduction and Management Network at the World Bank.

Ngaire Woods is Fellow in Politics and International Relations at University College, Oxford, Senior Research Associate of Queen Elizabeth House and Chair of the Working Group on the International Financial Institutions of the Global Financial Governance Initiative at the International Development Research Centre, Ottawa.

Acknowledgements

In early 1994, the UK Economic and Social Research Council (the ESRC) launched the Global Economic Institutions (GEI) Research Programme, with the objective of funding academic research on the functioning of multilateral economic organisations and about the global institutional structures within which economic activity takes place. As part of this programme, a group of researchers has been considering the structure and policies of the World Bank. This book, which brings together that work, is edited by Christopher Gilbert (Vrije Universiteit, Amsterdam, Queen Mary and Westfield College, London and CEPR), who has led the research, and David Vines (Balliol College, Oxford, Australian National University and CEPR), who is Director of the GEI Programme.

The initial presentation of some of this work took place at the 1996 American Economic Association meetings in San Francisco, and a further discussion meeting was held in the World Bank in February 1997. This led to a workshop on 'The Future of the World Bank' at the Foreign and Commonwealth Office in London on 24 June 1997. The success of that meeting led us to embark on the project of assembling this book. All but two of the chapters have been commissioned, and written, specially for the book. The two editors visited the Bank on a number of occasions in the course of 1998 and 1999, to discuss the contents of the book with economists, and with operational staff, within the Bank. As their work was beginning, they were asked by Jan Gunning (Oxford University and Vrije Universiteit, Amsterdam) and Paul Collier (Oxford University, now at the Bank) to write a chapter on the future of the Bank for a 'Special Feature' of the *Economic Journal* on the Changing Roles of the World's International Financial Institutions that appeared just as this book went to press; a greatly revised version of that paper has become chapter 2 of this book.

We are glad to acknowledge the funding by the ESRC of work in this important area. We would also like to express our thanks to Barry Eichengreen for his invitation to present the initial work in San Francisco and to Huw Evans, then UK Executive Director at the IMF and the World Bank, for organising the meeting at the Bank in February 1997, We are much indebted to Jim Rollo, then Chief Economist at the UK Foreign and Commonwealth Office, for hosting the June 1997 meeting, and to the Centre for Economic Policy Research and the Oxford Policy Institute (and in particular Andrew Graham, of Balliol College, Oxford) for their assistance in organising it. The editors appreciate, too, the courteousness with which many Bank staff have dealt with our requests for information and assistance, and the interest which large numbers of Bank staff have shown in this work as it edged towards completion.

At Cambridge University Press, Ashwin Rattan and Chris Harrison worked hard to expedite our plans, and arranged for three referees to comment on initial drafts of a set of chapters. We are grateful for those comments, since they helped us to considerably improve the general shape of the book. The production of the book would also not have been possible without the continuing assistance and unflagging enthusiasm of the Publications staff at CEPR. Sue Chapman, Lorna Guthrie and Lisa Moss have all worked hard to make this book happen, and to them we express our sincere thanks.

Last, but not least, we are grateful for the interest which Joe Stiglitz has shown in our project from the beginning, and for his assistance in helping us to secure some of the chapters for the book. In the week that the final chapters of the book are being sent to press, we have learned of Joe's pending departure from the Bank. The loss, both to the Bank and to the wider international community, will be considerable. As Chief Economist, Joe was always keen to provoke debate, even on issues which others would have preferred to regard as settled. His pivotal position in Washington stamped these criticisms with an authority which seldom derives from an academic position. There may be fewer ruffled feathers in the future, but we must hope that the spirit of openness and debate that Joe encouraged within the Bank will outlast his departure.

The editors and publishers thank the following for permission to reproduce copyright material.
World Development, for figure 6.1, from F. Bourguignon, J. de Melo and
  C. Morrisson 'Poverty and Income Distribution during Adjustment: Issues and Evidence from the OECD Project' (1991).

Oxford University Press, for figure 11.1, from R. W. Anderson, C. L. Gilbert and A. Powell, 'Securitizing Development Finance: The Role of Partial Guarantees and Commodity Contingency', in T. Priovolos and R. C. Duncan (eds.), *Commodity Risk Management and Finance* (1991).

The World Bank, for figure 12.1, from P. Collier and D. Dollar, 'Aid Allocation and Poverty Reduction', *Policy Research Working Paper*, **2041** (1999); for data in tables 6.2–6.5, 6.7, 6A.1–6A.6, from C. Jayarajah and W. Branson, *Structural and Sectoral Adjustment: World Bank Experience, 1980–92* (1995) and C. Jayarajah, W. Branson and B. Sen, *Social Dimensions of Adjustment: World Bank Experience, 1980–93* (1996), in table 6.6, from D. Dollar and J. Svensson, 'What Explains the Success or Failure of Structural Adjustment Programs?', *World Bank PRWP*, **1938** (1998), in table 6.7, from *WDR 1997* and *World Development Indicators* (1998) and in table 6.8, from M.L. Ferreira, 'Poverty and Inequality during Structural Adjustment in Rural Tanzania', *World Bank PRWP Working Paper*, **1641** (1996); for data in tables 9.7 and 9.8, from D. Kaufmann and Y. Wang, 'Macroeconomic Policies and Project Performance in the Social Sectors', *World Development*, **23** (1995) and in tables 9.10–9.13, from J. Isham, D. Kaufmann and L.H. Pritchett, 'Civil Liberties, Democracy, and the Performance of Government Projects', *World Bank Economic Review*, **11** (1997).

STICERD/DARP, for data in table 6.9, from F.H.G. Ferreira and J.A. Litchfield, 'Growing Apart: Inequality and Poverty Trends in Brazil in the 1980s', *STICERD/DARP Discussion Paper*, **23** (1996).

Quarterly Journal of Economics, for data in table 9.1–9.5 and 9.9, from J. Isham and D. Kaufmann, 'The Forgotten Rationale for Policy Reform: The Productivity of Investment Projects' (2000).

Review of Income and Wealth, for data in table 6.1, from R. Summers and A. Heston, 'A New set of International Comparisons of Real Product and Price Levels: Estimates for 130 Countries, 1950–1985' (1988).

Brett House, for data in figure 2.1.

Christopher Gilbert
David Vines
Amsterdam and Oxford
January 2000

Introduction

JOSEPH E. STIGLITZ

The 1990s have seen radical changes in thinking about development policy, as compared with the ideas inherited from the 1980s. At the end of that decade an approach to development emerged which became known as the 'Washington consensus': its aim was, roughly, 'to promote sound money and free trade, to free up domestic markets, and to encourage policy-makers to go home early and stop interfering with markets'. The experience in the 1990s of both the Asian miracle and the Asian crisis has shown without a doubt the inadequacy of this approach as a guide to development policy.

During the 'Asian miracle' period, the governments of Asian high-growth economies had clear priorities and did not hesitate to intervene (through subsidies, trade restrictions, administrative guidance, public enterprises, or credit allocation) (see World Bank, 1993; Stiglitz, 1996). More than this, the successful high-growth economies systematically subsidised investment; '[t]he...realistic presumption is that a range of market failures kept investment at a level below what would have been socially sub-optimal' (Rodrik, 1999: 55). And it is now widely agreed that the crisis of 1997–8 was largely created by the liberalisation of credit markets in the absence of adequate regulatory frameworks (Furman and Stiglitz, 1998; Stiglitz, 1999b). Both of these events – Asia's miracle boom and its unprecedented crash – have brought home the inadequacy of the simplistic Washington consensus as a framework for thinking about development policy.

Thinking on the Bank's role in delivering good development policy advice and assistance in this new 'post-Washington-consensus' climate is still in its infancy. The rejection of the 'Washington consensus' entails not only a questioning of the policies (and underlying assumptions) required for successful growth, but also a re-examination of development objectives, strategies, and processes (Stiglitz, 1998, 1999a).

The earlier theories saw development as a result of the solution to certain technical problems – improved resource allocation and increased resources. To be sure, at different times, emphases concerning what was the principal source of inefficiencies and what was the principal resource gap changed. In the era of development planning, attention focused on market failures: how, for instance, in the absence of a complete set of markets, government planning was needed to ensure the efficient allocation of resources, and how imperfections in capital markets prevented the efficient flow of capital from developed countries to less developed countries (hence the rationale for international lending institutions such as the World Bank). In the Reaganite–Thatcher years, government (including private rent-seeking activities directed at obtaining the largesse of government) was the chief culprit, with the obvious prescription – get the government out of the way. In the years following the oil price shocks, with the resulting macroeconomic instability (including huge variations in interest rates and in the developed countries which induced macro-instability in developing countries, especially those with heavy short-term indebtedness) it was this instability that was the core problem that had to be addressed.

The new development paradigm sees development as a more fundamental transformation, and one which will not necessarily be achieved simply by the solution to these technical problems. A mine in a remote corner of a country might lead to increased GDP, but is likely to have little impact on the development transformation. More generally, a country that has isolated pockets of, say, heavy industry, but whose rural sector remains largely untouched, is not undergoing a development transformation. As I put it in my Prebisch lecture (Stiglitz, 1998): 'A dual economy is not a developed economy.' Development entails changes in ways of thinking, in economic and social organisation, entailing, among other things, an acceptance of change.

The new paradigm puts greater emphasis on a variety of aspects of social and political organisation – it was, for instance, the deterioration of social and informational capital that in part accounted for the dismal performance of so many economies in transition in the past decade. Thus, the fact that the development transformation entails massive changes in society does not imply that traditional culture should be rejected outright; rather, successful development is evolution, building on existing institutions. Similarly, since changes in ways of thinking cannot be imposed, successful development cannot be based on conditionality. And successful development requires that the changes withstand the vicissitudes of the political process, that they be politically sustainable. Accordingly, greater emphasis is being placed on ownership and participation in the decision-making processes, and the development of capacities within countries to create and direct their own development programmes. And greater emphasis is being placed on the necessity of those programmes being (and being viewed as) equitable.

Paralleling these changes in the nature and processes of development are changes in perspectives on development strategies. It has come to be recognised that successful, isolated projects, as valuable as each might be to those who benefited directly from them, are simply not up to the scale of the problem facing the developing world, even if goals are modest, such as preventing the increase in absolute poverty; they are surely not up to the Development Assistance Committee goals, which include halving the number of those in extreme poverty by the year 2015. One has to go beyond projects towards policies. But good policies, as necessary as they are to successful development, also do not suffice. There need to be good institutions — such as judicial institutions which fairly and efficiently arbitrate disputes; good regulatory institutions, which ensure that markets, where possible, are competitive; and good financial institutions, which mobilise savings and allocate them efficiently. Where there is a natural monopoly, that monopoly power needs not to be abused, and so forth. While it is easy to identify the outcomes of good institutions, and to cite examples of institutions which work well and those which do not, it remains far from clear how to go about creating these 'good' institutions. As a result, the international community has increasingly resorted to exhortations for 'good governance in the public and private sector' but without correspondingly clear prescriptions of how to achieve that goal in general. In one area, in particular, however, there has been increasing consensus: corruption, and its adverse effects on growth and investment. Earlier, discussions of corruption would have been off limits for the World Bank, which was generally proscribed from engaging in political matters not directly related to development. But the new thinking argues that there is no bright line of demarcation: corruption, though a matter of politics, is at the heart of underdevelopment. But once that line has been broached, the limits of what should be in the Bank's purview are no longer clear. Openness, transparency, and democratic processes provide an important check on the operation of special interest groups and the extent of corruption.

Increasingly, the changes in the ways of approaching development, including the new relationships between the international financial institutions and the developing countries, have come to be seen from a broader historical perspective: 50 years after the supposed beginning of the end of colonialism, it appears that many vestiges of the colonial mentality have remained. For their part, nations in the developing world have had to struggle with overcoming their colonial heritage; it is not necessarily the case that everything that the colonists left behind – including their economic theories – was flawed; and it is not necessarily the case that the economic theories of those that supported the struggle for independence were sound. This was brought home forcefully by the collapse of the Soviet empire, which made those countries which had not yet become disillusioned by the failure of socialist development strategies re-examine their approach to development. Conditionality – including the manner in which conditions have often been imposed – has come to be seen by many, especially within the developing world, as part of the new economic colonialism which has succeeded the old.

With democratic institutions in an increasingly large number of developing countries, there is an increasingly strong imperative that the international financial institutions find ways to support democratic processes. An essential aspect of that is *democratic pluralism*. This has two central features. When the evidence concerning the consequences of a policy or the design of an institution is ambiguous, and there are alternative views, the country should be presented both with the alternative perspectives and with a realistic assessment of the risks and uncertainties. And when different policies impact different groups differently, as they almost inevitably do, the choice of the appropriate policy should be left entirely in the hands of the country and its political system. Outside advisers can clearly take strong positions against Pareto-inferior policies but, even then, a word of caution is necessary. The reform process is a dynamic one, occurring over time. What appears to be a Pareto-dominant policy in a static context may not be in a more dynamic one, and conversely. The country (its political leaders, its civil society) is likely to be in a better position to judge – and affect – those dynamic consequences, which often entail the formation of new political coalitions and/or the dissolution of old ones. This approach of democratic pluralism stands in marked contrast to the policy which has characterised the institutions during the first half-century of their existence. When the system worked 'well', the International Monetary Fund (IMF) and the World Bank would meet behind closed doors to decide on a unified view concerning what conditions to impose on the country, or what policies to recommend to the country. Divergences in views were frowned upon; it was suggested that such disagreements were confusing to the country. Views about the appropriateness of the policies were presented with a false sense of confidence in their efficacy. Alternatives, with different risk and distribution consequences, were not presented to the country for its own choice. To be sure, this characterisation is an exaggeration, as the actual programme was typically negotiated, but it was a bargaining process in which the

power was one-sided, especially when a desperately poor country franti-
cally needed funds. The only saving grace was that the conditions were
typically only imperfectly enforced.

In the approach of democratic pluralism, not only is it acceptable that
different courses of actions be offered up ('recommended') by different
international agencies, but also it should be expected that this would
frequently be the case, since the different international agencies have
different objectives and different governance structures. Indeed, if they
had the same objectives and the same governance structures, it would be
hard to justify the existence of separate agencies, except as competitive
producers of similar products. But then again, it is desirable that alternative courses of action be proffered, partly for reasons of *competitive
pluralism*, in the terms that the Asian Development Bank (ADB) has
used. To be sure, those in any market have a desire to reduce competition, to reduce the information base on which one can judge their com-
petency and effectiveness. But these attempts to suppress competition
should be recognised for what they are: self-serving attempts by the
agency to reduce the effectiveness of accountability. This is especially
the case for the IMF, whose governance structure includes a large role
for Central Bank governors, who typically are neither representative of
the population as a whole nor, increasingly, directly accountable to the
electorate. Indeed, it is ironic that in an era in which we increasingly
speak of democratic accountability, one of the major international organisations, with a tremendous potential effect on the global economy, has
been striving hard to reduce its accountability. In effect, it has been
waging a campaign to reduce its own direct accountability to democratic
processes. These are matters of controversy, but it is a controversy which,
unfortunately, has been suppressed for too long.

The differences in the institutional mandates of the World Bank, the
IMF, and the UNDP and the other international organisations are as
apparent as the differences in their governance. For instance, the IMF is
charged with maintaining the stability of the global financial system: in
practice, in the past, it has seemed to have had a strong concern to ensure
the creditors got repaid, resisting the use of bankruptcy and bankruptcy-
like proceedings even in private-to-private credit flows, as in the 1997–8
East Asia crisis. (Though this is not formally part of its mandate, the
assumption of this responsibility is not surprising, given its governance
structure). By contrast, the World Bank's mandate is to enhance developing country growth and reduce poverty. Policies that are well designed
for one objective (and that minimise risks to that objective) may be
poorly designed for another. Indeed, one of the long-standing criticisms
of IMF programmes is that in many countries they have led to increased

poverty – higher levels of poverty than would have occurred in pro-grammes with alternative designs.

Differences in mandates in turn lead to differences in views of the world, differences in models. This can be seen once we recognise the importance of uncertainty: as Bayesians, the probability judgements depend on loss functions, and institutions with different mandates will have different loss functions. Different models – views of the world – may also arise for other reasons, just as different firms in an economy may have different business strategies, based on different judgements concern-ing the evolution of markets. It is in this arena that competitive pluralism again takes on central importance. There is, for instance, a widespread view that the particular set of models that the IMF uses have been inappropriate in many situations (in the crisis in East Asia, for example, it is clear that their forecasts concerning the countries affected by the crisis were badly misguided). Within the World Bank, an alternative perspective, which turned out to be far more accurate, was stressed. But, regrettably given the official stance that such disagreements be not aired in public, there was no public debate about the appropriateness of the alternative perspectives. Even after the fact, debate within the institu-tions has been relatively muted though, fortunately, within academia, such a debate is now emerging.

One critical component of new thinking on development is the World Bank's new 'Comprehensive Development Framework', or CDF (see Wolfensohn, 1999; World Bank, 1999). The CDF approach to develop-ment attempts to be comprehensive in two respects: across different aspects of development, and across participants in the development pro-cess. The Bank clearly cannot do everything, and coordination among donors can ensure complementarity in the development effort within a coherent overall approach. Comprehensiveness across participants is envisaged: if government, the private sector and 'civil society' all become participants in the process, then identification with, and ownership of, the development process will be the outcome.

Some have argued that the Bank faces two big challenges in imple-menting the CDF. The first is how to coordinate, and prioritise, within the Bank, the Bank's own contributions to this comprehensive 'big-push' approach to development assistance. The second is how actually to coor-dinate the many other stakeholders who are to be involved in this approach to development policy. Who will be in charge when there are disagreements of analysis between the stakeholders, and – what is worse – straight conflicts of interest between them? But the very formulation of the challenges in this way reveals how hard it will be to change thinking about the aid process. The developing country should be in charge of its own aid strategy, and it should play the pivotal role in coordination and dispute resolution. To be sure, each donor has its own accountability: public agencies have fiduciary responsibilities, and must decide whether the funds allocated to a country – given that country's development programme – satisfy its own fiduciary standards.

This book brings together some of the latest thinking about these vital contemporary debates. It comes at an opportune moment: because of these debates the future of the World Bank is under more detailed scrutiny than at any time in the recent past. The authors have assembled an international group of front-rank writers to help carry these debates forward. A number of the chapters in the book are by members of the staff of the World Bank itself. These authors set out their vision for the role of the institution – its structure and its policies – and the ways in which they see these evolving. Their contributions take forward the task of putting Bank thinking about its reorientation as an institution into the public domain. In addition, the editors have commissioned a number of studies which provide an 'outside view' of the Bank.

Chapter 1 provides an introduction to the issues which are discussed in the body of the book. Part One discusses the Bank as an institution. Historically, the Bank has been a lending institution – as Keynes said, 'the Bank is a Fund'. But the editors, together with Andrew Powell, insist in chapter 2 that the Bank should instead see its core mission as that of a development agency. Chapter 3, by Kanbur and Vines, reviews the place of poverty alleviation within such a mission (something which we see currently as assuming a higher profile than recently). Many have argued that the Bank's worth as a development institution arises from its unparalleled knowledge of and experience in development, and its ability to deliver advice and assistance based on this knowledge – the Bank as a 'Knowledge Bank'. Lyn Squire, who was Director of the World Bank's Research Department from 1993 to 1997, provides a description and advocacy, of this aspect of the Bank's work in chapter 4. An organisation which does this kind of work will be intrinsically difficult to govern and to manage; Ngaire Woods in chapter 5 provides a thoughtful discussion of the issues which these difficulties raise.

Part Two is about the Bank's development assistance policies. A major debate is under way about the effectiveness of multilateral aid in stimulating growth and in assisting in poverty reduction (see World Bank, 1998). Some in this controversy have argued that policy conditionality is seldom effective, few now believe that it achieves all that its proponents once sought from it. This part of the book attempts to provide a balanced assessment of the debate on this issue. In chapter 6, Ferreira and Keely look at the early emergence, in the 1980s, of concerns about the effectiveness of structural adjustment lending. Chapter 8, by Burnside and Dollar, reviews the relationship between aid and growth, arguing that, on average, aid does not influence growth, and that there is a positive influence of this kind only in the presence of good policies. Chapter 7, by Devarajan and Swaroop, presents one reason why this is so: aid is fungible. Isham and Kaufmann in chapter 9 present further supporting evidence on how policies and institutions affect project performance, and Jones in chapter 10 examines the success of Sector Adjustment Programmes (SAPs) as one method of improving the effectiveness of development assistance. Two further chapters, chapter 11 by Hopkins, Powell, Roy and Gilbert, and chapter 12 by Collier, stand back from the issues raised by the earlier chapters, and attempt to present some conclusions. They advocate a radical reorientation of international aid policy away from a 'conditionality' that is detailed and micro-interventionist – and which saps the ability of borrowing countries to take ownership of their own development strategy – towards a conditionality based only on good policies and which encourages cooperative engagement between lender and borrower. This is a debate in which development economists are now deeply engaged: the present book will carry forward that debate to a wider audience.

The issues raised in this book will be central to the Bank's evolution in the first decade of the twenty-first century. They relate to questions which are being asked by the governments and taxpayers who currently fund the Bank's activities, and by the Bank's current and potential clients in the developing world. By taking a view from outside the Bank, and away from Washington but, at the same time, by drawing extensively on experience within the Bank, the book aims to make an important contribution to these discussions.

REFERENCES
Furman, J. and J. Stiglitz (1998). 'Economic Crises: Evidence and Insights from East Asia', *Brookings Papers on Economic Activity (Macroeconomics)*, **2**, Washington, DC: Brookings Institution
Rodrik, D. (1999). *The New Global Economy and Developing Countries: Making Openness Work*, Washington, DC: Overseas Development Council
Stiglitz, J. (1996). 'Some Lessons from the East Asian Miracle,' *World Bank Research Observer*, **11(2)**:151–77
  (1998). 'Towards a New Paradigm for Development Strategies, Policies and Processes', Prebisch Lecture, UNCTAD, Geneva, 19 October
  (1999a). 'Participation and Development: Perspectives from the Comprehensive Development Paradigm', paper presented at the

International Conference on Democracy, Market Economy, and Development, Seoul, 27 February

(1999b). 'Must Financial Crises be this Frequent and this Painful?', chapter 12 in P.-R. Agénor, M. Miller, D. Vines and A. Weber (eds.), *The Asian Financial Crises: Causes, Contagion and Consequences*, Cambridge: Cambridge University Press

Wolfensohn, J. (1999). 'A proposal for a comprehensive development framework – a discussion draft', available at < http://www.worldbank.org/cdf/cdf-text.htm >

World Bank (1993). *The Asian Miracle*, Washington, DC: World Bank

(1998). *Assessing Aid: What Works, What Doesn't and Why?*, Oxford: Oxford University Press

(1999). 'Comprehensive development framework: questions and answers' < http://www.worldbank.org/cdf/cdf-faq.htm >

1 The World Bank: an overview of some major issues[1]

CHRISTOPHER L. GILBERT AND DAVID VINES

The World Bank (henceforth 'the Bank') is an institution whose objective is the promotion, world-wide, of sustainable economic development and poverty reduction.[2] It pursues these objectives through lending, through the production of research and economic analysis and through the provision of policy advice and technical assistance.[3] The purpose of this book is to critically examine the rationale of this institution and to describe the policies which it currently carries out, in order to examine whether its objectives are best served by its current mix of activities.

Our intention is not just to look backwards, but to examine future options and to advocate choices among them. It has often been said that the Bank lacks a coherent vision, and that, as a consequence, it suffers from a dysfunctional proliferation of objectives. We agree. In response to this, we argue that the Bank should be organised around a vision of itself as a 'Knowledge Bank'. To some extent, this has already happened. But it has only partly happened; making it really happen would radically transform the Bank's priorities, and its activities in the field, way beyond any changes currently in train. In particular, far less manpower would be devoted to analysing loan proposals and outcomes, and far more would be devoted to giving advice about development strategies and to providing help with their implementation.

The Bank recently celebrated its fiftieth anniversary. It has always been controversial. Throughout its life it has been seen variously as: promoting statist and socialist regimes and as imposing free market ideologies; as having far too little money to lend and as being profligate with taxpayers' funds; as being an arm of the US Treasury; and as being an institution which can protect aid allocations from donor government agendas.[4] Those on the left (see Wade, 1990) have viewed it as an imperialist institution for imposing one view of the development process, and have also criticised its record on the environment, poverty reduction and other social issues. Those on the right (see Walters, 1994) have also argued that it is a hangover from the interventionist early post-war era, that what it does is overly political (although what is identified as worrying is different from what vexes those on the left), that it interferes with the operation of effective market-led economic development and that it should be shut down.

This volume does not concern itself with these polemics. To that extent, it is an 'insider's' book, one which adopts a deliberately sympathetic view of the Bank's purposes and activities.

Our vision of a future for the Bank is presented in detail in chapter 2 in this volume (p. 39).[5] In order to underpin the argument in that chapter, we have commissioned a number of papers, from both authors inside the Bank and authors outside it (we have in fact helped to write two of those papers ourselves). Not all of the authors of those papers will agree with the proposals for the future of the Bank which we set out in chapter 2. But all of them support – we believe – our view that the issues surrounding these proposals deserve to be aired.

The purpose of the present chapter is to provide an introduction to the issues which are discussed in the body of the book, without here reaching any particular conclusions on them. First there are two introductory sections. In section 1 we explain the structure of the Bank. Section 2 briefly provides some history: of the Bank's activities and of ideas within the Bank. Much of the material in these two sections will be familiar to many of our readers. We set it out in order to emphasise some key features of structure and history which are relevant to our concerns. These sections are also designed to provide background for those who know less about the Bank than more specialist readers. Sections 3 and 4 review the contents of the two substantive parts of the book; in doing so we describe the place of these two parts of the book in the overall argument which we as editors present in chapter 2. Section 5 sets out our idea of what a 'Knowledge Bank' is and also describes our claim that the Bank is already to some extent such an organisation, but in section 6 we move to the Bank's response to global crises and its relationship with the IMF. Section 7 probides a succinct summary of all the subsequent chapters. Section 8 concludes, and also provides a bridge to our core argument in chapter 2, namely that the Bank has further to go if it really is to become a 'Knowledge Bank'.

1 The institutional organisation of the Bank

The Bank is a large organisation employing over nearly 10,000 people. It comprises an amalgam of four organisations – the 'World Bank Group' – operating under a common board but with different functions.

(1) The International Bank for Reconstruction and Development (IBRD) was founded in 1946. It is the original and central member of the World Bank Group. Its main activity is to borrow funds and lend these on to qualifying member governments or to public sector institutions for agreed projects. The loans are medium-term (normally up to 10 years but sometimes as long as 20 years) and are at a small mark-up over the Bank's AAA borrowing rate. The size of this mark-up is intended to ensure profitability of IBRD lending. The resulting rates are nevertheless generally substantially lower than would be obtainable from the private sector, although the loans often involve extensive conditions and monitoring. IBRD lending is concentrated in Latin America, the Middle East and North Africa, and in East Asia. Providing IBRD loans remains the Bank's main activity.

(2) The second component of the Bank is an aid agency the International Development Agency (IDA) — which was established in 1960. IDA activities are confined to a group of 60 'IDA countries' – mainly in Africa and South Asia – which have a low GDP per head.[6] IDA credits are very long-term (up to 40 years) and are at heavily concessional interest rates – i.e. they contain a large grant element. IDA staff are integrated with those of the IBRD, so that the same staff are involved in both non-aid and aid work, but the accounts of the two institutions are kept separate. IDA lending is financed from the profits of the entire World Bank group and by grants from member governments.

(3) The third component of the Bank is the *International Finance Corporation* (IFC), founded in 1956.[7] This lends to private sector institutions without any governmental guarantee, and also takes equity shares in private sector enterprises.

(4) The *Multinational Investment Guarantee Agency* (MIGA), created in 1988, is the fourth organisation in the World Bank Group.[8] MIGA guarantees private sector investors against expropriation and repatriation risks in developing countries. It is relatively small, but its capital base was doubled to coincide with its tenth anniversary. Its creation followed the debt crisis of the 1980s, which gave prominence to sovereign risk problems as causes of the high interest rates that

many developing countries were obliged to pay in order to borrow, and of the lack of access of countries to markets for new loans even at high rates.[9]

Mason and Asher (1973: 980) describe the distinction between the IBRD and IDA as 'an elaborate fiction' and, as already noted, the staff of the two organisations are almost entirely coextensive. The two organisations have slightly different voting structures, but since IDA membership is confined to IBRD member governments, the effects are minimal. Nevertheless it would be wrong to claim that the distinction between these two parts of the World Bank group is little more than an accounting device. This is because both the criteria for the disbursement of funds and the source of the loaned funds are quite different. The Bank, as IDA, provides both development assistance and development aid while, as the IBRD, it provides assistance and enhanced access to capital.

The limited degree of separation between the IBRD and IDA contrasts with the IBRD's relationship with the IFC. The latter two organisations differ both in the way that they borrow and the way that they lend. The IBRD borrows against member government guarantees and either lends or guarantees loans to member governments or to public sector institutions against governmental guarantees. By contrast, the IFC borrows in its own name without member government guarantee and lends to private sector institutions, again without any governmental guarantee. The IFC's articles emphasise its separate identity from the IBRD but also indicate that the IFC should be able to draw on IBRD staff and facilities for administrative support. In practice, this has happened relatively little. The IFC is therefore a separate organisation working together with the IBRD under the umbrella of the World Bank Group, while the IDA and the IBRD are essentially the same organisation operating with different lending regimes and subject to different capital structures.

The general perception of the World Bank Group is of the IBRD–IDA complex, and the focus of the present book is on that complex. This is not to deny that there are important concerns about the future directions of the IFC. A frequently heard complaint about the IFC is that its development focus can be drowned out by its merchant banking objectives. In order to circumvent this problem, Gilbert et al. (1996) proposed that the IFC should also share a common staff with the IBRD–IDA. However, they further proposed that the capital structure of the IFC should be further differentiated from the capital structures of the IBRD and IDA through partial privatisation of the IFC. However these issues are largely independent from our concerns in this book, and as a result we will have very little to say about that organisation.

2 The history of the Bank

It was unclear in 1946 whether the Bank's role would be temporary, covering the post-war reconstruction period, or be more permanent; whether it would lend funds directly or would guarantee funds lent by private sector institutions; and whether or not it would be able to borrow in its own name (as it does) or issue its own partially backed SDR-like 'notes' (as it does not). Some, but not all, of these questions have recurred during the initial 50 years of the Bank's life and, indeed, remain with us. But other questions, not anticipated in 1946, have also come to the fore. The result has been that the Bank has adapted its role both to changing economic challenges and to changing perceptions of the contribution that a multilateral public sector institution can make to the development process.[10]

Harry Dexter White, the US Treasury official who, in the 1940s, had written the initial draft of the plan for a world bank,[11] saw its primary objective as to 'provide or otherwise stimulate long-term, low-interest-rate loans for reconstruction and for the development of capital-poor areas' (Oliver, 1975). However, post-war reconstruction was the primary objective and 'development' may have been an afterthought.[12] At that time, the Bank was just the IBRD.

Reconstruction dominated the initial decade and a half of the Bank's life. The political priorities in this period were set by the intensification of the Cold War and the need to bolster the democratic world against the Soviet threat. Economically, the 'dollar shortage' (Kindleberger, 1950) implied that, at least until the 1950s, almost all countries outside North America remained capital-poor. Much of Africa, Asia and the Caribbean remained under colonial administration.

The world was a different place by the early 1960s. The boundaries of the Soviet empire had been largely settled by the Berlin airlift in 1949 and the western-led defence of South Korea in 1951–2. By the late 1950s, prosperity had returned to western Europe making the Bank's reconstruction role redundant. Moreover, convertibility of the European currencies, attained in the mid-1950s, allowed relative free flows of capital throughout what was now starting to be called the 'developed world'. But decolonisation, particularly in Africa, created in the 'underdeveloped countries' a new group of client states with an agenda of rapid development. It was natural, therefore, that the IBRD should shift its priorities from reconstruction to development and from Europe to the developing world. This evolution forms the main element in the story told by Mason and Asher (1973) in the volume written to commemorate the first 25 years of the Bank.

The 1960s also saw the start of a trend which is apparent to any visitor to Washington – the growth of the Bank. In 1961 the Bank had 400 employees, but by 1971 this became 1,300. By the end of FY (i.e. end-June) 1998, full time staff numbers had grown to 9,262. The IMF and the Bank are seen as the two major pillars of Bretton Woods, but the Bank is many times larger in terms of both budget and payroll: the IMF reported a staff number of 2,181 for December 1997, less than a quarter of the Bank's complement. Similarly, the World Bank's budget for 1997–8 amounted to $1.35 billion against the IMF's administrative budget of $0.52 billion.[13]

Development lending in the first 25 years of the Bank's existence was concentrated on projects with clearly quantifiable pecuniary returns (Gavin and Rodrik, 1995: 333), even if these were not always directly appropriable. The main rationales for development lending were those advanced by White: the investments required typically had a longer horizon than could easily be financed on the private market, and private funds, if available, would be offered only at interest rates which would make these investments unattractive. In this period, therefore, the primary justification for World Bank activity can be characterised as overcoming perceived capital market deficiencies. This was to change significantly during the 1970s.

A major impetus for the 1960 creation of IDA was the difficulty of finding projects in many of the poorer (now renamed) 'developing' countries which would generate rates of return compatible with repayment of IBRD loans. With the creation of IDA, the Bank effectively repositioned itself, to some extent reluctantly,[14] as a development agency rather than a public sector bank lending for development-related projects. Lending, even through the IBRD, was now justified not only, and often not mainly, in terms of capital market deficiencies, but rather in terms of the character and direction of the development process.

This shift in emphasis became consolidated under the influential McNamara presidency (1968–81) which also saw a major growth in development research. Left-wing critics of the development orthodoxy argued at the time that growth tended to exacerbate often already wide income differentials in the developing countries and might even result in an absolute deterioration of the standard of living of the poorest groups (see, e.g., Hayter, 1971). These criticisms were felt within the Bank itself and were instrumental in forcing a redefinition of Bank priorities during the 1970s (Morawetz, 1977; Mosley, Harrigan and Toye, 1995; see also chapter 3 in this volume). As a consequence, Bank lending began to emphasise rural development, urban infrastructure, education and health (Ayres, 1983), areas in which lending previously had been at a relatively low level; and in addition, action against poverty.

The 1980s were dominated by the issues of debt and adjustment. Private sector capital flows to developing countries all but disappeared, and net flows reversed back to the developed world. The immediate problems for the multilateral agencies were those of sustaining the payments positions of the indebted countries in such a way as to prevent outright default. This involved a combination of debt rescheduling in conjunction with new loans, the primary purpose of which was to pay the interest on old debt. Developmental objectives became secondary. From the World Bank's perspective, this involved a move away from project to programme lending. But often the agreed reform programmes were rationalisations rather than justifications for the lending.

By the end of the decade, the debt problem was approaching resolution, not so much because the indebted countries had paid off their debt, but because the developed country creditor banks had engineered sufficient improvement in their balance sheets to be able to mark their developing country debt to market. The Brady Plan, foreshadowed in a March 1989 speech of US Treasury Secretary Nicholas Brady, organised official support for the replacement of debt to commercial lenders by lower-value bonds which governments would undertake to honour.[15] This substitution of non-performing loans with what became known as Brady bonds enabled the banks to recommence lending to the developing world.

Subsequently the 1990s became the decade of the emerging markets, and later of submerging markets. The problem for many middle-income countries became the management of volatile inward capital flows rather than the absence of adequate levels of foreign investment. The consequence for the Bank was that, at least until the start of the 1997 Asian crisis, Bank lending *per se* became much less important than it had been a decade earlier except, of course, for the IDA countries. The implication of this was that supposed capital market imperfections no longer provided an adequate justification for the Bank's IBRD functions. If there were no other justification, it began to be said, should the Bank be privatised, or even abolished?

The dominant philosophy of the multilateral donors during the 1990s has often been referred to as the 'Washington consensus' (Williamson, 1990). However, perhaps as with every supposed consensus, there was less agreement as to what the 'Washington consensus' actually was. The term is generally interpreted as referring to the neo-liberal belief that the combination of democratic government, free markets, a dominant private sector and openness to trade is the recipe for prosperity and growth.

However, John Williamson, who introduced the term, actually did so as a way of signifying what he took to be a shift in beliefs *away* from this position, and towards a recognition that markets will not deliver everything, and that governments must conjoin their commitments to free and open markets with a recognition of their responsibilities in the areas of health, education and poverty reduction (Williamson, 1999). Nevertheless, the neo-liberal agenda was in fact dominant in Bank thinking at least up until 1995.[16] Ravi Kanbur and David Vines discuss the reasons for this in chapter 3.

There was a change to this at the start of James Wolfensohn's first term as Bank President in 1995. Although it is still to early to deliver a final judgement, Wolfensohn does appear to have radically shifted both Bank rhetoric and Bank action towards the neglected half of the 'Washington consensus': poverty reduction now has at least equal status in Bank financing decisions with the promotion of growth; serious consideration is given to environmental concerns; ownership has been embraced (see p 77); and a serious dialogue with the NGOs has begun.[17]

It is also recognised that market liberalisation by itself is insufficient – it must go hand in hand with, and perhaps even be preceded by, capacity building, market regulation and often more effective law enforcement, and it is no longer accepted as axiomatic that all countries are best advised to open their doors to all inward capital flows all the time. These are issues discussed by Joseph Stiglitz in his preface to this book. While not denying the basic liberal stance of the 'Washington consensus', this 'post-Washington consensus' view moves the emphasis to those parts of the original position which were previously relegated to the footnotes.

3 The World Bank's structure: the Bank as an institution

3.1 The Bank as a financial institution

The Bank is first and foremost what its name says: it is a Bank, a financial intermediary. Accordingly it is important for us to describe and analyse the Bank's financial structure and lending its operations. This we do in chapter 2.

But the discussion there is short and we actually have relatively little to say about this obviously key aspect of the Bank. This may seem surprising. There are two reasons that we proceeded this way. One is that there is a very good discussion of this issue in the World Bank *History* (KLW, 1997a, chapters 14–16). But a second, much more important, reason is as follows. As already noted, the original purpose of the Bank was to over-come capital market imperfections: to 'provide or otherwise stimulate long-term, low-interest-rate loans for reconstruction and for the develop-ment of capital-poor areas'. We believe that there is no longer any justi-fication for an organisation with this (sole) purpose. This proposition – that the capital market-imperfections justification for the Bank is no longer valid – and its implication that the Bank needs some other justi-fication for its existence – is a major motivation for the argument we develop in chapter 2 in this volume. In an era in which the flow of private direct investment into developing countries is highly elastic – with the implication that countries where the marginal productivity of investment is high and profit repatriation is unproblematic receive very large flows – the traditional capital market-failure argument no longer provides the rationale for the Bank's lending activities. Instead, the Bank's role becomes that of extending the beneficial effects of these inward flows to a wider range of countries, where returns are less secure and where either the nature or the uncertainty of government policy provides a less welcoming environment for private flows; and of ensuring that the invest-ment that is undertaken, in both successful and less successful countries, contributes to growth and to poverty reduction.

3.2 Poverty

Poverty alleviation was not part of the original mandate for the Bank. Instead, poverty reduction came onto the Bank's agenda only gradually, with the creation of the IDA and, in particular, through the champion-ship of McNamara. It is now the Bank's core mission.[18] But progress to this position has not been linear: over the 50-plus years since the Bank's foundation, there have been radical shifts of view about how the Bank might best promote poverty alleviation.

Since views on this issue so deeply underpin all other views on the Bank's purposes and operation, we devote a key early chapter in this volume (chapter 3) to this issue. The story told in that chapter is a fascinating one. In the Bank's early days, loans were made for particular projects (and later for particular programmes), and the justification of these loans was in terms of the returns on these investments; the effect on poverty reduction was meant to 'trickle down' from the effects of good investment projects. McNamara's war on poverty, begun in the early 1970s, involved a rejection of this view. The new view was that the Bank should be explicitly concerned, in justifying any particular piece of lending, with the effects on poverty reduction. But then in the 1980s trickle-down re-emerged, albeit it in a new and decisively different version. This view held sway, during the time of the 'Washington consensus', through to the early 1990s. Recently this trickle-down view has, again, been rejected. What has now replaced it is the view that certain forms of poverty reduction are, in fact, necessary conditions for sustained growth.

These changes in the realm of ideas have, of course, had a profound impact on the practical realm of development assistance. They have affected both the Bank's sense of what it should and should not be doing, and also what the Bank has actually done. Chapter 3 charts these connections. It concludes by suggesting where the poverty reduction agenda points for the future.

3.3 Research

If the Bank's role were purely that of a financial intermediary, research would be redundant. Instead, the research department has taken on a pivotal role, of an educational kind. The target audience has in part comprised client governments, but the research department has also had its sights on operational divisions of the Bank, and on the development community at large. Gradually, the Bank has taken upon itself the role of defining and propagating a model of best development practice. As Gavin and Rodrik (1995: 333) note, despite the fact that this role was not anticipated in the Bank's charter, by 1994 its research budget was nearly double the economics research budget of the US National Science Foundation ($26 million against $16 million). They also stress that the Bank's contribution in research is not in the originality of its ideas, for which they see little evidence, but in propagation: 'Once the Bank gets hold of an idea, its financial clout ensures that the idea will gain wide currency.'

What justifies such substantial expenditures by the Bank on development research? Would this money have been better spent on development assistance? Or if the outcomes of the research are needed ones, might not research of the same or higher quality be obtained at lower cost by commissioning it from universities or from consulting firms? Particular answers to these questions are central to our claim – made in chapter 2 – about the Bank as a 'Knowledge Bank'. In writing that chapter we have drawn in important ways on the ideas in Chapter 4, which is called 'Why the Bank Should be Involved in Development Research' This chapter is by Lyn Squire, who was himself Director of the Bank's Research

Department from 1993 to 1997. Squire emphasises the link between the Bank's research and its activities in the field. Adopting a principal–agent perspective, it is natural to suspect that if the Bank's research were sub-contracted to universities or to consulting firms, then the outcomes would in part address the agendas of these agents, rather than those of the principal (i.e. the Bank). Furthermore, Squire argues that, for research to actually influence policy in the field, it requires a 'champion' within the Bank. If the identity of the researcher and the champion are the same (whether this be an individual or a team) then that will tend to generate more effective use of research results. Raul Hopkins and his co-authors in chapter 11 stress an additional point: the positive feedback from research to project returns.[19]

3.4 Governance

The Bank is a *multilateral* institution which enables richer countries – in particular, of course, the United States – to assist with the development problems of the poorer countries without entering into direct bilateral political power relations with them. By enabling arm's-length relations to be maintained between countries in the world's core on the one hand, and its developing periphery on the other, it enables development assistance to be conducted while at the same time avoiding the worst excesses of imperialism. It is against the background of this fact that the governance of the Bank should be discussed.

The IBRD's capital is subscribed by member governments, and IBRD lending is to governments. Voting is approximately proportional to GDP with the consequence that the developed countries effectively control lending policies Changes to the IBRD's articles required an 80 per cent majority, with the consequence that the United States was the only country with a vote in excess of the 20 per cent required for a veto. When, in 1989, the US share fell to 17 per cent, the majority required for amendment was increased to 85 per cent. Active management is in the hands of the Executive Board. Large, or otherwise important, shareholders have their own Executive Director who is a board member,[20] while other countries form 'constituencies'. The US voting power, and also to some extent its veto power, puts the US Executive Director in a very powerful position and makes the relationship between the Bank and the US Treasury central to the effectiveness of the Bank's performance (Gwin, 1997: 248).

Ngaire Woods (chapter 5) discusses the 'delicate balancing of political forces' as the Bank simultaneously acknowledges the interests and wishes of the United States, its largest funder, but at the same time, strives to maintain the independence (particularly from the United States) which confers legitimacy on it. It is this legitimacy which provides the justification for US governments to channel taxpayers' funds through an institution which is not directly accountable to US voters. At the same time, this argument will remain cogent to future US administrations only provided the World Bank continues to adopt policies which are in line with perceived US interests. This generates a Seattle-style tension between increased legitimacy, which may be seen as implying more open and democratic decision-making in which developing country governments exercise greater influence, and the utility of this legitimacy as a device for allowing the United States to fund development at arm's length. The clear danger is that Congress would decide to reassert direct control over US development assistance if the Bank comes to be perceived as failing to promote free enterprise and democracy in borrowing countries.

4 The World Bank's policies: the effectiveness of World Bank aid

4.1 Project lending versus policy-based lending

The major evolution which took place in the second 25 years of the Bank's existence was the shift from project-based to policy-based lending, in particular through the device of structural adjustment programmes. In part, this was an implicit acknowledgement that financial assistance is always to some extent fungible (see p. 61). However, as noted in section 3, the timing of the shift to programme lending in the early 1980s arose out of the pressing need at that time in many indebted developing countries for balance of payments assistance rather than for project finance.[21] Shifts in the perception of the riskiness of overseas investment can result in very large swings in international capital flows. Reversal of large outward movements of capital requires a much more rapid response than is available from the process of identifying and specifying financeable projects. Structural Adjustment Loans (SALs), and later Sectoral Adjustment Loans (SECALs) permitted rapid disbursal of funds which would at least partially replace absent private sector flows.

The transition to sectoral adjustment loans reversed the pre-structural adjustment roles of lending and conditionality. In the first 25 years of Bank activity, conditionality was imposed in order to ensure the success of projects and to guarantee that their potential benefits were captured. By the mid-1980s, the imperative was to channel dollars to indebted countries in order to enable them to service their debt. However, lending also required justification in terms of a more conventional return on investment and was often justified in terms of the benefits of the policies that were to be imposed through conditionality clauses attached to loans. These (reformist) policies would result in adjustment costs, and other transition costs, and it was the purpose of the loans to offset these provided to the governments. Policies in effect became projects, with investment in economic policy-making infrastructure replacing investment in physical infrastructure.

Initially, adjustment policies were primarily macroeconomic and were specifically directed towards the balance of payments but, over time, the shopping list became longer, and included policies with little direct payments impact (KLW, 1997a: 524). Trade liberalisation, which does affect the balance of payments, also figured more centrally, and later privatisation, where the immediate impact is on the fiscal deficit, also became a target.

The move to policy-based lending has often been attributed to the election of right-wing governments in the United States, Britain and Germany. Mosley, Harrigan and Toye (1995) argue that the moves towards policy-based lending in fact originated from within the operational divisions of the Bank and were prior to the US–UK–German rightward shift. Indeed, the Executive Board of the Bank resisted these changes for several years. Mosley, Harrigan and Toye (1995) record that operational managers had become disillusioned about the effectiveness of the existing policy dialogue process with borrowers. In particular, they became frustrated when economic deterioration in sub-Saharan Africa resulted in a situation in which it often became impossible to identify any projects which would be potentially profitable even at subsidised interest rates. Both because of these pressures and of the need to mobilise balance of payments support in the wake of the debt crisis, structural adjustment lending assumed major importance from 1983 on.

The success of the Bank's structural adjustment programmes is discussed by Francisco Ferreira and Louise Keely (chapter 6 in this volume, p. 159). They argue that the Bank did not succeed in purchasing much reform, largely because of insufficient focus on the supply side. This anticipates the consensus on the conditionality debate. But at the same time, what happened should be seen in the context of the rapid disbursement required if SALs were to address balance of payments concerns. KLW (1997a: 523) claim that adjustment lending had two purposes: promotion of reform and provision of flexible foreign exchange. The failure to purchase effective reform suggests that the first of these objectives was subordinate to the imperative of getting the money out quickly.[22]

More recently, in response to a series of critiques of the Bank's lending practice, there has been a move towards an increasingly programmatic approach in place of traditional project lending. This has involved new instruments, notably Sector Adjustment Strategies (SASs), which support sector-level government expenditure programmes rather than individual projects (see Stephen Jones, chapter 10 in this volume). One may see instruments of this type as recognising the lessons of aid fungibility – which we are about to discuss – but as also being driven by sectoral development prospects rather than payments or debt scheduling imperatives.

4.2 Aid fungibility

Discussing the immediate post-war reconstruction period, KLW (1997a: 13) note Paul Rosenstein-Rodan's comment that 'he could never understand why bankers took the link between particular loans and particular assets so seriously'. If a particular lending programme has a high return, it is likely that government would have undertaken it in the absence of a Bank loan. Governments may generally be expected to respond to aid-financing of this activity or sector by diverting their own resources to other activities or sectors.

Substantial evidence, summarised by Shantayanan Devarajan and Vinaya Swaroop (chapter 7 in this volume, p. 196) indicates that this is generally true of both bilateral and multilateral development lending. Projects may appear to perform well on their own terms but the overall impact of external assistance may be less impressive if these funds are diverted to marginal projects. The implications for development lending are less clear. The negative view is that, since aid money is effectively spent on things other than those for which it was intended, and these diversionary uses will typically have lower returns than the intended project (otherwise, they would have been financed in any case), the developmental impact of Bank lending will typically be less than that anticipated by Bank economists. The alternative view is that the Bank should recognise fungibility and lend to governments of countries where developmental returns are generally high, rather than focusing on narrowly defined project returns. It is this latter view which underlies the shift away from project lending and towards programme and sector lending (see Jones, chapter 10 in this volume, p. 266).

4.3 Policy conditionality

Policy-based lending and policy conditionality are two sides of the same coin. The premise of adjustment lending is that the country needs to undertake reforms, but either these will be costly, or there will be a lead time before which the beneficial results come through. Either way, the country requires support over the reform process, and this support will have the incidental benefit of reducing payments pressures and allowing debt service. Policy conditionality sees reforms as a precondition for aid, often required for the same balance of payments and debt service purposes. The difference is more than semantic: in adjustment lending there is a claim that the returns to the policy reform justify the loan, whereas conditionality-based lending sees reforms as increasing project returns to acceptable levels (i.e. there is project which might in principle have been financed even in the absence of reforms). Policy conditionality originated with the IMF (Killick, 1998: 1) and initially had a relatively specific macroeconomic focus, in particular relating to budget targets and the exchange rate regime. In Killick's terminology, policy commitments on these matters were either preconditions or triggers for the release of finance, the requirement for which followed from a payments or debt-servicing crisis which forced the government into the IMF's arms. Furthermore, the crisis situation gave the IMF substantial bargaining power, and the nature of the reforms limited the possible extent of back-sliding. Over time, IMF conditionality became broader, moving into such areas as reduction of price subsidies and removal of price controls, seen as concomitants of budgetary control.

Bank lending had always imposed some element of conditionality in recognition of the fact that there is little merit in lending to finance a project if the potential benefits arising from it are dissipated through upstream or downstream inefficiencies.[23] However, the move to SALs and SECALs made the policy reforms central to project justification. Killick (1998: 2) notes that: 'once it got started in the business of policy conditionality the World Bank was never anything other than ambitious.' He records that adjustment loans disbursed in 1989 specified an average of 56 reforms.

Aid-conditionality on the part of multilateral organisations dominated by the rich countries has been seen as 'neo-colonialist' imposition of western values and ideology on developing countries. The political reality is, however, that use of taxpayers' money must be justified in the national parliaments of 'Part I' countries.[24] In any case, NGOs, which have often been vocal in this criticism, have lobbied for alternative conditions in Bank lending and have also both imposed conditions of their own on their assistance. The pragmatic issue is therefore whether and to what extent policy-based lending has been effective. These arguments pit standard economic and political economy considerations.

Economic theory suggests that a benevolent government should adopt the best policies without external coercion. If a potentially beneficial reform is too costly, the government will rationally choose not to implement it. Haggard and Kaufman (1992: 18) state: 'The central political dilemma of reform is that though significant benefits may accrue to society as a whole, policy adjustment involves significant startup costs and the reduction of rents to particular groups.'

If governments are required to adopt policies or reforms which they would not choose unilaterally, this requires that one of the following conditions holds:

(1) the multilateral agency can reduce the costs of adjustment, for example, by lowering interest costs (a standard capital market 'imperfection' view deriving from sovereign risk considerations)
(2) the agency can reduce the costs or increase the benefits of reform through its superior knowledge and experience (the 'Knowledge Bank' view)
(3) aid conditionality can allow governments to pre-commit and thereby avoid time- consistency problems; they can also, to a more limited extent, commit their successors
(4) the agency can oblige a government to adopt reforms which are in the best interests of its population, but run against the narrow interests of the government or its clients.

The first three justifications amount to 'agreed conditionality', while the fourth implies 'imposed conditionality'.[25] It is imposed conditionality that is problematic.

The central question in the political economy of reform is why governments do not adopt policies which are in the best interests of their populations. One answer is that the 'unitary actor' model fails to accord with political realities (Bates and Krueger, 1993: 455). Instead, legislatures conflict with executives, civil governments with military establishments, and interest groups with other interest groups. Furthermore, groups whose interest are threatened are often more organised than potential groups who would benefit from reform – 'crucial sectors that might constitute the core of reform coalitions, such as small peasants and landless labourers, informal sector workers, and non-traditional export industries, are less well organised and must overcome significant barriers to collective action to become politically effective' (Haggard and Kaufman, 1992: 19). These considerations may be exacerbated by electoral cycles. In environments of this type, policy conditionality may be seen as strengthening the hand of the pro-reform groups.

Economists have tended to emphasise a different and more Machiavellian mechanism. If the World Bank is offering money for policy reform, developing country client governments need policies or sectors which require reform. Furthermore, strategic considerations and support from developed company champions (often the ex-colonial powers) confer governments with a degree of monopoly power in the supply of reforms. A rational government will, in these circumstances, withhold reforms to increase their price. Furthermore, less than complete success in implementation can result in reforms being recycled. There is no doubt some truth in this view, but it features relatively little in political economy accounts of reform processes. This is probably because only a few countries have sufficient monopoly power to be able to extract good prices – more normally, adjustment reform offers 'stringent reform for a modest amount of financing' (Kahler, 1990, 1992).

Overall, therefore, we subscribe to the political economy view that the frequent failure of governments to adopt beneficial policies is due to the fact that the economic status quo reinforces the political interests which are its beneficiaries. This is not a problem that is confined to developing countries, but it is often exacerbated by weak democratic institutions, government control of media and low levels of political education. It provides the context in which we need to examine the effectiveness of policy-related aid.

4.4 Aid effectiveness

Aid effectiveness has formed the subject of a major debate over the 1990s, and this volume brings together a number of studies relating to this debate. The most authoritative summary of the Bank's own view on the subject may be found in World Bank (1998a). The general conclusion is an overall scepticism that multilateral lending, and World Bank lending in particular, has achieved any notable effect on the performance of borrowing governments. This conclusion is based on detailed studies, on internal assessments of loan outcomes and on econometric analysis of the relationship between growth and aid.

The evidence in that book is summarised, and extended, in the chapters in this volume by Craig Burnside and David Dollar (chapter 8) and Jonathan Isham and Daniel Kaufmann (chapter 9). Burnside and Dollar's results relate to the impact of development assistance from all sources on growth and poverty outcomes, while Isham and Kaufmann's results relate specifically to the effectiveness of Bank lending in achieving particular lending objectives. In both cases, these will include project and policy lending. The negative nature of these results reinforces the more anecdotal evidence of Mosley, Harrigan and Toye (1995) and Killick (1998) that policy-based lending is seldom effective.

There are two possible approaches to these findings. The historical approach, stressed by Paul Collier (chapter 12 in this volume), stresses the context in which policy-based lending emerged and argues that strict compliance with aid conditions may often have been regarded as voluntary. The Bank was more concerned with filling 'payments holes' than with the policies it was purchasing. This is consistent with the view (not held by Collier) that although policy conditionality was not sufficiently well applied in the past, it would now be possible to apply it more rigorously.

The alternative, ahistorical, approach regards conditionality as intrinsically flawed. One reason is that, if the conditionality is 'imposed', in the sense defined above, the same interests that impose adoption will also have to impose implementation. Economists have tended to recast this explanation in terms of the principal-agent problem. The donor institution is the principal, but decisions are implemented by the borrowing government acting as agent. Imperfect monitoring, at least until late in the project, allows the agent to divert resources (project resources, or its own management or resource inputs) to its own ends.

Many of the comments on policy conditionality have stressed lack of 'ownership' by the implementing institutions. It is difficult to find any precise definition of 'ownership', even in Killick (1998), who devotes two pages to explaining the concept, but broadly it relates to situations in which the agent's priorities are sufficiently different from those of the principal as to compromise reform outcomes (lack of effective monitoring and control by the principal being taken as given). A general conclusion is the importance of increasing ownership if reforms are to be successful. One view is that this will require incentive regimes which overcome principal-agent conflicts. An alternative, and not incompatible, view is that the Bank will need to educate governments, civil servants and voters on the benefits of reform resulting in at least a partial reappraisal of perceived interests.

The most recent econometric work has added an important qualification to the generally prevalent scepticism about the success of development assistance in general, and policy-based lending in particular. This qualification is as follows. The econometrics finds that aid (in general) has, on average, been ineffective. But it also finds that it *is* effective in the context of 'sound' policy, where this is crudely identified (for the purposes of the econometrics) with the outcomes of openness, low inflation and a low government deficit – see Burnside and Dollar, 1996, and chapter 8 in this volume).[26] This finding suggests that where governments are reform-minded and policy conditionality is of the agreed type, it can be effective.

The implication for aid effectiveness is that aid should be directed towards governments of countries where there is an effective policy regime in place. These are countries in which further reforms will be owned and are likely to be effectively implemented. That being the case, there is little need for detailed monitoring, nor for any great concern with possible fungibility. But it requires a move away from the philosophy that aid can buy reform.

This approach may seem brutal since many countries, including many of the poorest countries, do not have good policy regimes, and are unlikely to develop good regimes in the near future. Does this imply that the World Bank should abandon such countries? Squire (chapter 4 in this volume) suggests not and Isham and Kaufmann (chapter 9) provide evidence that project returns are high in countries which make improvements to their policy environments over the period of project implementation. However, the emphasis in these countries should, in the first instance, be on development advice and on education with aid flows following the commitment to reform. On this view, the 'Knowledge Bank' will march hand-in-hand with the new-style 'Conditionality Bank'.

As Hopkins *et al.* (chapter 11 in this volume) note, if conditionality in some form is unavoidable, it is important to examine the costs and benefits of alternative forms of conditionality. Policy-change conditionality, in which lending is conditioned on prospective changes in the borrowing government's policies, has not been very effective, and there is no reason to expect this to alter. On the other hand, policy-level conditionality, in which lending is conditioned on the current policies of the borrowing government, limits aid to countries with 'good' policy environments, and this may conflict with the Bank's poverty mandate. But what makes policy-level conditionality particularly difficult to apply is that many (perhaps most) developing country governments will fall into the category of having neither wholly bad nor wholly good policies, and lending is likely to result in the same sorts of decisions and bargains as previously.

This debate may be recast in terms of the Bank's new 'Comprehensive Development Framework' or CDF (Wolfensohn, 1999). The CDF proposes a holistic and collaborative approach to development assistance in which multilateral donors, NGOs, government and 'civil society' will work together for agreed development objectives. To the extent that this is successful, reform will be donor-driven and ownership will be enhanced. Mutually agreed targets will replace aid conditions, implying an approach similar to Killick's (1998) agreed conditionality. The problems which may arise in the CDF framework were indicated in Stiglitz's introduction (p. 1) and are further discussed by Hopkins *et al.* in chapter 11 (p. 282). In addition, the CDF framework puts a premium on openness and participation, and some governments may see this as a new form of conditionality. Moreover, where there are strong vested interests ranged against reform, it is difficult to see how the various parties can arrive at a mutually agreed CDF, while the financial imperative of reaching agreement will increase the probability of subsequent backsliding. The issues will not change, but the debates over these issues may be more open and perhaps less confrontational.

5 The 'Knowledge Bank': a unifying framework

The idea of the World Bank as a 'Knowledge Bank', which we develop in chapter 2, provides a unifying framework which can tie together a description of what the Bank does, and which can also suggest ways in which it might further re-position itself.

The Bank combines lending and advisory functions in a way which is incompatible with the profit-oriented incentives of private sector institutions (either banks or consulting firms), and with a commitment and mandate which is denied to other public sector institutions (universities, government aid agencies). The Bank's knowledge and cumulated experience of the development process provides the justification for a continuing role for the World Bank in an era where international capital markets appear overliquid rather than underliquid. The Bank is in a position to give advice which is more disinterested than that provided by professional consultants, more professional than that provided by academics and more comprehensive than that provided by NGOs. The fact that this advice is linked to lending implies that the Bank is committed to favourable outcomes. And the ending of Cold War tensions implies that the

Bank can afford to walk away from countries which are disinclined to accept its advice. One possible conclusion is that this 'power to walk away' needs to be used more frequently than has been the case in the past.

The now generally accepted finding that aid has, on average, been ineffective in promoting growth demonstrates that aid by itself is insufficient. The institutional preconditions for growth and poverty reduction, in terms of institutional capacity and the quality of governance, stressed by Joe Stiglitz in his preface, have been well documented over the past decade. Private sector funding cannot address these issues but, unless they are addressed, private sector investments will not be profitable. A modern approach to development would stress neither the absence of capital nor the absence of profitable projects but the difficulty of realising the profits which are potentially available on the capital which is available to be invested. The World Bank cannot by itself solve these problems, but it does have the knowledge and experience to help those governments who are committed to obtaining a solution. The Bank's new CDF may be interpreted as seeking to ensure that the Bank does indeed behave in this way. If the Bank does do this, then it can show the way forward; it will thereby provide initial funding for reforms, in a way which will stimulate the private flows that will sustain development and enable poverty reduction.

We take up these issues at length in chapter 2.

6 The World Bank and crises

The first quarter-century of the Bank's operations coincided with a period of relative stability and predictability in the world economy. But the subsequent quarter-century has witnessed a sequence of spectacular shocks. The largest three of these all caused major disruptions to the Bank's lending programme – the 1980s' debt crisis, the 1994–5 Mexican crisis, and the 1997–9 emerging markets' crisis. The common feature of these crises is that they required rapid disbursement of large sums of money. These disbursements could be justified in terms of promised adjustments or restructuring operations which would reduce the probability of future crises but, as argued above in the context of SAL lending in the 1980s and early 1990s, financing requirements were the dominant consideration.

A possible argument, which we discuss in chapter 2 and which is taken up by Collier (chapter 12 in this volume) is that crisis relief is properly the IMF's territory, and the Bank should not be distracted from its longer-term development objectives by short-term crisis imperatives. It is complemented by the view expressed by US Treasury Secretary Larry Summers that the Fund should concentrate on crisis management and move away from longer- term adjustment assistance.[27] There is merit in these arguments, but both require qualification. With regard to the Bank, any crises will inevitably generate a large and urgent financing requirements which the IMF by itself will have difficulty meeting – there would be no crisis if the IMF could provide the required funds within its normal budgets. Since it is politically impossible for the Bank to stand aside, the issue it has to face is how to insulate its normal activities from emergency crisis requirements while, at the same time, not doing anything which could jeopardise its AAA status. In relation to the proposal that the Fund move away from longer-term assistance, there is an important issue as to whether a period of, say, 12–18 months would be sufficient for adjustment if the crisis reflects structural problems in the crisis-hit countries, and not simply contagion-induced capital volatility *per se*.

For the Bank, the answer must lie in maintenance of a sufficient reserve level which, in World Bank terms, translates into sufficient lending 'headroom'.[28] As we discuss in chapter 2, the Bank usually aims to have sufficient headroom so as to be able to increase lending by normal amounts in normal times; some of this increase can be temporarily diverted into crisis lending, and can be further augmented by temporarily departing from the normal process of adding to reserves so as to provide for growing headroom in the future. But this can provide only a temporary breathing space; the scope for it is severely limited.

7 Plan of this volume

The chapters of the book have all been mentioned in passing in this introduction. Here we summarise by describing the chapters one by one.

The book falls into two parts. Part one is concerned with the World Bank as an Institution. It comprises four chapters. Chapter 2, by Christopher Gilbert, Andrew Powell and David Vines describe the Bank as a 'Knowledge Bank' – a bundled organisation, which brings together lending, research and development assistance functions – and argue that it should move further in this direction. In chapter 3, Ravi Kanbur and David Vines trace the Bank's evolving views on poverty reduction and look to the future role that poverty alleviation will play in the Bank's strategy. Chapter 4, by Lyn Squire, asks whether the Bank should be involved in research, and provides a strongly positive answer. Finally, in chapter 5, Ngaire Woods considers the Bank's governance.

The chapters in part two of the book are all concerned with the question of the effectiveness of World Bank assistance to borrowing countries. Francisco Ferreira and Louise Keely (chapter 6) look at the emergence of concerns, in the 1980s, about SAL effectiveness. Shantayanan Devarajan and Vinaya Swaroop (chapter 7) argue that aid will frequently be fungible since governments will generally undertake high-return projects even in the absence of assistance. This provides support for the view that donors should support good governments rather than fund good projects. In chapter 8, Craig Burnside and David Dollar summarise and extend their previous work on the importance of the policy regime for aid effectiveness and in chapter 9, Jonathan Isham and Daniel Kaufmann provide additional evidence from the Bank's own internal review procedures on these issues. Stephen Jones, in chapter 10, takes a forward-looking view on how Sector Adjustment Policies (SAPs) can increase aid effectiveness. In chapter 11, Raul Hopkins and his co-authors attempt to reconcile a traditional view of the importance of conditioning aid on policy with the current emphasis on ownership evident in the new CDF. Finally, in chapter 12, Paul Collier brings this set of arguments together and provides some perspective.

8 The past and the future

This introduction has been written in the closing months of the closing year of the century. The World Bank has been involved in development, as distinct from post-war reconstruction, for four decades. An end-of-century report would record some development successes, particularly in Asia and the most southern part of Latin America, but would also indicate that the Bank's role in these successes was not large. It would note promising developments elsewhere in Asia and Latin America where the Bank is more active. And it would record other areas, particularly in Africa, where progress has been slow despite heavy Bank involvement. It would also record new concerns, particularly in relation to the environment, which complicate and sometimes compromise development objectives. The writers of this report might even pose the question as to whether the overall return had been positive.

Some readers of such a report might argue that it had posed the wrong question. Poverty involves us all – they might say – and, although the Bank has an obligation to obtain a high return on its capital, the developed countries owe a commitment to the developing world on poverty reduction – whatever the outcome. Others readers might make a similar argument on a basis of self-interest: we share one world, interaction is inevitable and this is best achieved on an equitable basis.

There would be merit in both of these responses. But we would like to conclude this introduction by suggesting a third position. This is that there has been a clear and substantial return on Bank resources, over and above any direct return, in the quality of our understanding of how to assist with the development process. That development economics is now more codified, more systematic and more clearly based on detailed and scientific empirical evidence is, in no small measure, due to the integration of development funding, development research and development assistance within the Bank. The Bank which enters the new century has already partly become a 'Knowledge Bank': a special, and important, kind of development agency, one that is a repository of best practice in development assistance.

In the chapters which follow we (the editors) set out to justify this assertion.[29] We aim to do this by means of the arguments which we ourselves, and other 'outside' authors, present. We also aim to do this through using this book as a means of presenting important work by Bank economists to a wider audience.

But we wish also to go beyond this assertion. We suggest that the Bank's reinvention as a 'Knowledge Bank' has not gone far enough. This is a large claim. It is with substantiating this, second, big, claim that will be concerned in chapter 2.

NOTES

1 We have benefited from useful comments on a preliminary draft of this introduction from Francisco Ferreira, Raul Hopkins, Daniel Kaufmann, Lyn Squire and Ngaire Woods; and also from suggestions from three anonymous referees approached by the publishers.

2 'Our Mission: To fight poverty with passion and professionalism for lasting results ... The main focus is on helping the poorest people and the poorest countries' < http://www.worldbank.org >.

3 See < http://www.worldbank.org/html/extdr/whatis.htm >.

4 See the narrative account in chapter 1 of Kapur, Lewis and Webb (hereafter, KLW) (1997a).

5 Chapter 2 is written jointly with Andrew Powell.

6 In FY1999, the list of IDA countries contained those countries with a GDP per head of $925 or less (see World Bank, 1998: 155). In addition, IDA lends to some small island economies with somewhat higher GDP per head.

7 See < http://www.ifc.org/about/ >.

8 For a history of MIGA, see < http://www.miga.org/welcome.htm >.

9 The fifth organisation under the umbrella of the World Bank Group is the International Centre for Settlement of Investment Disputes (the ICSID). It plays a juridical function and we do not discuss it further.

10 To celebrate 50 years of this evolution, the Bank commissioned a two-volume official *History* (KLW, 1997a, 1998b). This pair of large volumes makes fascinating, at times even riveting, reading. It is rich in detail, and provides much insight; at the same time it is tightly focused analytically. We have made extensive use of it in our researches for this book. The present short section cannot begin to do justice to the narrative presented by its authors. Note, however, that there is some further historical narrative in chapter 3 in this volume by Kanbur and Vines on the evolution of the Bank's thinking, and work, in its agenda on poverty reduction.

11 See Gardner (1969).

12 When asked about what would happen when reconstruction was completed, White replied 'Let's have it there for after' (KLW, 1997a: 57).

13 World Bank (1998b: 109, 153); IMF (1998: 100, 103).

14 KLW (1997a: 1120).

15 See KLW (1997a: 651–61).

16 It was also dominant in the Fund until Managing Director Michel Camdessus' conversion to poverty reduction at the 1999 Bank–Fund joint meetings. It is not entirely clear how this new commitment meshes with the proposal that the Fund should in future focus on crisis resolution (see section 6, p. 000).

17 Non-Governmental Organisations, who had previously tended to see themselves as in opposition to the Bank.

18 'To fight poverty with passion and professionalism for lasting results' < http://www.worldbank.org/html/extdr/mission.htm > .

19 In doing so they note that these feedbacks should be expected to spill over onto private sector projects, which leads to the additional point that a private sector development bank would therefore spend insufficient on research.

20 Countries with their own Board members in 1999 were China, France, Germany, Japan, the Russian Federation, Saudi Arabia, the United Kingdom and the United States.

21 See KLW (1997a: 503–12) and Armandariz de Aghion and Ferreira (1993).

22 See Svensson (1998) who argues that heavy indebtedness was the most important determinant of lending.

23 Ryrie (1995: 58) goes somewhat further. Speaking of Eugene Black, Bank President from 1949 to 1962, he says: 'although Gene Black was quite capable of refusing a loan to a country whose fiscal policies were lax, this had more to do with credit-worthiness and the security of the Bank's money than with promoting sound macro-economic policies for development reasons.'

24 IDA member countries are classified as Part I or Part II, depending as to whether they were, in 1960, lending or borrowing countries (see KLW, 1997a: 191–2).

25 'Pro forma' and 'hard core' conditionality in Killick (1998).

26 This conclusion depends crucially on the significance of a policy-aid interaction coefficient in a panel Barro growth regression.
27 Speech at the London Business School (14 December 1999), reported in *The Economist* (18–30 December 1999: 153).
28 'Headroom' measures the extent to which the IBRD can make additional loans subject to the constraints imposed by its Articles and the requirement to add to the funds available to IDA. IDA funds are always fully committed.
29 The over-arching views set out in this introduction do not necessarily reflect the views of the other contributors to this volume, or to the institutions that they represent.

REFERENCES

Armanderiz de Aghion, B. and F. Ferreira (1993). 'The World Bank and the Analysis of the International Debt Crisis', STICERD *Development Economics Paper*, **51**

Ayres, R.L. (1983). *Banking on the Poor: The World Bank and World Poverty*, Cambridge, MA: MIT Press

Bates, R.H. and A. O. Krueger (1993) *Political and Economic Interactions in Economic Policy Reform*, Cambridge, MA: Blackwell

Gardner, R.N. (1969), *Sterling–Dollar Diplomacy: The Origins and Prospects of Our International Economic Order*, New York: McGraw Hill

Gavin, M. and D. Rodrik (1995). 'The World Bank in Historical Perspective', *American Economic Review, Papers and Proceedings*, **85**: 329–34

Gilbert, C.L., R. Hopkins, A. Powell and A. Roy (1996). 'The World Bank: Its Functions and its Future', *CEPR Global Economic Institutions Working Paper*, **15**

Gwin, C. (1997). 'US Relations with the World Bank, 1945–92', in D. Kapur, J. P. Lewis and R. Webb, *The World Bank: Its First half Century, 2: Perspectives*, Washington, DC: Brookings Institution

Haggard, S. and R. Kaufman (1992). *The Politics of Economic Adjustment*, Princeton: Princeton University Press

Hayter, T. (1971). *Aid as Imperialism*, Harmondsworth: Penguin

Hopkins, R., A. Powell, A. Roy and C. L. Gilbert (1997). 'The World Bank and Conditionality', *Journal of International Development*, **9**: 507–16

IMF (1998), *Annual Report*, Washington, DC: IMF

Kahler, M. (1990). 'Orthodoxy and its Alternatives: Explaining Approaches to Stabilization and Adjustment', in J. M. Nelson (ed.), *Economic Crisis and Policy Choice*, Princeton: Princeton University Press
    (1992). 'External Influence, Conditionality, and the Politics of Adjustment', in S. Haggard and R.F. Kaufmann (eds.), *The Politics of Economic Adjustment*, Princeton: Princeton University Press

Kapur, D., J. P. Lewis and R. Webb, R. (1997a). *The World Bank: Its First Half Century, 1: History*, Washington, DC: Brookings Institution
    (1997b). *The World Bank: Its First half Century, 2: Perspectives*, Washington, DC: Brookings Institution

Killick, T. (1998). *Aid and the Political Economy of Policy Change*, London: Overseas Development Institute

Kindleberger, C.P. (1950). *The Dollar Shortage*, Cambridge, MA: MIT Press

Mason, E.S. and R. E. Asher (1973). *The World Bank Since Bretton Woods*, Washington, DC: Brookings Institution

Morawetz, D. (1977). *Twenty-five Years of Economic Development 1950–75*, Baltimore: Johns Hopkins University Press

Mosley, P., J. Harrigan and J. Toye (1995). *Aid and Power: The World Bank and Policy-Based Lending*, 2nd edn., London: Routledge

Oliver, R.W. (1975). *International Economic Co-operation and the World Bank*, London: Macmillan

Ryrie, W. (1995). *First World, Third World*, London: Macmillan

Svensson, J. (1998). 'Aid Tournaments', Development Research Group, Washington, DC: World Bank, mimeo

Wade, R. (1990). *Governing the Market*, Princeton: Princeton University Press

Walters, A. (1994). 'Do We Need the IMF and the World Bank?', *Current Controversies*, **10**, London: Institute of Economic Affairs

  (1999) 'What Should the Bank Think about the Washington Consensus?', World Bank, July, mimeo

Williamson, J. (1990). 'What Washington Means by Policy Reform', in J. Williamson (ed.), *Latin American Adjustment: How Much Has Happened?*, Washington, DC: Institute for International Economics

  (1999). 'What Should the Bank Think about the Washington Consensus?', World Bank, July, mimeo

Wolfensohn, J. (1999). 'A proposal for a comprehensive development framework – a discussion draft', available at < http://www.worldbank.org/cdf/cdf-text.htm >

World Bank (1998a). *Assessing Aid: What Works, What Doesn't and Why?*, Washington, DC: World Bank

  (1998b). *World Bank Annual Report 1998*, New York: Oxford University Press

Part One

The World Bank's Structure:
The Bank as an Institution

2 Positioning the World Bank

CHRISTOPHER L. GILBERT, ANDREW POWELL
AND DAVID VINES

1 Introduction and summary

The World Bank (henceforth 'the Bank') is dedicated to the promotion, world-wide, of sustainable economic development and poverty reduction.[1] It pursues these objectives through lending, through the production of research and the provision of economic analysis, and through policy advice and technical assistance.[2]

The initial rationale for the Bank was that a source of lending, in support of the objective of economic development, was justified by market failures in the international capital market. We argue that this justification can no longer be sustained. Our justification for the existence of an institution like the Bank dedicated to poverty reduction, is, instead, that it can help to resolve global market failures in the development process. As a consequence, we identify three key 'rationales' for the Bank: the rectification of government failure, the rectification of information failures and the provision of global public goods. But we also believe that a Bank with these rationales needs to reposition itself.

The Bank is a complex organisation; a continuing line of criticism has been that it is too sprawlingly complex.[3] Oliver's (1971, 1975) accounts of the Bretton Woods and subsequent negotiations show that differences of opinion about how the Bank should pursue its central objective, both between the Americans and the British, and also within the US administration itself go right back to the Bank's very origins. Naim (1994) accuses current World Bank practices of generating dysfunctional 'goal congestion'. The implication of a long line of such criticism (see KLW, 1997a, chapter 14) is that it might be desirable if the Bank could better define its focus. We agree.

Our view, which we will develop in detail in this chapter, is that a certain amount of complexity is essential. This is partly because 'development and poverty reduction' is a diffuse and complex agenda. But it is also centrally because the Bank needs to 'bundle' together a group of rather different 'behavioural activities' in order to solve the three market failures identified above. We will distinguish three different types of behavioural activities that are necessary for the Bank: the Bank as a bank – i.e. as a financial intermediary; as a development research institution, producing both research and economic analysis; and as a development agency, providing development assistance, attaching conditions to loans and monitoring performance, and also contributing to the provision of global public goods.

We will use the label 'Knowledge Bank'[4] to describe an organisation which sees itself as:

(1) delivering this threefold bundle of services, in order to
(2) solve the three market failures which we have identified, in order to
(3) promote, world-wide, sustainable economic development and poverty reduction.

We develop the analysis in this chapter, with the aid of this label, in two parts. First we present a descriptive claim that the Bank has already partly become a 'Knowledge Bank'. Second we argue, normatively, that the Bank could, and should, go much further in this direction. As part of this second argument we will examine Bank President James D. Wolfensohn's Comprehensive Development Framework (CDF) (Wolfensohn, 1999). In particular we will ask whether Wolfensohn's strategy of committing the Bank to CDF principles is one which is properly focused on the task of repositioning the Bank as a 'Knowledge Bank'. Our answer will be 'only partly'. We say this because properly reinventing the Bank as a 'Knowledge Bank' would radically transform the Bank's priorities, and its activities in the field, long beyond any changes currently in train. In particular, far less manpower would be devoted to analysing loan proposals and outcomes, and far more manpower would be devoted to giving advice about development strategies, and to providing help with their implementation.

The crisis in international capital markets which broke in the summer of 1997 unleashed a new challenge for the Bank: and this certainly made it hard to keep the Bank's objectives properly in focus. This is not only because of the enormity and urgency of the crisis and but also because of controversy about the role played in it by both the Bank and the International Monetary Fund (IMF) (hereafter, the Fund). A central theme of Wolfensohn's address to the Bank's Board of Governors in October 1998 was the need not to let concerns with this crisis unduly divert the Bank from its objective of promoting long-term growth and development (Wolfensohn, 1998). In our view, a helpful response to this challenge is that one should think of the Bank as having two ways of pursuing its objective, one appropriate for times of calm water sailing and the other appropriate for hurricane, and that one should analyse these problems essentially independently.

Accordingly, in the first and longer part of this chapter (sections 2–5) we concentrate on the long-term fair weather objective. The second substantive part of the chapter (section 6) discusses the Bank's role in relation to financial crisis, and its relationship with the Fund (which clearly has the major responsibility for the avoidance of and resolution of crises). There are issues of demarcation which we examine. Section 7 brings threads of our discussion together in order to discuss the Bank as an institution.

2 Rationales for an institution like the Bank

2.1 Redistribution and development

We shall see that the IBRD provides loans to its clients somewhat below market rates and that the IDA provides concessional loans with a very large aid component. There are arguments in favour of global redistribution of this kind, such as the arguments in favour of the welfare state within one nation (see Rawls, 1971; Sen, 1987). Such arguments in favour of global redistribution become arguments in support of a multilateral institution such as the Bank, because it provides a conduit for funds which enables richer countries to give aid to poorer countries, without this leading to direct bilateral political power relations with them.[5]

However, the application of arguments for intra-national redistribution to the whole world are not uncontentious.[6] Furthermore, in contrast to a number of important NGOs,[7] the Bank has never seen itself as a global social security organisation. Rather, to the extent that the Bank is involved in redistributing the world's income and wealth, it does this because it is involved in promoting growth and the alleviation of the *causes* of poverty, rather than just alleviation of the *symptoms* of poverty. Reduction of poverty in this way has been an avowed Bank objective from at least 1972 (see Stern and Ferreira, 1997: 542). However, as discussed in chapter 1, the interpretation of this objective has varied over the Bank's history. Most recently, the view has gained currency that poverty reduction through 'capability building' is necessary precondition for sustainable development – see Kanbur and Vines (chapter 3 in this volume).

This view, that development and poverty reduction are complementary, implies that we can provide a rationale for the Bank's activities in poverty reduction if we can, in turn, provide convincing rationales for its activity in promoting growth and development.[8]

2.2 Correcting capital market imperfections

One possible line of argument identifies capital market imperfections. The Bank was created at the Bretton Woods conference of 1944 as an institution for funnelling capital to the war-torn global periphery in the face of liquidity-constrained capital markets.[9] However, with the integration of global capital markets which has taken place in the past 30 years, this initial conception of the Bank now makes little sense. For IBRD (middle-income) developing countries, although experience over the 1990s has demonstrated that private capital flows to them countries are volatile and undependable, we argue in section 3 (p. 44) against any view that what is needed is to permanently supplement such flows with official lending. For IDA countries who clearly are still credit-constrained – what matters is not just the money but the ability (or not) to use it to transform policies. Thus, we will argue, supposed capital market imperfections no longer *on their own* provide a major rationale for the Bank lending.

Instead we see the Bank's activities as directed towards intervening *in the borrowing countries,* towards influencing both market outcomes, and government policies towards the market.

2.3 Correcting market failures

The most basic rationale for intervention to promote development is to internalise externalities. (See Rosenstein-Rodan, 1943; Hirschman, 1958; Murphy, Shleifer and Vishny, 1989; Krugman, 1999a.) In the early stages of development, externalities arise particularly because of the complementarity between activities, any one of which may only become profitable only when the others are already established. Private sector enterprises may be unable to capture the social returns from potential investments; governments can undertake such investment projects in which private returns fall short of social returns. By doing this, they may raise potential returns not only on their own investments but also on those undertaken by the private sector (national and international). In this way, government investment projects may not only be of value in themselves but may crowd in private sector investment. The provision of public goods – health, education, infrastructure – can be thought of in this way as well. But why can the Bank, a global, multilateral institution, be usefully involved in the above kinds of activities, which are normally identified as the functions of national government? In making such arguments, it is useful to distinguish market failures at the national level from failures at the international level.

2.3.1 Correcting government failure

A first answer to this question lies in the weak powers of the state in developing countries. Government may lack the capacity to adequately perform the functions just described. The Bank may provide this extra capacity to intervene. Furthermore, rent-seeking and political opposition may prevent the state from adequately intervening in the manner suggested by the above arguments; Bank participation in investment projects may raise the expected level of both social and private investment returns and hence 'crowd in' additional private sector investment. And to the extent that government fails to acknowledge the interests of the poor, social rates of return may exceed private rates, providing a direct justification for the Bank's concern with poverty reduction.

The government-failure view leads naturally to a focus on the ability of the Bank to impose conditions on its loans, to monitor the projects in which it invests, and to attempt to ensure that its contractual lending terms are met. It also leads directly to criticisms of the Bank as being paternalistic (equals neo-colonialist?) and of usurping the proper powers of sovereign governments. This view of the Bank as imposing 'conditionality' on its clients will be extensively discussed below.

2.3.2 Rectification of information failures

A second potential type of national market failure is informational. Investment in emerging markets is significantly more risky than in developed markets, although potential returns are also often very high. Identification of those markets where the risk–return ratio is most favourable constitutes one of the major problems for potential private sector investors. It is possible that the Bank's development knowledge and experience allows it to make this identification more accurately than can the private sector. If this is indeed the case, and if Bank disbursements are guided by these appraisals, private sector investors can benefit by taking Bank investments as a signal. Since the overall risk–return ratio on private sector investment will improve, the Bank will again crowd in the private sector. Note that in this case there need not be any alteration to individual project returns (i.e. there need be no externality or public goods aspects to the projects) and also that the imposition of 'conditionality' is not crucial to the Bank's intervention.

2.3.3 The provision of global public goods at the world level

The externality and informational considerations discussed above operate at the level of the individual country. But in addition to these there are what we see as global public good aspects of good development policies. We identify two aspects of these. The first is to do with knowledge about what constitutes good development policies. This is to a large extent generic rather than country-specific, because what works in one country will, at least to some extent, work elsewhere. Knowledge of this kind has aspects of a global public good, requiring a global solution to the provision problem. Additionally, and in a quite different vein, there are 'global commons' problems in development which also require a global solution. Examples are environmental pollution, the management of global capital flows and the elimination of drug trafficking. The analysis of these problems and the brokering of solutions to them involves the provision of a rather different form of global public good which requires institutional support.

3 Understanding and justifying the Bank's current activities

We identify three very different kinds of activity currently carried out in the Bank as it now exists: lending, development research and development assistance. In this section, we examine whether these three activities can be justified in terms of attempting to rectify one or other of the market failures described in subsection 2.3. And we then ask whether, to do this, the activities currently carried out in the Bank really need to be bundled together in the one institution.

This argument is a difficult, but also an important, one. It is difficult because, since the three kinds of activity carried out in the Bank are very different, the Bank can (and does) mean different things to different people within it. (This would be much less so in the case of the IMF and the World Trade Organisation.[10]) It is important because policy-makers – and, in particular the Board of the Bank – face the need for prioritisation across activities and this is difficult when the rationale for each activity is confused.

3.1 The Bank as a multilateral lending institution

The Bank borrows at AAA rates on international markets and then on-lends the funds at a small margin to countries which would otherwise have been able to borrow only on significantly less favourable terms, if at all. The IBRD, which is the original kernel of the Bank and remains the institution within the World Bank Group with the largest capitalisation and lending, continues to operate in this way. This is the first – and largest – of the Bank's major lending activities. With the 1960 creation of IDA, the Bank was empowered to lend to poorer countries on concessional terms from funds contributed by developed country governments and from its own accumulated profits. This added a second major remit to the Bank's lending activities

3.1.1 The Bank's financial structure

The Bank's actual lending (i e the total of its disbursed and outstanding loans) stood at approximately $100 billion in 1997. There was a further net lending disbursement of $8 billion in 1998.The Bank is able to borrow funds at below LIBOR because it has a buffer of callable capital.[11] It lends these funds to governments on a cost-pass-through basis, with a margin over the cost of funds to make a contribution to the Bank's operational costs. Until recently, this margin was set at 50 basis points but, in practice, approximately half of this amount has been waived. But in addition, there has also been a one-off commitment fee. Taken together, these have led to a lending margin of around 50–60 basis points in recent years. In 1997, this margin stood at around 60 basis points.[12]

The *gross income* of the Bank has two very broad components: loan-related income and income on capital. Loan-related income is what the Bank would have earned if all of its loans had been debt-funded. Taking a simplified picture of the Bank, we can say that, on the basis of the total of disbursed and outstanding loans in 1997 of $100 billion, and with a spread of about 60 basis points, this would have given rise to an income in 1997 of approximately $600 million. Income on capital is the notional income due to the Bank from its risk capital (which is equal to paid-in capital plus accumulated reserves). In 1997, this stood at $22 billion.[13] At an average interest rate of 6 per cent, this yielded a notional income of around $1.3 billion. Taking the two components of gross income together, along with small 'other income' items, the Bank's gross income in 1997 was $2.1billion in 1997.

IBRD expenditure, or operating costs, has two broad components: gross administration costs (which includes research) and loan-loss provisioning. In 1997 the figures for these stood at $800 million and $60 million, respectively.

If we deduct expenditure from gross income we obtain the Bank's *net income.* In 1997 this stood at approximately $1.2 billion. There are two competing claims on this income.[14] First comes the Bank's contribution to reserves. It is a prudential requirement of the Bank's Articles that it build up a reserve position which is in accord with the size of and risks in its business. In 1997 the addition to reserves was $500 million.[15] Second comes the Bank's grants in support of its development priorities, including the Bank's contribution to IDA, its contribution to the HIPC scheme for reducing the debt of the least developed group of countries and some other smaller grants. In 1997 the first two of these contributions stood at $304 million and $250 million, respectively; whilst other contributions were somewhere between $100 and $150 million.

Notice that in 1997 the Bank's loan income, $600 million, fell significantly short of its gross administration costs, namely $860 million. Taking all administration costs to be variable costs in the long run, the policy of cost-pass-through lending for IBRD lending, as it has been implemented until recently, has resulted in IBRD lending being priced at significantly less than long-run marginal cost.[16] Recent price increases, discussed at the end of the chapter, will change this. At the same time they will serve to increase the Bank's capability to make grants in support of its development priorities.

3.1.2 The size and significance of Bank lending

The Bank is a major source of finance for developing countries, but it would be wrong to see it as the predominant source. Figure 2.1 charts net transfers ($billion, deflated to constant 1995 values using the US producer prices, all-items, index) for 1985, 1990 and 1995.[17] Figure 2.1 shows the massive growth in private transfers to developing countries since the mid-1980s. In 1985, official flows only just offset the value of negative private transfers, but by 1995 private flows amounted to over 80 per cent of total flows. The Bank is responsible for only around 30 per cent of official flows. (But bilateral flows are not entirely motivated by developmental objectives. Of course, these aggregate figures disguise substantial

Figure 2.1 *Net transfers, 1985, 1990 and 1995*

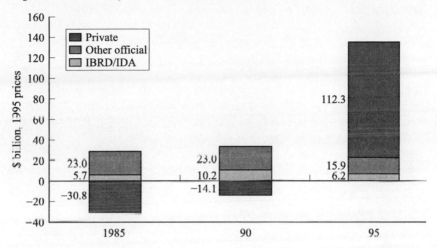

inter-country variation; the Bank is much more important than this for certain countries.)

3.1.3 The justification of Bank lending

Can the Bank's lending activity be justified in terms of trying to solve the market failures identified in subsection 2.3? We need to consider this question in three stages: as it applies to IBRD lending, to IDA lending and finally to IFC and MIGA lending.

The historic justification for the Bank's IBRD lending has been in terms of supposed capital market imperfections (although to the extent that IBRD lending has been subsidised it has also been possible to deploy a redistributional argument). But the early 1990s saw a reversal of this situation and private sector flows came to dominate capital flows to developing countries. Indeed, until the Mexican financial crises of 1994 5 and the 1997–9 crisis in international capital markets many middle-income developing countries often preferred to borrow from the private sector, even at a somewhat higher rate than they would pay the Bank, in order to escape the surveillance and interference which borrowing from the Bank brought with it. In the light of this radical change, it appears that there is no longer normally a role for public sector development lending *as such*, at least to middle income developing countries. Such countries who just want money – as distinct from wanting assistance with as well as money – can 'graduate' to private sector borrowing – a view on which some of us expounded in Gilbert *et al.* (1996).[18]

It is true that Bank lending through the IBRD window was crucially important through the 1980s when, as a consequence of the 'debt crisis', net private sector transfers to developing countries became negative. The recent international financial crisis made borrowing for even middle-income developing countries either impossible or subject to extra risk premia of hundreds of basis points. This experience has led some to argue the liberalised international capital markets of the 1990s are still inadequate as a way to funnel capital to developing countries. But the right conclusion to draw is that developing countries face issues of crisis avoidance and crisis management which concern how to lessen and to deal with the volatility of private capital flows, rather than needing to permanently supplement such flows with official lending. These problems are primarily the responsibility of the IMF rather than the Bank; we deal with this question in section 6 (p. 65). The relevant point for now is that the problem is one of adjusting to the vagaries of free and open capital markets, rather than to their absence. Thus, we believe, supposed capital market imperfections no longer provide a rationale for the Bank's IBRD lending.

The revival of private international capital movements has largely eschewed the IDA countries and their demand for Bank lending remains as strong as ever. The IDA was created in response to the perception that it was very difficult to identify projects which would earn commercial rates of return in the least developed group of countries, but, at the same time, these were (and remain) the countries which most require development assistance. This indicates that the justification for IDA lending was always more in terms of redistribution than capital market imperfections. However, we have noted that redistribution is not a sufficient rationale for Bank lending. It is therefore important to understand whether the Bank's concessional lending does actually promote growth and reduce poverty and, if so, what features of Bank lending result in this outcome. In fact, there is now widespread scepticism that concessional assistance does have positive effects on growth, poverty reduction or environmental quality. We discuss this evidence in section 4 (p. 54) and consider its implications for the Bank's future. The simple relevant point here is that what matters for aid is not just the money.

The IFC and the MIGA do address very specific capital market imperfections. The IFC is the Bank's private sector investment vehicle. One of its major activities is the development of financial markets in developing countries. It is not unreasonable to claim that the IFC pioneered emerging market investments. Here the imperfection is that of 'missing markets'. MIGA offers guarantees to private sector investors and therefore specifically addresses the sovereign risk issue. In fact, it has never been required to pay out on these insurance contracts – it is better seen as an efficient fire brigade, which puts out fires before they cause damage, than as a fire insurance agency. However, with these two exceptions, Bank lending cannot be justified by invoking capital market imperfections. The implication is that the rationale for Bank lending must be found in its being bundled with other activities.

3.2 The Bank as producer of knowledge about development

In 1996 the Bank's research budget was $25 million, or about 2.5 per cent of operating expenditure.[19] In addition, economic analysis of a more instrumental kind is carried out in operational divisions – according to Squire (chapter 4 in this volume), this Economic and Sector Work (ESW) has accounted for around 30 per cent of the Bank's operational budget in recent years. Although the Bank's (non-ESW) research budget has tended to decline over recent years,[20] the Bank remains the largest development research institution in the world. Fischer (1995) claims that Bank research and publication is 'quite influential in developing countries and ... has had an increasing impact on the academic community in the United States in recent years'.

The Bank has been instrumental in promoting debate, and fostering consensus, on the conditions and policies which will result in sustainable growth. (Ferreira, 1992; Stern and Ferreira, 1997). A famous example is the role played by the Bank in the early 1980s in the promotion of open liberal trade policies (see Nogués, 1997). More recently, in its study on the *Asian Miracle,* the Bank was responsible for probing the underpinnings of the 'Washington consensus' on 'sound money and open markets', a questioning role which continued with the advent of Joe Stiglitz as Chief Economist at the Bank. Despite this, few new or original ideas appear to have originated within the Bank – instead the Bank's multilateral nature has given it a comparative advantage in accessing data and in testing theories, often developed elsewhere.[21] One may thus think of the Bank as having been involved primarily in the 'development of ideas' component of development R&D rather than pure research component.[22] The Bank's 'knowledge development' activity has created an understanding about good policies which it would have been very difficult for countries to develop on their own. Squire (chapter 4 in this volume) gives examples of the content of this research on matters as varied as: on public policy towards ageing, on AIDS and public health, on education reform. A recent publication (World Bank, 1999) brings together the results of a large body of important research in the Bank on the effectiveness of aid, some of it reviewed in sections 4 and 5 below.

How can these research activities be rationalised? Specifically, why should this knowledge development be done within a multilateral lending institution like the Bank, rather than it all being done in private sector consultancies, in universities, or in research institutes? We believe, following Squire (chapter 4), that there is a role for a significant in-house research capacity. The argument has at its core the public-goods justification for a Bank-like institution discussed in subsection 2.3: knowledge has aspects of a public good, and knowledge about best-practice development is a global public good, requiring a global solution to the provision problem.

But a further step is required. Why should the Bank be involved in the production of this public good, rather than merely paying for others to create it? We see two reasons for this.

The first is a principal–agent point: 'it is difficult to structure incentives such that outside research institutes will deliver the kind of research that the World Bank [wants]' (Squire, chapter 4 in this volume, p. 108). Part of this agency problem is simply that outside consultants have their own objectives which will be only imperfectly aligned with those of the Bank: academics are motivated to research the kind of problem which leads most easily to publication in leading academic journals; private consultants not operating in a peer-review world may, for example, face the dysfunctional incentive to do safe work in the hope of repeat business. Part of the agency problem relates to the very significant economies of scale and scope in the development of knowledge about development, with the implication that an optimal-sized supplier will have quite high overhead costs. Because of this, any knowledge development outside the Bank will be concentrated in a small number of organisations; it is thus not as if the Bank would face a competitive or even contestable market of suppliers. Insurance considerations would then suggest grounds for some in-house supply, and scale and scope concerns then lead one to suggest that this capacity should not be too small. At the same time the outside suppliers that exist will find it difficult to carry the requisite overhead costs, partly because separating themselves from 'low-quality' rivals may be difficult, and also because much of the requisite overhead will be embodied in mobile human capital.[23] Perhaps the most serious part of the agency problem relates to the intersection of these two points. Being an organisation (be it university department, research institute, or consulting organisation) whose purpose is to sell research which fosters best-practice development is quite different from being a development institution with public purposes like the Bank.[24] In the former kinds of organisation there will always be cost-minimising pressures to cut the knowledge overhead – subject merely to satisfactory product (i.e. research) quality. By contrast, in the Bank the development mission can be pursued as the primary objective. And the institution can, at least in principle, guard against short-run cost-cutting pressure because of its income on capital. Against all this, of course, Bank staff themselves may be motivated as much by their own career objectives as by the Bank's development mission. All of this suggests that complete reliance on either internal or external staff is probably ill-advised. The difficult issue is that of finding the appropriate balance.

A second, quite different, reason for an in-house research capability has been put forward by Squire (chapter 4 in this volume, p. 108): 'without an in-house capacity, integrating the results of research into the World Bank's everyday operations and making those results available to policy-makers in developing countries does not happen. This usually requires an in-house champion, and the best champion is usually the best researcher.' This is an explicit bundling argument. The integration which is sought can, probably, best be achieved in an institution which lends money for projects and programmes and is involved in their implementation. Lending enables the ideas to be put into practice because the projects and programmes coming with the money carry the ideas.

3.3 The Bank as a global development agency

There are two rather different activities which the Bank carries out as a global development agency.

The first – and most straightforward – is illuminated by the observation that the Bank does not just lend money and produce ideas: it packages the ideas and the money together. We refer to this as the 'Bank in the Field'. In this mode, the Bank provides development skills, including skills in project and programme management, bundled together with its loans in a package which would otherwise be unavailable to the Bank's low- and middle-income client countries.

However desirable it is for countries to obtain this technical assistance, can we justify this activity in terms of the Bank trying to solve the market failures identified in subsection 2.3 above? Such activities may be rationalised either in terms of overcoming informational failures – by virtue of its development knowledge and experience, the Bank can improve the returns on investment, and can ensure better project selection (thereby raising average returns) – or in terms of internalisation of externalities. The task of a 'Bank in the Field' carrying out such activities is to deliver services at the country level, one by one.

The World Bank's President, James Wolfensohn has proposed a 'Comprehensive Development Framework' or CDF (Wolfensohn, 1999) as an operating framework within which these skills might be delivered. The CDF approach to development assistance attempts to be comprehensive in two respects: across different aspects of development, and across participants in the development process.[25] It appears that the Bank faces two big challenges in implementing the CDF. The first is how to coordinate, and prioritise, within the Bank, the Bank's own contributions to this comprehensive big-push approach to development assistance. The second is how actually to coordinate the many other stakeholders who are to be involved in this approach to development policy. Who will be in charge when there are disagreements of analysis between the stakeholders, – and what is worse – straight conflicts of interest between them?[26]

In contrast to the traditional development agency role just described, the Bank carries out a second kind of role as a global development agency. This is as a provider of global public goods – and, in particular, as a contributor to the solution of externality problems which arise at a super-national level. (See Reinicke, 1997, 1998a, 1998b; Braithwaite and Drahos, 1999; Kanbur and Sandler, 1999; Kaul, Grunberg and Stern, 1999; and < http://www.globalpublicpolicy.net/ >; this issue is also discussed in Wolfensohn, 1999). In section 1 (p. 39) we noted that an increasingly important number of goods necessary for development are global public goods which can only be effectively provided at the global level. We gave as examples pollution control, financial regulation and the prevention of drug trafficking; another example is forest conservation. There is a lack of congruence, across a wide range of areas, between an increasingly globalised private sector and the delivery of development strategies, public goods and even governance, at the national level. Global public policy responses appear increasingly necessary in response to this disjunction. But, in the absence of global government, this requires new forms of governance. Reinicke (1997) proposes the formation of what he calls global public policy networks and Reinicke (1998a) gives examples of the operation of such networks from three diverse areas: financial markets (the Basle Accords), money laundering (where there is now an increasing number of international cooperative agreements) and dual-use (civilian–military) trade in which, again, there are also now agreements. Braithwaite and Drahos (1999) provide a wealth of other examples, including nuclear safety, drugs and air transport. They discuss the emergence of global 'regulatory webs' to deal with these issues.

The Bank's role in such activities has been, and can be, part provider of disinterested research backup and also as broker of solutions. One example of this is provided by the Commission on Dams which, under the auspices of the Bank, came up with guidelines for dam development which the participants agreed to be bound by. Other examples requiring both research and brokerage might include free trade areas, and liberalised international transport. We believe that an increasingly important part of the Bank's role over the next decades will be to facilitate understanding about, and delivery of, such global public goods.

3.4 The Bank as a bundled institution

The common perception is probably that the Bank's rationales are those of development lending and redistribution. Our arguments suggest that, in the modern world of open capital markets, there is no longer a market failure which rationalises development lending *per se*, and that redistribution *per se* has never been part of the Bank's agenda. That the Bank is involved in these activities is obvious, but supposed capital market failure and need for redistribution do not, we believe, provide a rationale for the Bank's continued existence. Instead, we have pointed to the internalisation of externalities and the provision of 'local' public goods in the development process, to the provision of the global public good development knowledge and to provision of a wider class of global public goods as three arguments which provide more durable rationalisations for the Bank.

In what follows, we suggest that development lending is bundled with the internalisation of development externalities and the provision of public goods because this is the way that these activities are most effectively provided. We see poverty reduction as a beneficial joint product of the promotion of development in this way. Thus we think of the Bank as rather like an Oxbridge college, or a private American university, which uses an endowment income to subsidise its research and teaching. The IBRD provides subsidised loans to its clients while the IDA provides highly concessional loans with a grant component. The Bank also invests in the production and dissemination of development knowledge and provides direct development assistance. It simultaneously combines the activities of financial intermediary, development research institution, consulting company and inter-governmental agency. It finances all its varied activities from income earned from its subscribed capital and accumulated reserves. In certain circumstances, this will imply that the Bank's prime function is lending; in some others, specific policy advice will be more important; while in others, its main contribution will be aiding in the provision of the national or international framework within which development, and development assistance, will take place. Why this should all be done in the one institution is the key issue to which we now turn.

4 Two paradigms: the 'Conditionality Bank' and the 'Knowledge Bank'

Section 3 described the Bank's activities as a lending institution, as a producer of knowledge about development and as a global development agency. Each of these activities exists to some extent outside the Bank in other institutions – many private sector banks are active in lending to developing countries, much development research takes place in universities, a large number of international consulting firms offer project management and overall development assistance and many NGOs are involved in the provision of global public goods. We must thus now tackle the question of why these activities should be brought together under the one roof.

We consider two possible answers to this question. These answers are not necessarily mutually exclusive, but judgement as to the balance between them has important implications for how the Bank ought to position itself.

The first answer, which reflects a widely accepted aspect of the Bank's oral tradition, we call the 'Conditionality Bank' view of the Bank as an institution. It is set out in Gilbert et al. (1996) and Hopkins et al. (1997), both of which draw upon Rodrik (1995), Gavin and Rodrik (1995), and Mosley, Harrigan and Toye (1995). According to this view, which we refer to below as the GHPR view, the lending, research and development agency activities of the Bank are all necessary parts of an institutional practice which is bound together by the conditionality attached to the Bank's lending. This conditionality is designed to influence the behaviour of, and correct the failings of, the governments who borrow from the Bank. Policy conditionality, which must be at least partially successful, raises the Bank's returns, and also raises the returns of private sector lenders who benefit from the same policy improvements.

According to the second view, the key to the justification of the Bank's lending is its research and accumulated development experience. The unifying element which justifies the functional bundling is the Bank's development knowledge and experience. This gives the Bank a comparative advantage over other institutions in adopting a central role in the development process. On a narrow interpretation of the term 'Knowledge Bank', it implies that the Bank's knowledge and experience enables it to identify and implement projects and programmes which would be deemed too risky or infeasible by private sector organisations. On a somewhat broader interpretation, the 'Knowledge Bank' view also sees the Bank as providing public goods, both those to do with knowledge about what constitutes good development policies, but also in responding to 'global commons' problems. On this account, the bundling of research and development assistance is rationalised in terms of the principal–agent argument already discussed in subsection 3.2. The bundling of lending with these activities is based on the idea that lending enables ideas to be put into practice because the projects and programmes coming with the money carry the ideas. At its broadest, the concept sees the Bank's development knowledge and experience, as distinct from its sheer size, as giving it a comparative advantage over other (nationally or regionally-based) development agencies in taking the lead role in development planning and assistance.

4.1 The 'Conditionality Bank'

The conditionality view of the Bank may be expressed as follows: the Bank's distinctiveness and strength derives from the way it bundles together three activities: lending, development research and development assistance. By lending for approved development projects, it is able to assist governments in benefiting from its development experience. That experience ensures a higher success rate on loans than might otherwise be attained. And under the IBRD policy of cost-pass-through lending, this translates into a higher level of lending than would otherwise be possible.

In more detail, the 'Conditionality Bank' argument runs as follows. The Bank's status as a multilateral development agency improves the prospects for its debt servicing and repayment, enabling it to lend to sovereign developing world borrowers at only a modest margin over its borrowing rate. The GHPR argument relies on the claimed ability of the Bank to favourably influence government policies through policy conditionality. According to this view, the importance of the Bank's development agency function is that the Bank is potentially able to address the market failure of *policy risk*. This has two aspects. First, because of its knowledge base in relation to development, the Bank is able to devise conditions on loans and to impose these conditions. Second, the Bank has the ability to monitor loans and projects and so to ensure that contractual lending terms are met. In the absence of Bank conditionality, project returns may not be sufficient to induce investment. In particular, in the absence of Bank surveillance, policy-makers may – so the argument runs – find it difficult to prevent monopolisation of returns in ways which have an anti-development bias, or even to prevent plain rent-seeking from depleting the returns themselves. This suggests that the effects of policy conditionality will be to raise the expected level of both social and private investment returns and hence 'crowd in' additional private sector financing.

The ability to impose conditionality is therefore, according to this view, central to the Bank's effectiveness. Its ability to impose such conditionality, like that of the IMF, arises fundamentally from its legitimacy as a multilateral Bretton Woods treaty institutions. The proponents of this view do not claim that conditionality is always effective. But the Conditionality Bank view of the Bank as an institution rests on a claim that it is at least partly effective.

On the conditionality view, the importance of the World Bank as an *institution* arises from the fact that it can capture some of the gains from its conditionality. By doing this, it adds value to the projects for which it lends. In this paradigm, the role of knowledge and experience is in informing policy conditionality, and the bank's research activities are in turn supported by the (private) return to the Bank from the imposition of conditionality. This argument suggests that, if the Bank did not exist, or it were privatised, then neither the research nor the development-promotion activities would survive, since they both support, and are supported by, the imposition of conditionality, which could not itself survive.

Notice that conditionality – if it is effective – will not only raise expected repayments to the Bank, as the enforcer of conditionality, but in forcing the adoption of good policies, it will increase returns to private sector banks who lend alongside it. The Bank can therefore generate an externality, which further promotes development by encouraging the inflow of private funds into its client states. In due course the supply of funds to its borrowing clients will increase, both as development proceeds and as funds are attracted as a result of the Bank's own actions. This, in turn, will mean that the Bank's clients will, subsequently, be able to obtain funds from private markets without the need to submit to the Bank's conditionality.

4.2 The 'Knowledge Bank'

Returns from investment in developing countries are inevitably uncertain. Economic science, moderated by practical experience across a wide range of countries, will reduce this uncertainty and allow more accurate discrimination between projects and across countries. At one level, the Bank's development knowledge and experience should ensure superior country and project selection. This will result in development finance being better focused than in the absence of a multilateral bank, while lower risk will result in an overall higher level of lending. All of these observations would apply equally well to private banks and consulting companies as to a multilateral institution like the Bank. However, private banks have no incentive to disseminate their knowledge and make their experience widely available, and consulting firms do so only at a price substantially in excess of the marginal cost of dissemination. The Bank, and other multilaterals, can do such dissemination; thus increasing the benefits from the availability of better information. In this way, the Bank's investment decisions, and the research on which these are based, may provide a signal to private sector banks thereby raising the profitability and productivity of their investments.

The 'Knowledge Bank' sees the Bank's knowledge and experience as enabling it to identify and implement projects and programmes which would be deemed too risky or infeasible by private sector organisations. But more than this, the 'Knowledge Bank' view also sees the Bank as providing public goods. There are several ways in which this can happen:

(1) Whereas the 'Conditionality Bank' is able to raise returns above those which private sector lenders would obtain, the 'Knowledge Bank' obtains the same returns but is better able to identify the high-return projects. If there are externalities affecting private sector lenders, these operate through (positive) intra-country or intra-sector correlations across project returns which enable private lenders to follow the Bank's lead.

(2) Knowledge about what constitutes good development policies is to a large extent generic rather than country-specific: what works well in one country will, at least to some extent, work elsewhere. Knowledge of this kind has aspects of a global public good, requiring a global solution to the provision problem.

(3) Global public goods, of the kinds discussed in subsection 3.3, raise the prospects for development across the range of participating countries. However, it is difficult for individual governments to provide these goods, in particular since these will often require cooperation

between governments, each of which has an individual incentive to depart from the cooperative solution. Provision of these global public goods will raise returns on investments, both those undertaken by the Bank, and also those undertaken by private lenders.

The common feature of these strands of the 'Knowledge Bank' conception is that they see the Bank's crucial activity as the production and dissemination of knowledge about the process of economic development and the policies best calculated to promote it. On this account, the bundling of research and development assistance and lending money is rationalised in terms already explicitly stated above.

4.3 Which Bank?

Both the 'Conditionality Bank' and 'Knowledge Bank' arguments rationalise bundling and emphasise that the private sector benefits from an efficient multilateral bank. This may suggest that, from a policy standpoint, it may not matter which view of the Bank is correct. However, if conditionality is effective but the effects of improved knowledge are relatively minor, the Bank may be overinvesting in research while, at the same time, failing to realise its potential by being insufficiently committed to coercing governments in the direction of reform. This view would imply possible pruning of the Bank's Washington-based activities in order to move more resources into field-based monitoring. It would justify a tougher stance in negotiations with borrowing governments and, in particular, a greater willingness to cut off finance when there is policy backsliding. By contrast, if conditionality does not work then an institution like the Bank would need to base itself on 'Knowledge Bank'-type arguments and the expenditure of additional resources would be wasteful and perhaps even counter-productive. Bank staff are best employed in identifying good projects and programmes, in producing knowledge and seeking to disseminate: they should not spend their time attempting to salvage poor investments.

Clearly evidence on conditionality is important here. This evidence is the subject of section 5.

5 The ineffectiveness of conditionality: evidence and implications

5.1 Policy conditionality and time-inconsistency

The 'Conditionality Bank' concept rests on the supposed effectiveness of policy. An important series of recent papers has questioned – at both *a priori* and empirical level – whether conditionality is likely to be effective.

The central problem with conditionality is that it results in time-inconsistency. Recipient governments may agree to *ex ante* policy conditions if they see this as a means of attracting future loans or aid support. However, once the aid is disbursed these incentives are diminished. In certain cases, governments may simply renege on the conditions to which they had previously agreed, but more typically, lack of ownership will imply that the reform process receives less priority than Bank officials may have wished, and becomes subject to compromise within the context of domestic policy debates.

The lender's natural response to this problem is to restructure its decisions as a repeated game. The Bank has done this by designing aid programmes which include shorter horizons and more detailed conditions. The disbursement of aid has been broken into multiple tranches, with the release of each tranche contingent on the prior achievement of policy reforms.

However, it is arguable that this *ex ante* 'bargaining' approach to reform has actually tended to exacerbate the problems associated with conditionality, not solve them. This is because such *ex ante* conditionality induces a conflictual approach to the Bank's relationships with borrowing governments in which the governments 'sell' reforms to the Bank. In such an environment, governments have the incentive to maximise the price at which reform can be sold both by holding back from unilateral action and by exaggerating the costs of reform. These effects can be so deleterious as to actually cause governments which would otherwise be proponents of reform to become opponents. Furthermore, conflicts associated with conditionality can undermine the ownership of those reforms which are undertaken, with the consequence that these reforms are less successful than would otherwise have been the case. At the same time, once the initial tranche of a loan has been made available, Bank staff have a strong incentive to make the loan 'work'. This is partly because their own success depends on effectively managing aid disbursements and partly because punishments which imposed by the Bank for failing to meet conditions imposed by the Bank lack moral legitimacy. The threat not to make subsequent tranches available therefore has relatively low credibility, and the Bank learns to accept partial success. Furthermore, an agile government may be able to sell the same reform several times – Collier (chapter 12 in this volume) suggests examples of this.

Opponents of conditionality often frame their objections in a principal–agent framework in which the Bank is principal and the borrowing government is the agent. It is arguable that this exaggerates the monolithic nature of many governments and that, instead, policy is often the outcome of competing pressures within government which contains both advocates and opponents of reform. In that case, there is no inevitable clash of interests between principal and agent, and the role of conditionality is to 'tip the balance' towards the reformers, or even to strengthen government in adopting policies which are acknowledged as necessary but which are difficult to sell to an uninformed public.

An alternative response is to argue that the 'Conditionality Bank' argument and, indeed, the entire academic discussion of conditionality exaggerates the importance of policy conditionality in Bank lending. In many countries in which the Bank leads, there is and never has been any attempt to influence policy, this being regarded as broadly satisfactory.

5.2 Evidence

Evidence on the claimed ineffectiveness of World Bank conditionality comes in three forms – from case studies, from the Bank's own assessments and from econometric studies. In each case, the evidence points in the same direction.

A substantial body of case study evidence has been assembled, in particular by Mosley, Harrigan and Toye (1995) and Killick (1998). Mosely, Harrigan and Toye (1995) examined whether conditionality changed the policies of recipient governments, and whether this actually improved outcomes. Their answer to both questions was 'a little, but not as much as the Bank hoped' (Mosely, Harrigan and Toye, 1995: 305). In particular, they found that structural adjustment lending was typically successful in raising export growth, but often resulted in lower aggregate investment with the consequence that overall output growth was little affected. Killick (1998) analysed the experience of 21 countries, and concluded that governments typically comply with Bank conditionality only when they perceive this as in their own interests.[27] In their view, 'conditionality is not an effective way of improving economic policies in recipient countries' (1998: 165). Killick acknowledges that conditionality can sometimes tip the balance towards reform, but finds relatively few examples of this (1998: 166).

The Bank has its own internal evaluation unit, the Operations Evaluation Department (OED), which ranks project outcomes as either successful or unsuccessful depending whether the desired outcomes are achieved [28] Around two-thirds of projects are judged successful. Dollar and Svensson (1997) investigated the determinants of success econometrically. They show that variables representing Bank supervision have no significant effect on success which, instead, is affected by variables representing political stability. Isham and Kaufmann (chapter 9 in this volume), who also use OED data, show that projects are particularly likely to generate poorer returns than anticipated in the presence of an overvalued exchange rate, low public sector expenditure (implying a lack of complementary activities) and lack of openness to trade.

The OED-based studies consider success in terms of achievement of prior objectives. This is relatively straightforward for traditional projects, but less satisfactory for programme lending, where there will in general be multiple and often broadly defined objectives. An alternative and complementary approach is to consider the effects of aid on overall economic performance. This is the approach, anticipated in Mosley, Harrigan and Toye (1995), that has been followed in the most recent work. A major study by Burnside and Dollar (1996, hereafter, BD) examines the effects of aid on growth rates. Their measure of aid covers both multilateral and bilateral aid and is constructed as the aid component of concessional loans. BD conclude that, although on average, aid has no discernible effect on growth rates, it significantly raises growth rates in 'good' policy environments but reduces growth in 'bad' policy environments. The conclusion that, on average, aid does not affect growth arises by averaging across countries with different policy environments; the implication is that aid *can* be effective when directed to places where the policy environment is good.

The BD study is complemented by work by Feyzioglu, Swaroop and Zhu (1996, hereafter, FSZ) on aid fungibility. Donors care strongly about being able to affect the budget of the recipient country: conditions stipulate that aid is given for a particular purpose in order to ensure that the recipient actually does spend more on that purpose. FSZ find that, with the single exception of projects in the transportation sector, aid dollars are completely fungible.[29] A dollar of project aid in the health sector has the same impact on health expenditure as a dollar to the education sector, or a dollar of free resources in the hands of the government: every dollar received for a particular purpose simply frees a dollar for the government to spend in some other way. Donors may believe they are affecting budgetary composition by earmarking – but in general they are not. On the one hand, the FSZ results suggest a reason for the BD results. Since aid is not necessarily used for the purposes for which it is intended by the donor, governments with good policies can use it well but governments with poor polices are free to use it badly. On the other hand, they imply that the Bank may be wasting the resources it currently devotes to project design and monitoring.

Even conceding the BD and FSZ results, aid may nevertheless have a beneficial effect on policy by improving the policies of recipient governments. This could happen either because aid changes policy (through conditionality) or because growth itself causes improvements in policy. The BD study makes a first step in the investigation of this question. Although their primary focus is the link between aid and growth, the authors do control for the possible endogeneity of policy by estimating a policy equation. Their estimated equation supports the conclusion that the quality of policy is not affected by aid. The BD and FSZ results, together with the earlier work by Mosley, Harrigan and Toye (1995) and the OED analyses, make a powerful case that policy conditionality is ineffective. Not only is aid not necessarily used for what it is directly intended, but on average it has no effect on growth, either directly, or indirectly through improved government policies. What matters is the policy environment, but lending appears to have little direct impact on this.

5.3 Ex post conditionality?

The negative empirical results on the effectiveness of Bank conditionality have prompted two opposing responses. The first, adopted by Mosley, Harrigan and Toye (1995), is to argue for more effective conditionality. They argue that conditionality should be more appropriate and simpler, and that 'punishments' on renegers should be applied more consistently. This is to implicitly view conditionality as essential to the Bank's operations, but its application to have been flawed. 'Ownership' is regarded as crucial for effective policy reform and, to that end, it is proposed that reforms be proposed by governments rather than imposed by the Bank. This 'positive conditionality' view implies that governments will propose projects or programmes to the Bank, perhaps with Bank staff assistance, and that policy reforms will form a part of such proposals.

An alternative view, currently receiving considerable prominence, is that the Bank should give up on policy conditionality in its current form, on the grounds that this can never be effective (BD; Collier, 1997; and chapter 12 in this volume). In what initially seems a paradoxical argument, it is claimed that the Bank would actually obtain a superior outcome to the repeated game precisely by committing not to impose detailed conditions on the use of its funds. Instead, the Bank should recognise that there are 'good' types and 'bad' types of countries and it should direct aid at the 'good' types rather than to trying to alter turn the behaviour of clients (all of whom are assumed to be to a greater or lesser extent 'bad'). But this does not imply that the Bank should cease to interest itself in the details of client government policies. Indeed, the Bank should continue to advocate and push for the adoption of policies which are consistent with its accumulated knowledge and practical experience. Governments will have an incentive to pay heed to this advice, both because Bank advice benefits from its accumulated knowledge, and because following this advice will induce future assistance from the Bank.

The Bank can best work towards the achievement of good policies,[30] it is argued, if it directs its aid selectively towards countries which have demonstrated that they have good policies, and if it works on making widely known what good policies are. Furthermore, there may be regional spillovers – countries which reform and grow may drag their trade partners along in their wake and demonstration effects – success may encourage others to emulate good policies. One may characterise this latter mode of operation as 'ex post' conditionality, a name chosen in order to sharply contrast what is proposed from current practice, which is described as 'ex ante conditionality'. On this view, the Bank should adopt a set of policy indicators in order to determine aid allocation: the Bank should provide development assistance only to countries which have followed sound policies, as measured by these indicators. BD adopt a policy index comprising openness, low inflation and a satisfactory fiscal position. The ex post conditionality view implies that borrowers who have demonstrably good policy, as measured by an index of these indicators, should not face further conditions on their use of funds. This would be the only form of conditionality which the Bank should seek to impose.

According to its advocates, this approach would clearly have the potential to transform the ownership of reform. Countries would find themselves in charge of their own reform programme rather than, as currently, bargaining with it with the Bank. Reforming governments would be those that had chosen to reform – rather than being unwilling recipients of 'reforms' thrust upon them. They would own their reforms and would therefore have the incentive to make them successful. The Bank would sharpen these incentives by rewarding success with continued funding, and would be able to reduce its own expenditure on project design and monitoring.

Ex post conditionality of this kind, it is claimed, would reduce domestic credibility problems for a reforming client government while allowing it to send a clear signal to foreign investors of its genuine reform credentials. It might also lead to a relatively quick reduction in financial risk ratings for strong reformers.[31] And since the Bank currently devotes considerable resources to monitoring compliance, a shift to *ex post* conditionality has the potential of releasing these resources, which would then be available for lending to (and assistance in) countries whose governments are judged to have good policy. It might even be possible to downsize the Bank to such an extent that it could entirely fit into its newly refurbished H Street building.

5.4 Implications for the Bank as an institution

It is arguable that a move to *ex post* conditionality is likely to be over-brutal, by forcing a large number of 'poor-policy' countries to fare for themselves, at least until they learn to reform. The 'Knowledge Bank' view emphasises the role of the Bank as educator. But just as it has become generally accepted that schooling should be universal, the Bank cannot confine its educational activities, which are the vehicle for its lending activities, to the deserving. This suggests that there should be a two-pronged approach to future Bank lending.[32]

There should be a change in the way that the Banks deals with the governments of countries which have good policy regimes in place and where it is judged that past lending has been properly used. Governments of these countries should make proposals to the Bank, and these will typically be framed in conjunction with Bank staff, but grants to them should not be conditional on anything other than regular reporting to ensure that funds are employed as specified in the loan agreements. In particular, this form of lending would not involve policy conditionality.

By contrast, a large component of Bank activity in countries with poor policy environments will be educational. The Bank will stand ready to advise governments, to participate in policy discussions, and to involve itself in training and related activities (for example, university courses). But projects are also a means of transferring knowledge, and the Bank will look for projects in which it can lead governments. Within this view of the Bank's operation, projects become a vehicle for transferring knowledge to client governments.[33]

Education is labour-intensive, and the Bank is income-constrained. The 'Knowledge Bank' would put more staff in the field, particularly in countries where policy is weak. This will require staff economies elsewhere – this must be in the Bank's dealing with countries with good policy environments and good recent growth experience. Paradoxically, therefore, the 'Knowledge Bank' would move its human resources to countries where average Bank staff productivity is low, while the *ex post* conditionality school would do the contrary. This is because if the policy environment can be changed by a sufficiently large push, capital productivity will be increased substantially.

In summary the lesson is that Bank lending to countries should be explicitly designed so as to transfer knowledge to help countries design their own reform programmes.[34] In thinking about foreign assistance much of the discussion should be about getting the *right* combination of money and knowledge. In the countries with good policies and strong institutions, the emphasis should be on money. In countries where the policy environment is poor, either because of an unsatisfactory macro-economic and trade framework, or because of poorly performing public institutions, the emphasis must be on getting these policy and institutional prerequisites right.

All of this has important implications for the Bank's administrative structure and for its budget. Knowledge transfer is staff-intensive. In policy-poor countries, the ratio of staff-time to lending dollars will be very high, suggesting a costly, and possibly increasingly costly, operation, which will require financing. One way will be to economise on staff input into the administration of loans to countries with good policies. But there may be implications both for the pricing of loans to these countries and also for how much capital the Bank needs. We take up these issues in section 7.

6 The Bank's role in the light of the emerging market financial crisis

6.1 The conjuncture

The emerging market financial crisis of 1997 and 1998 significantly changed international capital markets and the environment in which the Bank operates; the lack of market access for many emerging market economies has opened the debate as to whether the world needs an international lender of last resort (see Fischer, 1999). The actions of the Fund in coordinating very significant rescue packages for crisis-hit countries, and the establishment of the Contingent Credit Line (CCL), have moved the Fund inexorably towards playing this role, albeit with very limited resources in comparison to private capital flows.[35]

This raises the question of whether the Bank should also play an active part in helping to remedy this deficiency of the global architecture. In practice, the Bank became involved through 1998, simply 'because it was across the road' from the IMF. In total, the Bank provided around $8 billion in short-term liquidity financing in the packages of lending to Thailand, Indonesia and Korea. This 'defensive' lending had very little to do with promoting development (in the normal sense of that expression). If it were to be repeated, such emergency liquidity lending could severely destabilise the Bank's normal development lending (see subsection 7.2, p. 74). Ideally, therefore, the direct provision of 'lender of last resort' financing should be the preserve of the Fund.

Instead the Bank has, we believe, two kinds of role to play. In the recent crises real shocks have been exacerbated by financial shocks. The interaction between a negative real and a weak financial sector led to a sharp withdrawal of (or refusal to roll over) credit by international capital markets. This, in turn, led to a deeper financial crisis and to a larger adjustment than that required to absorb the original real shock (see Gavin and Powell, 1997; Radelet and Sachs, 1998; Alba *et al.*, 1999; Corbett and Vines, 1999a, 1999b; Krugman, 1999b). The Bank can contribute to a solution to these problems by (1) helping to establish the regulatory structures within which emerging markets countries are safe places to lend and (2) helping to construct facilities, *ex ante*, which enable emerging market economies to continue to access private markets at times of crisis. The construction these structures and facilities has significant global–public goods aspects: Bank involvement in these activities is a good example of the kind of role envisaged for the Bank in subsection 3.3.

6.2 Financial regulation

The Bank has consistently acknowledged the importance of the financial sector in developing economies and has aimed to support financial development.. This has often taken the form of encouraging the growth of equity finance, where the private sector-oriented IFC arm of the Bank has taken the leading role. However, bank finance remains dominant in most middle income countries, and here the emphasis is in ensuring the integrity of the banking system. The Bank may be the natural institution to work with emerging countries to design appropriate safety net policies, to ensure institutional separation between banks and industry, to aid countries with bank privatisation and to advise and provide technical assistance to enhance banking regulation and supervision.

We argue that the Bank should, in addition, prioritise the development of corporate and financial infrastructure. In this, we include assisting countries to move towards internationally accepted accountancy procedures and auditing rules, to develop creditor protection laws and to clarify bankruptcy procedures in line with international practice. Development of infrastructure laws and procedures becomes extremely difficult in a financial crisis when urgency and the perceived need to protect special interests can result in expensive compromise.

The recent financial crises have strained relations between the Bank and the Fund over which institution should have the lead role in financial sector surveillance and reform issues. It is clear that whilst such surveillance is absolutely necessary for the Fund's 'stability' mandate (and, indeed, the Fund has been asked to incorporate a higher level of financial sector surveillance in the context of Article IV consultations) it is the Bank – and not the Fund – which has had the experience and the on the ground knowledge of financial sector work in many emerging markets. This observation led to the idea (embodied in a British proposal[36]) of merging the financial sector staff of the Bank and the Fund and creating a new third institution that would be specifically responsible for financial sector work.

This proposed split between surveillance activity and lending activity would mirror the split between some national banking sector regulators and the relevant Central Bank. For example, there is such a split between the Bundesbank and the German banking regulator and the separation in the United Kingdom since 1997 is similar. We favour such a split at the global level, for two reasons. First, there are clear difficulties in making the lender of last resort also the regulator. Second to concentrate such regulatory – as distinct from educating and institution development-promoting – activity in the Bank would overbalance an institution which already suffers from goal congestion. We recognise that it will be difficult to make such a radical institutional change. But it appears to be an important long-run objective.

6.3 Crisis prevention and crisis resolution

The recent series of crises have been particularly severe precisely because, in current international circumstances, liquidity crises have amplified the initial real shocks. In such circumstances, liquidity is an important asset. Indeed, at the extreme, if a crisis is sparked only by a liquidity shock – owing, say, to contagion in international capital markets – pre-arranged access to international liquidity might have completely prevented it. Pre-arranged international liquidity could at least reduce the amplification of a real shocks, through an accompanying liquidity crisis.

The Asian experience has shown that, with open capital markets, the amount of reserves required to defend quasi-fixed exchange rate regimes may be extremely high. The maintenance of a peg may give the private sector a false sense of security that it is not exposed to currency risk. This may encourage the private sector to borrow abroad in foreign currency, thereby incurring exchange rate risk, or to borrow in domestic currency from the banks who take in foreign deposits, thus themselves shouldering the exchange rate risk. More generally emerging country borrowers normally face a choice; borrow short-term in domestic currency or longer-term in foreign currency. Whatever route is chosen the consequent foreign exchange or liquidity risks open up the possibility of self-fulfilling crises as investors attempt to be first out when trouble threatens. Naturally, when large exchange rate depreciations do occur, the effect on firms' balance sheets is such that domestic governments feel obliged to intervene and bailout financial (and in some case non-financial) institutions to avoid widespread bankruptcies. One of us has argued elsewhere (Corbett and Vines, 1999a, 1999b, Corbett, Irwin and Vines, 1999) that the Asian crisis became a collapse precisely when the bailout obligations caused by currency falls went beyond, or were thought to go beyond, the fiscal capacity of the country concerned. This in turn caused currency depreciations to turn into currency collapse, as markets feared monetisation of deficits which might spiral out of control. The liquidity required to prevent such crises may be impossibly large, implying that quasi-fixed exchange rate regimes may no longer be viable.

This has led to the view – which we largely share – that viable exchange rate regimes are corner solutions – either truly flexible or truly fixed through, say, a currency board arrangement. Irrespective of which regime is adopted, however, international liquidity remains a vital commodity for emerging countries. This is because the two alternative exchange rate regimes are still intrinsically risky. Truly floating exchange rates have been shown to be subject to very large degrees of volatility, and this is particularly the case for emerging economies, where external capital plays a highly significant role and markets are thin, and where – if there are perceptions of policy weakness – movements may become self-fulfilling. Currency boards, on the other hand, imply that countries lose an unlimited domestic lender of last resort and hence the banking sector may be more vulnerable to a self withdrawal of funds. Moreover, it will continue to be the case that emerging countries will be able to borrow only short-term in their own currencies, and longer-term in foreign currencies and hence maturity mismatches or currency mismatches should be recognised as an inevitable consequence of capital inflows. It thus appears that, whatever exchange rate regime is chosen, emerging market economies may need much larger international liquidity than had been supposed prior to the recent crisis.

Taking the world as a whole, if emerging market economies all self-insure by accumulating reserves, then this will lead to an inefficiently large aggregate level of reserves. Purchase of liquidity insurance is an alternative to relying on accumulated reserves. Policies of this sort have recently been implemented by Argentina and, to a more limited extent, Mexico.[37] In these schemes, private banks stand ready to provide liquidity for a commitment fee plus a payment if the facility is used against collateral issued by the purchasing government. Provided governments have appropriate collateral, this is likely to be a much less expensive means of accessing liquidity than accumulation of reserves. However, many developing countries may lack appropriate collateral. By offering partial collateral insurance in arrangements of this type, the Bank can enhance the value of these facilities making them more attractive to both the insuring banks and the insured countries.[38] These facilities should, however, remain private sector driven and private sector priced. They then serve a complementary role to the Fund's 'products'. The private sector monitoring will complement official surveillance which, together with the availability of a stock of liquidity, will reduce the likelihood of a crisis occurring. If a crisis does occur then such facilities 'bail-in' private sector funds automatically.

In this context, a problem with Bank procedures is that guarantees are treated as if they were disbursements. This is paradoxical since the purpose of a guarantee is to avoid having to make a disbursement. However, as a consequence of this very conservative treatment of guarantees, very few have been granted. It would be preferable to regard guarantees as call options in which case they would be equivalent to loans in proportion to the implied delta. If the Bank were to move to a delta-based system, this would further enhance its ability to provide such cover.

6.4 A new compact between the Bank and the Fund?

Overlap between the Fund and the Bank is unavoidable. Necessarily, economists of the two institutions will use the same data and analyse similar topics (although perhaps with a different focus). However, this overlap should not be seen in terms of a turf battle between the two institutions but rather in terms of two institutions which share common ground, with each having the right to the same type of analysis. Naturally this should be done in a cooperative fashion possible with extensive information-sharing and exchange of views in a frank and transparent manner.

Nevertheless, the history of Bank–Fund 'cooperation' suggests that conflict between the two institutions is likely unless there is a formalised process of cooperation between them. The chapter by Jacques Polak in the Bank *History* (Polak, 1997) discusses, from the point of view of a Fund 'insider', the friction concerning structural adjustment lending which dogged the relations between the two institutions during the 1980s, and which led to open conflict between them in the case of the loan to Argentina in 1988; the Bank *History* itself (KLW, 1997a: 527–21) gives an account of what happened, which is interestingly different from that given by Polak. This is a story which almost exactly mirrors the conflict which erupted in 1998 between the Bank and the Fund over the Fund's handling of the Asian debt crisis. In the case of Argentina in 1988 'the Fund, in [a] ... standby to Argentina, impose[d] strict conditionalities, which Bank personnel found so rigorous that they alerted the Fund that the government was sure to fall short ... [T]he Bank people, who had been spending more time in Argentina than their Fund counterparts, found the latter's macroeconomic analysis stereotypical, excessively short-ranged, and thin.' (KLW, 1997a: 530). In the case of Asia in 1998, Joe Stiglitz publicly criticised the Fund's role in Indonesia, Thailand, Korea and elsewhere for excessively tight policies, both monetary and fiscal, based on what he claimed was inadequate analysis of Asia's particular circumstances. In response to the Argentine problem, a formal concordat was drawn up in 1989 between the Fund and the Bank, which delineated the areas of 'primary responsibility'; 10 years later, something similar is again needed.

We propose that the two institutions have core missions: the Fund on macroeconomics and crisis resolution and macro-policy advice; and the Bank on longer-term development – including microeconomics and trade and industry issues – and poverty reduction. This proposal embodies a view that the Bank should not be distracted from its longer-term development objectives by short-term crisis imperatives; it complements the view expressed by US Treasury Secretary Larry Summers that the Fund should concentrate on crisis management and move away from longer-term assistance.[39] Of course there are complications which need to be addressed. With regard to the Bank, any crises will inevitably generate a large and urgent financing requirement which the IMF by itself will have difficulty meeting – there would be no crisis if the IMF could provide the required funds within its normal budgets. Since it is politically impossible for the Bank to stand aside, the issue it has to face is how to insulate its normal activities from emergency crisis requirements while, at the same time, not doing anything which could jeopardise its AAA status. In relation to the proposal that the Fund move away from longer term assistance, there is an important issue as to whether a period of, say, 12–18 months would be sufficient for adjustment if the crisis reflects structural problems in the crisis-hit countries, and not simply contagion-induced capital volatility.

To deal with such inevitable complications we suggest that, beneath the statement of core missions, there would be an *agreed list of competencies* and a *division of lead responsibilities* between the institutions. For example, the Bank would be responsible for trade liberalisation and, perhaps, the Fund for privatisation. But in all areas there would be a *formal obligation to consult*. For example, in the design of Macroeconomic Adjustment Programmes (MAPs), the Fund is already *obliged* to consult with the Bank on Social aspects, both *ex ante* and *ex post*. *Ex ante* the Fund can expect analysis and cooperation from the Bank on designing the programme so as to minimise social consequences. *Ex post* the Bank is to monitor social effects, and the Fund is to consider the Bank's judgement on whether the programme had acted as intended. Quite deliberately the Fund in this example has the power and the Bank acts as consultant. But also, deliberately, the party with the power is obliged to formally consider the views of the consultant. In the case of trade liberalisation the Bank would have the power but would be obliged to consult with the Fund. The structure of such obligations can, and should, be generalised.[40]

There may also be an important 'division of style' between the Bank and the Fund. Within the IMF, considerable effort is devoted to the review of country programmes by functional departments (in particular, the Fiscal Affairs Department and, especially, by the Policy Development and Review Department). The purpose of this is to ensure consistency of treatment of countries in similar circumstances. Before the Asia crisis, many observers had commented on the coherence and consistency of the internal IMF intellectual tradition which underpinned its advice (see

Clark, 1996a; Eichengreen and Kenen, 1994) This state of affairs was well summed up in the mid-1990s by the current Managing Director who stated 'the intellectual discipline will be maintained while I am here – we deal with crises and we cannot have our troops rethinking strategy on the field of battle' (quoted in Clark, 1996b: 23). The Bank is a very different kind of organisation. This is because the bundle of competencies brought together in the Bank's core activities are more complex and difficult to manage than those of the IMF: 'development and poverty reduction' contains a much more diffuse agenda than macroeconomic stabilisation and crisis management. In a revealing contrast drawn before the recent crisis, Arnold Harberger has suggested that 'while [the image] of the Fund is like a commercial bank in that there is a single corporate line in dealing with the outside world', that of the Bank 'is something like a travelling seminar' (cited in Clark, 1996b: 23).

The recent financial crisis has accentuated these differences. It has also suggested that there may be disadvantages in being too much like an army. New events can require nimble footwork and the Fund appears to be too rigid as an organisation to respond rapidly to new and different challenges. There is now widespread agreement that the Fund was mistaken in aspects of its strategy in relation to the Asian crisis, and that as an institution it was slow to learn and slow to respond to its inadequacies.[41] The Bank does not suffer from this difficulty. During the last two years it has often seemed a good thing that the Bank does sit across the road from the Fund on 19th Street. Furthermore, to be a 'Knowledge Bank', the Bank has to be – much more than the Fund needs to be – an organisation where new, and possibly unorthodox, thinking can flourish. We have reviewed above what we think such new thinking needs to involve. An enduring legacy of Joe Stiglitz's term as Chief Economist at the Bank will be his assertion of the need for this new thinking.

7 The Bank as an institution

We have argued that the Bank as an institution is like an Oxbridge college or a private university. It is involved in the education business and uses an endowment income – obtained from its subscribed capital and accumulated reserves – to subsidise its provision of knowledge and of public goods. This metaphor helps us to understand the bank's institutional structure, motivates us to ask whether it has enough money, and leads us to think about its overall vision. We conclude this chapter by considering these three issues in turn.

7.1 Institutional structure

A Bank which was only a 'Conditionality Bank' would – it seems – be able to get by without the income from endowment. A 'Conditionality Bank' would be one in which policy conditionality translated into enhanced profitability on project lending, allowing these profits to be used to finance the research which feeds into the policy conditions, without the need for a large endowment. But a 'Knowledge Bank' – which is what we have argued the World Bank should increasingly see itself becoming – does not have such a luxury. To transfer knowledge and to supply public goods, which is the mission of a 'Knowledge Bank', is costly, and it is not right to expect returns on loans to cover these costs entirely. It therefore requires an endowment, and cross-subsidisation from income on capital to its operating accounts. A 'Knowledge Bank' is best seen as trying to maximise its output of knowledge and global public goods, subject to a financing constraint.

We have also (in subsection 5.4) explored a tension here. Some higher-income developing countries, with good policies and strong institutions, will require that relatively little knowledge provision and relative few public goods are bundled together with their loans from the Bank. The 'Knowledge Bank' has an incentive to take profits on these loans. These profits can be used to add to the income on capital to subsidise operations in policy poor countries, where the emphasis will be on knowledge transfer and income will not cover costs.

This issue has implications for a question raised in subsection 3.1. There it was suggested that middle-income countries, with good policies and strong institutions, should 'graduate' to borrowing from the private sector instead of borrowing from the Bank. But, arguably, the Bank should instead seek to sustain its loans to such countries, in order to improve its loan portfolio: so as to obtain profits on this sort of lending which can help to sustain an IBRD surplus for transfer to IDA or HIPC. Such loans, of course, bring the Bank into direct competition with the private capital market. In the face of such competition, the Bank may still expect to make profits on these loans which it can use to cross-subsidise those of its activities where the financial return falls short of the social return. The profitability of its lending to middle- income countries arises from the Bank's low cost of capital (for reasons discussed in subsection

3.1) and because it has repayment privileges which come from being a multilateral institution established by government treaty. Nevertheless this aspect of the Bank as an institution seems relatively vulnerable in the longer term to erosion by private sector competition, with implications for the Bank's longer-term structure. We do not attempt to resolve this tension. Instead we simply note that the balance of advantage in IBRD lending to middle-income countries will be improved the greater the profitability of this lending.

7.2 Does the Bank have enough money?

This brings us to the next questions. Would the Bank's capital be sufficient to satisfy its creditors if it were to be wound up? And does its capital generate sufficient income to enable it to carry out the business which its shareholders wish it to?

The first question is easy to answer. As already noted in section 3, the Bank's Articles of Agreement require that the ratio of its total subscribed capital and accumulated reserves to its outstanding loans, loan participations and loan guarantees be beneath unity. The 1997 figures, quoted in section 3, put this ratio at $100/(186 + 14) = 0.5$. Although the Bank can call this capital without seeking the consent of member governments, these governments are anxious to minimise this possibility. Nevertheless, this calculation suggests that the IBRD's capital would certainly be sufficient to cover any needs to pay the Bank's creditors in the event of its insolvency.[42]

The second question is the more relevant one and leads to more demanding tests. These have two aspects. First, the Bank is obliged by its Articles of Association to add each year to reserves an amount consistent with the projected growth of its loan book. In practice, this is interpreted as a requirement which should bind in normal years. Second, the Bank has a loan book which is highly concentrated in loans to particular sovereigns, some of which are high-risk; the covariance risk of these loans is also high (because a global economic downturn could affect a number of sovereign states simultaneously). The Bank needs to be confident, in an abnormal year in which there is a large shock resulting, say, from a number of its loans becoming non-performing that that it will be able to continue with its core business.

In section 2, we noted that the Bank's *net income* in 1997 stood at approximately \$1.2 billion, and that, after an addition to reserves of \$500 million, the Bank was able to make contributions to IDA and to the HIPC scheme of $304 million and $250 million, respectively. The Bank would like, at the very least, to be able to continue to spend the same amount on IDA and HIPC and on its other development priorities. At the same time, it may well wish to increase the output of those public goods which it does not bundle with loans on which it can earn an interest mark-up. This is in the context of a world of low and declining interest rates which will reduce the Bank's income from capital. Furthermore decisions already in the pipeline mean that from 1997 to 2000 the Bank's loan book grew considerably, perhaps to as much as $140 billion, and became more risky, at least in the sense of becoming more concentrated. In the new steady state, the Bank needs to be able to add enough to reserves to permit a reasonable rate growth of its loan book from this higher base.

Analysis along these lines led, in 1998, to a pricing policy review by the Bank which resulted in a significant price increase for normal IBRD loans. The margin over cost of funds has been raised to 75 basis points, of which only one-third was waived for fiscal year 1999, and, in addition, a front-end fee of 1 per cent was added. Furthermore, 'extraordinary' crisis loans were priced at substantially higher rates: the Bank has created a new instrument, the Special Structural Adjustment Loan (SSAL) which will be priced at 400 basis points above cost, plus a front-end fee of 100 basis points, and a commitment fee of 75 basis points. Loans of this type will also not be eligible for interest waivers. These price increases should enable the Bank, in a normal year, to add to reserves as required.

We also understand that analysis in the Bank has clearly shown that, in an abnormal year, the Bank would be able to safely withstand the serious downturn in loan income which would result from some of its major borrowers going into non-accruals. Nevertheless straightforward arithmetic suggests to us that this could, depending on its seriousness, jeopardise either the Bank's ability to grant waivers on existing loan interest, or its ability to make contributions to IDA and to the HIPC scheme, or both. It could also call into question the ability of the Bank to make new emergency loans. It is clear that the Bank would be most likely to experience such a downturn in its income at a time of systemic crisis, and that this is precisely when such new loans would most be needed.

It is therefore our conclusion that – if the Bank really is to do what is described in the agenda in this chapter, and if it is still to remain flexible enough to be able to meet needs for emergency financing – then it may need to seek an increase in its paid-in capital. It is worth pointing out that the sums involved are small. A 25 per cent increase in (usable) paid-in capital and reserves would require less than $6 billion. Spread across all of the Bank's Class 1 contributing shareholders, this would not be a large sum.

7.3 *Institutional organisation and institutional strategy*

At the time of writing, James Wolfensohn has been in office as President of the World Bank for over four years, and he has just been given a second five-year term. His first moves in office led to the much publicised 'Strategic Compact', unveiled in February 1997. The thrust of this review was primarily internal. Wolfensohn aimed to reorganise the Bank and to continue the push, begun before his time, for the Bank's internal structures to move towards those appropriate for a 'learning institution': to change the skill mix of its personnel, to give greater presence on the ground, with fewer staff in Bank's offices, delivering better products. He envisaged then that perhaps 10 per cent of current Bank staff would have to leave, aiming to replace them by recruits who better combined finance skills and development experience.

At the time it seemed that Wolfensohn had produced only part of a strategy. He had identified some of the questions which needed to be addressed: what products should the Bank be selling to which clients, and at what prices? He also addressed the cost side of the institution. By setting up an internal employment market, the Bank has become much more able to identify those staff whose contribution falls short of their employment costs.[43] But a crucial component of the strategy then seemed to be missing: the revenue side. The Board needed – and shareholder governments needed – a clearer answer than they got at the time of the Strategic Compact to the question: 'What is the Bank's mission and how should it be pursued?'

The components of an answer to this question are now clearer. Conditionality has not worked – or, at least, has not worked to anything like a sufficient extent to make this the main instrument by which the Bank advances development. The Bank has therefore learned that it should therefore step back from attempting to coerce developing country governments into adopting good policies. In our view, it should adopt a twofold strategy. First, it should make available policy advice, based on best practice and on experience, to all countries. This advice should be treated as a public good and should be subsidised or free to recipients (certainly to low income recipients) financed, as currently, from the Bank's income from capital. Second, the Bank should finance good projects proposed by potentially good borrowers. Governments should propose projects to the Bank and then manage these projects, although Bank staff will often participate in the designing of these projects and even the writing of the proposals.

One expression of how this might be done can be found in Wolfensohn's proposal for a Comprehensive Development Framework (CDF) (see Wolfensohn, 1999). Borrowing countries are encouraged to develop matrix-based development plans jointly with donor organisations, NGOs and civil society to ensure that development objectives are comprehensively covered, that donor activities mesh with each other and that local ownership is maximised. Success in designing a CDF is likely to become a precondition for Bank finance. This will require government itself to commit to the CDF objectives. In particular, it is likely to require governments to commit themselves to raising the quality of their public institutions, and to adopting macroeconomic policies which encourage development rather than protect vested interests. In this context, it seems likely that Bank staff will spend a considerable amount of time in the design and coordination exercises from within which the CDFs emerge.

This amounts to a two-pronged strategy for the 'Knowledge Bank'. It will continue to transfer money to developing countries, and it will also transfer development knowledge and experience. The balance between these activities will differ across countries. In countries with good growth experience and a favourable policy environment, the Bank will lend more heavily but with relatively low staff input. Countries with poorer policy environments will receive proportionately more advice. In such countries, lending will be primarily an instrument for transferring knowledge. This is an educational activity, the returns from which will not be entirely appropriable by the project itself.

Wholehearted adoption of criteria of this sort would lead to a significant redistribution of Bank resources. Although it would result in a less equitable distribution of Bank funds than hitherto, it would not imply that the Bank is abandoning countries where the political system has resulted in poor outcomes. (This would have been the outcome of merely adopting so-called *ex post* conditionality proposal.) Instead, the distribution of staff resources would be skewed towards educational activities in the poorer policy countries, while the distribution of lending would be skewed towards countries where there is greater certainty of high development returns. Many countries will be towards the middle of this range, and might see little difference. However, the overall strategy would be to invest money where the development returns are greatest, and to invest educational resources in other countries to bring them to the point where aid investment is productive. Effectively, this would require that their governments understand and own a growth-supportive environment.

All of this refers to what we have called the 'fair weather Bank', but we have also discussed what the Bank should do in bad times. We have argued that it is the Fund that must be principally concerned with crisis management, and that it is essential that the fact that the Fund will inevitably be short of resources must not divert the Bank from its long-term development objectives. At the same time, the Bank cannot ignore crises. Most obviously, it has an important role to play in crisis prevention.[44] But if it is required, as presently, to make funds available for emergency purposes, these should be lent at an interest rate which enables the bank to increase its Bank's capital, so as as much as possible not to circumscribe the Bank's ability to fund development assistance.

NOTES

An earlier version of this chapter appeared in the *Economic Journal* Policy Forum on the IMF and the World Bank (1999), and that paper itself drew upon Gilbert *et al.* (1996). We are grateful to Mark Baird, Paul Collier, Paul David, Stan Fischer, Jan Gunning, Raul Hopkins, Ravi Kanbur, Nirmal Paul, Wolfgang Reinicke, Lyn Squire, T. G. Srinivasan, Joe Stiglitz, John Todd, and John Wilton for helpful discussions. We acknowledge support from the Global Economic Institutions (GEI) Research Programme of the ESRC.

1 Our Mission: To fight poverty with passion and professionalism for lasting results ... The main focus is on helping the poorest people and the poorest countries' < http://www.worldbank.org/html/extdr/whatis.htm > .

2 See < http://www.worldbank.org/html/extdr/whatis.htm > .

3 See the narrative account in chapter 1 of Kapur, Lewis and Webb (hereafter, KLW) (1997a).

4 The term 'Knowledge Bank' has a long history, but tends to mean different things to different authors. We deliberately use it in a precise, but broad, way. That definition focuses on the activities of the Bank's Research Department. While we do not wish to minimise the importance of this department, the definition adopted in this chapter refers to the role of development knowledge and experience across the entire range of the Bank's activities.

5 Channelling aid through a multilateral agency enables donors to precommit not to impose political conditions or economic conditions (such as tying the aid to purchases of the donor country's goods, see Cassen, 1994).

6 Communitarians might argue that large-scale redistribution is likely to be possible only within communities which share an explicit democratic political process and government (see Majone, 1993).

7 Non-Governmental Organisations.

8 Pragmatically, contribution to poverty reduction is one of a number of hurdles that projects require to surmount if they are to obtain Bank finance and, while with some projects, this is relatively straightforward, for others, where poverty reduction is not the prime objective, this requirement forces both borrowing governments and Bank lending officials to give poverty greater priority.

9 See van Dormael (1978) for an absorbing account of the negotiations leading up to the creation the Bank and the Fund, and, more generally, see KLW (1997a, 1997b).

10 For a comparison of the purposes, activities and agendas of the Bank, the IMF and the WTO see Vines (1997).

11 The Bank's Articles of Agreement require that it have a total of subscribed capital (paid-in capital and callable capital) plus accumulated reserves that is greater than its total of outstanding loans, loan participations and loan guarantees.

12 The relationship between the Bank's pricing and the margin which it actually receives on its loans is not completely straightforward. This is because (1) there are still a small number of high interest rate fixed-rate loans on the Bank's books that were committed prior to 1982; (2) the Bank's billing process tracks its cost-of-funds-plus-margin with a six-month lag which can generate a higher margin in cash flow terms at a time of falling interest rates and (3) the Bank reports its income in US dollars but not all loans and loan income are dollar-denominated.

13 At the (June) end of its 1997 fiscal year, the IBRD had 'subscribed capital' of $186 billion This is money that provided by member governments. But 94 per cent of this is in the form of callable guarantees – i.e. this is money that governments have stated that they will provide in the event of major default on Bank loans to meet the IBRD's obligations. The IBRD's actual paid-in capital amounted to only $11 billion, but only about $8 billion of this is usable. (Some is in promissory notes and or in weak or non-convertible currency.) In addition, however, the Bank had accumulated reserves of approximately $14 billion. As a result, subscribed capital plus accumulated reserves totalled $200 billion in 1997 while 'risk capital' (i.e. usable paid-in capital plus accumulated reserves) amounted to approximately $22 billion.

14 Waivers on loan interest are also in a sense a claim on income, but these have already been subtracted in the above calculation of net income.

15 This is the same figure as that for 1994; the reserve additions in the intervening two years were somewhat lower.

16 Some parts of gross administration costs are clearly not loan-related, and there is a grey area as to which parts of research should be treated as loan-related. Even after allowance for this point, this statement remains true.

17 Source: World Bank, *World Bank Annual Report*, IMF *International Financial Statistics* (various issues). IBRD-IDA figures relate to the Bank's financial year, while the remaining figures are on a calendar year basis with adjacent years averaged to give a number centred on the Bank calendar year. We are grateful to Brett House for compiling the data presented in figure 2.1. IBRD loans are almost invariably for a maximum of 10 years, whereas IDA loans can extend for up to 40 years – the average maturity of outstanding IBRD loans was 4.7 years at the end of the Bank's 1997–8 financial year while that of IDA loans was 17.2 years (figures derived from World Bank, 1998b). The southern Asia group of countries is the largest single destination of IDA

funds while Latin America and the Caribbean is the most important destination for IBRD loans.

18 But there is a view is that the Bank requires low-risk, high-return, IBRD loans to middle-income countries to provide finance for its higher-risk, low-return, IDA loans. We revert to this question in section 7 (p. 72).

19 It is worth noting that, in 1994, the Bank's research budget stood at $26 million, exceeding the National Science Foundation's economics budget of $16 million by a wide margin. (See Gavin and Rodrik, 1995: 333)

20 The World Bank *Annual Report* (1996: 153) records that the research budget had dropped by 30 per cent from a peak of $36 million in 1992 to less than $25 million in 1996.

21 'The Bank was highly instrumental in generating empirical evidence for the testing of many ideas, through its access to country data and the monitoring of its own programmes' (Ferreira, 1992, abstract).

22 It is interesting that this contrasts with the IMF which, during the 1950s and 1960s was where both the Mundell-Fleming open economy macroeconomic model and the monetary approach to the balance of payments were developed.

23 The ability of the World Bank to employ non-US citizens without 'green-card' status gives it an advantage over private sector consultants in this respect since the majority of World Bank staff are not easily able to obtain alternative employment in the United States.

24 Understanding why a non-private sector organisation like the Bank is valuable for the development of knowledge about development is akin to understanding why some other kinds of institutions like universities, hospitals and broadcasters, can best carry out their activities in the not-for-profit sector.

25 As Joe Stiglitz argues in the Introduction, comprehensiveness across participants is clearly important: if government, the private sector and 'civil society' all become participants in the process, then identification with, and ownership of, the development process will be the outcome.

26 Jones (chapter 10 in this volume) discusses detailed implementation issues.

27 The Killick (1998) study relates to the multilateral agencies in general, and not just the World Bank.

28 This paragraph draws on Ferreira, and Keely (chapter 6 in this volume).

29 This exception appears to result from the fact that transport projects are very big – the scope for government to make offsetting reductions in its own transport commitments is limited.

30 'Policy' is to be interpreted widely throughout this discussion. It includes not only explicit government policy, but also the reliability and transparency of the legal framework, absence of corruption, modern bankruptcy laws, standard accounting practice and reporting and other prerequisites for economic activity.

31 This approach would create the possibility for like-minded governments to work together along regional lines to pursue reform. The example of the Asia Pacific Economic Cooperation (APEC) process could be perused here. In its successful years in the early 1990s, the APEC process operated so as to assist

neighbouring countries in the bolstering of each other's reform efforts. They did this by committing to growth and trade- enhancing reforms which were of reciprocal benefit. It is clear that this 'club' approach was – for a while at least – effective in promoting reform.

32 We are grateful to Lyn Squire for helping us clarify our views on this section.

33 This contrasts with a simple 'Knowledge Bank' view in which knowledge is simply the means of making projects more effective.

34 This is the central message of *Assessing Aid* (World Bank, 1998a).

35 We note that the eligibility criteria of the IMF's CCL is a clear example of multilaterals making loans available on conditions to be satisfied *ex ante* rather than *ex post*.

36 See Eichengreen (1999) for a description of various proposals on international financial architecture.

37 The Argentine contract is the larger of the two and currently stands for a total of $6.7 billion (just under 10 per cent of the Argentine deposit base). It involves 14 international banks. It is constructed as a contingent repo facility and gives the Argentine Central Bank the option to sell dollar-denominated, Argentine government bonds for dollars cash subject to a repurchase clause with an implicit fixed cost of funds. If the facility is used, it will cost on average LIBOR + 200 basis points. In addition, there is an annual commitment fee paid averaging 32 basis points (see Central Bank of Argentina, 1998).

38 For example, the Central Bank of Argentina has negotiated a $1 billion enhancement from the World Bank and the Interamerican Development Bank (IDB).

39 Speech at the London Business School (14 December 1999), reported in *The Economist* (18–30 December 1999: 153).

40 In the light of this proposal we suggest that the Fund's 'conversion' to a commitment to poverty reduction, announced by Managing Director Michel Camdessus at the 1999 Bank–Fund joint meetings, is unfortunate. Although the Fund should *take account* of poverty issues in the manner described above, concern with these issues should not be part of its core mission.

41 In our view such criticism, if it is to be both legitimate and effective, must be accompanied by an argument about how the Fund could have done better. One of us has attempted to provide such an argument (see Corbett, Irwin and Vines, 1999). The Fund has itself publicly defended its own role (see Lane *et. al.*, 1998).

42 The test can be refined to include callable capital only from member governments who themselves have an AA or AAA rating, and is still easily passed.

43 It is not clear to us that the Bank has got this issue quite right. One aspect that is notable in the Fund – as a complement to discipline and loyalty – is security of tenure. By contrast, as part of a move to an internal market, most Bank employees are on short-term contracts. There is substantial anecdotal evidence that this is distorting incentives away from creative thinking and towards career-path management.

44 This presupposes a demarcation between Bank and Fund, although in practice they will often be required to cooperate closely. The historical record of Bank–Fund relations suggests that such cooperation may be more forthcoming if it is channelled through protocols requiring mutual and formal consultation.

REFERENCES

Alba, P., A. Bhattacharya, S. Claessens, S. Ghosh and L. Hernandez (1999). 'The Role of Macroeconomic and Financial Sector Linkages in East Asia's Financial Crisis', World Bank; chapter 1 in P.-R. Agénor, M. Miller, D. Vines and A. Weber (eds.), *The East Asian Financial Crisis: Causes, Consequences, and Contagion*, Cambridge: Cambridge University Press

Agénor, P.-R, M. Miller, D. Vines and A. Weber (1999). *The East Asian Financial Crisis: Causes, Consequences, and Contagion*, Cambridge: Cambridge University Press

Bretton Woods Commission (1994), *Bretton Woods: Looking to the Future*, Washington: Group of Thirty

Braithwaite, J. and P. Drahos (1999). 'Global Business Regulation', Australian National University, draft manuscript

Burnside, C. and D. Dollar (1996). 'Aid, Policies and Growth', Policy Research Department, Washington, DC: World Bank, mimeo

Cassen, R. (1994). *Does Aid Work?*, Oxford: Clarendon Press

Central Bank of Argentina (1998). 'Argentina and the Contingent Repo. Facility', Central Bank of Argentina, October

Centre for Economic Policy Research (1998). 'Financial Crises and Asia', *CEPR Conference Report*, **6**, London: CEPR

Clark, I. (1996a). 'Should the IMF Become more Adaptive?', *Working Paper*, **WP/96/11**, Washington, DC: International Monetary Fund

(1996b). 'Inside the IMF: Comparisons with Policy-making Organisations in Canadian Governments', mimeo

Collier, P. (1997). 'The Failure of Conditionality', in C. Gwin and J Nelson (eds.) *Perspectives on Aid and Development.* Washington, DC: Overseas Development Council

Corbett, J. and D. Vines (1999a). 'Asian Currency and Financial Crises: Lessons from Vulnerability, Crisis, and Collapse', *World Economy,* **22**: 155–77

(1999b). 'The Asian Crisis: Lessons from the Collapse of Financial Systems, Exchange Rates and Macroeconomic Policy', chapter 2 in P.-R. Agénor, M. Miller, D. Vines and A. Weber, *The East Asian Financial Crisis: Causes, Consequences, and Contagion*, Cambridge: Cambridge University Press

Corbett, J., G. Irwin and D. Vines (1999). 'From Asian Miracle to Asian Crisis: Why Vulnerability, Why Collapse?', in L. Gower and Gruen (eds.), *Capital Flows and the International Financial System,* Sydney: Reserve Bank of Australia

Corsetti, G., P. Pesenti and N. Roubini (1998). 'What Caused the East Asian Financial Crisis?', New York University, mimeo; chapter 4 in in P.-R.

Agénor, M. Miller, D. Vines and A. Weber, *The East Asian Financial Crisis: Causes, Consequences, and Contagion*, Cambridge: Cambridge University Press

Dollar, D. and J. Svensson (1997). 'What Explains the Success or Failure of Structural Adjustment Programs?', Washington, DC: World Bank, mimeo

Eichengreen, B. (1999). 'Toward a New International Financial Architecture: A Practical Post-Asia Agenda', Washington, DC: Institute for International Economics

Eichengreen, B and P. Kenen (1994). 'Managing the World Economy under the Bretton Woods System: An Overview' in P. Kenen (ed.), *Managing the World Economy: Fifty Years after Bretton Woods*, Washington, DC: Institute for International Economics

Eichengreen, B. and R. Portes (1995). *Crisis, What Crisis? Orderly Workouts for Sovereign Debtors*, London: Centre for Economic Policy Research

Ferreira, F.H.G. (1992). 'The World Bank and the Study of Stabilisation and Structural Adjustment in LDCs', LSE, STICERD Development Economics Research Programme, *Working Paper*, **41**

Feyzioglu, T., V. Swaroop and M. Zhu (1996). 'Foreign Aid's Impact on Public Spending', Policy Research Department, Washington, DC: World Bank, mimeo

Fidler, S. and M. Wolf (1998). 'Emerging with Credit' (interview with James Wolfensohn), *Financial Times*

Fischer, S. (1995). 'The World Bank and the IMF at Fifty', in H. Gensberg (ed.), *The International Monetary* System, Heidelberg: Springer Verlag

   (1999). 'On the Need for an International Lender of Last Resort', IMF, mimeo

Gardiner, R. N. (1956). *Sterling Dollar Diplomacy*, Oxford: Clarendon Press

Gavin, M. and A. Powell (1997). 'On Domestic and International Lenders of Last Resort: Constructive Ambiguity and Cheap Talk', Central Bank of Argentina, mimeo

   (1998). 'Should the International Lender of Last Resort be Privatised?', Central Bank of Argentina, mimeo

Gavin, M., and D. Rodrik (1995). 'The World Bank in Historical Perspective', *American Economic Review, Papers and Proceedings*, **85**: 329–34

Gilbert, C.L. (1996). 'The World Bank at Fifty Two', *Newsletter of the ESRC Global Economic Institutions Research Programme*, **3**, London: CEPR

Gilbert, C.L., R. Hopkins, A. Powell and A. Roy (1996). 'The World Bank: Its Functions and Its Future', *CEPR Global Economic Institutions Working Paper*, **15**, London: CEPR

Haq, M., R. Jolly, P. Streeton and K. Haq (1995). *The UN and The Bretton Woods Institutions*, London: Macmillan

Hirschman, A. (1958). *The Strategy of Economic Development*, New Haven, CT: Yale University Press

Hopkins, R., A. Powell, A. Roy and C.L. Gilbert (1997). 'The World Bank and Conditionality', *Journal of International Development*, **9**: 507–16

Hopkins, R., A. Powell, A. Roy and C.L. Gilbert (1999). 'The World Bank, Conditionality and the Comprehensive Development Framework', chapter 11 in this volume

House, B. and D. Vines (1997). 'Reforming the World Bank', *Newsletter* of the Global *Economic Institutions Research Programme*, London: CEPR: 2–7

Kanbur, R. and D. Vines (1999). 'The World Bank and Poverty Reduction: Past, Present and Future', chapter 3 in this volume

Kanbur, R. and T. Sandler (1999). 'The Future of Development Assistance: Common Pools and International Public Goods', *ODC Policy Essay*, **25**, Washington, DC: Overseas Development Council

Kapur, D. J. Lewis, and R. Webb (1997a). *The World Bank: Its First Half Century, 1: History*, Washington, DC: Brookings Institution

 (1997b). *The World Bank: Its First Half Century, 2: Perspectives*, Washington, DC: Brookings Institution

Kapur, D. and R. Wade (1998). 'Paying for Privilege' *Financial Times*, October

Kaul, I., I. Grunberg, and M. Stern (eds.) (1999). *Global Public Goods: International Cooperation in the Twenty First Century*, New York: Oxford University Press

Killick T. (1998). *Aid and the Political Economy of Policy Change*, London, Routledge.

Krueger, A. (1997) *The World Trade Organisation: Its Effectiveness as an Institution*, Chicago: University of Chicago Press

Krugman, P. (1999a). 'The Fall and Rise of Development Economics' (revision of a 1994 essay, < http://web.mit.edu/krugman/www/dishpan.htm >)

 (1999b). 'Analytical Afterthoughts on the Asian Crisis < http://web.mit.edu/krugman/www/MINICRIS.htm >

Kuznets, S. (1971). *economic growth of Nations: Total Output and Production Structure*, Cambridge, MA: Harvard University Press

Lane, T., A. Ghosh, J. Hamann, S. Phillips, M. Schulze-Ghattas and T. Tsikata (1998). 'IMF-supported Programmes in Indonesia, Korea and Thailand: A Preliminary Assessment', Washington, DC: IMF, mimeo

Little, I.M.D. (1982). *Economic Development*, New York: 20th Century Fund

Little, I., T. Scitovsky and M. Scott (1970). *Industry and Trade in Some Developing Countries*, Oxford: Oxford University Press

Majone, G. (1993). 'The European Community: Between Social Policy and Social Regulation', *Journal of Common Market Studies*, **31**

Mosley, P., J. Harrigan and J. Toye (1995). *Aid and Power*, 2nd edn., London: Routledge

Murphy, R., A. Shleifer and R. Vishny (1989). 'Industrialisation and the Big Push', *Journal of Political Economy*, **97**: 1003–26

Naim, M. (1994). 'The World Bank: Its Role, Governance and Organisational Culture', in Bretton Woods Committee, *Looking to the Future*, **C273-86**, Washington, DC: Bretton Woods Committee

Nogués, J. (1997). 'Comment on Paper by David Vines', in A. Krueger, *The World Trade Organisation: Its Effectiveness as an Institution*, Chicago: University of Chicago Press

Oliver, R.W. (1971). 'Early Plans for a World Bank', *Princeton Studies in International Finance*, **29**, Princeton: Princeton University.

(1975). *International Economic Cooperation and the World Bank*, London: Macmillan

Polak, J. (1997). 'The World Bank and the IMF: A Changing Relationship', in D. Kapur, J. Lewis and R. Webb, *The World Bank: Its First Half Century, 2: Perspectives*, Washington, DC: Brookings Institution

Portes, R and D. Vines (1997). *Coping with International Capital* Flows, London: Commonwealth Secretariat

Radelet, S. and J. Sachs (1998). 'The Onset of the East Asian Crisis', Harvard University, mimeo

Rawls, J. (1971). *A Theory of Justice*, Cambridge, MA: Harvard University Press

Reinicke, W. (1997). 'Global Public Policy', *Foreign Affairs*, **76**: 127–38

(1998a). *Global Public Policy: Governing without Government?*, Washington: Brookings Institution

(1998b). 'Global Public Policy: A Vision for Multilateralism in the 21st Century', Washington, DC: World Bank, mimeo

Rischard, J.-F. (1998). 'Multilateral Banks and Global Public Networks: Speculations for the Next Century', *Cahiers* Papers, **3**: 82 9

Rodrik, D. (1995). 'Why is There Multilateral Lending?', in M. Bruno and B. Pleskovic (eds.), *Annual World Bank Conference on Development Economics*, Washington, DC: World Bank: 167–93

Rosenstein-Rodan, P. (1943). 'Problems of Industrialisation of Eastern and South-eastern Europe', *Economic Journal*, **53**: 202–11

Sen, A. (1987). *On Ethics and Economics*, Oxford: Blackwell

Stern, N. and F. Ferreira (1997). 'The World Bank as an "Intellectual Actor"', in D. Kapur, J.P. Lewis and R. Webb, *The World Bank: Its First Half Century, 2: Perspectives*, Washington, DC, Brookings Institution: 473–609

Stiglitz, J. (1998a). *Macroeconomic Dimensions of the East Asian Crisis*, in Centre for Economic Policy Research, 'Financial Crises and Asia', *CEPR Conference Report*, **6**, London: CEPR

(1998b). 'Sound Finance and Sustainable Development in Asia', Keynote Address to the Asia Development Forum and Chief, Manila, 12 March (available at < http://www.worldbank.org/html/extdr/extme/jssp031298.htm >)

(1998c). 'IFIs and the Provision of International Public Goods', *Cahiers* Papers, **3**: 116–33

van Dormael, A. (1978). *Bretton Woods: Birth of a Monetary System*, London: Macmillan

Vines, D. (1997). 'The WTO in Relation to the Fund and the Bank: Competencies, Agendas, and Linkages', in A. Krueger, *The World Trade*

Organisation: Its Effectiveness as an Institution, Chicago: University of Chicago Press

Wade, R. (1990). *Governing the Market*, Princeton. Princeton University Press

Walters, A. (1994). 'Do We Need the IMF and the World Bank?', *Current Controversies*, **10**, London, Institute of Economic Affairs

Wolfensohn, J. (1998). 'The Other Crisis' (address to the Board of Governors, October 1988), Washington, DC: World Bank

(1999). 'A Proposal for a Comprehensive Development Framework A Discussion Draft', available at < http://www.worldbank.org/cdf/cdf-text.htm >

World Bank (1996). *Annual Report 1996*, Washington, DC: World Bank

(1998a). *Assessing Aid: What Works, What Doesn't and Why?* Washington, DC: World Bank

(1998b). *World Bank Annual Report*, New York: Oxford University Press

3 The World Bank and poverty reduction: past, present and future

RAVI KANBUR AND DAVID VINES

1 Introduction

The mission of the World Bank is to achieve a 'world without poverty'. Over the 50-plus years since the end of the Second World War when the Bank was founded, there have been radical shifts in views about how this might best be achieved. In this chapter we chart the highly non-linear development of thinking: from the 'trickle-down' views of the early 1950s, to McNamara's war on poverty, to a new version of 'trickle down' again in the heyday of the 'Washington consensus' in the early 1990s, to the current re-rejection of this view. Thinking about this issue is complicated by the fact that we must think not only about the effects of growth on distribution and poverty but also about the effects of distribution and poverty on growth. It will be a central claim of this chapter that we should think of these links as consisting of a twofold reciprocal relationship.

The World Bank is not independent of either the intellectual world or the political world in which it operates. The Bank's thinking on poverty thus closely parallels academic concerns with poverty, and its actions with regard to policy relief reflect the political priority afforded to poverty in the world at large. That being said, there has never been unanimity in the economics profession about policy issues, and at every point of time a wide range of political positions has been in evidence. Furthermore, the Bank can lead as well as lag; it is large enough to influence both academic opinion and the political climate. Thus the links between the Bank's thinking on poverty and the academic and political context are far from being a one-way street running from a consensus on external positions to influence on internal thinking and activity. Nevertheless it is with views external to the Bank that we begin our discussion.

87

The chapter is set out as follows. Section 2 reviews general thinking about poverty reduction over the past 50 years, concentrating on the most recent period. World Bank thinking about poverty is discussed in section 3. Section 4 examines the recent behaviour and actions of the Bank in relation to poverty, and looks at the current crusade within the Bank to make poverty reduction the core issue in the Bank's agenda at the beginning of the new century.

2 A brief history of thinking about poverty reduction

It is possible to identify four phases in thinking about the reduction of poverty since the Second World War.

2.1 Phase 1

This runs from 1945 to approximately 1955, and can be described as 'growth does it all'. The central idea here came from Rosenstein-Rodan's paper 'Economic Backwardness in Historical Perspective' (Rosenstein-Rodan, 1943),[1] which gave the impetus for 'big push' ways of thinking about development. Loosely, this consisted of the view that development is a virtuous circle driven by external economies – that is, that modernisation breeds modernisation. Some countries, according to this view, remain underdeveloped because they have failed to get this virtuous circle going, and thus remain stuck in a low-level trap. There is consequently a powerful case for government activism as a way of breaking out of this trap.[2]

There were disputes, now famous, over the nature of the policies that might be required to break a country out of a low-level trap.[3] But whatever the exact policies needed and adopted, it was argued that the growth and development which they would bring about would, of itself, lead directly to poverty reduction. Furthermore there was no other way to bring this about:

It was the common sense of American board and seminar rooms that economic growth was the indispensable and principal tool for reducing poverty in developing countries, and that efforts to short-circuit this by raising expenditure on welfare would be counterproductive. Such measures would be temporary palliatives, at the expense of savings and productive investment; direct and immediate attacks on mass poverty would only squander limited national resources. Conversely, growing production would mean a gradual but inevitable rise in living standards. These beliefs, that growth would spread or 'trickle down', and that there existed a trade-off between growth and distribution, served to rationalize patience in the face of poverty. (Kapur, Lewis and Webb, hereafter, KLW, 1997a: 115)

Radical alternatives to neoclassical theories were equally unsupportive of policies which might have favored the rural or urban poor ... Raúl Prebisch ... added to the bias against agriculture by pressing the urgency of import substitution based on protection ... Marxist theory accepted low wages and growing inequality as the inevitable concomitant of capitalist growth. (KLW, 1997a: 118)

2.2 Phase 2

This ran from the mid 1950s until the end of the 1970s, and saw a questioning of the trickle-down approach. The Lewis model (Lewis, 1954), on the one hand, and Kuznets' empirical work (Kuznets, 1955), on the other, led to the idea that growth and inequality were inseparable. Lewis' theoretical model suggests that inequality is necessary to generate the surplus required for the accumulation of capital. Kuznets' empirical work suggests that there is an inverse U-shape relationship between growth and poverty. In the early stages, growth would not just require, but lead to, a worsening of income distribution, but then there would come a stage in which income inequality would begin to fall again: the idea is that primarily agricultural economies start out with an initially equitable distribution with a low average, but that as they develop, portions of the population migrate to other sectors with greater inequality but higher averages. Initially, this causes inequality to worsen. But, as countries continue to progress, more of the rural sector moves out of agriculture and inequality eventually decreases.[4] Fishlow's work on Brazil in the 1960s suggested a confirmation of these ideas. Brazil grew steadily at 6 per cent or 7 per cent per annum but the result was increasing income inequality (Fishlow, 1972). There was, as a consequence, a debate on whether the consequent rise in inequality would become so great that it would undermine the objective of poverty reduction. The discussion then centred on the kinds of interventions necessary to prevent this undermining: food subsidies, highly progressive taxes, welfare, state support, etc.

By 1970, however, the questioning had become more insistent. There was by this time a widespread loss of confidence that national economic growth was a sufficient means of reducing poverty. A wide range of data were brought forward to support this revisionist hypothesis which showed rapid population growth, widening income distributions, and limited growth in industrial employment:

The new paradigm was old wisdom for much of the world. Outside the small but powerful development establishment centered in Washington and in the prestigious Anglo Saxon Universities, intellectuals and officials were more inclined to skepticism than belief in the proposition that market-based economic growth would equally spread to the masses. [The c]ontrary affirmation – that the poor were not sharing and were unlikely to share in growth – was widely held, and the belief was sustained by a substantial body of conceptual and empirical study. (KLW, 1997a: 225)[5]

As the 1970s wore on, a series of studies made major efforts to dent the trickle-down view. These included *Industry and Trade in Some Developing Countries* (Little, Skitovsky and Scott, 1970). This focused on the cost of excessive protection, which it implicated as a cause of limited job creation. A lively academic debate on the 'choice of technique in developing countries', which was paralleled by a more popular debate on 'intermediate technology' (see KLW, 1997a: 231), argued that deliberate choice of more labour-intensive methods of production was necessary if growth was to lead to poverty reduction. There was even a willingness to sacrifice some growth to this end.[6] Furthermore, the rethinking of development policy was more general than this. The Tanzanian experiment and the Yugoslav model, both of which featured in lively debates at the time that the present authors were students, seemed to offer alternative paths to poverty reduction. The 'Green Revolution', on the other hand seemed to offer the prospect of growth-promoting, but inequality-inducing, mechanisation. In addition there was a more general perspective. Albert Hirschman has suggested that many development economists were becoming concerned that rapid growth could have deleterious side effects:

The series of political disasters that struck a number of third world countries from the 1960s on were clearly somehow connected with the stresses and strains accompanying development and 'modernisation.' These development disasters, ranging to from civil wars to the establishment of murderous authoritarian regimes, could not but give pause to a group of social scientists. (cited in KLW, 1997a:231)

The result, as will be documented in the next subsection, was the emergence of a development strategy deliberately directed towards reducing poverty.

2.3 Phase 3

However, in Phase 3, which ran from the beginning to the end of the 1980s, things changed again; a reaction set in against policies directly targeted towards poverty reduction. The first reason for this was that the analytical basis of the 'Kuznets' curve' was questioned (Anand and Kanbur, 1991, 1993).[7] Also, and more importantly, this was a period during which there was a very pronounced series of macroeconomic shocks: the first energy crisis and subsequent global recession; the second rise in oil prices which flowed from the time of the Iranian revolution; the resulting global recession which spawned the Latin American debt crisis; and the period of very low commodity prices which subsequently resulted, in the mid-1980s. Such instability was a natural counterpart to, indeed a consequence of, the end of the previous Bretton Woods regime; there was a period of 15 years of deep incoherence in the global macroeconomic policy framework. The effect of this on the Third World was to require large changes in macroeconomic policy, and also substantial changes in microeconomic policy as macro-adjustments required the removal of distortions and rigid policy frameworks, in particular overvalued exchange rates and the dismantling of parastatal enterprises. The consequence was that primary attention came to be given in the Third World to policy discussion centred on the removal of microeconomic and macroeconomic rigidities. The 1980s became the 'adjustment decade'.

Parallel to this, prominence was given to the view that removing these distortions would be good for growth and that this would lead to poverty reduction. There was also a footnote that many of the distortions were themselves the consequence of rent-seeking by the relatively well-off policy elite and thus that the removal of these distortions themselves would be inequality-reducing. This was part of the mindset of the Thatcher–Reagan–Kohl era.

Out of this era grew the years of the 'Washington consensus'.[8] A central part of this consensus involved the view that openness and liberalisation would lead to growth.[9] The part of the 'Washington consensus' that is relevant for the present discussion is the additional argument that the growth which would result from openness would in turn lead to poverty reduction. That is, the new neo-liberal agenda proposed the following line of causation: openness leads to growth leads to poverty reduction. We are back to a kind of 'trickle-down' argument, with the analysis turning a full circle to embrace a variant of the 1950s' ideas. But whereas, in the 1950s, the growth which was meant to cause the trickle down was to be promoted by a big push, the growth to produce the trickle-down was now to be promoted by openness. This analytical argument was buttressed by two strands of empirical work. The first of these showed that growth had no effect on increasing inequality (Anand and Kanbur, 1993; Li, Squire and Zou, 1998). Second, growth could be convincingly shown empirically to have a strong effect on poverty reduction (Ravallion and Chen, 1997). The implication was that higher *per capita* income would be associated with an upward shift in income at all levels and thus that there would be a decisive reduction in the number of people experiencing any given low level of *per capita* income.

The intellectual implications of the 'Washington consensus' were profound. It spawned an attitude in this area similar to the attitude to distribution in pre-modern public economics. This is the world of Meade's *The Intelligent Radical's Guide to Economic Policy* (Meade, 1972), in which the growth-promoting parts of the policy community can get on with promoting growth whilst the distribution branch concerns itself with promoting greater income equality, preferably through lump-sum taxes. This view of the world descends ultimately from Arrow–Debreu, in whose model the issues of efficiency and redistribution can be analytically separated. The empirical work gave grounds for the belief that growth and distribution could indeed be separated. (Kanbur and Lustig, 1999). What was needed for poverty reduction was growth, *and* what was needed for growth was liberal, open markets.

2.4 Phase 4

Phase 4, which we are now in, involves a reaction against this neo-liberal agenda. It does this by arguing that at least to some extent a form of reverse causation is important: that poverty and inequality in turn has an effect on growth. The way of making this argument relies on variants endogenous growth theory. There are a number of ways of pursuing it.

2.4.1 Basic services

One way of constructing this argument is to note that the provision of basic services – health and education – is vitally important for growth.

Consider health. The specific way in which the poor participate in growth tends to be through increased or more productive use of 'their most abundant asset', labour. But one of the intrinsic characteristics of poverty – poor nutrition and health – also contributes to a reduction in capacity for work. Measures of nutritional status and health status have been shown to have important impacts on wages and productivity, and these impacts are greater for the poor than the non-poor. Strauss and Thomas (1997) show that controlling for a range of factors, taller men in the USA earn more – a 1 per cent increase in height is associated with a 1 per cent increase in wages. The same relationship for Brazilian males is much more powerful – the same 1 per cent increase in height implies a 7 per cent increase in wages. In their survey of the literature, Strauss and Thomas (1998) conclude that improvements in health do result in increases in productivity and wages (and, more importantly for present purposes, the 'effects are likely to be greatest for the most vulnerable – the poorest and those with little education'). Without these basic building blocks, the poor are unable to take advantage of income-earning opportunities that come with growth.[10] At the same time, society suffers the loss of their potential contributions. The provision of basic social services, besides being important in its own right, therefore constitutes an important precondition for growth.

Something similar is also true for education and the accumulation of human capital. There appear to be strongly increasing social returns to the acquisition of human capital, and yet the private return may actually be negative at low levels of income, meaning that the socially advantageous formation of human capital does not happen. Poverty reduction then solves a collective action problem in the accumulation of human capital.[11] Several recent empirical studies at the household level using panel data provide support for a strong interaction between human development and growth in incomes. For example, a panel of 891 households in Peru was studied during the period 1994–7. The study found that the higher the education of the household head in 1994, the larger the growth in *per capita* expenditures in the subsequent period (Bourgignon, Chong and Hentschel, 1999). Similarly, panel data for 2,678 Vietnamese households covering the period 1993–8 came to the same conclusion – while on average those households whose head had no education saw expenditure *per capita* decline, on average all households whose head had primary education or more saw *per capita* expenditure increase, with the increase for those with upper secondary education being three times that for those with primary education (Zaman, 1999). Third, income inequality may lead to crime which may be a disincentive to the creation of a sufficiently supportive environment for capital accumulation and growth (Bourgignon, Chong and Hentschel, 1999).

Where countries have put in place incentive structures and complementary investments to ensure that better health and education lead to higher incomes, the poor have benefited doubly they are healthier and better educated, and they have increased their consumption. Most of the East

Asian countries, prior to the recent crisis, illustrate what can be achieved. Poverty fell dramatically in East Asia from 1975, when roughly six out of 10 East Asians lived in absolute poverty, to 1995, when only about two did. At the same time, and in part propelling these achievements, governments invested in human capital through public expenditures on education and health. Over the same 20-year period, life expectancy increased by more than nine years, the average years of education rose by 60 per cent and infant mortality fell from 73 per thousand births to 35.[12] While these achievements may be eroded to some extent during the current crisis, their lasting impact will still represent a degree of progress not seen elsewhere.[13]

2.4.2 Security

Other types of evidence provide broader grounds for this kind of argument. One version has been put forward by Rodrik (1999). He argues that, in a volatile world, success in maintaining growth goes to those who are able to adjust. What is it then that explains which countries have the capacity for adjustment? The claim is that the capacity for domestic economic management really matters. Rodrik then links this capacity for domestic management, and for adjustment, to the capacity of a country to handle distributional changes. His empirical work on this issue directly challenges the Sachs–Warner (1995) openness-to-growth correlation (see Rodrik, 1999, chapter 4; 1998). Rodrik reconstructs the Sachs–Warner data and suggests that their openness measure picks up macroeconomic stability – or, even more relevantly to his argument, picks up proxies for mechanisms for the management of distributional difficulties thrown up by needs for adjustment.

Rodrik allies to this argument a claim that more openness in a country leads to more volatility and thus increases the exposure of its citizens to risk. One aspect of poverty which is not captured in the level of incomes is the risk associated with volatility of incomes. The particular importance of poverty is not just as a state of having little, but also of being vulnerable to losing the little one has. Sources of risk range from irregular rainfall and epidemics to crime and violence, as well as the structural vulnerability of homes and civil conflict. But recent Asian economic history has emphasised the fact – if it was not already clear – that openness increases the exposure of an economy to risk: risks of trade shocks, risks in shocks to capital flows and risks attached to the policies which need to be adopted to cope with these shocks. Evidence suggests that the poor suffer disproportionately in the face of the macroeconomic dislocations which such shocks can set in train (Lustig, 1999).

Alongside the importance of macroeconomic volatility the literature of the 1980s and 1990s, helped considerably by the increasing availability of household panel data for developing countries, has also highlighted the importance of micro-level risk and vulnerability for poor households. It has been shown that these risks are considerable, that they are relatively larger for poor households, and their consequences are to adversely affect the medium-term prospects of households to grow out of poverty (see, for example, Grootaert and Kanbur, 1995; Morduch, 1995; Hoddinott and Kinsey, 1998; Jalan and Ravallion, 1999).

The emerging empirical growth literature buttresses this challenge to the neo-liberal consensus. This new literature points out, in the light of the above theory, that one would not expect there to be a correlation between the *change* in inequality and the change in growth – as predicted if the causality runs from growth to inequality – but between the *level* of inequality and the rate of growth – which is what is predicted if inequality influences growth. While the empirical terrain remains untidy there is at least some support in the literature to suggest that there is indeed an effect from the level of equality to the growth of GDP (Kanbur and Lustig, 1999).[14]

We may summarise where the beliefs in Phase 4 lead. They point to the argument that addressing both structural inequalities and the vulnerability to risk is a prerequisite for accessing the opportunities of globalisation and new technology. This is a complete flip around from 'trickle down' and the 'trickle-down-plus' agenda which has that it is growth which leads to reduced poverty, and which would merely acknowledge that redistributive policy might be tacked on to augment the effects of growth on poverty. This new literature says that you will not get sustainable growth if inequality or poverty is too severe.

3 World Bank thinking on, and policy actions towards, poverty

As we noted at the start of this chapter, the World Bank does not operate in an intellectual or a political vacuum. It is greatly influenced by the tides of professional opinion and political possibilities, particularly in its major shareholder countries. In this section we relate thinking and action within the World Bank to the evolution of thinking on development and poverty reduction which we laid out in section 2. In doing so, we will rely primarily on the official *History* of the World Bank, but we also offer our own interpretations, particularly for the more recent periods, when we have ourselves been personally involved with the institution.

3.1 The early years

Chapter 3 of the Bank *History* (KLW, 1997a) conveys the flavour of the Bank's behaviour in the early days:

The canvas of the developing world was ... a scene of frontal, energetic and life-and-death engagement with rural poverty and human development. [But] against this backdrop, and with a great deal of conviction, the Bank set out on an independent course, not to the rural and human welfare front lines of the war on want, but instead to the tasks of ordinance and logistics to build roads, railways, ports and power stations, and to teach governments to balance budgets, pay debts, plan expenditures, and repair roads. (KLW, 1997a: 114)

This very much mirrors the framework of ideas in 'Phase 1' discussed above. KLW (1997a) conclude that 'in avoiding agriculture, social services and redistribution and concentrating on economic infrastructure, the Bank was swimming with the intellectual current in the 1950s' (KLW, 1997a: 119).

3.2 The McNamara years: the end of trickle down and 'waging war on poverty'

Things changed when Robert McNamara become President of the Bank in April 1968:

Robert McNamara, during his long term as President ... until June 1981, applied himself with energy, talent and single mindedness to expand the bank, to redefine it as a 'development agency' and – most controversially – to move poverty up front, from the rear of the bus. (KLW, 1997a: 215)

This move was signified by McNamara's Nairobi speech in 1973 (see KLW, 1997a; 263, 415), which led to the agenda of the 1970s with projects directly targeted to the poor. Immediately after the Nairobi speech, the Bank set out to identify ways to reach the poor, both in the cities and in agriculture (KLW, 1997a: 263); there was a rapid growth in the Bank's 'poverty projects' – i.e. lending for social purposes (see, for example, KLW, 1997a: 274–82). In tandem with this a fundamental rethinking on policy began in 1976 with the emergence of the 'basic needs' approach to development assistance (KLW, 1997a: 265). In addition, in a very wide range of borrower countries the Bank set about attempting to influence policies so that they paid more attention to promoting greater income equality and to reducing poverty. According to the Bank *History*, one of the most visible and sustained attempts to do this came in Brazil, where inequality was extreme (KLW, 1997a: 274).

Nevertheless, for all the attention given to poverty eradication in the 1970s, the *History* concludes that the results were 'surely disappointing': at the end of a chapter on the 1970s entitled 'Waging War on Poverty', one finds the following downbeat comment on what was actually achieved:

In practice, intervention in distributive policies proved difficult. National agendas were crowded with long-run development goals and with immediate, circumstantial needs. Other variables affected the outcomes, such as the political interests of the Bank's shareholders and the institutional concerns of the Bank itself. Poverty projects proved equally frustrating. In the end, project eggs were placed in a surprisingly small number of baskets: rural development projects, urban housing for the poor, and water supply projects. Though these categories conceal important differences, and many other kinds of lending also made a contribution to direct poverty alleviation, a retrospective view must necessarily wonder that a social, and global, revolution – seeking to eradicate poverty in developing countries – could have been expected from so limited a tool kit. This reflection influenced the Bank's approach when it returned to poverty alleviation in the next decade. (KLW, 1997a: 329)

3.3 The 1980s and 1990s: trickle down returns, but then so does explicit concern with poverty

By 1980 the emphasis had begun to shift away from direct poverty reduction projects. This was partly due to doubt in the Bank about the poor performance of the previous decade's poverty-oriented lending innovations. But the Bank history tells us that it was partly associated with a change to a more conservative leadership under Clausen who:

did little to suggest an energetic, urgent concern for and belief in the possibility of rapid poverty alleviation. Instead his speeches, and the institution's *World Development Reports*, stressed stabilization, balance of payments adjustment, and the market economy, all of which seemed consistent with a former private banker's priorities. (KLW, 1997a: 336)

The change also happened because of external events. The 1980s were the 'adjustment period'; this was the turbulent, post-Bretton Woods world which, as noted above, was replete with shocks, to which adjustment was necessary. But, clearly, there was one further reason, too. All of this happened at a time when the ideology of the age was moving towards freer markets. This was, after all, the decade in which Ronald Reagan,

Margaret Thatcher and Helmut Kohl were elected leaders of the most influential shareholder countries of the World Bank. Indeed, following the tradition that the President of the World Bank is appointed by the United States, Clausen was in fact appointed by Reagan. And the *History* is in no doubt as to the consequences: 'Arriving at this juncture, Clausen found it relatively easy to bring about a change of stance. The poverty mission was now rapidly abbreviated and downgraded' (KLW, 1997a: 339). An extended section of the *History* (KLW, 1997a: 339–57) describes and documents this process.

By 1987, however, the circle had begun to turn again:

The Bank itself ... decided most firmly that it had strayed from its poverty mission. This message was amplified and transmitted in several major reports, beginning with a status report requested by Barber Conable [the new President] five months after his appointment was announced. (KLW, 1997a: 352)

During the five years of his Presidency, Conable staked out a middle ground. In 1986 'he ... stressed that growth was necessary for social improvement ... that growth was the 'healing antidote' to the poison of poverty' (KLW, 1997a: 360). But by 1987 he had gone further and said:

'growth, by itself, is not enough'. It was a return to McNamara's starting point. Conable went on to outline direct poverty-alleviating measures in the style of McNamara. Over the rest of his term, the institution engaged in a repetition of McNamara's early search for an operational poverty strategy: this was the institution's second attempt to find ways to improve on trickle-down. (KLW, 1997a: 360)

But the momentum of the push of the late 1970s and early 1980s to generalised policy reform and market liberalisation remained strong. The idea that it was these reforms which would help growth and hence poverty reduction remained. The *History* quotes the unofficial No. 2 at the Bank at this time, Ernest Stern, as saying that 'Adjustment Programs are very beneficial to lower income groups'. It also points to a whole range of research reports which attempted to detail this connection, for example through the impact of overvalued exchange rates on agriculture (KLW, 1997a: 353, 354).

A synthesis, of sorts, of this 'rededication to poverty in the light of the experience of the adjustment decade' was launched in the *1990 World Development Report* (World Bank, 1990). The report tried to square the circle through a two-part strategy for poverty reduction, based on 'labor-intensive growth' and 'widespread provision of basic social services'.

One of us wrote a review of the *1990 WDR* at the time, from which we now quote at length:

Before designing policies to help the poor it is important to understand the characteristics of the poor ... The broad conclusion [of the *1990 WDR*] is that whilst the poor are heterogeneous, certain general conclusions can be drawn from the evidence ... Poverty is primarily a rural phenomenon. In Africa and in Asia, the incidence of poverty is far higher in rural areas, and the rural poor account for the vast majority of all those in poverty. In Latin America the situation is less extreme, primarily because of the higher degree of urbanisation. However, so far as non-income achievements are concerned, even in Latin America rural areas lag behind urban areas ...
Since poverty is primarily a rural phenomenon, it is also primarily an agricultural phenomenon. A related characteristic of the poor is that they lack assets. They either have very small amounts of unproductive land, or no land at all. They lack human capital and are therefore reduced to selling unskilled labor, largely in an agricultural setting. This means that the main sources of income for the poor are from agriculture and (in both rural and urban areas) the sale of labor. Those who are income poor also turn to be poor in other dimensions – they do not have as great an access to public services such as health and education as do the non-poor. This in turn affects their earning capacity.
Based on these very general characteristics ... the WDR proposes a two-pronged strategy for alleviating poverty. Firstly, increasing the demand for the poor's most abundant asset – their labor power – through a policy of broad based, labor- intensive growth. Secondly a concerted program of social expenditures to increase access of the poor to basic health and education. (Kanbur, 1990: 11, 12)

There was extensive discussion in the report of individual-country experience. The reading of this evidence was strongly influenced by the what was then happening in the Asia Pacific region; the report highlighted Indonesia as a leading example of a country which had seen dramatic reductions in poverty, as a result of a strategy of broad-based growth and infrastructure expenditure. The *Human Development Report* of 1990 (*1990 HDR*, UNDP, 1990) had a very similar thrust to that of the *1990 WDR*. It summarised the conclusions from country experience in terms of six lessons:

First, growth accompanied by an equitable distribution of income appears to be the most effective means of sustained human development ... Second, countries can make significant improvements in human development over long periods – even in the absence of good growth or good distribution – through well-structured social expenditures by governments ... Third, well-structured government social expenditures can also generate fairly dramatic improvements in a relatively short period ... Fourth, to maintain human development during recessions and natural disasters, targetted interventions may be necessary ... Fifth, growth is crucial for sustaining progress in human development in the long run, otherwise human progress may be disrupted ... Sixth, despite rapid periods of GNP growth, human development may not improve significantly if distribution of income is bad and social expenditures are low. (Kanbur, 1990: 13, 14)

In sum, the *1990 WDR*, and the *1990 HDR* alongside it, represented the consensus of the time that economic growth was necessary but not sufficient for poverty reduction. There was a clear statement that the provision of basic health and social services, and of safety nets, was also necessary. For the World Bank, the *WDR* provided a bridge between the two major trends of the previous decades – the direct attack on poverty through projects in the 1970s, and the market liberalisation zeal of the 1980s. A strategy based on these two elements had strong attractions for the Bank. It allowed the Bank to support both liberalisation and direct action on poverty reduction. Not surprisingly, the Bank increased its lending to the social sectors over this period (see Kanbur, Sandler and Morrison, 1999), as well as pushing countries to liberalise their internal markets and their external trade.

One would have thought that these developments of the late 1980s and early 1990s, including a repositioning of the Bank's strategy astride the market liberalisation and human development tracks, would be broadly acceptable. And yet the World Bank came under increasing criticism in the lead-up to the 50th anniversary of its founding in 1994 – indeed, one of its most vocal critics was a broad grouping of civil society organisations called 'Fifty Years is Enough'. Why?

In our view, the main reason is that there remain significant disputes, professionally and ideologically, around the liberalisation part of the agenda, and within the 'market liberalisation' mindset, formed in the 1980s, which still dominates in the operational part of the World Bank. It is worth exploring the nature of this mindset:

- First, following on from the range of reports produced by the World Bank in the 1980s, culminating in the *1990 WDR*, it sees *rapid market liberalisation* as the basis of growth.
- Second, it does not take a nuanced and contigent view of the likely beneficial impacts of rapid liberalisation. It tends not to take on board the realities of market segmentation and missing markets – in other words, the *actual circumstances of developing countries*. John Williamson (1999), as we saw above, has puzzled about how his term 'Washington consensus', coined in 1990 to reflect what he saw as a move away from market liberalisation orthodoxy, came to be associated in the 1990s with the neo-liberal agenda. One of us (Kanbur, 1999), has argued that there is no puzzle. The operational mindset of

the Bank is one built up in the 1980s, in which the core task is to do 'battle' against statist development strategies. In this 'battle', nuance is beside the point. On the ground, the main negotiators of the Washington institutions in the 1980s did indeed have a mindset which viewed developing country governments as deeply committed to statist ideologies. In this setting, a negotiating stance, rather than a dialogue based on mutual comprehension, was appropriate. So the negotiators from Washington always took a more extreme stance than their real, more nuanced, understanding would have allowed them. 'Give them an inch of nuance, and they'll take a mile of status quo', seemed to be the mindset and the stance.

- Third, partly as a result of the lack of nuance, this mindset did not pay close attention to the *short-run negative consequences of such liberalisation* and had a 'band-aid' approach to dealing with these consequences. The *1990 WDR* did discuss the role of 'safety nets', but these were not at all prominent in the strategy which it proposed. In the operational mindset there is insufficient realisation of the fact that liberalisation may bring enhanced risks to the poor, and that these must be managed as part of a liberalisation strategy if the human development part of the strategy is not to be endangered by the liberalisation part.
- Fourth, despite the entreaties of the *1990 WDR*, the market liberalisation and human development parts of the strategy continue to be generally seen, in the operational parts of the Bank, as *separate entities*.

For all of these reasons, despite an avowed mission to eradicate poverty, and a seemingly pro-poor strategy, by the mid-1990s the World Bank came increasingly to be regarded by civil society advocates as the enemy of the poor.

4 Poverty reduction and the Bank at the turn of the century

Where do things now stand as we enter the twenty-first century? What is likely to be the Bank's stance in the next decade?

The changes which started in the late 1980s and early 1990s now look as though they are gathering full steam. As always, the roots of these changes lie in political and intellectual evolution outside the Bank. Politically, in 1995 a Democratic US administration appointed James D. Wolfensohn as President to succeed the previous Republican appointee. In 1999 Wolfensohn was reappointed by the same Democratic administration until 2005.

At the same time, as we discussed in section 2 (p. 88), the professional and analytical literature has been evolving in interesting ways over the last decade. The efficacy of market liberalisation in its raw form has been seriously questioned by the brutal experiences of the consequences of liberalisation in the transition economies and in the East Asia crisis (Stiglitz, 1999). The less than satisfactory experiences of liberalisation in generating growth in Latin America and Africa, and the growing concern with increasing inequality and increasing volatility owing to changes in technology and trade, are also the basis of much reassessment that is taking place. Looking back it is now possible to see how contingent was the steady progress made by the countries which liberalised in the 1960s, 1970s and 1980s. The management of external volatility,[15] and of internal distributional conflict, was at the core of the successes of this period.

The increased interest in, and analytical support for, the causal connection from inequity and volatility to growth is also influencing thinking inside the Bank. Wolfensohn has put forward a 'Comprehensive Development Framework' (CDF) which emphasises the institutional dimension of development strategies (World Bank, 1998). The CDF approach to development attempts to be comprehensive not just in this way alone. Comprehensiveness across participants is also an aspiration: if government, the private sector and 'civil society' all become participants in the process, then it is hoped that a greater degree of identification with, and ownership of, the development process will be the outcome.

So things are changing. It is our hope that the new century will see strategies for poverty reduction which go beyond the mantra of 'market liberalisation leads to growth and growth leads to poverty reduction', or even the mantra of 'market liberalisation plus social investment'. Rather, the analytical literature and experience on the ground suggest that a different mindset is needed. This is a mindset which makes equity and security, in their different dimensions, the starting point for growth-promoting policies, including market liberalisation policies. It discusses equity and security first, since it recognises that not only do they have a direct impact on growth, but that addressing them as a priority allows market liberalisation measures to play their full role in growth and poverty reduction. Also it leads to a more cautious attitude: to privatisation, if the appropriate ownership structure is not in place, and to trade liberalisation, if the appropriate macroeconomic strategy is not in place.

The lessons of the 1960s and 1970s, including many disastrous statist interventions in the name of equity and security, must not be forgotten.

Critics of what we advocate here will no doubt suggest that it advocates a return to these dark days.[16] But, with care, an emphasis on equity and security as a prerequisite for market liberalisation is, paradoxically, more likely to lead to policies which deliver growth in the next century than a mindset which takes market liberalisation as *the* prerequisite for all of growth, equity and security.

NOTES

This chapter draws on Kanbur and Squire (1999) and Kanbur (1999). We have made extensive use of the *History* of the World Bank (KLW, 1997a, 1997b), and would like to acknowledge the marvellous resource which this study provides.

1 See also Murphy, Shleifer and Vishny (1989); Krugman (1999).

2 Krugman (1999, p.1).

3 Rosenstein-Rodan and others (e.g. Nurkse, 1953) argued as follows. (The paragraph which follows is taken, with adaption, from Krugman, 1999) Modern methods of production are potentially more productive than traditional ones, but their productivity edge is large enough to compensate for the necessity of paying higher wages only if the market is large enough. However the size of the market depends on the extent to which modern techniques are adopted, because workers in the modern sector earn higher wages and/or participate in the market economy more than traditional workers. So self-sustaining modernisation can be got going only if it is started on a sufficiently large scale. This view appeared to imply that a coordinated, broadly-based investment programme would be required. Hirschman (1958) disagreed, arguing that a policy of promoting a few key sectors with strong linkages, then moving on to other sectors to correct the disequilibrium generated by these investments, and so on, was actually the right approach. This led, in due course, to Mahalanobis' work on the need to improve the efficiency of the machines that would make the machines that would make the machines (Mahalanobis, 1963).

4 Kuznets' work was based, by his own account, on about 5 per cent empirical information and 95 per cent speculation. It suggested explanations for – and theoretical arguments against – his scant data. What is now known as the Kuznets' curve or Inverted U Hypothesis actually comes from a hypothetical numerical exercise.

5 KLW (1997a: 225; see especially nn. 22, 23).

6 'In present circumstances, when the employment problem is already crucial, it may thus be necessary, to some extent, to be ready to sacrifice growth of output for more early employment' (Little, Scitovsky and Scott, 1970, p. 92, cited in KLW, 1997a: 226).

7 The analysis in these two papers was undertaken in the second half of the 1980s.

8 John Williamson (1999) has revisited the strange history of this term, which he invented. As he notes: 'I have slowly become conscious that the term is often being used in a sense significantly different to that which I had intended, as a

synonym for what is often called "neo-liberalism" in Latin America, or what George Soros (1998) has called "market fundamentalism." ' This is the sense in which we are using the term here. For a further discussion of this term, see below.

9 Balassa (1985) is an example of the literature of the 1980s. More recent support for this view is presented in Dollar (1992) and Edwards (1993); a restatement of the basic argument is to be found in Krueger (1998). Rodrik (1999) reviews and then critiques the empirical literature claiming to support the connection between trade liberalisation and growth.

10 For example, Ravallion and Datt (1999) show that non-farm economic growth in India's states was less effective in reducing poverty in states with poor basic education.

11 See Zysman (1978); see also van der Ploeg (1987).

12 Population-weighted averages for Indonesia, Korea, Malaysia, Philippines, Thailand and Taiwan.

13 But note that the structure of incentives and the complementary investments to ensure that society, and especially the poor, reap maximum benefit, including increased incomes, from investment in education and health may not be in place (Squire, 1993). There is evidence in support of this view, especially for education. Thus, cross-country regressions suggest that the impact of growth in educational capital on growth in GDP per worker are 'consistently small and negative' (Pritchett, 1996). Pritchett squares the circle between the apparently positive effect of education at the individual level and its apparently insignificant effect at the aggregate level by distinguishing between rent-seeking and productive activities (Murphy, Shleifer and Vishny, 1989). If the returns to being educated are to be found at least in part in rent-seeking then the individuals receiving education will enjoy increases in income but national income will not necessarily rise. According to this view, countries such as Sri Lanka have enjoyed the immediate benefits of better and more education but have not realised the increases in income that could accompany them.

14 It should be noticed that the studies that try to get to structural inequalities and their effect on growth do better than simply looking for an effect of *straight* income inequality on growth (Kanbur and Squire, 1999). 'Structural inequality' here refers to the distribution of assets and wealth as distinct from the mere distribution of more income.

15 Even although the growth of world trade was far from steady in the 1970s and early 1980s, developing countries which liberalised were not then exposed to the volatility of capital flows to which such countries are now exposed.

16 See Srinivasan (1999).

REFERENCES

Anand, S. and S.M.R. Kanbur (1991). 'Public Policy and Basic Needs Provision in Sri Lanka', in J. Drèze and A. Sen (eds.), *The Political Economy of Hunger, III: Endemic Hunger*, Oxford, Clarendon Press

(1993). 'Inequality and Development: A Critique', *Journal of Development Economics*, **41(1)**: 19–43

Balassa, B. (1985). 'Exports, Policy Choices and Economic Growth in Developing Countries After the 1973 Oil Shock', *Journal of Development Economics*, **18(2)**: 23–35

Bourguignon, F., A. Chong and J. Hentschel (1999). 'Bundling of Basic Services, Welfare, and Structural Reform in Perú', DECRG and PREM, Washington, DC: World Bank, unpublished paper

Dollar, D. (1992). 'Outward-oriented Developing Countries Really Do Grow More Rapidly: Evidence from 95 LDCs, 1976–85', *Economic Development and Cultural Change*, **40**: 523–44

Edwards, S. (1993). 'Trade Orientation, Distortions, and Growth in Developing Countries', *Journal of Economic Literature*, **31(3)**: 1358–93

Fishlow, A. (1972). 'Brazilian Size Distribution of Income', *American Economic Review*, **62**: 391–402

Grootaert, C. and R. Kanbur (1995). 'The Lucky Few Amidst Economic Decline: Distributional Change in Côte d'Ivoire as Seen through Panel Data Sets, 1985–88', *Journal of Development Studies*, **31**: 603–19

Hirschman, A. (1958). *The Strategy of Economic Development*, New Haven, CN: Yale University Press

Hoddinott, J. and W. Kinsey (1998). 'Child Growth in the Time of Drought', Washington, DC: International Food Policy Research Institute, unpublished paper

Jalan, J. and M. Ravallion (1999). 'Are the Poor Less Well Insured? Evidence on Vulnerability to Income Risk in Rural China', *Journal of Development Economics*, **58**: 61–81

Kanbur, R. (1990). 'Poverty and Development: the *Human Development Report* and *The World Development Report, 1990*', *Discussion Paper*, **103**, University of Warwick, November

(1999). 'The Strange Case of the Washington Consensus: A Commentary on John Williamson's 'What Should the Bank think about the Washington Consensus?', World Bank, July, mimeo

Kanbur, R. and N. Lustig (1999). 'Why is Inequality Back on the Agenda?', *Working Paper*, **WP 99-14**, Department of Agricultural, Resource and Managerial Economics, Cornell University

Kanbur, R., T. Sandler and K. Morrison (1999). 'The Future of Development Assistance', *Policy Essay*, **25**, Washington, DC: Overseas Development Council

Kanbur, R. and L. Squire (1999). 'The Evolution of Thinking about Poverty: Exploring the Interactions', World Bank, September, mimeo

Kapur, D., J. Lewis, and R. Webb (1997a). *The World Bank: Its First Half Century, 1: History*, Washington, DC: Brookings Institution

(1997b). *The World Bank: Its First Half Century, 2: Perspectives*, Washington, DC: Brookings Institution

Krueger, A. O. (1998). 'Why Trade Liberalisation is Good for Growth', *The Economic Journal*, **108**: 1513–22

Krugman, P. (1999). 'The Fall and Rise of Development Economics', < http:/ www.web.mit.edu/krugman/www/dishpan.html >

Kuznets, S. (1955). 'Economic Growth and Income Inequality', *The American Economic Review*, **45(1)**: 1–28

Lewis, W.A. (1954). 'Economic Development with Unlimited Supplies of Labor', *Manchester School of Economic Studies*, **22**: 139–91

Li, H., L. Squire and H. Zou (1998). 'Explaining International and Intertemporal Variations in Income Inequality', *Economic Journal*, **108**: 1–18

Little, I., T. Skitovsky and M. Scott (1970). *Industry and Trade in Some Developing Countries*, London: Oxford University Press

Lustig, (1999). 'Crises and the Poor: Socially Responsible Macroeconomics', Presidential Address, LACEA, Santiago, Chile

Mahalanobis, P. (1963). *The Approach of Operational Research to Planning in India*, Bombay

Meade, J. (1972). *The Intelligent Radical's Guide to Economic Policy*, London: Allen & Unwin

Morduch, J. (1995). 'Income Smoothing and Consumption Smoothing', *Journal of Economic Perspectives,* 9(3): 103–14

Murphy, R., A. Shleifer and R. Vishny (1989). 'Industrialization and the Big Push', *Journal of Political Economy*, **97**: 1003–26

Nurkse, R. (1953). *Problems of Capital Formation in Underdeveloped Countries*, Oxford: Blackwell

Pritchett, L. (1996). 'Where has All the Education Gone?', *Policy Research Working Paper*, **1581**, Washington, DC: Policy Research Department, World Bank

Ravallion, M. and S. Chen (1997). 'What Can Survey Data Tell Us about the Changes in Distribution and Policy?', *World Bank Economic Review*, **11**: 357–82

Ravallion, M. and G. Datt (1999). 'When is Growth Pro-poor? Evidence from the Diverse Experiences of India's States', World Bank, mimeo

Rodrik, D. (1998). 'TFPG Controversies, Institutions, and Economic Performance in East Asia', in Y. Hayami and M. Aoki (eds.), *The Institutional Foundations of Economic Development in East Asia*, London: Macmillan

(1999). *The New Global Economy and Developing Countries: Making Openness Work*, *Policy Essay*, **24**, Washington, DC: Overseas Development Council

Rosenstein-Rodan, P. (1943). 'Problems of Industrialization of Eastern and South-Eastern Europe', *Economic Journal*, June–September

Sachs, J. and A. Warner (1995). 'Economic Reform and the Process of Global Economic Integration', *Brookings Papers on Economic Activity*, **1**: 1–95

Soros, G. (1998). *The Crisis of Global Capitalism: Open Society Endangered*, London: Little Brown

Squire, L. (1993). 'Fighting Poverty', *AEA Papers and Proceedings*, **83(2)**: 377–82

(1998). 'Health, Nutrition, and Economic Development', *Journal of Economic Literature*, **36**: 766–817

Srinivasan, T. N (1999). 'Variety of Routes to Development already Known', letter to *Financial Times,* 28 September

Stiglitz, J. (1999). 'Whither Reform? Ten Years of the Transition', Annual Bank Conference on Development Economics, Washington, DC: World Bank

Strauss, and Thomas (1997). 'Health and Wages. Evidence on Men and Women in Urban Brazil', *Journal of Econometrics*, **77**: 159–85

(1998). 'Health, Nutrition and Development', *Journal of Economic Literature*, **36**: 766–817

United Nations Development Programme (UNDP) (1990). *Human Development Report*, New York: Oxford University Press

van der Ploeg, F. (1987). 'Trade Unions, Investment and Employment: A Noncooperative Approach', *European Economic Review*, **31**: 1465–92

Williamson, J. (1990). 'What Washington Means by Policy Reform', in J.Williamson (ed.), *Latin American Adjustment: How Much Has Happened?*, Washington, DC: Institute for International Economics

(1999). 'What Should the Bank Think about the Washington Consensus?', World Bank, July, mimeo

World Bank (1990). *World Development Report 1990*, New York: Oxford University Press

(1998). *East Asia: The Road to Recovery*, Washington, DC: World Bank

Zaman, H. (1999). 'Who Benefits and to What Extent? An Evaluation of BRAC's Micro-credit Program', PhD thesis, University of Sussex

Zysman, D. (1978). *Politics, Markets and Growth: The Politics of Industrial Change*, Ithaca: Cornell University Press

4 Why the World Bank should be involved in development research

LYN SQUIRE

1 Introduction

My years as Director of the World Bank's Research Department from 1993 to 1997 gave me ample cause to contemplate the issue raised in the title of this chapter. In most institutions that are engaged primarily in operations – whether it be production or, as in the case of the World Bank, lending – some staff inevitably view research and other analytical work as a luxury. Budget reallocation brings calls for a reevaluation of such 'frills'. These circumstances require that the research programme be kept active and effective. In this chapter, I spell out why the World Bank should be involved in development research and, wherever possible, illustrate how it has lived up to its potential. Evidence shows that on the whole the effort has been a success, and widely recognised as such.

Economics tells us that the creation and dissemination of knowledge has the key attributes of a public good. Knowledge is non-rivalrous because my use of a piece of knowledge does not preclude its use by others. Thomas Jefferson put this well when he said: 'He who receives an idea from me, receives instruction himself without lessening mine; as he who lights his taper at mine, receives light without darkening me.' Knowledge is also non-excludable – it is often difficult for the creator of knowledge to prevent others from using it. As is well known, these two attributes result in undersupply – individuals and firms will underinvest in the creation of knowledge because they receive only a small part of the total benefits to society, but they bear the full costs. If the investment is worthwhile for society as a whole to make, then the government can step in. But in some instances, knowledge is an international public good – the benefits of generating a particular piece of knowledge may spill over from the producing country to other countries. In these circumstances, no single country or private organisation has the incentive to undertake

108

the research necessary to create such knowledge. International institutions can help fill this gap. This, then, justifies the World Bank's involvement in development research – international institutions may be able to solve what otherwise would be a difficult problem of coordinating the actions of many countries to create and disseminate knowledge that the developing world needs.

There is nothing in the preceding argument, however, to suggest that 'involvement in development research' need take the form of in-house production of research. Research could be funded by the World Bank and other international institutions but undertaken by others – universities, research institutes, individual consultants, and so on. Why should the World Bank undertake research itself rather than support research in other institutions? The main reason is that it is difficult to structure incentives such that outside research institutes will deliver the kind of research the World Bank seeks to promote. Given its mandate, the World Bank needs research that is relevant to developing countries, that is of high quality and that, once created, is shared and used by others. It thus faces a principal–agent problem that has three dimensions – relevance, quality and follow up.

The Bank may feasibly set incentives to ensure that outside research is relevant to developing countries. For example, it could identify specific topics and then call for the submission of proposals. In this way, it funds only research that it believes to be relevant to developing countries. It could also rely on third-party, peer review to ensure quality both to select among proposals and to assess final output. Requiring submission of papers to refereed journals would be one simple mechanism for checking quality. (In fact, the Bank does precisely this to test the quality of its own research.) Thus, the Bank can probably devise incentives to deal with the issues of relevance and quality.

But without an in-house capacity, integrating the results of research into the World Bank's everyday operations and making those results available to policy-makers in developing countries does not happen. This usually requires an in-house champion, and the best champion is almost always the researcher. This then supplies the primary rationale for an in-house research capacity at the World Bank. The in-house researcher has more knowledge about operational departments in fact, researchers at the World Bank spend about one-third of their time working directly with operational units. And the in-house researcher has a longer-term interest in the institution and will therefore be more committed to the institution's goals than, say, maximising publications.

Self-selection ensures that in-house researchers on average have a greater interest in integrating the results of their research into the

Bank's operational work and its policy advice. A researcher obliged to participate in operational missions and contribute to operational reports, or required to engage in extensive dissemination of key policy results will stay in the Bank because she finds such work professionally rewarding. As a result, the Bank has developed a clear comparative advantage in certain types of research. The Bank focuses on applied, policy-oriented research often with a strong, cross-country dimension. The flip side, of course, is that more fundamental, theoretical research is left to academia. As Gilbert, Powell and Vines (1998) aptly comment, along the spectrum of R&D the Bank has focused on the 'D' component the development of ideas produced elsewhere – rather than pure research.

Accepting that the World Bank should undertake research in-house, the question that then arises is: how much research? In principle, one could work out the optimal scale. There are almost certainly economies of scale and of scope – research involves fixed costs, and researchers benefit from broad cross-fertilisation – but we have little real information on the shape of the production technology. Nor do we have precise measures of benefits. In the absence of this information, determining the level of research will inevitably be arbitrary and approximate.

One approximation begins with the choice of areas in which the World Bank wants to have impact – trade, poverty, pollution, and so on. It then asks what level of research is required to ensure at least some impact in each of these areas. In this approach, one stays within the broad framework of cost–benefit analysis, but judgements rather than quantitative measures drive the outcomes. This is the approach followed by the World Bank to set priorities and determine funding levels.

The rest of this chapter elaborates these points. It begins by describing the World Bank's research and economic work: the content, size of the effort and allocated budget. The next section elaborates the arguments presented above and illustrates them with specific examples. The final section turns to the difficult task of assessing the worth of World Bank research. Ultimately, this is the only way to assess the merit of the arguments advanced in the chapter. Several imperfect measures are used – number of publications in peer-reviewed journals, citations, the use of World Bank material in university courses, client surveys, and so on. But in none of these cases are we able to arrive at a quantitative measure of impact. In the one case where we do have such a measure, we find that the World Bank's economic analysis improves the quality of lending programmes significantly, especially compared to costs.

2 World Bank research and analysis

The World Bank undertakes research chiefly in its research department, but most departments throughout the institution perform some research. World Bank staff, primarily in the operational departments, carry out Economic and Sector Work (ESW) in support of their lending operations and policy dialogue. While the focus of this chapter is on research, we will offer some comments on ESW.

World Bank research covers a range of topics nearly as wide as Bank operations. In recent years, economic management, poverty and human resource issues have been the leading subjects of research, but work on environment and sustainable development has expanded. Nearly three-quarters of Bank research is located in units under the direction of the Bank's Chief Economist, who has overall responsibility for the Bank's research programme. About two-thirds of Bank research is carried out as part of an integrated multi-year research programme within the Development Economics complex. Recent examples of World Bank research output include: 'Averting the Old Age Crisis' (World Bank, 1994); 'Confronting AIDS' (World Bank, 1997); and 'Saving Across the World: Puzzles and Policies' (Schmidt-Hebbel and Serven, 1997). The examples convey the flavour of World Bank research: it is policy-oriented and usually empirical.

The World Bank undertakes ESW on all developing countries that are members this amounts to well over 150 countries ranging in size from Chad to China. The work undertaken on each country is specific to that country but could include: a Country Economic Memorandum, a comprehensive account of economic performance and prospects and/or more topic-focused reports such as Poverty Assessments, Public Expenditure Reviews, Labour Market Studies, as well as a wide range of sectoral studies. In general, the more aggregate studies underpin the World Bank's policy advice while the sectoral studies Reviews of the Transport Sector, Health and Education Sector Reports, and so on provide the foundation for lending operations in those sectors.

Undertaking this range and magnitude of work is expensive – since 1975 the World Bank has used about 22,000 staffweeks a year on ESW. Table 4.1 shows the amounts spent on research and ESW in US dollars, and the size of their budgets relative to the operational budget for the past six years. Three points are worth noting: first, together, research and ESW amount to a significant share of the total operational budget – around 30 per cent in the early 1990s – although most of this is the ESW managed by operations. Second, resources allocated to research and ESW have declined significantly over the 1990s. Research has fallen from $US29.8 million in 1992 to $US24.6 million in 1997, while ESW has fallen from $US105.5 million to $US81.0 million over the same period. That said, the third point remains: at $US100 million in 1997, this amount of research and ESW makes the World Bank one of the largest sources of such analysis for the developing world.

3 The World Bank and development research

In this section we elaborate the arguments set out in the introduction to justify the role of the World Bank in development research. To make the arguments as concrete as possible, we offer examples to illustrate each point. We begin with three examples to demonstrate that World Bank research is indeed creating knowledge that has the characteristics of an international public good. We then illustrate what we believe is the critical justification of in-house research – the role of the champion. Turning to the 'production technology' for research, we show how a relatively large pool of researchers can undertake analysis and produce outputs that perhaps would not be feasible for smaller, specialised research groups. These arguments justify a substantial, in-house research capacity at the World Bank. That said, some types of research of great importance to developing countries ought to be undertaken elsewhere. To conclude this section, we present two examples of research that the World Bank is actively encouraging in other institutions. One involves the development of local research capacity. In the other, scientific expertise clearly rests with others.

3.1 International public goods

Every change in policy creates knowledge that can be of value to other countries considering similar changes. Every project, whether successful or not, also creates knowledge about what works and what does not work. The transfer of local knowledge from one country to another has the potential to unleash powerful development forces. Learning from others, assimilating that knowledge, and adapting it to local circumstances offer the opportunity to make rapid advances without repeating others' mistakes. However, carrying out rigorous analyses of the policy experiments of dozens of other countries or assessing the merits

Table 4.1. *Bank resources devoted to research in relation to other Bank analytical work and the administrative budget, FY 1992–1997*

Item	1992		1993		1994		1995		1996		1997	
	Million dollars	per cent of operational budget	Million dollars	per cent of operational budget	Million dollars	per cent of operational budget	Million dollars	per cent of operational budget	Million dollars	per cent of operational budget	Million dollars	per cent of operational budget
Research	29.8	5.8	32.4	5.6	29.8	4.6	28.0	4.1	25.5	3.9	24.6	3.8
Economic and sector work	105.5	20.5	123.8	21.4	126.8	19.6	109.1	16.0	93.1	14.2	81.0	12.5

Source: Planning and Budgeting Department reports on 'World Bank Budgets by Major Programs', and Research Advisory Staff.

of alternative project interventions is beyond the capacity of most developing economies. It is also beyond the self-interest of any single country because the global benefits of a systematic analysis of policy experiments exceed those that accrue to the originating country. International institutions and other providers, then, have a role in helping countries *exchange* knowledge about policies, projects, and the development process itself (World Bank, 1999).

The policy research of development institutions aims to fill part of this gap by analysing and codifying policy reforms around the world so that this information can be used world-wide. For example, it was only in the late 1970s that development agencies began to fully appreciate the value of openness to international markets as a spur to economic growth. In the two decades since, development agencies have undertaken research to establish the benefits of a reasonable degree of openness, encouraging insular economies to learn from the success of the more open ones. Of 35 countries that undertook major trade liberalisations over this period, almost all were influenced by the successful cases that had gone before (World Bank, 1999). This influence would have been much less potent without systematic efforts to demonstrate and disseminate the lessons of success and failure (see p. 126 below).

Turning to projects, the World Bank has an established capacity to evaluate projects by drawing on cross-country evidence and experience. Project evaluation benefits the country in which the project is located, particularly if the feedback results in continuous improvement. And when properly disseminated, the results of careful evaluation can benefit other countries as well. In fact, much of the value of development projects comes through the *ex post* evaluation of innovative activities, whether successful or unsuccessful. Thorough evaluation includes listening to project beneficiaries and taking into account their measures of a project's success or failure. It also requires analysis, which means not only recording perceptions of what constitutes 'best practice', but also digging into what really works, why it works and what the most important contributing factors are. Analysis is needed not only to ensure continual improvement, but also because all too often what is 'best practice' depends on both the details of a programme and the context in which it is applied. Only careful analysis can determine which practices suit which contexts.

Countries may undertake projects on their own, or may implement projects funded and supported by outside institutions such as the World Bank. Especially when it is directly involved in funding, the World Bank has a unique opportunity and responsibility to compare similar projects across countries and carry out impact evaluations.

Other countries benefit from such analysis, and the World Bank itself thus enhances the success of its new initiatives. In 1998–9, for example, a research team composed of research staff, in-country counterparts and international consultants completed impact evaluations of five World Bank-financed projects that support reforms in the education sector, either through decentralisation or privatisation. The research project adopted a common evaluation design and instruments, where possible, for comparability across cases, but also used a variety of methods that illustrates the range of alternative evaluation approaches that can be used under different circumstances. They used both random and matched comparison groups, tracked programme participants over time and conducted qualitative studies such as focus groups to supplement the quantitative findings. Now the group is embarking on a project to synthesise and disseminate the findings of the study, in part to inform future decentralisation reforms and privatisation programmes, encourage similar research in the academic communities in different countries and foster capacity-building and collaboration with national education evaluation teams. Already, as a result of the close partnership with Bank operations staff and in-country researchers, there has been an early dissemination of the research results within the Bank and the countries (World Bank, 1998b).

One other area of knowledge exchange deserves mention – knowledge about the development process itself. For example, the long-standing debate about whether rising income in the early stages of development leads to higher levels of inequality has suffered from a lack of adequate data on distribution. The Bank has recently put together the most extensive database to date on inequality. Starting with over 2,000 observations on a distribution of varying degrees of quality, a final data set of 682 high-quality observations was identified. An observation was considered to be of 'high quality' if it was from a national household survey in which an attempt had been made to account for all sources of income. Armed with these data, it was possible to show that rising incomes are not necessarily associated with higher levels of inequality and that increases in mean income are almost always associated with increases in the incomes of those in the poorest quintile of the population. Policy-makers can thus be assured that the package of policies used to promote growth in these countries will in general reduce poverty as well (Deininger and Squire, 1996).

Quite apart from any analysis the Bank may do itself, a further contribution that it can make is to place these data in the public domain. This generates valuable externalities – researchers who might not otherwise focus on development may be attracted by the availability of good data.

The Bank's data on inequality are available from its Web server < http://
www.worldbank.org/ > .

3.2 *The role of champion*

The impact of research both on Bank operations and on the developing
world depends critically on the efforts made by researchers themselves to
'sell' their ideas. Publication in scientific journals is not enough. Some of
the most successful examples of research results being translated into
action arise when researchers are willing and able to take the time to
work with operational staff and policy-makers in developing countries.
This seems to work best when the research is undertaken within an
institution that also has an operational mandate, and is therefore a com-
pelling argument for an in-house research capacity. The principal–agent
problem that would otherwise arise if the World Bank relied exclusively
on external research is thus solved through self-selection. Researchers
inside the Bank are expected to incorporate the results of their research
in the Bank's operational activities and the policy dialogue. Knowing
this, researchers attracted to the Bank are those most interested in this
style of research.

One famous example of someone who championed the implementation
of research results was Bela Belassa. During the 1980s, his ideas about
prices and trade and the damaging effects of distorting either were translated into the Bank's stance on promoting trade liberalisation, as noted
above. At the same time, he saw ahead of the bulk of the economics
profession in his arguments for government support of the positive
externalities of manufacturing industries and in his insight that tariff
reduction ought to proceed gradually. Belassa personally acted as consultant to a number of countries, applying his perceptions and priorities
(Stern and Ferreira, 1997).

More recently research on pension reform exemplifies the way basic
research translates into meaningful policy changes by means of cooperation among researchers, operational staff and policy-makers. Many
developing economies have public pension schemes that operate on a
pay-as-you-go basis, with current contributions paid out mostly to current recipients. The benefit–tax ratios of these schemes remain viable as
long as there are many workers and few retirees, but will become unwork-
able as the ratio of retirees to workers climbs. A 1994 World Bank report,
'Averting the Old Age Crisis' (World Bank, 1994), contributed signifi-

cantly to the policy debate on pension reform, providing a blueprint for Bank staff and policy-makers alike (World Bank, 1996a).

A wide range of countries – among them virtually every country in Eastern Europe and Central Asia, and Argentina, China, Mexico and Uruguay – have studied the long-term fiscal and distributional consequences of their old-age security systems. These countries were able to draw on the lessons of, for example, the successful Chilean pension reform. Once the public understood that current benefit–tax ratios were not sustainable, political support for reform increased. Hungary and Poland have adopted systems based on the Report's recommendations after much discussion about how to reform their problem-laden pension plans. Hungary started the decentralised competitive funding in 1998 and Poland started in 1999. Peru revised its 1992 Pension Reform in response to advice from the Bank. Much of this was supported by an intensive effort on the part of the lead researcher herself to translate the research findings into practical policy guidance through numerous missions and follow-up activities. Since 1994, she has participated in about 100 presentations and seminars on pension reform, given abundant press conferences, radio and TV interviews in countries all over the world, written 14 journal articles and edited a special issue of a journal on pension reform (James, 1998a; and see, for example, the survey article, James, 1998b).

In some cases, Bank researchers work directly with implementing agencies in developing countries. This is perhaps one of the most effective means of ensuring that research has impact. A good example is Indonesia's Programme for Pollution Control, Evaluation, and Rating (PROPER), launched in 1995 (World Bank, 1995). It assigns a colour rating to a factory based on the government's evaluation of its environmental performance. A blue rating is given to factories in compliance with regulatory standards, and green to those whose emissions controls significantly exceed standards; the gold rating (yet to be awarded to any firm) is for world-class performers. Factories that fall somewhat short of compliance receive a red rating, and black is for those that have made no effort to control pollution and have caused serious environmental damage.

The Indonesian government publicised these ratings. The simple act of making this information public caused firms to change their behaviour. More than 30 per cent of the first 187 factories rated moved from red or black to blue status in 15 months. PROPER actually expanded during the 1998 financial crisis, keeping pollution in check as plant managers cut back on maintenance and operations in pollution abatement. Bank researchers were instrumental in designing PROPER and assessing its progress and are now sharing this example of public information in action with other countries. Indeed, the Philippines has started its own public disclosure program called ECOWATCH, while Colombia and Mexico have initiated pilot ratings and Bangladesh, Thailand and China have pledged to begin the process as well, with the help of Bank researchers.

3.3 Production technology

The self-selection of researchers noted above results in a package of skills at the World Bank that leads to particular strengths. Whereas theoretical analysis is mainly the province of universities and research institutes, the Bank has a comparative advantage in applied research and policy analysis. And because the Bank's mandate extends to 'development' in the broadest sense, it takes a comprehensive approach, which has implications for both the scope and the scale of its research. Its unique collection of competence in microeconomics, sectoral studies, macroeconomics and particular country expertise thus proves more valuable than outstanding talent in one dimension when undertaking such activities as applied empirical research; cross-country, cross-regional and global trend studies and evaluation of project and national performance. As an integrated entity, the World Bank profits from economies of scope and of scale.

One example of how economies of scope work in favour of Bank research is a report entitled 'Assessing Aid' (World Bank, 1998a). Macroeconomists, public finance analysts and poverty experts worked on different aspects of the impact of aid, and these analyses were then brought together to construct an integrated view of what works, what does not, and why. From the macroeconomic side, researchers reported that the effect of aid on growth was neutral or even negative until they separated countries with good economic management from those with poor economic management. With good management, an additional 1 per cent of GDP in aid increases growth in *per capita* income by 0.5 percentage points.

Changes in GDP affect income *per capita* and thereby the number of people in poverty, as reported by the poverty experts. They cited recent evidence that the benefits of growth do accrue to the poor as well as to the wealthy as countries develop. All expanding economies in a study of 67 countries saw *per capita* income grow and poverty decline, and every country experiencing a drop in *per capita* income also suffered an increase in poverty (Ravallion and Chen, 1997). Armed with these and similar results, the researchers were able to show that an extra 1 per cent of GDP in aid can lead to a decline in the level of poverty of 1 per cent in well managed economies, but in a poorly managed country there is no marginal impact for that amount of aid.

With the help of public finance analysts, the reasons for the variable effects of aid are elucidated: typically, aid is 'fungible', so that only part of a dollar of aid goes to the intended project or sector. Thus, to a large degree, aid finances the public budget. This helps to explain why sound policies and institutions – good economic management – determines the impact of aid. In well managed countries, it is probably easier and more sensible for donors simply to provide general budget support. In average or poorly managed countries, financial aid is not likely to be effective. In this case, aid should take the form of institution-building and knowledge transfer, so that the country can improve the efficiency of its service delivery and in the future use general aid more effectively.

To summarise: in well managed countries, aid contributes to growth and growth increases *per capita* income and reduces poverty, because governments allocate the aid sensibly and deliver public services efficiently. Aid has little or no effect in poorly managed countries. By assessing aid from many different standpoints, the report provides insight into what aid does, why it matters, how it does it, who should receive it and which approach works best for different countries. Implementing such a broad research programme was made easier by the presence of many researchers with different skills and areas of expertise in a single department.

Along with such economies of scope, World Bank research benefits from economies of scale. The institution naturally amasses large quantities of detailed data from client countries, forms a multitude of contacts across the world and in the development community, and retains a sizable staff. These features give the Bank a comparative advantage in the assembly and analysis of cross-country data, allowing for better cross-country and cross-region regressions, comparative development analyses and global trend analysis.

For example, the World Bank produces an important source of data for all development researchers the World Development Indicators at the back of the *World Development Reports* (*WDR*s). These data constitute an important reason why the reports have such a wide circulation. The tables cover 64 indicators for 148 economies, and draw data from the United Nations, the IMF, the World Trade Organisation (WTO), the OECD, private organisations and the statistical offices of more than 200 economies, as well as the Bank's own cross-country experience and sectoral knowledge. The Bank directly collects data from living standards surveys and external debt reports, as well as country economic reports, sector and project work and research papers. It is difficult to imagine that this level of data assembly could be undertaken by any other institution.

The considerable concentration of staff and resources also contributes to in-country research. For example, in 1980, the World Bank established the Living Standards Measurement Study (LSMS) to explore ways of improving the type and quality of household data collected by government statistical offices in developing countries. The objectives of the LSMS were to develop new methods for monitoring progress in raising levels of living, to identify the consequences for households of current and proposed government policies, and to improve communications between survey statisticians, analysts and policy-makers. As of 1997, surveys with several, if not all, of the hallmarks of the LSMS had been conducted in about two dozen countries. The World Bank research group assists in implementing new surveys, archives and disseminates data from LSMS surveys to eligible users, periodically produces written materials on the lessons from LSMS implementation experience and supports the LSMS *Working Paper Series* which publishes papers on issues relevant to the collection or analysis of multi-topic household surveys. To date, 134 working papers have been written using the LSMS, and several hundred research reports have been published that draw on LSMS data. Again, organising and implementing a data-collection exercise on this scale is probably beyond the capacity of any other institution (see Grosh and Glewwe, 1998).

3.4 Supporting research elsewhere

The preceding arguments for a strong, in-house research capacity do not mean that research should never be outsourced. Indeed, there are two reasons why the Bank actively encourages research in other institutions. The first arises from the desire to build research capacity in developing countries. The second arises when the technical expertise to undertake the research clearly rests elsewhere.

Policy-makers and communities in developing countries often have information, or local knowledge, that is not readily transferable to international institutions. It is often most efficient for development institutions to transfer internationally available knowledge to well trained government officials or other local residents, who can then merge that knowledge with local knowledge to devise locally appropriate policies or projects. For this reason, donors often help create domestic capacity for policy analysis and devise mechanisms that allow a strong civil society to engage government in a dialogue on policy.

To this end, the Bank has supported the creation of Regional Research Consortia throughout the developing world. While each is designed with region-specific circumstances and needs in mind, there are two key underlying principles. The first is to encourage networking among local research institutes through conferences, workshops, publications, and so on. The second is to support a competitive allocation of research funds through peer review.

The African Economic Research Consortium, which supports research by Africans on African economic policies, is universally regarded as an extraordinarily successful capacity-building institution (Thorbecke, 1996; Henderson and Loxley, 1997). It provides grants to African researchers on a competitive basis and organises region-wide conferences and workshops in which Bank staff have long been involved as peer reviewers and mentors. The Consortium now has an annual budget of $US8 million. The Economic Research Forum in Cairo serves a similar purpose for the Arab countries, Iran and Turkey. Organised along the lines of the American Economic Association, it hosts an annual conference, topic-specific workshops and training sessions for younger researchers and provides grants for research on a competitive basis. Its research fellows, numbering close to 150 and drawn from all over the region, have to meet certain professional standards and are expected to assist with the professional development of younger researchers. The Forum's annual budget is now $US1 million. Greater competition and enhanced analytical skills should accelerate the rate at which good policies are learned from international experience, adapted to local conditions and adopted. Similar networks are being established in the other regions of the developing world.

In addition to building research capacity in developing countries, the World Bank also supports research on issues of importance to developing countries that may not be undertaken by private researchers and which require technical expertise clearly not available in the Bank. The Consultative Group for International Agricultural Research (CGIAR) is an outstanding example of an organisation created to provide an international public good: agricultural knowledge. By researching higher-yielding varieties of staple crops for developing countries, the CGIAR was instrumental in sowing the seeds of the 'green revolution'. A survey in southern India concluded that thanks to the new high-yielding varieties, the average real income of small farmers increased by 90 per cent between 1973 and 1994, and that of landless labourers – among the poorest in the farm community – by 125 per cent (Foster and Rosenzweig, 1996).

On many knowledge frontiers, the skewed distribution of global wealth implies that the strongest incentives for private research are for innovations that interest primarily the richer countries. These innovations may or may not be high priorities for poorer countries, particularly in the area of health research. Some major diseases – malaria and tuberculosis, for example – afflict poorer countries far more than they do richer ones. Yet the World Health Organisation (WHO) has estimated that, in the early 1990s, 95 per cent of health-related R&D was devoted to issues of concern primarily to the industrial countries, and only 5 per cent to the health concerns of the far more populous developing world.

One international effort seeks to develop an inexpensive vaccine for AIDS. If technical changes to combat AIDS were already moving rapidly in the right direction, there would be little justification for public action. But the evidence suggests that existing, market-based incentives are biased in favor of developing a profitable treatment for AIDS, and against developing an inexpensive vaccine to prevent it. The reason is that effective demand for new treatments is strong, coming from AIDS patients in high-income economies, whereas demand for a vaccine from those at high risk in developing countries is weak. The tragedy is that a vaccine promises far greater spillover benefits: by limiting the spread of AIDS it protects even those who never purchase or use the vaccine. An ounce of prevention is thus still worth a pound of cure, but in this case the unequal distribution of global income distorts the terms of that trade.

In this case, it makes sense to modify the incentives for private pharmaceutical companies that already have the capacity and technical staff to carry out the work. To this end, the World Bank and other development institutions are investigating a new financing mechanism: a contingent loan. Under a contingent loan scheme, the international community would make binding commitments to lend to developing countries sufficient funds to buy large amounts of an AIDS vaccine, once such a vaccine has been invented and demonstrated as safe and effective. By assuring the pharmaceutical firms a future market, the scheme would reduce the risks to which those firms are exposed, giving them a stronger incentive to conduct the necessary research.

4 The bottom line: quality and impact

The arguments for an in-house research capacity at the World Bank would all be for naught if the quality and impact of the research were found wanting. High-quality, high-impact output does not necessarily substantiate the arguments but it would seem to be a reasonable minimum expectation. That said, measuring the quality and especially the impact of research is extraordinarily difficult. In this section we discuss the available evidence, starting with the quality of research. Here, we rely mainly on the external review by experts within the profession to which most World Bank research is exposed. Turning to impact, we provide evidence on citations, we draw on surveys of clients, and we present one – indeed, the only one known to us – quantitative assessment of the impact of economic and sector work on the net present value of World Bank loans.

4.1 Quality

Research projects undergo a rigorous evaluation *ex ante*, assuring quality control, and *ex post*, contributing to an understanding of the state of overall Bank research. The effort to ensure quality begins with the Research Committee sending all research proposals to outside experts. The reviewers are asked to assess the quality and importance of the proposal in the context of the wider literature and current research on these issues. Good proposals have well defined goals relevant to developing and post-socialist countries, reflect current knowledge on the topics addressed and possibly improve on previous methodological approaches and are adequately designed to deal with the issues they raise (their hypotheses and methods of analysis are well defined and appropriate, the data are reliable and the work schedule is well designed). Careful reviews of research proposals are effective screening mechanisms that carry great weight in the Committee's funding decisions. Once a project has been approved and undertaken, mid-term reviews ensure that they proceed according to plan or improve to adapt to new conditions.

After taking these measures to ensure the quality of research, the Bank seeks evidence of that quality. One test is acceptance in peer-reviewed journals. Many articles written by World Bank researchers first appear as informal working papers circulated for comment before revision and final publication. About two-thirds of the Bank's Policy Research Working

Papers then are submitted for formal publication. One-half of those, or about a third of the working papers, go on to be published in professional journals.

The Bank also asks external experts to conduct periodic evaluation of research funded by the central Research Support Budget. The 1997 round of evaluations encompassed 61 research projects that were evaluated by 14 non-Bank reviewers. The results were published in 1997 and circulated to researchers Bank-wide. Overall, the reviewers found the range and quality of Bank research to be very impressive, and were especially laudatory about the emphasis on empirical and policy-relevant topics, praising some Bank projects for their valuable contributions to policy formulation and the broader store of information and empirical data. At the same time, the reviewers had several suggestions for improvement, including closer linkages with operations, more frequent use of local researchers and better dissemination. Research Committee policy has been revised in response to these evaluations.

4.2 Impact

In trying to tackle the issue of impact we face the same problems that confront efforts to evaluate research more generally. The literature on this topic takes the view that spending on research is an investment that should produce measurable economic returns. The difficulty, of course, arises with the word 'measurable'. Traditionally, economists have relied on two approaches – the production function approach and the consumer surplus approach (Averch, 1994). Both rely on market outcomes to provide measures of the benefits of research. Often, however, this is not possible. Research is frequently trying to create more basic knowledge that, like all public goods, proves difficult to value. This happens to be true in our case. Economic studies and policy advice creates and disseminates knowledge, the ultimate impact of which can be far-reaching but is usually difficult to trace.

An alternative approach is to focus more directly on the immediate outputs of research: reports generated or articles published (Wise and Agranoff, 1991). For example, the National Science Foundation identified a set of indicators that included publications, citation, data archiving and sharing, software development and sharing and education and pedagogy (National Science Foundation, 1995). The World Bank has also relied on this approach. In addition, the World Bank has made use of client surveys to assess impact. In the following, we use these approaches to assess the impact of World Bank research on three different sets of clients operational staff, policy-makers and the development community more broadly and university students.

Starting with operational staff, the Bank's Research Advisory Staff conducted a study in 1997 to investigate the internal impact of research. After identifying major issues in focus groups of research and operations staff, the study asked research staff to identify research outputs they considered to have had an operational impact, and then surveyed operations staff about the usefulness of the cited studies. Of 89 research projects identified as having operational impact, 69 had been used by a sample of operations staff reached for questioning. Across the sample of 69 research projects, the Research Advisory Staff found that more than 80 per cent of the studies were used in more than one phase of operations (the four phases were identified as economic and sector work; discussions with and advice to clients; the lending programme; and best practice, training, and Bank policy). More than half were used in three or more phases, altogether the 69 studies had contributed to at least 177 operations activities. Economists and specialists in operations use research most commonly in discussions with clients, and often in the other phases of operations.

Following interviews and surveys of the Bank's Lead Specialists, Lead Economists and regional Principal Economists, the Advisory Staff found that many respondents have contacts with researchers, directing queries and suggestions to them, drawing on them for advice and direct support and receiving requests to comment on research topics. Researchers allot an average of 30 per cent of their time to support operational colleagues, and were generally found to be accessible, helpful and useful. Clients find the researchers' broadly based knowledge and experience in many countries pioneering new policies and projects particularly helpful in their policy discussions (World Bank, 1998d).

Turning to policy-makers and the development community more generally, Bank research in the outside world, according to available evidence, is broad in its coverage of topics, influential among policy-makers, well regarded by other researchers, heavily used as teaching material in development economics courses and widely disseminated in a variety of publications produced by the Bank and others (World Bank, 1996a). Bank research publications are among the most widely distributed of Bank publications with the *World Development Report (WDR)* continuing as the Bank's flagship publication and the first two policy research reports among the 10 most widely distributed Bank publications in 1994 and 1995. Distribution makes publications available, but tells little about their use, especially when they are free. A 1995 readership survey indicated that the Bank's most widely distributed publications are also the most frequently read. After the *WDR*, the research journal *World Bank Economic Review* is the second most widely read Bank publication overall, and the most widely read in borrowing countries. Bank research is also disseminated through many non-Bank publications; Bank authors published nearly 300 articles in professional journals in each of FY 1994 and 1995. In a two-way transfer, Bank research also draws much expertise from the external research community. A third of Bank research projects involve local counterpart research institutes and consultants (World Bank, 1996a).

Bank research influences policy in client countries through the Bank's policy papers, economic and sector work and summaries of best practice, as well as through research publications themselves. Case studies of policy change in pension reform, girls' education and electrification programmes in several countries provide strong evidence of the many linkages from research to policy-makers, and these are just a few of many possible examples. In a preliminary pilot survey conducted with 48 high-level policy-makers in 11 countries, 79 per cent said they were familiar with World Bank papers and reports, and 75 per cent reported that these had contributed to policy development in their agencies. In general, World Bank research was evaluated as influential by 79 per cent of the respondents (Abt Associates Inc., 1998).

Other quantitative measures can also be used as indicators of the impact of Bank research. Analyses of the number of citations of Bank work in journal articles show that Bank-authored journal articles are cited from 10–50 per cent more than the average for economics articles. Articles in the *World Bank Economic Review* and the *World Bank Research Observer* are cited more than articles in any other development economics journal; they rank near the thirtieth percentile of all economics journals by this measure (figures obtained using technique by Laband and Piette, 1994, reported in World Bank, 1996a). The citation rate of papers in the *Proceedings of the World Bank Annual Bank Conference on Development Economics* exceeds that of the Bank journals. Bank research also receives press coverage, which extends its dissemination to the general development community. The *Financial Times* and *The Economist* are most likely among newspapers and magazines to carry a story on Bank research and to draw on Bank statistics (World Bank, 1996a).

Influencing the next generation of leaders is often key to future reforms. Bank-authored studies, particularly Bank books, are well represented on reading lists in university courses in economic development (World Bank, 1996a). In a collection of 25 (mostly graduate-level) development course reading lists published in 1995, one-sixth of the entries were by Bank authors (Tower, 1995). The Bank's Economic Development Institute draws heavily on Bank studies in its courses, workshops, and seminars – attended by more than 6,600 people in FY 1995. Even the education of high school students is influenced by World Bank research output: in 1997, the National Council on Economic Education released a curriculum for teaching social studies, economics, and business classes that drew heavily on the World Bank's 1996 *World Development Report: From Plan to Market* (World Bank, 1996b).

None of the above measures provides the basis for a cost–benefit analysis of World Bank output – benefits are not quantifiable and hence cannot be compared with cost. We conclude this section by reporting on the only study we know that provides at least a partial assessment of the value of the World Bank's ESW. This analysis uses the performance of World Bank projects to show the value of the effort that goes into producing the economic memoranda, public expenditure reviews, poverty assessments and other reports that underpin the policy dialogue with government, and of the wide range of sectoral reports that provide the foundation for specific lending operations (Deininger, Squire and Basu, 1998). Even after statistically controlling for differences among countries, sectors, economic conditions and amounts of staff input for project preparation and supervision, this research finds that analytical work – both macroeconomic and sectoral – improves project performance. Indeed, one additional week of analytical work by World Bank staff increases the benefits of an average-size Bank-financed project by four to eight times the cost of that week of staff time, or between US $12,000 and US$25,000 for a cost of no more than US$3,000. And because analytical work typically relates to more than one project, the overall benefit is even larger: up to 12–15 times the cost (Deininger, Squire and Basu, 1998). Moreover, these are just the benefits to projects financed by the Bank. The changes inspired by the Bank's analysis may affect other donor-financed projects, or even perhaps all government projects as well as policies, resulting in very high returns to analytical work.

5 Conclusion

We started this chapter by pointing to the tension that inevitably arises between the operational (lending) and research sides of the Bank. This issue has now been absorbed into a larger debate about the future of the World Bank and in particular the emphasis to be placed on the new roles implied in being a 'Knowledge Bank' as opposed to a Lending Bank (see Wolfensohn, 1996, for an introduction of the 'Knowledge Bank' idea). This question clearly depends to some extent on our assessment and justification of Bank research. If research is of low quality or has little impact, then the World Bank should obviously not emphasise its role as a 'Knowledge Bank'. But the evidence tells us otherwise: Bank research is subject to rigorous tests of quality and is widely used. In that case, when should the World Bank put on the face of a 'Knowledge Bank'? Some of our own (high-quality, high-impact) research provides clear guidance on the future direction for the Bank, and it is to this issue that we turn in this final section.

What is the primary purpose of the World Bank? If it is to transfer resources to developing countries, then doing so through projects is a very inefficient mechanism. It typically costs about US$1 million to process a World Bank project and on top of that we must add the costs incurred by the recipient country (World Bank, 1998c). The reason that the Bank and other donors use projects is, of course, because they want some control over the use of funds. But, as research presented in the 'Assessing Aid' report (World Bank, 1998a) shows, funds are at least partially fungible. So even project lending ends up funding the public budget as a whole. Therefore, it seems to be more efficient to simply transfer funds to the recipient government and avoid the administrative costs associated with processing loans.

'Assessing Aid' goes further, telling us why this expedient is too simplistic. Transferring resources to countries with relatively weak economic management brings no benefit. A country that is misallocating domestic resources is unlikely to use foreign resources effectively. But transferring resources to countries with relatively good economic management does yield substantial benefits. Thus, for these countries it does make sense to transfer large amounts of financial resources without much administration (and hence with lower administrative costs).

The real 'action' in development, of course, lies in the countries with relatively weak economic management. Governments and development institutions face the puzzling task of improving policies and strengthening institutions. The transfer of financial resources has very little chance of bolstering this effort (see, for example, Collier, 1999). But the transfer of knowledge through analysis of policy options, technical assistance and projects aimed toward capacity-building may well make a difference. Knowledge transfer entails a substantial commitment of staff resources for economic and sector work, research and technical assistance over a long period of time and involves little transfer of financial resources.

Typically, the Bank finances its economic and sector work and its research from its net income, earned at least in part from charges related to the size of loans. Here, however, we have argued for a large staff commitment with relatively small financial transfers. The question that immediately arises is: how will the commitment of staff resources be paid for? We can balance the equation by noting that in countries with strong economic management we have called for the opposite – large financial transfers with little staff input. These should generate substantial amounts of income that in turn can finance the knowledge transfer to countries with weak economic management.

In this model, both the 'Lending Bank' and the 'Knowledge Bank' have a clear role. We can think of the transfer to recipient countries as a combination of finance and knowledge. In countries with strong economic management the combination should emphasise finance. These countries can use substantial inflows effectively. But in countries with weak economic management the emphasis should be on the transfer of knowledge. Their most urgent need is to acquire knowledge that will best help them to improve their policies and strengthen their institutions, without which it is impossible for them to use external financial assistance effectively. Assuming the improvement in institutions and policies results in better use of domestic as well as external resources, the returns to knowledge transfer will be incalculable.

NOTE

The excellent research assistance of Noémi Giszprnc is gratefully acknowledged. I would also like to thank Chris Gilbert and Greg Ingram for valuable comments on an earlier draft.

REFERENCES

Abt Associates Inc. (1998). 'Final Report: Pilot Test of Use of Research in Policy Making in Developing Countries', paper prepared for Clara Else, DECRA, World Bank, 12 November

Averch, H. (1994). 'Economic Approaches to the Evaluation of Research', *Evaluation Review*, **18**

Collier, P. (1999). 'Conditionality, Dependence and Coordination: Three Debates in Aid Policy', chapter 12 in this volume

Deininger, K. and L. Squire (1996). 'A New Data Set Measuring Income Inequality', *World Bank Economic Review*, **10**: 565–91

Deininger, K., L. Squire and S. Basu (1998). 'Does Economic Analysis Improve the Quality of Foreign Assistance?', *World Bank Economic Review*, **12**

Foster, A. and M. Rosenzweig (1996). 'Technical Change and Human Capital Returns and Investments: Evidence from the Green Revolution', *American Economic Review*, **86**: 931–53

Gilbert, C. L., A. Powell and D. Vines (1998). 'Positioning the World Bank', paper prepared for an *Economic Journal* Policy Forum on the IMF and the World Bank, 11 December

Grosh, M. and P. Glewwe (1998). 'Data Watch: The World Bank's Living Standards Measurement Study Household Surveys', *Journal of Economic Perspectives*, **12**: 187–96

Henderson, D. and J. Loxley (1997). 'The AERC Research Programme: An Evaluation', *AERC Special Paper*, **25**, Nairobi: African Economic Research Consortium

James, E. (1998a). 'The Political Economy of Social Security Reform: A Cross-country Review', *Annals of Public and Cooperative Economics*, **69**

  (1998b). 'New Models for Old-age Security: Experiments, Evidence, and Unanswered Questions', *World Bank Research Observer*, **13**: 271–301

Laband, D. N. and M. J. Piette (1994). 'The Relative Impact of Economics Journals: 1970-90', *Journal of Economic Literature*, **32**: 640–66

National Science Foundation (1995). Report of NSF Stakeholders' Panel in Linguistics

Ravallion, M. and S. Chen (1997). 'What Can New Survey Data Tell Us about Recent Changes in Distribution and Poverty?', *World Bank Economic Review*, **11**: 357–82

Schmidt-Hebbel, K. and L. Serven (1997). 'Saving Across the World : Puzzles and Policies', *World Bank Discussion Paper*, **354**

Stern, N. and F. Ferreira (1997). 'The World Bank as 'Intellectual Actor', in D. Kapur, J. P. Lewis and R. Webb, *The World Bank : Its First Half Century, 2: Perspectives*, Washington, DC : Brookings Institution

Thorbecke, E. (1996). 'The AERC Research Programme: An Evaluation', *AERC Special Paper*, *21*, Nairobi: African Economic Research Consortium

Tower, E. (1995). '*Development I: Reading Lists*', Chapel Hill, NC: Eno River Press

Wise, L. R. and R. Agranoff (1991). 'Organisational Characteristics and Productivity Measurement in Research Organisations', *Public Productivity and Management Review*, **15**

Wolfensohn, J. D. (1996). '1996 Annual Meetings Speech', Washington, DC, 1 October; available at < http://www.worldbank.org/html/extdr/extme/jdwams96.htm >

World Bank (1994). 'Averting the Old Age Crisis: Policies to Protect the Old *and* Promote Growth', *Policy Research Report*, Washington, DC: World Bank

  (1995). 'What is *PROPER*? Reputational Incentives for Pollution Control in Indonesia', *Policy Research Report*, Washington, DC: World Bank

  (1996a). 'Report on the World Bank Research Program Fiscal 1994 and 1995', *Report* **15296**, Washington, DC: World Bank

  (1996b). *World Development Report: From Plan to Market, 1996*, Oxford: Oxford University Press

(1997). 'Confronting AIDS : Public Priorities In A Global Epidemic', *Policy Research Report*, New York : Oxford University Press, Washington, DC, published for the World Bank

(1998a). 'Assessing Aid: What Works, What Doesn't, and Why', *Policy Research Report*, Washington, DC: World Bank

(1998b). 'A Dissemination Proposal for "Impact of Education Projects: Decentralisation and Privatisation Issues" (RPO 679-18)', Washington, DC: World Bank

(1998c). *World Bank Annual Report 1998* , Washington, DC: World Bank

(1998d). 'Report on the World Bank Research Program Fiscal 1996 and 1997', *Report* 17306, Washington, DC: World Bank

(1999). *World Development Report: Knowledge for Development, 1998/99*, Oxford: Oxford University Press

5   The challenges of multilateralism and governance

NGAIRE WOODS

1 Introduction

From the 'Wapenhans Report' (World Bank, 1992b) to the Strategic Compact of 1998, the World Bank has over the past decade closely examined how to achieve its development objectives more effectively. This is more difficult for the World Bank than for many private sector actors since the Bank is more than a development agency (see Hopkins *et al.* chapter 11 in this volume). It is also multilateral institution which must represent and implement the will of the governments who are its members. For this reason, the Bank's ability to undertake and fulfil its economic purposes depends on a number of political forces. The institution requires the ongoing support of its most powerful members, while yet satisfying 'an increasingly vocal and demanding senior shareholder', the Bank must also retain its status as a technical and multilateral agency which requires the support of all its other members (see Feinberg *et al.*, 1986).

This chapter examines the relationship between political pressures exerted on the Bank and its independence. In particular, the chapter analyses the characteristics of the Bank which enhance its autonomy so as potentially to counter-balance the Bank's reliance on the support of its largest shareholder. The characteristics examined include the Bank's financial structure, its research and expertise and the rules governing its lending operations. The chapter notes that by the end of the 1980s all the above had become subject to political influences, thus challenging the Bank's status as a multilateral and technical agency. In the 1990s, the Bank was called upon to become more accountable, more transparent, more democratic and to prove its competence across a wide range of issues including population, gender, environment, governance, corruption and education (Le Prestre, 1989; North–South Roundtable, 1993;

132

Commission on Global Governance, 1995; Nelson, 1995; Griesgraber and Gunter, 1996; Fox and Brown, 1998). Yet, as will be seen below, its response to these demands has not necessarily relieved the tensions which arise from its special relationship with the United States.

2 The United States and the Bank as a multilateral institution

2.1 The special position of the United States

The Bank relies on a delicate balancing of political forces in order to maintain itself. Above all, it must pay attention to its most powerful member – the United States. The United States planned and created the World Bank in the last phase of the Second World War, seeing it initially as an institution far more important than the IMF.[1] The organisation's headquarters were placed at the seat of the US Federal government in Washington, DC, and the Bank's Charter and its operational policies enshrined US views of how the world economy should be organised , how resources should be allocated and how investment decisions should be reached (Gwin, 1997). The distribution of voting power within the institution, although ostensibly based on measurements of national income, foreign reserves and international trade, was from the outset according to US political preferences (Mikesell, 1994). Subsequent adjustments have also been highly political (Lister, 1984; Ogata, 1989; Buira, 1996; Rapkin and Strand, 1996).

Today, the influence of the United States is felt throughout the Bank. On the 24-member Executive Board of the IBRD, the US has 16.68 per cent of the votes – the largest share of any country.[2] This is not counterbalanced by Japan's vote which is 8 per cent, nor by the vote of European countries especially since they do not vote collectively as the European Union. The United Kingdom has 4.38 per cent of votes, as does France, while Germany has 4.57 per cent. Thus even if the United Kingdom, France and Germany vote together their collective vote is still less than the United States. All other EU countries are represented in groupings with other countries. Italy, Greece and Portugal, for example, are represented along with Albania, and Malta by an Executive Director who wields a total of 3.47 per cent of votes. Austria and Belgium are represented in a group which also includes Belarus, the Czech Republic, Hungary, Kazakhstan, Luxembourg, the Slovak Republic, Slovenia and Turkey, and has a total of 4.83 per cent votes (World Bank, 1998).

The voting share of the United States is not only the largest of any country but also confers a veto power on the United States over all decisions which require a special majority of 85 per cent. The United States is the only country to enjoy such a veto, and indeed the maintenance of this veto is itself the result of political negotiations in which the United States has succeeded in prevailing (Lister, 1984; Ogata, 1989). In practice, the Board of the Bank operates by 'consensus' (albeit strongly underpinned by an awareness of relative voting strengths) and US influence is often exercised less formally. When the United States does not approve of a loan or a policy, it is unlikely even to come before the Board (interviews with Executive Directors; see also Ayres, 1983). Rather, a less direct form of influence over the staff and management of the Bank will prevent the staff even proposing the loan.

Among the management and staff of the Bank, the US influence is more subtle. In the original US vision of the Bank, a powerful Executive Board, on which the US Director would be dominant, was envisaged as a controlling force over the President and senior management of the institution (Gardner, 1969: 258–9). In actual fact at times this was the case, thus 'the normal thing [was] for an applicant for a loan to stop on his way to the Bank and get the support of the US Director' (Davidson Sommer, cited in Gwin, 1997: 199). Yet successive Bank Presidents (in spite of being appointed by US administrations) have fought against this tendency, struggling instead to increase the political independence of the institution.

The Bank's first President, Eugene Meyer, resigned out of frustration over his own powerlessness *vis-à-vis* the US Executive Director and US government. His successor, John McCloy, succeeded in increasing his power as President as a precondition of taking the job. Specifically, McCloy demanded that the United States would not interfere in loan negotiations nor give prior indication of US positions on loan applications; that he would have a free hand in hiring and firing of staff and administration; and that he would nominate the US Executive Director (Bird, 1992: 283). Today there are still complaints about the informal US consent needed for any loan proposal to go forward to the Board with any chance of success. It is still the case that: 'Any signal of displeasure by the U.S. executive director has an almost palpable impact on the Bank leadership and staff, whether the signal is an explicit complaint or simply the executive director's request for information on a problem' (Ascher, 1992: 124). The Bank's first line of defence against such influence is probably the strength and independence of its President even though, as mentioned above, Bank Presidents are always US citizens appointed by the US government. The cases of McCloy and subsequent Presidents such as Robert McNamara demonstrate that a strong President can play an important role in enhancing the independence of the organisation.

2.2 The requirements of multilateralism

Although the United States has a uniquely influential position within the Bank, it does not enjoy full control over the institution's nature and activities. Indeed, if the United States had control over the organisation, or indeed was perceived to, the Bank would be of little use to the United States. As two scholars of international relations write: 'powerful states structure such organisations to further their own interests but must do so in a way that induces weaker states to participate' (Abbott and Snidal, 1998). To be effective, the World Bank relies on the participation of most states in the world. Such participation, in turn, requires continued belief in the Bank's 'legitimacy': the perception by its members that the agency not only has a particular technical expertise but also that it has a certain degree of independence, a genuinely international character and that it acts in a rule-based way rather than according to US discretionary judgements.

The advantages to the United States of multilateralism have been obscured in recent debates over abolishing or privatising the Bank.[3] Yet the United States benefits in several obvious ways from its participation. In the first place, the United States needs multilateral institutions like the World Bank to achieve objectives (both national and collective) which it could not achieve acting alone.[4] Such uses of international institutions have been elaborated in the political science literature on inter-state cooperation using game theory (Stein, 1983; Snidal, 1985; Oye, 1986; Morrow, 1994). The objectives the United States seeks to achieve through the World Bank include continuing to encourage trade liberalisation and better 'governance' in developing country markets, and the mitigation of environmental degradation stemming from development projects. In each of these areas, the coordination of information and policy undertaken by the World Bank has been crucial to promulgating policies and could be achieved unilaterally only at much greater cost and with a much lower level of effectiveness.

A second reason for a multilateral approach to these and other issues is that it lowers the transactions costs of many policies and permits them to be shared. By centralising cooperation, the World Bank makes the formulation and implementation of policies easier and less expensive. It brings all parties together under one roof, sharing information and developing expertise, standardising procedures, speeding up response time and saving member governments from time-consuming sequential bilateral negotiations. Economies of scale are reaped through the sheer volume of development lending. At the financial level, the pooling of capital contributions and commitments enables the Bank to access resources on world capital markets at advantageous rates and lend them on to borrowers to facilitate development. The Bank thereby pools the risk of its wide-ranging portfolio of loans, reducing the risks borne by any one member. The burden on the United States in particular is a light one, compared to the level of influence it enjoys in the Bank[5]: the US share of contributions and commitments in the IBRD is about one-sixth of the total (reflecting its voting share).

Finally, the United States benefits from the multilateralism of the World Bank because the institution plays a vital role in making US-supported aims and policies more acceptable to the rest of the world. To cite one scholar, this is 'because its neutral and apparently technical advice may be less offensive to national sentiments than direct intervention by the United States', 'sparing the USA the unsavory epithets of ... "aid with strings", "arm-twisting political pressures", etc.' (Ascher, 1992: 118). The World Bank as an international organisation has more legitimacy (insofar as it sustains a reputation for being independent) than any US government department acting alone in advocating particular policies or reforms.

Of course, there are some costs to participation in international institutions which accrue to the United States. As recently demonstrated in the World Trade Organisation (WTO), once a powerful state creates an institution and a set of rules which serves its overall interests, it will have to show itself willing to subject itself to those rules even when they do not further its interests if the institution is to retain legitimacy. This is the essential distinction between a multilateral 'rule of law' and a simpler form of power politics in which 'might is right'. In the World Bank, as will be seen below, the United States created an institution which has often served its interests. During the Cold War, for example, it was able to use the institution for political purposes it shared with the Western alliance. Occasionally, however, the United States has also had to accept that the institution will act according to its own Articles of Agreement and rules even where they do not concur with US policy preferences.

In summary, the World Bank's close relationship with the United States creates tensions for the institution, which must both please its most powerful political master and at the same time maintain its independence and credibility both as a technical agency (with technical expertise as opposed to political/ideological solutions), and as a multilateral organisation. In order to be effective, the Bank needs to be perceived by all its member countries as a legitimate multilateral organisation, pursuing predominantly developmental objectives in a rule-based way. It needs recognised credibility and expertise in economic policy based on the scope and depth of its research. In order to enjoy this legitimacy, the Bank also needs a visible degree of political independence from interference by its most powerful members.

The question that follows from this is whether the World Bank in fact enjoys this kind of independence. What features of the institution give it scope to enjoy a relative autonomy from its political masters? The existing literature in political science has little to say about the pro-active and autonomous role that international institutions such as the World Bank can play.[6] Similarly all too few attempts have been made to dissect the potential and actual sources of autonomy and political independence of organisations such as the World Bank. It is to this task that this chapter now moves.

3 The relative autonomy of the Bank

There are several characteristics of the Bank and its work which underscore a significant potential autonomy. This section analyses the relative independence of the Bank which accrues owing to its financial structure, its research role and its lending operations. In each case, however, the Bank faced a challenge at the end of the 1990s: to reverse the erosion of its autonomy which occurred in the 1980s and early 1990s and in so doing to strengthen its status, credibility and effectiveness.

3.1 The Bank's finances

Unlike the IMF and other international institutions, the World Bank does not rely directly on contributions from its member governments to fund its activities. Rather, the Bank is primarily a financial intermediary which borrows on capital markets and lends to members in need of development assistance, thus generating its own income (Purcell and Miller, 1986). National governments contribute a small fraction of the Bank's lending through their paid-in capital subscriptions, yet even these have diminished over the years.[7] The major contribution government members make lies in the contingent liability they take on by guaranteeing all Bank lending. It is these guarantees which permit the Bank to borrow at the lowest market rates available 'applying the sovereign credit of its rich shareholders – in the form of their capital guarantees of about $90 billion – to market borrowings, $110 billion of which remained outstanding as of 1995' (Kapur, Lewis and Webb, hereafter, KLW, 1997a: 902).

As a result of its financial structure, the Bank enjoys a potential autonomy unrivalled by most other international institutions. Other organisations rely on members' contributions in order to carry out their core activities and administration. Hence, they must always act with an eye to the pleasure or displeasure of contributing national governments. By contrast, from its inception, the World Bank's lendable resources have come primarily from financial markets. This has meant that the institution must focus on winning and maintaining a high credit rating. Having done so, the Bank has then been able to increase its equity and surpluses, borrowing cheaply and lending long-term and untied funds in the face of very little competition.

A crucial exception to the Bank's relative financial independence lies in its 'soft loan' facility – the International Development Association (IDA) which was created in 1960 and opened up a new channel through which the Bank could be pressured by its government members. The United States has used threats to reduce or withhold its own funding in periodic replenishments of the fund to influence Bank policy. During the late 1970s, for instance, the Bank was forced to promise not to lend to Vietnam in order to prevent the defeat of IDA 6 (the negotiations on the sixth replenishment of the Bank's concessional lending agency), and in 1993, under pressure from Congress, the US linked the creation of an independent inspection panel in the World Bank to IDA 10 (the tenth replenishment of the Bank's concessional lending agency). As one writer puts it: 'with the Congress standing behind or reaching around it, the American administration was disposed to make its catalogue of demands not only insistent but comprehensive on replenishment occasions' (Gwin, 1997: 1150). Further strengthening US leverage is the fact that other members often pro-rate their contributions to IDA to those of the United States. Hence, if the United States diminishes its contribution, the effect is subsequently magnified.

Political pressures have also been applied in determining how the Bank's own-generated surpluses should be spent. Although the Bank's income is generated by payments from its borrowing members, the surpluses have been spent largely at the behest of its largest, and most powerful, non-borrowing members. Examples of this include assistance extended to the former Soviet Union, in Gaza and in Bosnia and

Herzegovina. These are all undoubtedly worthy causes, but they also reflect strong foreign policy preferences of the United States and its major allies, leading to the suspicion that 'the institution's net income looks like a convenient source for funding foreign policy objectives, such as those posed by the emergencies in Bosnia, Mexico, Palestine, and the former Soviet Union' (KLW, 1997a: 47).

It bears noting, however, that the Bank has also demonstrated a capacity to turn down political pressures to take on new, large lending commitments. In the 1940s, the Bank refused to become the major provider for reconstruction in Europe. At the end of the 1990s, the Bank's President rejected the proposal that the institution expand its lending to include emergency assistance packages in tandem with the IMF.

In summary, the Bank's financial structure gives it the potential for an autonomy which few other international institutions enjoy. This independence has been eroded by the structure of IDA, which has been used by the United States to exert direct influence over the policies and structure of the Bank. The need to gain periodic approval for contributions to IDA has opened the World Bank up to direct pressure from the US Congress and US-based NGOs. This poses serious problems for the governance and representativeness of the institution, which will be further examined below.

3.2 The Bank's technical expertise and research

Since its creation, the Bank's technical expertise has been vital to its independence and its legitimacy. In its operations around the world, the Bank provides both money and advice to developing country governments who are often jealous in guarding their sovereignty. These governments would not wish to argue for very long that they are forced to take World Bank advice because they have no choice, or are too weak to do otherwise. And they do not need to, for the Bank's advice is based on a wealth of technical knowledge, information and research. The Bank can answer the question 'why should a government follow its advice?', by pointing to the fact that it undertakes research in well over 150 countries, bringing together the world's largest concentration of development economics specialists and producing some of the most definitive research in the field (Ranis, 1997; Squire, chapter 4 in this volume). This research capacity is what makes the Bank a legitimate advisor: the Bank's status as a technical agency gives governments a publicly acceptable reason for accepting its advice.[8]

The Bank's expertise has broadened over its lifespan. In its early years the Bank was known for its high-quality project work performed by specialists of good professional pedigree. Under Robert McNamara, the Bank expanded its research capacity through administrative and organisational changes and growth. Today, the staff of the Bank undertakes sophisticated project analysis but also does research which extends beyond the institution's operational requirements, disseminating ideas and contributing to ongoing debates about development, as well as asserting authoritative positions on issues of economic policy.[9] The Bank has more recently expanded this research agenda to encompass issues such as education, environment and gender.

For the purposes of this chapter, the central question is to what degree this research and expertise is free from political influence. It is worth noting that direct political influence over specific policy prescriptions of the Bank is not widespread. In their operational work, the Bank's officers prepare projects and policies for approval by their political masters – the national government members – in the Executive Board. The staff tend to present detailed technical analyses of proposals and, interestingly, in so doing they preserve an independence from political control. Executive Directors who wish to question particular aspects of a proposal, or to propose alternative approaches, soon find themselves in deep (technically detailed) water. Since Bank staff present only analyses which back their own proposals – and not, for example, analyses of a borrowing government's proposed alternatives – Executive Directors find it difficult to argue credibly for an alternative (interviews with Executive Board members; see also Ascher, 1992). Direct political influences on loans thus tend more to determine simply whether or not a loan goes ahead (and, later, determine how tightly conditionality will be applied), as opposed to fashioning specific policy elements of the loan.

The research basis for loans, however, is not without a less direct form of political influence. Early in the Bank's history the United States was able to resist pressures for there to be any national quotas for hiring, and to establish a commitment to nothing but English as a working language. Recent historians of the Bank argue that this skewed employment in the Bank significantly, not just geographically (favouring south Asia over East Asia and Britain over other European countries), but also overwhelmingly towards graduates of institutions that taught in English (i.e. predominantly US and UK institutions) (KLW, 1997a: 1167). It is true that Bank staff are overwhelmingly US- or UK-trained in economics and finance.[10] However, many economists would argue that this simply reflects the fact that the best economics departments of the world are to be found in the United States, followed by the United Kingdom.

Perhaps more importantly, in elucidating political influence we need to examine the kinds of research and advice the Bank has fostered and promulgated in particular over the past two decades.

During the 1980s the Bank became a powerful advocate of what came to be known as the 'Washington consensus'. This consensus was forged by the US Treasury, the Federal Reserve and the International Financial Institutions (IFIs) as a way to deal with the debt crisis of the 1980s. Central to the approach was the belief that countries facing debt problems needed first and foremost to control inflation, to balance their budgets, to liberalise prices and to deregulate and reduce the role of the state in their economies. The priority placed on these policies was strongly pushed by the US administration (under President Reagan) which had come to power voicing a strong ideological commitment to reducing the role of the state, and relying on the private sector to foster economic growth.

The World Bank soon became a champion of the new orthodoxy, stressing the importance of careful price, trade, tax and institutional reforms for increasing the efficiency of resource allocation (see *World Bank Development Report*, 1983–7; Stern and Ferreira, 1997: 539). Institutionally, at the heart of the Bank a reorganisation of the Development Policy Staff was undertaken in 1982, with Anne Krueger brought in to head a renamed 'Economics Research Staff' which was strongly sympathetic to the 'Washington consensus' (KLW, 1997a: 1194). This set the tone for the World Bank's contribution to managing the debt crisis in the 1980s.

As one might expect, US policy-makers took the lead when events in Mexico in August 1982 sparked a crisis in confidence in Latin American debt repayments. The ensuing debt strategy emerged in three phases. In the first phase (1982–5) the debt crisis was seen as a liquidity problem, requiring immediate stabilisation in debtor economies and the IMF was called upon to orchestrate the solution. In the second phase (1985–9), US Treasury Secretary James Baker announced that the debt strategy needed to ensure growth and recovery in debtor economies, and thus the World Bank was brought to centre stage of what was known as 'the Baker Plan'. In the third phase (from 1989), Secretary of Treasury Nicholas Brady announced 'the Brady Plan', which involved recognising and supporting certain kinds of debt reduction schemes, relying once again on the participation of the World Bank. Throughout these phases, where important US interests were at stake, the United States was clearly in the lead, using both the IMF and the World Bank to legitimate strategies framed within the US Treasury.

Some time before the Brady Plan was announced, staff within the World Bank had begun to think about debt relief. However, in the mid-1980s the subject was taboo since policy-makers in Washington, DC would not entertain the idea – and, indeed, the banks' balance sheets had not recovered enough for debt reduction to proceed. Subsequently, a two-way process of influence between the Bank and politicians took place. In the first place, the Bank's research into debt reduction and relief was kept very quiet. To quote a senior Bank official '[t]he US squelched research on this [debt] issue during the mid-80s ... the institution was under political orders (not only from the US, also the Germans, and the Brits) not to raise issues of debt relief' (KLW, 1997a: 1195). Yet although research was 'squelched', it nevertheless became highly influential. When the US Treasury wanted to shift the debt management strategy, the Bank was able to contribute ideas to what an alternative policy might be. Hence, the Bank's (and other institutions') research into debt relief assisted the change in the US debt strategy at the end of the 1980s.

The experience of the 1980s suggests that there is a two-way flow of influence between the Bank (and its staff's expertise) and the politicians of Washington, DC; however, the US dominance spelt an erosion of the independence of the Bank. Throughout the 1980s the Bank tended to stick fairly closely to the 'Washington consensus' (or the neo-liberal model) as a prescription for economic policy applicable to all borrowers – as the US government wanted the Bank to do, even though from an advisory point of view the rationale for the model was not fully justified by empirical research. As the Bank's Chief Economist Joseph Stiglitz subsequently pointed out: 'some aspects of the neoliberal model might not even be necessary conditions for strong growth, and if undertaken without accompanying measures, say to ensure competition in relevant areas of the economy, they may not bring many gains and could even lead to setbacks' (Stiglitz, 1998b: 2)

The research of economist Dani Rodrik demonstrates that while some followers of the neoliberal model have not enjoyed especially strong economic performance, other countries who have 'ignored many of the dictates – at least with respect to the crucial details of sequencing ... have experienced among the highest rates of sustained growth the world has even seen' (Stiglitz, 1998b; Rodrik, 1996). The evidence that the cluster and sequencing of policies labelled the 'Washington consensus' was not always the best strategy for borrowers did not surprise all applied development economists. Even among the Bank's staff there had always been both believers and sceptics in the neo-liberal model. What is significant about the Bank's strong advocacy of the Washington consensus in the 1980s – at least for political scientists – is that it highlights the extent to which the institution is liable to sway towards the mindset and priorities prevailing in the US government at any period in time.

By the end of the 1990s, the Bank had shifted its advice, prioritising a 'second generation' of reforms focusing on institutional reform and the modernisation of the state. The Bank also responded to the criticism that the Washington consensus relied too much on 'top-down' policies which a small number of policy-makers would undertake to implement without needing to garner wider political support (Nelson and Contributors, 1994; Naim, 1995; Taylor, 1997). More specifically, the Bank accepted that effective implementation of policies required a very high level of cooperation and participation from governments as well as from local groups within borrowing economies – not only at the implementation stage but also in defining policies and projects. Without participation and the local sense of 'owning' policies which comes with it, Bank pro- grammes have been found to be much less effective (World Bank, 1992b, 1992c, 1996; Stevens and Gnanaselvam, 1995). Operationally, this think- ing has been reflected in repeated Bank expressions of commitment to ensuring, for example, greater involvement of 'key stakeholders' in the preparation of country assistance strategies (CASs), 'sharper client focus', and 'responsiveness to clients' (World Bank, 1998). Most recently this has been expressed in the Bank's 1999 initiative, the 'Comprehensive Development Framework' or CDF.

The problems of implementing a strategy of greater 'participation' by borrowers was highlighted by Bank staff some time ago:

Participation has often been equated with explaining the project to key stake- holders (individuals and groups who stand to gain or lose from the project), instead of involving them in decision-making. Borrowers are not committed to project goals. Their 'ownership' has been sought by making them responsible for preparation and implementation, instead of ensuring that the impetus for the project is local and that the process provides explicit opportunities for consensus building. (Picciotto and Weaving, 1994)

The challenge for the Bank in ensuring greater participation is a deep one. Taken seriously, it involves rethinking the Bank's own 'expertise' so as to place a greater value on local (and less prestigious) knowledge and skills. The Bank itself recognises that this is necessary in order to build deep consensus over policy and projects within borrowing countries. Yet this is difficult for an institution whose prestige and status have tradi- tionally been based on the technical research and expertise it brings to advising its borrowers. The new approach suggests a different role for Bank missions. Rather than bringing in brilliant experts and economists to define, plan and monitor projects and policies, Bank officers need to become more adept at facilitating and coordinating thinkers, activists and decision-makers in borrowing countries. In the 'participation model', the Bank's awesome catalogue of research and knowledge spanning over 150 countries can no longer be assumed to offer the Bank unique foundations for a policy blueprint for all countries. Rather the Bank's legitimacy and status as an adviser would come from its ability to work constructively with each borrower.

The signs that the Bank might rise to the challenge it has set itself are mixed. The 'Strategic Compact' which has been advanced by the Bank President aims further to shift resources from administration to front-line operations; to decentralise activities to borrowing countries; to improve the technical expertise of Bank staff and the circulation of information within the institutions; and to develop new services and create partnerships with other organisations. Indeed, the Bank has already made efforts to decentralise its operations by locating some of its management staff within regions.[11] At the same time, the Bank has heavily underlined its commitment to being a 'knowledge institution'. To cite the 1998 *Annual Report*: 'A central tenet of the evolving role of the World Bank is to build it into a world-class knowledge institution through a knowledge management system that extends across the World Bank and outside to mobilize knowledge and learning for better results' (World Bank, 1998). Clearly, the Bank is hoping both to retain its special place as *the* institution of knowledge, and at the same time to decentralise itself and give greater priority to local knowledge and initiatives. This dual project is not without difficulties and contradictions.

The difficulties for the Bank are highlighted in the search for and definition of a 'post-Washington consensus' (Stiglitz, 1998a). The institution has recognised that a great weakness of the 1980s 'Washington consensus' was the degree to which it was defined in Washington and relied for implementation on a small and relatively insulated group of policy-makers – interlocutors with Bank staff – in borrowing countries. Yet the temptation at the end of the 1990s may well be to fashion a new consensus which suffers from similar problems. The 1980s consensus dealt with macroeconomic stabilisation and adjustment. Many within the Bank see the institution's present challenge as one of defining and prescribing a better set of policies for its borrowers: policies which address institutional reform and strengthening. However, the deeper challenge for the Bank is in some ways to avoid doing just this and instead to find a way to apply a new more participatory approach to all its operations – from policy definition to implementation and monitoring.

3.3 Bank lending

So far, this chapter has analysed the Bank's potential autonomy from the point of view of its financial structure and its research and expertise. A third source of independence lies in the Bank's lending activities which in theory are insulated from political interference. The Bank's Articles of Agreement prohibit it from taking politics into account in its lending decisions. Article IV, section 10 states that the Bank and its officers 'shall not interfere with the political affairs of any member, nor shall they be influenced in their decisions by the political character of the member or members concerned'. Furthermore, the Articles also restrict the scope of the Bank to make loans in support of particular policies, requiring that all lending be for specific projects 'except in special circumstances'. These formal requirements reflect the concern about sovereignty held by member states in the Bank: the desire of governments not to have policy-making encroached upon by the Bank. In theory, therefore, the Bank enjoys a significant independence from political pressures and judgements in its lending activities. In reality, however, political considerations have been highly influential in determining who borrows from the Bank and (especially since 1979) the Bank has been highly active in policy-linked lending.[12]

The Bank was formed in 1944 at which time the Western alliance was still fighting side by side with the USSR in the Second World War. The early history of the Bank reflects the origins of the subsequent Cold War. As the relationship between the Soviet Union and the allies soured in the aftermath of the war against Germany, so too the plans for the post-war world altered. The original plan envisaged that the Bank (the International Bank for Reconstruction and Development, or IBRD) would be the lead institution in facilitating finance for reconstruction in Europe. However, this scheme was soon superseded by the Marshall Plan announced by the US government in 1947 which channelled bilateral, conditional funds to European governments. The sidelining of the Bank in Europe, however, did not leave the Bank immune from Cold War pressures elsewhere. Within the Western alliance, the Bank was soon seen as an important means of supporting and reinforcing allies throughout Asia, the Middle East, Central and South America and Africa.

In 1948, when Yugoslavia broke from the Soviet bloc, the World Bank stepped in with loans, fulfilling the advice of George Kennan (the architect of the US containment strategy) that the West should offer the country 'discreet and unostentatious support' (KLW, 1997a: 103). In Nicaragua, the US-supported Somozas regime received a disproportion-

ate number of World Bank loans (KLW, 1997a: 103) while offering the
United States a convenient base for prosecuting the Cold War in Central
America such as training for and launching of the 1953 overthrow of
Guatemalan President Jacobo Arbenz (seen as a Communist sympathi-
ser) and the 1961 Bay of Pigs invasion of Cuba (Lake, 1989). In the
Middle East, Iran was heavily supported whilst it offered an important
way to contain Soviet-sympathising Iraq. Indeed in the period 1957–74
Bank lending to Iran amounted to $1.2 billion in 33 loans (KLW, 1997a:
500). In Indonesia after General Suharto assumed power in March 1966,
the Bank immediately began a very close and special relationship. The
very substantial levels of corruption, the failure to meet World Bank
conditions regarding the state oil company Pertamina, not to mention
the regime's human rights record, were all overlooked. Rather more
important in explaining the Bank's relationship with Indonesia was the
backdrop of US strategic concerns about South East Asia and communist insurgency (Green, 1990). The right kind of government in
Indonesia, in the context of the Cold War, simply had to be assisted.

These examples give a flavour of the way in which the World Bank
became part of the Cold War. However, it must also be noted that the
Bank's closeness to Indonesia (and other countries) also developed out of
relations between Bank staff and a particular set of interlocutors: in
Indonesia a group of young US-trained economists (or 'technocrats' as
they came to be called) who were brought into government by General
Suharto. From the Bank's side, the most senior staff member in Jakarta
was given unprecedented powers to make loans and report directly to the
World Bank President (KLW, 1997a: 467–71). Significantly, once the
Bank's technocratic interlocutors lost some of their influence and
power so, too, Indonesia's relationship with the World Bank became a
more distant one. This story has been repeated in other countries allied to
the West with whom the World Bank formed close relations: Turkey,
Mexico, Iran (in particular in the late 1970s), and the Philippines, for
example. In all of these cases the issues of corruption, human rights
abuses and failure to meet conditions of loans were overlooked in favour
of close and generous treatment from the World Bank, closely supported
by the US Treasury and State Departments. Equally importantly, close
relations in each case were formed between Bank officials and 'technocrats' (often US economics-trained) in the borrowing government and
suffered when technocrats lost their positions or influence.

The political pressures of the Cold War heavily influenced World Bank
lending throughout the period 1948–90. However, the case of India illustrates that the exigencies of the Cold War did not completely override
other lending considerations for the Bank. In India, the Bank became

closely involved even though the country was not a Cold War ally of the West. The Bank's loans to India reflected concerns of the US aid community, but not US national interests as understood by the US Treasury, State Department or Executive. Indeed, the United States had earlier exerted considerable pressure on the IMF to reduce its assistance to India (James, 1996: 138). The case of India also highlights the importance of Bank relations with interlocutors (as mentioned above). In India, the limits of the Bank's policy influence came not so much from overriding US-defined political priorities foisted on the Bank, but rather from the lack of technocratic interlocutors in the Indian government (KLW, 1997a: 293–8, 463–7).

In the aftermath of the Cold War, one cannot say with confidence that the Bank has been freed from political influences in its lending policies. The end of the Cold War brought with it a raft of new geostrategic challenges and in particular the integration of Russia and the former Soviet bloc into the world economy: not just for economic reasons but in order to safeguard the West from a new nationalist (and still nuclear-armed) Russia (Gould-Davies and Woods, 1999). The World Bank very quickly became involved in this project (see *World Bank Development Reports*, 1992–8), which has been led by the United States. Indeed, it would seem that strategic and US-defined economic priorities are also influencing other lending decisions (as evidenced by the loans mentioned in subsection 2.1) to Gaza, and Bosnia and Herzegovina, as well as the deployment of Bank resources in the Mexican and Russian financial crises of the 1990s.

The political influences on Bank lending leave a serious challenge for the Bank at the end of the 1990s: how to establish more autonomy over lending decisions (especially now that Cold War imperatives have disappeared). Put another way, the Bank needs to reinforce its character as a rule-based, multilateral agency. A serious potential obstacle to this aim is the extent to which the Bank has become beholden to political pressures emanating from the US government and from the US Congress in particular, as further detailed below.

4 New challenges

The previous sections have described a running tension between the Bank's identity and work as a technical agency and the influence of the United States, which enjoys a sixth of the votes on the Executive Board of the Bank,[13] as well as informal influence in the institution. At the end of the twentieth century, we need to add to this equation the new challenges the Bank is facing – in particular, demands that the institution be more accountable and more transparent. In part this is a result of the drive for 'democratisation' which began at the end of the Cold War and which has been extended into arguments for democratising organisations (Commission on Global Governance, 1995; Boutros Boutros-Ghali, 1996). In part, it is also the result of a sustained campaign by the US Congress and US-based NGOs to bring about reforms in the way the Bank works, as well as new conditionalities in its lending.

It bears noting that arguments for democratisation affect the World Bank and the IMF more than most other international economic fora. Unlike the Group of Seven (G-7), the Group of Three (G-3), or Bank for International Settlements (BIS), the Bank and Fund are genuinely international organisations with near-universal memberships. Furthermore, their work directly affects the lives of people all over the world and theoretically these people are all represented by governments on the Boards of the institutions. Critics point out that this representation is too tenuous and that the institution needs 'democratising' so as better to represent and be accountable to those it affects. Some point to voting power on the Executive Board, emphasising that it underrepresents governments of developing country borrowers who are not only most affected by the Bank but also generate the major part of its income.[14] Others argue that government representatives from borrowing countries inadequately represent the groups and communities most affected by Bank policies and therefore the real challenge for the Bank is for it to become more open and accountable to grassroots, NGOs. It is this latter challenge that has elicited the strongest responses and reforms from within the Bank.

In 1993, the Bank established an independent inspection panel with the mandate to receive and investigate complaints about Bank-supported projects in which the Bank has not followed its own policies and procedures with respect to the design, appraisal, or implementation of a project (Shihata, 1994). The first case accepted by the inspection panel was the Arun III Dam project being undertaken by the Nepali government. The panel's findings questioned whether, in preparing this project, the Bank had followed its own indigeneous peoples' and resettlement policies. The project was very strongly supported by senior management in the Bank, yet in the end was rejected by the Executive Board (Fox and Brown, 1998). Critical to the Board's rejection of the project was the opposition of the US Executive Director, and the fact that the Bank's President James Wolfensohn overrode his own senior management. It seemed, therefore, that the NGOs had acquired some leverage, not only over the Bank but also over US policies within the Bank.[15]

By the end of 1998 the Panel had received 13 formal requests for inspection, 11 of which were found to be admissible and seven of which have been acted upon (World Bank, 1998). The Bank had also adopted a broad-ranging 'disclosure of information' policy. Both these policies have been largely brought about due to the pressure of NGOs: in the words of one scholar, the Bank has 'climbed onto the NGO bandwagon in a big way' (Nelson, 1995). Yet the Bank's new relationship with NGOs is not without problems for the Bank.

NGOs have played a vital role in prising the Bank open, increasing its transparency and introducing a new kind of accountability. However, as NGOs have come to play an increasing role – under the banner of democratisation – the question arises as to whether they are a constituency to whom the Bank ought to be accountable, and if so, why. Two kinds of argument are made for the inclusion of NGOs. The first suggests that the Bank operates within a very narrow a set of values and that issue-based NGOs raise a broader set of moral and ethical concerns that the Bank should be forced to consider. A second kind of argument proposes that NGOs should be included because for many people in the world – who are not represented or protected by their own governments (who sit on the Executive Board of the Bank) this is the only way in which their voice and concerns about Bank projects can be heard. There is a strong case to be made in favour of each of the above arguments (Nelson, 1995; Fox and Brown, 1998). However, the experience of NGOs in the Bank suggests that there are also dangers inherent in the way they have been included. The most serious danger is that the inclusion of NGOs will indirectly enhance the influence of the United States, thereby exacerbating the tensions of multilateralism already discussed in this chapter.

Importantly, the relationship between NGOs and the World Bank has been a triangular one including the US Congress. This has been highlighted in a detailed analysis of environmental NGOs and their relations with the Bank in the 1980s (Wade, 1998). Politically, the victory of the environmental NGOs in pushing for the inspection panel was possible only because of the unholy alliance they formed with US Senator Kasten (Rep., Wisconsin), Chair of the Senate Appropriations Subcommittee on Foreign Operations, otherwise known for his strong anti-foreign aid stance. In grouping with anti-World-Bank and anti-IDA forces in the US Congress, NGOs not only increased their own influence, but also that of the US Congress itself. The danger here is that the US Congress will continue, and perhaps augment, its demands for particular conditions to be imposed by the World Bank on borrowing countries:

whether it be concerning the environment or birth control. Such unilateralism can only erode the multilateral character and accountability of the World Bank, undermining the legitimacy of the advice and conditions it sets for its borrowers.

Perhaps equally importantly, it has been noted that the environmental values being pushed by NGOs in the 1980s were not necessarily universal – and that they were perhaps even essentially American. One scholar suggests to us that the environmental pressures put on the Bank in the 1980s reflected 'Sierra Club' values (e.g. the protection of endangered species) rather than developing country concerns say, about tropical agriculture and water (Wade, 1998). The underlying problem with this is that US values and beliefs already get a hearing through existing formal channels (on the Executive Board, and so forth). If US-based NGOs also get to propound these views through informal channels of communication in the Bank, then a kind of 'double-counting' is occurring. In essence, the danger is that the way in which NGOs are being included may well magnify the US voice within the Bank, rather than succeeding in opening the Bank to otherwise unheard voices.

5 Conclusions

Since its creation, the World Bank has steered a delicate course between courting and placating its largest shareholder, and fulfilling its developmental objectives in a genuinely multilateral way. Several characteristics of the Bank give it scope for relative autonomy. In the first place, the Bank's financial structure gives it a large degree of independence from political control. However, this independence is severely eroded by the concessional window within the Bank group (the IDA), whose periodic replenishment requires agreement from members. Replenishment negotiations have opened up a channel for political pressure which US politicians, in particular, have not hesitated to use.

A second source of independence for the Bank lies in its role as a technical agency dispensing neutral expertise and research. Here, however, there are also subtle political influences at work. This influence, it has been suggested, flows both ways between the Bank and US administrations; however, during the 1980s the latter tended to define the broad parameters within which Bank advice could proceed.

A further source of autonomy is conferred by the Bank's Articles which impose strict neutrality and independence from political factors in its lending decisions. Indeed, in practice the Bank has always legitimated its loans by defending them with reference to its rule-based procedures and criteria. Nevertheless, during the Cold War the Bank was perhaps best seen as part of the Western alliance system, and since the end of the Cold War political considerations seem still to apply.

Overall, the Bank can be said to enjoy a limited degree of independence which is crucial to its effectiveness both as a multilateral institution and as a technical agency. The Bank's position, however, is a delicate one and at the end of the 1990s it is clear that independence from its largest shareholder has been further challenged. As the Bank responds to over tures from NGOs and the US Congress, it is clear that the institution must understand and carefully delineate the legitimate representative and advisory role NGOs can play. If independence is not to be further eroded, distinctions must be made between NGOs who further the 'participation' objectives of the World Bank (i.e. agencies comprising local communities and direct stakeholders in Bank projects) and NGOs who represent wider concerns which can be (or already are) expressed through government stakeholders. Above all, the inclusion of NGOs must aim to enhance the legitimacy of the World Bank and not simply the Bank's popularity on Capitol Hill. As has been argued throughout this chapter, the Bank's legitimacy is a prerequisite for it effectively to pursue its core objectives in the world economy. This legitimacy in turn can be maintained only if the Bank is seen to retain an independence from its most powerful member, thus reinforcing its multilateral character and maintaining the status and credibility of its technical expertise.

NOTES

I am indebted to Chris Gilbert, Robert Wade, Rosemary Foot and Diana Tussie for their invaluable comments and suggestions on an earlier draft of this chapter.

1 Once the Bretton Woods Conferences took place, the IMF became the more central topic of discussion (James 1996: 40).

2 The policies expressed by the US Executive Director at the Bank are formulated in the US Treasury to which agency the Executive Director reports and which chairs the Working Group on Multilateral Assistance (created in 1973) which includes representatives from the departments of Treasury, State and Commerce, as well as the International Development Cooperation Agency, the Federal Reserve and the Export–Import Bank.

3 For example, see Eberstadt and Lewis (1995).

4 One domestic reason, it has been argued, was so that the US Treasury and State Department could retain control over international economic and financial affairs, using multilateral institutions to remove American policy from the control of Congress (James, 1996: 72).

5 As stated explicitly by Under-Secretary of Treasury for International Finance, Timothy Geithner to the Senate Banking, Housing and Urban Affairs Committee (9 March 1999).

6 Abbott and Snidal (1998): instead, institutions are seen either as sites of cooperation or as passive embodiments of norms or rules (see Keohane, 1984; Moravcsik, 1991; Garrett and Weingast, 1993).

7 As regards paid-in capital for the IBRD, there have been three general capital increases (1959,1979, 1989); however, along with each has been a decrease in the paid-in provsion from 10 to 7.54 to 0.3 per cent.

8 Some argue that for this very reason, World Bank research is sometimes compromised – since its advice is not disinterested, it is biased towards what will be publicly acceptable to governments (Wade, 1993).

9 The Bank has estimated that its own publications are cited 20–40 per cent more often than the average article in publications covered by the Social Science Citation Index (Stern and Ferreira, 1997: 590).

10 The results of a 1991 study of the Policy, Research and External Affairs Departments showed that some 80 per cent of senior staff trained in economic and finance at institutions in the United States and the United Kingdom (Stern and Ferreira, 1997).

11 Already the Bank has situated some 22 Country Directors in regions. During 1998, for example, the Bank relocated three of its country directors for Europe and Central Asia into the region (one for the Czech Republic, Hungary, Moldova, the Slovak Republic and Slovenia; the second for Poland and the Baltics; and the third for Russia) with the overall objective of strengthening the Bank's knowledge base, and laying the groundwork for more systemic interaction with local stakeholders (World Bank, 1998).

12 In fact, to some degree, policy conditionality has always been part of the Bank's work (Baldwin, 1965)

13 The World Bank's *Annual Report 1997* describes the Executive Board's oversight responsibility as covering

> virtually all Bank policy, so its role cannot be clearly separated from most of the Bank activities and initiatives [covered in this Report]. This oversight responsibility is exercised in part through the process of Board approval of each bank or IDA lending operation and the annual budget process. However, the Executive Directors also exercise an important role in shaping bank policy and its evolution. (World Bank, 1997b: 10)

14 Indeed, the share of votes held by developing countries has been proportionally diminished as basic votes have been eroded, and is also argued to be underrepresented owing to the GDP calculations used in determining quotas (Wagner, 1995; Patel, 1996).

15 Fox and Brown (1998) caution us from drawing too general a lesson from this action since the project was, in a sense, an easy one to cancel since it involved a small borrower, it had been prepared before Wolfensohn's appointment to the Bank and it was funded by IDA whose replenishment negotiations were looming ahead.

REFERENCES

Abbott, K. and D. Snidal (1998). 'Why States Act through Formal International Organisations', *Journal of Conflict Resolution*, **42**: 3–32

African Development Bank (ADB) (1994). *The Question for Quality: Report of the Task Force on Project Quality for the African Development Bank*, Manila: Asian Development Bank

Ascher, W. (1992), 'The World Bank and US Control', in M. Karns and K. Mingst (eds.), *The United States and Multilateral Institutions: Patterns of Changing Instrumentality and Influence*, London: Routledge: 115–40

Ayres, R. I. (1983). *Banking on the Poor*, Cambridge, MA: MIT Press

Baldwin, D. (1965). 'The International Bank in Political Perspective', *World Politics*, **18**: 68–81.

Bird, K. (1992). *The Chairman: John McCloy: The Making of the American Establishment*, New York: Simon & Schuster

Boutros-Ghali, B. (1996). 'Democracy: A Newly Recognized Imperative', *Global Governance*, **1**: 3–11

Buira, A. (1996). 'The Governance of the International Monetary Fund', in R. Culpeper and C. Pestieau, *Development and Global Governance*, Ottawa: International Development Research Centre, the North–South Institute

Commission on Global Governance (1995). *Our Global Neighbourhood*, Oxford: Oxford University Press

Eberstadt, N. and C. Lewis (1995). 'Privatizing the World Bank', *The National Interest*, **40**

Feinberg, R. E. *et al.* (1986). *Between Two Worlds: The World Bank's Next Decade*, Washington, DC: Overseas Development Council

Fox, J. A. and L. D. Brown (1998). *The Struggle for Accountability: The World Bank, NGOs, and Grassroots Movements*, Cambridge MA: MIT Press

Gardner, R. N. (1969). *Sterling–Dollar Diplomacy: The Origins and the Prospects of Our International Economic Order*, NewYork: McGraw-Hill

Garrett, G. and B. Weingast (1993). 'Ideas, Interests and Institutions: Constructing the European Community's Internal Market', in J. Goldstein and R. Keohane (eds.), *Ideas and Foreign Policy: Beliefs, Institutions and Political Change*, Ithaca: Cornell University Press

Gould-Davies, N. and N. Woods (1999). 'Russia and the IMF', *International Affairs*, **75**: 1–22

Green, M. (1990). *Indonesia: Crisis and Transformation, 1965–1968*, Washington, DC: Compass Press

Griesgraber, J. M. and B. Gunter (1996). *The World Bank: Lending on a Global Scale*, London: Pluto Press

Gwin, C. (1997). 'US Relations with the World Bank, 1945–1992', in D. Kapur, J. P. Lewis and R. Webb, *The World Bank: Its First Half Century, 2: Perspectives*, Washington, DC: Brookings Institution: 195–274

Helleiner, G. (Report by Commonwealth Study Group) (1983). *Towards a New Bretton Woods: Challenges for the World Financial and Trading System*, London: Commonwealth Secretariat

James, H. (1996). *International Monetary Cooperation since Bretton Woods*, Oxford: Oxford University Press

Kapur, D. (1995). 'The New Conditionalities of the IFIs', Washington, DC, paper prepared for the G-24

Kapur, D., J.P. Lewis and R. Webb (1997a). *The World Bank: Its First Half Century, 1: History*, Washington, DC: Brookings Institution
    (1997b). *The World Bank: Its First Half Century, 2: Perspectives*, Washington, DC: Brookings Institution

Keohane, R. (1984). *After Hegemony*, Princeton: Princeton University Press

Lake, A. (1989). *Somoza Falling*, New York: Houghton-Mifflin

Le Prestre, P. (1989). *The World Bank and the Environmental Challenge*, Selingsgrove, PA: Susquehanna University Press

Lister, F. K. (1984). *Decision-making Strategies for International Organizations: The IMF Model*, **20**, **book 4**, Denver: Graduate School of International Studies, University of Denver

Mikesell, R. F (1994). 'The Bretton Woods Debates: A Memoir', *Essays in International Finance*, **192**, Princeton; Princeton University, Department of Economics, International Finance Section

Moravcsik, A. (1991). 'Negotiating the Single European Act: National Interests and Conventional Statecraft in the European Community', *International Organisation*, **45**: 19–56

Morrow, J. D. (1994). 'The Forms of International Cooperation', *International Organisation*, **48**: 387–424

Naim, M. (1995). 'Latin America's Journey to the Market: From Macroeconomic Shocks to Institutional Therapy', *Occasional Papers*, 62, San Francisco: International Center for Economic Growth

Nelson, J. and Contributors (1994). *Intricate Links: Democratisation and Market Reforms in Latin America and Eastern Europe*, Washington, DC: Overseas Development Council

Nelson, P. (1995). *The World Bank and Non-governmental Organisations: The Limits of Apolitical Development*, London: Macmillan

North–South Roundtable (1993). *The United Nations and the Bretton Woods Institutions: New Challenges for the 21st Century* (Bretton Woods, 1–3 September), New York: North–South Roundtable

Ogata, S. (1989). 'Shifting Power Relations in Multilateral Development Banks', *Journal of International Studies*, **22**

Oye, K. (ed.) (1986). *Cooperation under Anarchy*, Princeton: Princeton University Press

Patel I.G. (1996). 'Some Thoughts on Our Present Discontents', in R. Culpeper and C. Pestieau, *Development and Global Governance*, Ottawa: International Development Research Centre, the North–South Institute

Picciotto, R. and R. Weaving (1994). 'A New Project Cycle for the World Bank?', *Finance and Development*, December

Please, S. (1984). *The Hobbled Giant: Essays on the World Bank*, Boulder, CO: Westview

Purcell, J. and M. Miller (1986). 'The World Bank and Private Capital', in R. Feinberg *et al.*, *The World Bank's Next Decade*, Washington, DC, Overseas Development Council

Ranis, G. (1997). 'The World Bank Near the Turn of the Century', in R. Culpeper, A. Berry and F. Stewart, *Global Development Fifty Years after Bretton Woods: Essays in Honour of G.K. Helleiner*, London: Macmillan

Rapkin, D. and J. Strand (1996). 'US–Japan Leadership Sharing in the IMF and the World Bank', paper presented at IS Conference (San Diego, 16–20 April)

Rodrik, D.(1996). 'Understanding Economic Policy Reform', *Journal of Economic Literature*, **34**: 9–41

Shihata, I. (1994). *The World Bank's Inspection Panel*, Oxford: Oxford University Press

Snidal, D. (1985). 'Coordination versus Prisoners' Dilemma: Implications for International Cooperation and Regimes', *American Political Science Review*, **79**: 923–42

Stein, A. (1983). 'Coordination and Collaboration: Regimes in an Anarchic World', in Stephen Krasner (ed.), *International Regimes*, Ithaca: Cornell University Press: 337–54

Stern N. and F. Ferreira (1997). 'The World Bank as "Intellectual Actor"', in D. Kapur, J. P. Lewis and R. Webb, *The World Bank: Its First Half Century, 2: Perspectives*, Washington, DC: Brookings Institution: 523–610

Stevens, M. and S. Gnanaselvam (1995). 'The World Bank and Governance', *IDS Bulletin*, **26**: 97–105

Stiglitz, J. E. (1998a). *More Instruments and Broader Goals: Moving towards the Post-Washington Consensus*, Helsinki: WIDER/United Nations University
(1998b). 'Knowledge for Development: Economic Science, Economic Policy and Economic Advice', paper presented at the Annual Bank Conference on Development Economics (20–21 April), Washington, DC: World Bank

Taylor, L (1997). 'The Revival of the Liberal Creed – The IMF and the World Bank in a Globalised Economy', *World Development*, **25 (2)**: 145–52

Tussie, D. (1995). *The Inter-American Development Bank*, Boulder, Co: Lynne Rienner

Wade, R. (1993). 'Managing Trade: Taiwan and South Korea as Challenges to Economics and Political Science', *Comparative Politics*, **25**
(1996). 'Japan, the World Bank and the Art of Paradigm Maintenance', *New Left Review*, **217**
(1998). 'Greening the Bank: The Struggle over the Environment 1970–1995', in D. Kapur, J. P. Lewis and R. Webb, *The World Bank: Its First Half Century, 2: Perspectives*, Washington, DC: Brookings Institution: 611–734

Wagner, N. (1995). 'A Review of PPP-adjusted GDP Estimation and its Potential Use for the Fund's Operational Purposes', *IMF Working Paper*, **WP/95/18**

Woods, N. (1999).'Good Governance in International Organisations', *Global Governance*, **5**: 39–61

World Bank (1983–7, 1992–6, 1998). *World Development Report 1983 ... ,* Washington, DC: World Bank

(1992a). *Report of the Ad Hoc Committee on Board Procedures* (26 May), Washington, DC: World Bank
(1992b). *Report of the Task Force on Portfolio Management* (3 November), Washington, DC: World Bank
(1992c).'World Bank Structural and Sectoral Adjustment Operations: The Second OED Overview', *Operations Evaluation Department Report*, 10870, Washington DC: World Bank
(1994). *Report of the Financial Reporting and Auditing Task Force*, Washington, DC: World Bank
(1997a). *World Development Report 1997*, Washington DC: World Bank
(1997b). *Annual Report*, Washington, DC: World Bank
(1998). *The Annual Report of the World Bank 1998*, Washington, DC: World Bank

Part Two

The Effectiveness of World Bank Assistance

6 The World Bank and structural adjustment: lessons from the 1980s

FRANCISCO H.G. FERREIRA AND
LOUISE C. KEELY

1 Introduction

For a large number of developing countries, particularly in Africa and Latin America, the 1980s are remembered not terribly fondly as the decade of debt and 'structural adjustment'. In many of these countries, the term is closely associated with the International Monetary Fund (IMF) and the World Bank. More recently, though, during the 'emerging markets' boom of the mid-1990s, structural adjustment – a set of policy reforms aimed at restoring internal and external equilibria to a crisis-hit economy, whilst simultaneously seeking to increase the efficiency with which its productive resources are allocated – seemed consigned to text-books of the economic history of the 1980s, along with the debt crisis that preceded it.

With the onset of the East Asian, Russian and Brazilian balance of payments crises during 1997–9, however, the topic generated renewed interest. Other chapters in this volume will address the Asian crisis specifically. This chapter looks back at the World Bank's experience with structural adjustment programmes during the 1980s – since the first Structural Adjustment Loan (SAL)[1] was launched in February 1980. We discuss the causes and the nature of the process of adjustment, and consider its main policy components in turn. We also review the evidence on the performance of the programmes during the 1980s. Where appropriate, we draw some lessons for the different – yet related – systemic crises and reforms of the late 1990s.

Section 2 briefly reviews the causes and nature of the processes of stabilisation and structural adjustment in the 1980s. In doing so, it suggests a useful distinction between demand-side, macroeconomic policies grouped under the general term 'stabilisation', and supply-side, largely microeconomic and institutional policies, referred to as 'structural adjust-

159

ment'. Section 3 then examines the policy framework underlying macro-economic stabilisation and assesses the performance of Bank lending in terms of the macroeconomic outcomes associated with different SAL and Sectoral Adjustment Loan (SECAL) programmes. Section 4 reviews the roles of (microeconomic) reforms designed to improve the efficiency with which resources were allocated and used within each adjusting economy. Section 5 considers the impact of the overall packages of macroeconomic and microeconomic policies on poverty and income distribution. Section 6 offers some conclusions.

2 The concepts, causes and nature of adjustment[2]

2.1 The concepts

Usage of the words 'adjustment' and 'stabilisation' has occasionally been loose and their meanings have changed over time. In the early 1980s they were used somewhat interchangeably and the *World Development Reports* (*WDRs*) *1980* and *1981* used 'adjustment' to refer to the *collective* response of the international financial system to the balance of payments disequilibria set in motion by the two oil price shocks of 1973–4 and 1979–80.

'Adjustment' in this context involved recommendations for all countries facing increased current account deficits to shift resources to the production of tradeables, but it also encompassed maintaining capital flows from the current account surplus countries (essentially the oil exporters) to those in deficit. The emphasis was on macroeconomic variables, specifically the balance of payments, and on policies of international – rather than purely domestic – scope.

The view soon emerged, however, that to achieve such macroeconomic targets in the context of highly distorted economies,[3] a great amount of change was necessary in their microeconomic structures. Adjustment had to focus, it was suggested, on property rights, the boundaries between the private and the public sectors, trade policy, institutional efficiency, the development and regulation of financial systems, management policies, and so on. This comprehensive set of economic reforms was termed 'structural adjustment' and stabilisation was then to be understood as the complementary efforts to achieve broad macroeconomic equilibrium through macroeconomic policy instruments. Stabilisation policies dealt mainly with the (aggregate) demand side, whereas adjustment referred to reforms of the supply side (see World Bank, 1991: 113).

That interpretation of the terms is the one we adopt in this chapter, namely that *stabilisation* policies are those which aim to achieve broad macroeconomic equilibrium – i.e. to reduce inflation and current account deficits – by affecting the level and composition of aggregate demand. *Structural* adjustment, on the other hand, refers to any set of policies aiming to increase the efficiency with which agents perform their roles and allocate their resources, and thus has more of a supply-side focus. Below, we discuss the causes and specific policies of adjustment in more detail, and summarise their effects.

2.2 The causes of adjustment

It has been (convincingly) argued that the ultimate, long-term roots of structural adjustment in the 1980s lie in the adoption by many countries, in the 1950s and 1960s, of import-substitution policies based on price and interest rate distortions, which eventually made it harder for firms in these economies to respond to changes in the external environment they faced. They either continued to be sheltered from changes in shadow prices by increases in the distortions which protected them, or simply lacked the managerial expertise to cope with shocks, after prolonged periods in 'industrial infancy' (see, for example, Little, 1982).

Be that as it may, the experience of stabilisation and adjustment in the 1980s cannot be understood without reference to its medium- and short-term causes: the oil price shocks of the 1970s, the period of international 'recycling' of funds that they set in motion, and the subsequent debt crisis. The oil shocks had a strong stagflationary impact on the world economy (see Bruno and Sachs, 1985). In addition, given the importance of oil in international trade, its price rise also caused significant changes in global terms of trade, giving rise to very large payments imbalances. Table 6.1 traces the evolution of oil prices, growth rates and current account surpluses for three categories of countries – industrial countries, oil-exporting developing countries, and other developing countries – from 1973 to 1982.

Table 6.1 illustrates that, whereas industrial countries tended to reduce their growth rates more sharply in response to dearer oil (and the subsequent inward shift of the factor price frontier), restoring their current accounts to balance relatively rapidly, LDCs largely responded to the negative terms of trade shock by borrowing in the international capital markets. These loans – in effect temporary transfers of tradeable goods – helped them register a much less pronounced fall in growth rates in the

Table 6.1 *Responses of developed and developing countries to the oil shocks of the 1970s*

	1973	1974	1975	1976	1977	1978	1979	1980	1981	1982
Oil prices[a]	2.70	9.76	10.72	11.51	12.40	12.70	16.97	28.67	32.57	33.49
Industrial countries										
– Growth rate[c]	5.59	0.02	−1.07	4.40	3.42	5.52	2.51	0.97	1.49	−1.19
– Current account surplus[b]	20	−11	20	1	−2	33	−6	−40	1	−1
Oil-exporting developing countries										
– Growth rate[c]	6.39	5.34	−1.29	5.93	1.50	−3.56	3.96	−4.66	−4.59	1.63
– Current account surplus[b]	7	68	35	40	30	2	69	114	65	−2
Other developing countries										
– Growth rate[c]	4.34	3.75	2.85	3.22	4.02	3.09	2.16	3.31	1.54	−2.11
– Current account surplus[b]	−11	−37	−46	−31	−29	−41	−61	−89	−108	−87

Notes:
[a]US$/barrel, for Saudi Arabian crude at Ras Tanura.
[b]US$ billion, in IMF (1983) definitions.
[c]Per cent. Weighted average growth rate of real GDP *per capita* (RGDP, Summers and Heston, 1988), with weights given by RGDPs as a share of group's RGDP.
Sources: IMF (1981, 1983, 1985); Summers and Heston (1988).

immediate aftermath of a shock, but allowed their current account deficits to grow almost tenfold, on average, from 1973 to 1981.[4] This increase was made possible by the availability of funds in the international financial system to finance those large and growing deficits. The funds originated from the large current account surpluses being run by the oil exporters and, although there was some increase in concessional flows, the surpluses were channelled predominantly through the Western commercial banking system.

These loans, often made at negative real interest rates, provided for the so-called 'recycling' of funds which was seen by many policy-makers in the developing world, as well as in the World Bank and many commercial banks, as a perfectly appropriate response to the shocks, in that it enabled a much smaller reduction in domestic absorption, effectively cushioning countries from the need to adjust to sharply lower terms of trade. A smaller cut in absorption was supposed to allow for investment aimed at shifting productive resources to the tradeables sector, while avoiding the slowdown in growth and decline in living standards which would have been inevitable if such reforms were to have taken place in the absence of any external financing. For the commercial banks, this was seen as a safe portfolio option, following the credo of CITICORP Chairman Walter Wriston, who famously stated that 'countries never go bankrupt' (see Sachs, 1989: 8).[5]

However, a combination of abrupt changes in the external situation at the turn of the decade conspired to drastically alter that perception. After the second oil shock in 1979, conditions deteriorated sharply. A weighted index of real (non-oil) commodity prices tumbled from 121 in 1977 to 81 in 1982 (1980 = 100), compounding the decline in terms of trade for most developing countries. The industrial countries responded to the inflationary pressures exacerbated by the second oil price shock with an unprecedented tightening of monetary policies. Combined with the expansionary fiscal policy pursued by the Reagan Administration, this tight monetary policy led real interest rates to rise to historically high levels: the real US prime rate rose from −0.6 per cent in 1977 to 12.8 per cent in 1981 (see Dornbusch and Fischer, 1987).

The subsequent recession in the industrial countries – the deepest since the 1930s – curtailed demand for imports and triggered protectionist pressures. Developing countries faced the need to expand export earnings at a time when both the unit value of their export basket had declined (the terms of trade effect) and the volume demanded had stopped growing (the volume effect). To make matters worse, both the proportion of developing country debt owed to commercial banks, and that in Variable Interest Rate (VIR) arrangements, had been growing steadily, so that the sharp rise in interest rates increased the debt service burden very rapidly. As a result, combined current account deficits for non-oil-exporting developing countries rose from US$41 billion in 1978 to US$108 billion in 1981. To keep debt service payments up, borrowing in the thriving international financial markets accelerated.

Since demand for exports was so weak, many LDCs had only two ways to deal with these deficits: to sharply lower imports, through economic contraction, or to finance them by borrowing. Most countries chose the latter course, given the political resistance to cuts in the growth rate (or indeed the *level*) of GNP. Commercial banks, whose exposure to sovereign debt had steadily risen during the 1970s, responded by a massive, albeit short-lived, increase in lending. As Jeffrey Sachs puts it: 'What is truly remarkable about the bank behaviour is not the lending during 1973–79, but rather the outpouring of new lending during 1980–81, even after the world macroeconomic situation had soured markedly ... In a mere two years, 1980 and 1981, total bank exposure nearly doubled over the level of 1979 in the major debtor countries' (Sachs, 1989: 9).

In August 1982, Mexico found it impossible to produce the necessary foreign exchange to make its service payments on time and the ensuing rescheduling sent shock waves throughout the international financial system. Virtually overnight, voluntary lending to most LDCs all but ceased. The age of concerted lending, aimed only at 'rolling over' existing debt, commenced. The large current account deficits in many LDCs could no longer be financed by foreign capital inflows. 'Adjustment' in the 1980s was to acquire a new face. It was no longer seen as a concerted global effort aimed at responding to terms of trade changes that had originated in the oil price shocks, and recycling the resulting surpluses across the international economy, for which borrowing was seen as a legitimate instrument. The causation now ran from debt – and the 'Debt Crisis' – rather than oil prices, to adjustment, and adjustment would be viewed as a fundamentally internal, country-specific process.

2.3 The nature of adjustment

With recourse to foreign finance sharply curtailed for most debtors, developing countries had no choice but to bring expenditure in line with income. Figure 6.1, adapted from figure 2 in Bourguignon, de Melo and Morrisson (1991: 1489), gives a stylised explanation of the effects of the shock and the necessary stabilisation response. Consider two economies, F (for flexible) and R (for rigid), both of which produce a tradeable good, T, and a non-tradeable good, N. They have identical

Figure 6.1 *Flexible and rigid responses to an external shock*
Source: Bourguignon, de Melo and Morrisson (1991: 1489).

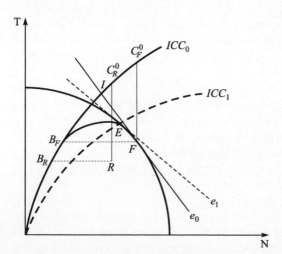

tastes, endowments and technologies, but different degrees of price rigidity. Their tastes are represented by an income–consumption curve (ICC), which maps the locus of tangencies between all isocost lines (for a fixed relative price) and indifference curves. There is thus one ICC for each relative price. Endowments and technology for both economies are represented by a common production possibility set.

F is an efficient economy with no price rigidities. R is an economy whose policies and institutions lead to significant X-inefficiencies and thus produces at R inside its PPF. This distinction between levels of efficiency will highlight the role of structural adjustment, *vis-à-vis* that of stabilisation. We return to this distinction below. Now let each economy initially receive an identical foreign income transfer (measured in terms of tradeables: $FC^F_0 = RC^R_0$). The transfer allows them to consume at C^F_0 (economy F) and C^R_0 (economy R). We can model an external shock straightforwardly as the suspension of that transfer, which previously allowed both economies to consume in excess of their production. The shock can be interpreted as a cessation of foreign lending, or an increase in interest rates leading to much larger debt service outlays.

As the transfer stops and the current account deficit can no longer be financed, both countries are faced with the need to reduce consumption in order to bring it into line with the income actually available to them. Furthermore, at ruling prices (the slope of e_0), there would be an excess demand for (supply of) tradeables (non-tradeables), as F would wish to consume at I, which is not feasible. If prices adjust fully flexibly, ICC_0 shifts to ICC_1 as the real exchange rate depreciates to e_1 and economy F reaches equilibrium at E. The cost of the shock, then, if there are no rigidities and prices adjust costlessly and immediately, is the value of the transfer that is lost to the economy. There are no secondary costs, that is: there are no costs of the adjustment process itself.

The adjustment process changes if rigidities exist in the goods, assets or factor markets. In the simplified framework of figure 6.1, this rigidity is represented by a fixed real exchange rate. Still considering the economy F, if the exchange rate stays fixed at e_0, consumption must take place somewhere along ICC_0. But the consumption level must derive solely from the country's own resources. If a devaluation is precluded by rigidities, consumption must come down further to lower imports. As noted above, given the prices implied by the slope of e_0, efficient production would take place at F, and consumption at I. In the absence of a capital account surplus, this is infeasible.

If e_0 will not adjust then total consumption must be brought down further. In other words, if expenditure switching won't occur, expenditure reduction must be even greater than would have otherwise been the case.

This happens through a contraction of the sector for whose output there is excess supply, N. The factors thereby released remain unemployed, as price signals do not induce producers in the tradeable sector to expand. This corresponds to a horizontal leftward movement from F to ICC_0. External equilibrium is reached at B_F. If there is partial relative price adjustment, the economy will end up somewhere along curve $B_F E$. Some costs of adjustment, measured in terms of lower or negative income *per capita* growth rates, reductions in the investment/GNP ratio, etc. can be captured by this move inwards in the production possibility set. They depend crucially on the existence of rigidities and market imperfections that preclude an immediate adjustment.

For the inefficient economy R, apart from stabilisation policies similar to those used by F, such as a real devaluation and expenditure reduction, structural reforms are necessary to improve X-efficiency. These policies, which are described below, are the constituents of structural adjustment, and are designed to improve resource allocation and use in a distorted economy. If R is successful in removing these distortions, and allows relative prices to adjust smoothly to reflect relative scarcities, it too could resume equilibrium at E. Otherwise, depending on exchange rate rigidity, it will be somewhere between B_R and E.

This picture – and the story it tells – suggest a schematic understanding of the processes of stabilisation and structural adjustment, and of the differences and complementarities between them. Stabilisation generally involves two components: expenditure reduction, usually through contractionary fiscal or monetary policies, and expenditure switching, through policies aimed at producing a devaluation of the real exchange rate. These policies are macroeconomic in nature, and focus on the demand side.

Structural adjustment, on the other hand, has come to be seen as encompassing a large range of policy reforms – macroeconomic, microeconomic and sectoral in nature – aimed at improving resource allocation and increasing economic efficiency. They are concerned with the performance of the supply side of the economy, and include:

- *Trade reform*, whereby systems of protection are reformed to bring about equal incentives to produce for sale in the domestic and foreign markets, by bringing prices closer to their shadow values
- *Price reform*, related principally to rationalising public sector pricing
- *Tax reform*, aimed both at increasing the efficiency (and equity?) of revenue raising, as well as often raising revenue itself
- *Financial reform*, aimed at improving the functioning and completeness of domestic capital markets

- *Privatisation,* aimed at redrawing the borders between the public and private sectors in accordance with new views as to their comparative advantages
- *Labour market reforms,* aimed at increasing flexibility and integration in and among these markets
- *Institution-building,* aimed to increase the administrative capacity of government.

Naturally, specific adjustment packages must be devised with careful consideration to the conditions of each economy at any given point in time, including different structural and sectoral make-ups, as well as different parameter values in any underlying models. To illustrate, consider some of the differences and similarities between this stylised description of adjustment (which refers to the 1980s), and the situation faced by the devaluing economies of the late 1990s (including Thailand, Indonesia, Korea, Russia and Brazil).

The history leading up to the current account deficits which precipitated the devaluations was very different in the 1980s and 1990s. Instead of borrowing from commercial banks to finance a larger import bill driven by oil price rises, countries in the 1990s received capital inflows (predominantly through equity and short-term debt instruments) to finance larger import bills driven by investment and consumption booms associated with growth and trade liberalisation. But the end result was similar in essence: a sustained transfer of tradeables from abroad, such as that portrayed in figure 6.1, which manifested itself through a current account deficit, necessitating an overvalued currency (with respect to the hypothetical equilibrium value of the exchange rate in the absence of the transfer). One country's particular problems (Mexico's default then, Thailand's bad investments in real estate and the ensuing deterioration in the balance sheets of its banks now) lead investors to fear a decline in the expected value of the payments associated with their transfers, and thus to reduce the value of the transfers, necessitating the devaluation, just as in figure 6.1.

There are also specific differences and general similarities as regards the microeconomic reforms. Asian countries have already taken very substantial steps in price and trade liberalisation. The same is increasingly true of at least some Latin American economies. The type of financial reforms now discussed is different from the 'financial liberalisation' proposed in the 1980s. Yet, although there are important differences in the specifics, there remains a fundamental analogy: just as in the early 1980s, in the 1990s the need for expenditure reduction and switching at a macro level is accompanied by recommendations for microeconomic and institutional reforms that make economies function more efficiently. If it was lowering trade barriers and privatising then, now it is redesigning banking supervision and strengthening regulatory institutions across the economy. Some reforms, such as privatisation, labour market reforms and pension reform are common to the agenda of the 1980s and the 1990s, even if the sectors being privatised might be different (e.g. telecommunications and power, instead of steel).

In sections 3–5, we return to the 1980s and review the World Bank's structural adjustment lending policies as attempts to improve the borrowing countries' macroeconomic stability and microeconomic efficiency. We also consider their likely impact on the distributions of assets and income. We discuss how policies evolved over time, as the Bank's policy focus changed, and how those policies affected equity. Whenever appropriate we point out analogies with the crises of the late 1990s. The final section 6 draws some conclusions.

3 Stabilisation policies

The stabilisation policies suggested by the World Bank, as part of its structural adjustment lending programmes, were intended to address the two basic macroeconomic imbalances described above: an internal disequilibrium associated with fiscal deficits and an external disequilibrium associated with current account deficits. These imbalances resulted from a failure to adjust expenditures to the reduction in real income caused by a negative terms of trade shock. They led, in turn, to two symptoms which, despite a diversity of specific country histories, were remarkably consistent: high inflation and a loss of foreign exchange reserves.

Unsurprisingly, the gist of the Bank's suggested stabilisation strategy was for countries to:

● Reduce inflation, by reducing the fiscal deficit.
● Increase the net inflow of foreign exchange and make the current account sustainable, by (1) devaluing the real exchange rate, so as to encourage a shift of domestic demand towards non-tradeables and of productive resources towards tradeables, thereby reducing the trade deficit; and (2) increasing domestic interest rates (towards international rates *plus* the market's expectation of currency devaluation *plus* any perceived additional domestic asset risks), so as to reverse the decline in capital account financing of the current account deficit.

Naturally, the specifics of this basic macroeconomic package depended on country circumstances. To the extent possible, the Bank and the governments sought to exploit synergies between these policies and the microeconomic and institutional reforms being undertaken as part of structural adjustment. For example, the Bank's advice during the 1980s increasingly pointed to the scope for reducing the fiscal deficit through identifying sources of inefficiency in both revenue-gathering, as part of tax reform, and in expenditure, as part of public sector reforms.

As awareness of the impact of expenditure reduction on the poor grew over the course of the 1980s (on which, see section 5), Bank-sponsored adjustment programmes also sought to take the sectoral composition of cuts more carefully into account. Whereas early SALs may have settled on aggregate fiscal deficit targets, later programmes sought to target cuts towards sectors less likely to hurt the poor such as administration payrolls, national defence and public sector pensions and away from key expenditures on health and education. In the more sophisticated programmes, intra-sectoral distinctions were made between, say, expenditures on tertiary versus primary education.

The importance of agreeing fairly specific targets for expenditure reduction, so as to minimise their impact on (often politically less powerful) poor groups is one lesson from the experience of adjustment in the 1980s. However, as other chapters in this volume discuss, the key factor in ensuring that the expenditure cuts actually take place at all, and then that they do so in the 'right' sectors, is the country's internal political balance. It is unclear that strict Bank conditionality can achieve much in the face of a government that cannot pass legislation through Congress, or that it is necessary in the face of a government that both wishes and is able to implement such policies.

Another class of problems relates to transitional dynamics. Adjustment policies which may lead to a desirable and sustainable steady state may often imply a short-term path for the economy which is socially disrupting and/or politically infeasible. And a third, but related, class of issues concerns optimal timing and sequencing of reforms, given the delicate pattern of inter-relationships between different components of a policy package. For example: devaluation and/or raising the interest rate can lead to a decline in domestic investment, as has been witnessed in a number of stabilising countries, both in the 1980s (see Jayarajah and Branson, 1995) and in the late 1990s (see World Bank, 1998a). Additionally, although a devaluation may be crucial to address the *flows* problem of the current account deficit, if a country's *stock* of debt is denominated in foreign currency, then *future* debt service payments rise in domestic currency terms. And as Brazil's experience in 1999

Table 6.2 *SAL and SECAL programme levels of funding, 1980–1990*

Constant US$million[a]		Africa	Asia	EMENA	LAC	Total
Board date	1980	218.4	443.0	333.7	66.7	**1,061.9**
	1981	286.0	385.0	330.0	64.9	**1,066.0**
	1982	208.2	414.5	315.5	79.0	**1,017.2**
	1983	824.6	780.9	578.1	1,185.4	**3,369.1**
	1984	203.1	308.0	506.6	110.7	**1,128.4**
	1985	375.7	165.4	557.6	604.1	**1,702.8**
	1986	935.9	246.4	273.7	1,779.2	**3,235.2**
	1987	743.1	979.3	343.3	2,165.5	**4,231.3**
	1988	361.9	422.7	295.9	338.1	**1,418.5**
	1989	436.7	425.2	0.0	403.2	**1,265.2**
	1990	0.0	191.3	153.0	133.9	**478.2**
	Total	**4,593.6**	**4,761.7**	**3,687.6**	**6,930.8**	**19,973.7**

Note: [a]Deflated by total urban CPI to 1982–4 average = 100, from *Economic Report of the President* (1997).
Sources: Jayarajah and Branson (1995); Jayarajah, Branson and Sen (1996); authors' calculations.

reminds us, when a government's debt-servicing requirements are both substantial and based on variable interest rates, necessary short-term monetary tightness may have disastrous fiscal consequences.

3.1 A review of the World Bank's SAL

Although the essence of the stabilisation policies recommended by the Bank in the 1980s was as outlined above, the instruments through which the Bank encouraged their adoption, as well as the degree to which they were successfully implemented, varied substantially, both over time and across regions, as tables 6.2–6.5 indicate.[6]

Adjustment lending increased overall and within each region until 1987 and then dropped off significantly at the end of the decade (table 6.2). Overall, Latin American and Caribbean (LAC) countries received the largest amounts over the decade, accounting for some 35 per cent of total adjustment lending. However, the percentage of overall funding going to LAC was low until 1982, then rose sharply with the debt crisis, and declined again after 1986 (table 6A.1, p. 190). In terms of decade totals, LAC was followed by Asia; Africa; and Europe, the Middle East and North Africa (EMENA), in that order. Overall, the Bank lent some

Table 6.3 *SAL and SECAL funding trends, 1980–1990*[b]

Funding level (constant US$ million)[a]

Board date	SAL	SECAL	Total
1980	776.7	282.2	1,061.9
1981	860.3	205.7	1,066.0
1982	830.7	186.5	1,017.2
1983	1,867.2	1,501.9	3,369.1
1984	414.8	713.6	1,128.4
1985	381.2	1,321.6	1,702.8
1986	823.4	2,411.8	3,235.2
1987	749.3	3,482.0	4,231.3
1988	241.2	1,177.3	1,418.5
1989	169.5	1,095.6	1,265.2
1990	153.0	325.2	478.2
Total	7,267.3	12,706.4	19,973.7

Notes:
[a]Deflated by total urban CPI to 1982–4 average = 100, from *Economic Report of the President* (1997).
[b]Although the last Board Date is 1990, the adjustment periods ran into 1993 in some cases.
Sources: Jayarajah and Branson (1995); Jayarajah, Branson and Sen (1996); authors' calculations.

US$20 billion (at constant 1982 4 average prices) through adjustment instruments during the 1980s.

The balance of lending instruments also changed over the period, as SECALs gradually replaced SALs in prominence (table 6.3). This change was particularly noticeable around 1983–4, and may have reflected a perception within the Bank at that time that SECALs were easier to monitor and implement. The change may, however, have had an impact on macroeconomic adjustment, since the conditions of sectoral adjustment lending tend to be less macro- and fiscal-oriented than the SAL conditions (17.3 per cent and 27.3 per cent of conditions, respectively, see table 6A.2, p. 190). There were also regional variations in the type of lending. Africa and Asia had an above-average emphasis on macroeconomic conditions in their SAL and SECAL lending, with 30.2 per cent and 32.0 per cent for SALs and 23.8 per cent and 28.6 per cent for SECALs, respectively (see table 6A.2).

How did these SAL and SECAL programmes actually perform during 1980–93? Consider the Bank's own internal evaluations, carried out by the Operations Evaluation Department (OED). The OED rating of adjustment projects is not based on implementation of specific conditions, but on whether the desired policy outcomes were achieved. The rating is dichotomous: 'successful' or 'unsuccessful.' (see World Bank, 1997, for a full explanation of the OED rating system). About two-thirds

Table 6.4 *Policies and results in a sample of countries, 1980–1993*

Policy:	Reduce fiscal deficit	Real devaluation	Reduce negative interest rate differential
Outcome:	Reduce inflation	Reduce CA deficit	Increase net foreign exchange reserves
Right policy, good outcome	27	39	32
Right policy, bad outcome	9	3	7
Wrong policy, bad outcome	10	2	8
Wrong policy, good outcome	7	4	1
Chi-squared test of differences	6.5^a	27.1	15.6

Note: [a]Test fails to reject the hypothesis that the differences in proportions for each policy category are statistically significant across outcome types, at the 5 per cent level, but (marginally) rejects at 10 per cent; other tests reject at the 5 per cent level.
Sources: Jayarajah, Branson and Sen (1996: 36); authors' calculations.

of the adjustment programmes over 1980–93 were rated 'successful' (table 6A.3, p. 191). Broadly speaking, the success rate of projects increased over the 1980–93 period. There was no systematic difference in the success rate across SAL and SECAL projects (see table 6A.4, p. 191).

While the OED ratings give information on the policy outcomes of adjusting countries, they do not necessarily give insight into the implementation of the right policies. Two OED studies (by Jayarajah and Branson, 1995 and Jayarajah, Branson and Sen, 1996) provide a rough tabulation of the association between the right macroeconomic policy and a good outcome (i.e. macroeconomic stability). The relevant table from the 1996 study is reproduced here as table 6.4 and shows that the right policy was more likely to lead to the good than the bad outcome. Similarly, the wrong policy was generally more likely to lead to the bad than the good outcome. Except for the case of inflation reduction, these differences were significant at the 5 per cent level in a standard chi-squared test.

But while they are informative, these partial associations between certain policies and outcomes are far too rough a set of indicators to understand what really determines the performance of an adjustment programme. The main plausible candidate factors include: regional characteristics; the breadth of conditions in each loan programme; existence of macroeconomic stability (as a necessary condition for the success of

Table 6.5 *OED average rating, by region, 1980–1993*

Region	OED rating				
	s	Per cent of total	*u*	Per cent of total	Total
Africa	37	55	30	45	67
Asia	21	78	6	22	27
EMENA	14	82	3	18	17
LAC	19	56	15	44	34
Total	**91**	**63**	**54**	**37**	**145**

Notes: *s* = successful, *u* = unsuccessful; one project was not rated.
Sources: Jayarajah and Branson (1995); Jayarajah, Branson and Sen (1996); authors' calculations.

allocative efficiency reforms); World Bank planning and supervision; and the commitment of the borrowing government to the programme (as proxied by political economy variables).

A study by Dollar and Svensson (1998) regressed OED outcome data on a number of variables proxying and instrumenting for these factors. Their main finding was that regional location, as well as World Bank conditionality, planning and supervision, did not have statistically significant impacts on the OED indicator of success for adjustment programmes. By contrast, variables related to the political economy of the borrowing country significantly influenced the policy outcome.

Although programmes in Africa and LAC were on average significantly less successful than those in Asia and EMENA (55 per cent and 56 per cent versus 78 per cent and 82 per cent, see table 6.5), once appropriate controls were introduced, regional dummies for Africa, LAC and East Asia were generally insignificant in the Dollar and Svensson (1998) regressions.

A proxy for the breadth of conditionality is the number of conditions. There is no clear *a priori* expectation of what the sign of the coefficient of this variable should be. Further, policy success may vary non-linearly with the number of conditions and the relationship may also depend on the type of conditions stipulated. The regression results of Dollar and Svensson (1998) show the number of conditions variable to be slightly positive and statistically insignificant.

One (plausible) test of the hypothesis that macroeconomic stability is a necessary condition for microeconomic reforms is whether there is a marginally positive effect of the percentage of macroeconomic conditions on policy success. Again, Dollar and Svensson find that the percentage of macro and fiscal conditions (in total conditions) did not have a statisti-

Table 6.6 *Dollar and Svensson (1998), empirical results*

Dependent variable: OED rating		
Variable	Estimated coefficient	t-statistic
Preparation (staffweeks)	0.323	0.24
Supervision (staffweeks)	−0.869	−0.67
Government crisis	−2.285	−4.29
Ethnic fractionalisation	7.763	4.04
Ethnic fractionalisation^2	−8.046	−3.79
Time in power	−0.113	−2.09
Time in power^2	0.004	2.02
Democratically elected	0.912	3.09

Source: Dollar and Svensson (1998: table 6.3, regression 5)

cally significant effect on the OED Evaluation Outcome variable (t-statistics were between 0.44 and 1.06 in various regressions, see Dollar and Svensson, 1998, table 3).

The earlier OED study emphasises the need for both parties' commitment to and 'ownership' of the programme, as well as of careful World Bank advance planning (Jayarajah and Branson, 1995: 130–1). The effects of these three elements are examined empirically in Dollar and Svensson (1998). They find that World Bank preparation and supervision had a statistically insignificant effect on the success of structural adjustment, with the sign on the supervision variable actually *negative*. On the other hand, political economy variables proxying for political instability, social division, government tenure and a democratically elected government were all found to be significant with the expected signs. It was therefore the ability and interests of the adjusting country's government that was statistically most important in the success or failure outcome of structural adjustment. Table 6.6 summarises some of the findings in Dollar and Svensson's study (from table 3, regression 5 of their paper). While Bank effort variables, such as preparation and supervision staff weeks, are statistically insignificant, the opposite is true of domestic political economy proxies.

In sum, it would appear that while individual macroeconomic policies advocated as part of adjustment programmes are associated with the desired outcomes (table 6.4), it is not clear that World Bank conditionality, planning and supervision determine their adoption (table 6.6). It seems that it not as much what the Bank does, but to whom the Bank chooses to lend, that affects the success of adjustment. This conclusion is reinforced by the findings described in chapter 8, by Burnside and Dollar, in this volume. They have found that neither growth nor infant mortality is affected by the level of aid alone. However, the level of aid interacted with an index of a country's macroeconomic and institutional management has a statistically significant effect on both growth and infant mortality reduction. While these political economy variables are generally not within the Bank's sphere of influence, whether to lend to a particular country or not should always be.

4 Adjustment and the efficiency of resource allocation

An internal review of the experience of the early adjustment programmes of 1980–2, based largely on OED evaluations of the first SALs, contributed to a change in the Bank's approach to adjustment lending, beginning around 1983 (see World Bank, 1986). These evaluations suggested that microeconomic (or 'structural') inefficiencies were commonly to blame for the failure of many adjusting countries to meet specific macroeconomic conditions or targets. In addition, the institutional and microeconomic aspects which had already been included in the design of early SALs – under the headings of 'effectiveness of resource use' and 'institution-building' – were found by the OED to be, on average, the most successful components of the programmes.

Combined with Anne Krueger's arrival as the Bank's new Chief Economist in 1982, and given her emphasis on the importance of a sound microeconomic environment for development, this perception led at that time to a substantial strengthening of the emphasis on the microeconomic efficiency aspects of structural adjustment.[7] Reflecting this tendency, the *WDR*s of the mid-1980s all stressed the importance of price, trade, tax and institutional reform in adjustment policies. These policies were now seen as crucial to induce a more efficient resource allocation, especially for investment.

The World Bank provided intellectual leadership during this period in applying basic microeconomic principles to reforms of the supply side of adjusting economies, with a focus on prices. These ideas were not new; indeed an emphasis on the importance of prices as signals and incentives, and on the efficiency of trade, had long lain at the heart of economics. They had been stressed by many prominent commentators, both in the profession and in the Bank. But in the mid-1980s, in the context of structural adjustment, the Bank became a prominent champion of many of the central tenets of the neoclassical resurgence. The *WDR*s of 1983 and 1985–7 all focus on microeconomic reforms to increase the efficiency of resource allocation (crucially, domestic investment) as a necessary element of structural adjustment. It was during the 1980s and on this topic that the Bank was seen to be leading the charge of the neoclassical resurgence.

In section 3 we reviewed basic trends in the SAL and SECAL programmes. We noted that SECALs replaced SALs in prominence and lending volume at around 1983–4. This can probably be seen as one reflection of the increased emphasis on the microeconomic aspects of reform. A focus on key individual sectors was viewed as an appropriate method by which to improve the efficient resource allocation across an economy.

Reforms can be classified into one of the following sectors: finance, public enterprise, industrial (including tradeables), agriculture or energy. Although there were stand-alone SECALs that dealt exclusively with one of these sectors, there were also microeconomic conditions as part of SALs that pertained to one or more of them. Tables 6A.5 and 6A.6 (p. 192) summarise the breakdown of sectoral conditions by region over the 1980s and early 1990s. In their regression-based analysis of the determinants of success in Bank-sponsored structural adjustment, Dollar and Svensson (1998) find that finance, trade and other sectoral conditions did indeed all have a marginally significant positive impact on the success of structural adjustment programmes.[8]

4.1 Review of SECAL projects, 1980–1993[9]

In both SALs and SECALs, agricultural policy conditions were the most important type of sectoral condition, making up 15 per cent and 30 per cent of total conditions, respectively. The prominence of the agriculture sector is not surprising since it is the largest sector in many developing countries. Under SAL projects, public enterprise conditions (14 per cent) and financial policy conditions (9 per cent) were also prevalent. Under SECALs, trade sector reforms (27 per cent) were emphasised.

The policies of *financial sector reform* affect interest rates, institutional regulation and the legal and institutional infrastructure. The most common reform was the liberalisation and rationalisation of interest rates to bring real domestic interest rates up to the international level. Regulatory reforms included: reducing high liquidity and reserve ratios, reducing directed and subsidised credit schemes and reducing explicit and implicit financial taxes. Among institutional reforms was increasing the efficiency of banking systems that were frequently highly concentrated and publicly owned. Another common institutional reform aimed at the development of capital markets, which included liberalising rules on foreign investment and banking as well as privatising financial institutions. The key lesson of financial sector reform is the need for a sufficiently long project life; these reforms can take several years to complete. Also important is the sequencing of the reforms, both within the financial sector and also relative to other reform projects. For instance, interest rate liberalisation will not have the desired effects without fiscal balance and stable inflation.

Public enterprise reform conditions were used more heavily at the end than at the beginning of the period 1980–93. Policies related both to those enterprises which would remain publicly owned as well as to those preparing and executing divestiture. The latter were given increased attention over time, as both the Bank and the client country governments acquired privatisation experience. Retained public enterprises underwent financial restructuring and organisational and management restructuring. Divestiture involves a complex process of restructuring, pricing and selling the enterprise. The success rates of public enterprise reforms, as judged by the OED, were approximately two-thirds, about on a par with the overall average for SAL and SECAL programmes. A key lesson was that public enterprise reform is an area where willingness and ability of the borrower government to implement the reforms is of paramount importance.

Industrial sector reform took place mainly in middle-income countries, where there was already a substantial industrial sector in place. These reforms most commonly included trade policy reforms, and less frequently reforms of domestic industry and constraints on direct foreign investment. The reforms were intended to help the borrower country reallocate resources towards those industrial sectors where they had a comparative advantage. The short-run impacts of industrial sector reform did at times include a decline in investment and slower growth, owing to frictions inherent in factor switching into the reforming sector. Less than one-quarter of countries implementing industrial sector projects were judged as unsuccessful by the OED, and an important determinant of successful reform seemed to have been the devaluation of the effective exchange rate. A major lesson of industrial sector reform is, once again, that sequencing of adjustment programmes should be carefully considered.

Agricultural sector reforms, as noted above, accounted for a significant share of total conditions. There were 12 agricultural SECALs over the period 1980–92. One of the difficulties faced in the design and implementation of agricultural reforms is that, because agriculture is such a large portion of the economy, these SECALs have sometimes served as surrogate SALs. In other words, macroeconomic reforms have been lumped in with the sectoral reforms. Half of the agriculture SECALs were successful by the OED rating, which is lower than the average for all SECALs. The lessons from agricultural reform therefore have a slightly more negative tone than those of the other sectors. Agricultural reforms may have been slowed by a lack of understanding of the sector prior to implementation. Because agricultural SECALs have included macroeconomic reforms that might have been part of a separate SAL, there may also have been less focus on the specific agricultural elements of programme design and implementation. Finally, the reforms proposed suffered from insufficient political feasibility, echoing one of the main findings in Dollar and Svensson (1998).

The *energy sector* was not a main focus of sectoral reform. Energy-related policies were part of adjustment in 13 countries and one-third of the programmes. Most of these reforms were a response to high oil prices and attempted to increase efficiency of the sector and encourage sustainable development. In contrast to agricultural reforms, energy sector reforms suffered from being, if anything, not comprehensive enough. Part of this conservatism may have been due to the fact that the energy sector tends to be government-owned. All of the energy sector reforms involved liberalising input and output pricing. Seven of the countries' reforms included improvements in the market environment such as deregulation, elimination of discrimination in the trade regime and clarification of the government's role as regulator and enterprise owner (given the obvious potential conflict of interest). The success of these reforms was mixed. At programme end, energy prices were generally still regulated by the borrower governments, with few exceptions. There were few significant changes in institutions regulating and owning the energy enterprises, leaving the borrower countries vulnerable to possible future energy price shocks.

In summary, one might say that there were three main lessons from the SECAL projects of 1980–93. The first lesson is what is referred to as a need for 'borrower ownership'. This recommendation comes from two pieces of evidence. One is the collection of evidence which derives from the experiences of implementing the various lending programmes (Jayarajah and Branson, 1995; Jayarajah, Branson and Sen, 1996). The other is the main result of Dollar and Svensson 1998, which finds borrower ability and willingness to implement (proxied for by several political economy variables) as the most important determinant of the success or failure of structural adjustment. Similar findings for the general effectiveness of aid on growth and poverty reduction are echoed on Burnside and Dollar (chapter 8 in this volume).

The second lesson is the need for an adequate time horizon in the lending programmes. Implementing projects to develop the financial sector or to privatise public sector firms are complicated and lengthy tasks. Quick-disbursement loans and time horizons of one or two years were not sufficient to implement these reforms properly.

The third lesson is that sectoral reforms do not exist in a vacuum. Evaluation reports often underlined the need for truly systemic reforms, addressing both macroeconomic stability and sector-specific microeconomic policies. Sequencing and policy coordination is crucial: on the whole, stabilisation policies such as fiscal contraction and real devaluations, aimed at establishing price stability and stopping the drain in foreign exchange reserves, must precede other reforms – or, at least, be achieved as the longer-term structural reforms begin. Conversely, the sustainability of these macro achievements – and the efficiency of the economy in terms of its ability to grow sustainably and reduce poverty – depend on the elimination of distortions, and on the range of sectoral reforms discussed above. Finally, both for its own sake and given the recurrent theme of the need for political support for reforms, attention to the impact of reforms on living standards across the income distribution is also paramount. We now turn to this subject.

5 Adjustment and equity

5.1 Conceptual links

The change in the value of the effective exchange rate; the reduction in aggregate demand as a result of expenditure reduction; and the system-wide reforms implemented under structural adjustment must – and indeed some are explicitly designed to – affect the rewards to factors in different sectors and activities in the economy. Government expenditure cuts and changes in its overall composition must also affect secondary incomes (e.g. transfers) and entitlements. In the presence of any price rigidities – as suggested in section 2 – the expenditure reduction policies can also affect the level of employment, both formal and informal. These and other effects virtually guarantee that income distribution is affected by structural adjustment.

However, adjustment is a dynamic process and, in assessing the various impacts that its component policies have on living standards, it is important to distinguish between those which are short-run, and those which are persistent. In other words, those which are attributes of a transitional period only – but which may nevertheless be important – and those which will persist into the new 'steady state'. In this regard, we note, once again, that adjustment programmes should be designed to restore internal and external equilibria, thereby returning the economy to some sustainable long-run growth path.

The widespread consensus is, of course, that economic growth is poverty-reducing (see, for example, Deininger and Squire, 1996; Ravallion and Chen, 1997). This is in fact true by definition if growth is distribution-neutral and, even though adjustment does have distributional consequences in the short and possibly even in the long run, the overwhelming evidence is that growth effects tend to outweigh increases in inequality *in the long run*. It follows that adjustment can hurt the poor in three ways: (1) it fails to restore the economy to a sustainable growth path; (2) it does eventually lead to increased growth, but with such large increases in the accompanying steady-state inequality that although absolute poverty may in due course decline, it is plausible that some measure of relative poverty (e.g. 0.4 times the median) potentially increases in the new steady state; or (3) it succeeds in lowering poverty in the long run, through faster growth, but it maps a transitional path characterised by a reduction in living standards and increases in poverty.

On the whole, case (1) is treated as an adjustment failure. It is not that adjustment hurt the poor, but rather that the economy failed to adjust. There are a number of examples of this case such as Jamaica (1982–5) and Uganda (1982–6). While this case consists of perhaps the most serious instances of all, they are not particularly interesting for understanding the effects of adjustment on the poor. There was no adjustment.

Case (2) is a theoretical possibility, but has not really been observed in practice. The mechanism through which it works, however, has been observed in practice, and is worthy of consideration. It is element (v) in our list of channels of impact below (see Ferreira, 1995a, for a model of distributional dynamics capable of generating this perverse result). Case (3) is the standard case one considers. Below, we list five interrelated – but conceptually distinct – channels through which these effects take place. In principle, channels (I)–(IV) refer to transitional mechanisms. Channel (v) relates to case (2) above.

(i) *Relative price effects*: The following policies are likely directly or indirectly to alter relative goods and services prices, thus changing consumption patterns, incentives for production and real incomes: changes in the real exchange rate (normally devaluations); trade reforms, by abolishing quotas, lowering tariffs, creating or altering export subsidies, and so on; price reforms, by raising public sector prices and often farmgate prices paid to agricultural producers; and tax reforms, in particular by redesigning subsidies and indirect taxes. Factor prices are considered separately below.

(ii) *Labour market effects*: These are impacts upon a crucial set of factor prices, the wage rates in different sectors or for different types of labour (i.e. formal or informal, skilled or unskilled), as well as any effects on the level of employment itself. The policies which affect it most directly are expenditure reduction, in all its varieties, by affecting the aggregate level of activity and the demand for labour. However, if factor mobility is not perfect, or if price rigidities exist, as shown in figure 6.1, expenditure- switching policies will also affect employment levels. Naturally, trade policies also affect wage rates, through Stolper–Samuelson-type effects. From the supply side, privatisation and labour market reforms are also likely to affect wages and employment.

(iii) *Asset prices and capital gains and losses*: Bourguignon, Branson and de Melo (1992) noted that an important channel for impact of structural adjustment upon the distribution of wealth is through changes in asset prices. Portfolio shifts in response to expected asset price changes can generate capital gains and losses which redistribute wealth. The authors suggest shifts toward foreign currency-denominated assets (e.g. capital flight) as one example. Another is the differentiated ability to hedge against inflation. If there are barriers to enter the markets for some interest-bearing assets, so that the poor have less ability to protect their wealth against the inflation tax, inflation may have a strong redistributive impact. That becomes important when choosing between different adjustment packages that yield different rates of inflation (see table 4 in Bourguignon, Branson and de Melo, 1992: 24). Evidence for Brazil, presented by Ferreira and Litchfield (1996), illustrates the importance of this effect.

(iv) Public expenditure effects on entitlements: Expenditure reduction policies have microeconomic effects, as well as contractionary macroeconomic consequences. Governments do not normally cut all elements of their expenditure equiproportionately, and different programmes benefit different groups or classes. Hence, cuts in food subsidies or basic health care are likely to affect the poor more heavily than the rich. The difference between the former and the latter, when public health care is provided free of charge and seen as a highly inferior good, is that the cut in subsidies is captured as a price effect, under (i) above. But the latter, although it will surely affect welfare, by increasing queues, lowering the standard of service – and, indeed, its value to the consumer – will not be captured by price changes.

Some expenditure cuts, particularly in the areas of education, health services and infrastructure (irrigation schemes, rural roads, etc.), affect the level and distribution of welfare in ways which are not captured by the conventional budget constraint, in terms of prices or income changes. Much of the emphasis on the effects of public expenditure cuts on the welfare of the poor, such as in Drèze and Sen (1989) and Cornia and Stewart (1990), is of this type, and has to be estimated or measured beyond the effects of relative price changes, asset price changes, or labour market effects.

(v) *Long-term effects on the accumulation of capital*: It has been noted that the decline in the investment/GNP ratio during adjustment may have detrimental effects on the intertemporal distribution of income, by lowering the growth rate (see, for example, Demery and Addison, 1987). But another long-term impact is that on the future (*intra*-temporal, cross-section) distributions of income and assets, as a result of different rates of capital accumulation, both physical and human. It has long been widely accepted that human capital, or skills, should be seen as an important input and determinant of growth (see Lucas, 1988; Uzawa, 1988). There is also evidence of declines in government expenditures on health and education during adjustment, with a measurable impact on enrolment rates and health standards.

If, as suggested above, publicly provided health and education services are inferior goods, then these cuts are likely to affect rates of human capital accumulation among the poor especially severely. Similarly, if capital market imperfections preclude the access of the poor to some assets, then the rates of physical capital accumulation will also differ. This is an effect separate from that on their current welfare, under (iv), as it will lower their future wealth and the return on their human assets in the future. If the poor are more affected than other social groups, this may have an inequality augmenting effect over time. Ferreira (1995b) explores a possible setting in which the combination of effects (iv) and (v) above may lead to both a reduction in the economy's overall growth rate and to an increase in income, wealth and consumption dispersion within the society.

5.2 The evidence, and why there is relatively little of it

Despite the various mechanisms described above, when these programmes were first designed as SALs by the World Bank in 1980, little
attention was paid to distributional impacts. This neglect was largely due
to informational deficiencies. As discussed in Bourguignon, de Melo and
Morrisson (1991), neither the analytic tools nor an understanding of how
adjustment programmes would impact income distribution were well
developed. Furthermore, the policies themselves were not aimed specifically at distributional issues. More recently, adjustment policies have
been designed with heightened awareness about the effects on income
inequality (see Ferreira, 1996).

The early view was that, provided external finance was available to
soften the expenditure reduction and spread it over time, adjustment
could be expected to reduce poverty over the medium to long term.
This was because it intended to remove distortions that impeded faster
growth, and because there was a general perception that poor people
produced mostly tradeables (as in agriculture), and would hence benefit
from an increase in their relative prices.

Concern with negative distributional impacts grew as evidence from
countries undergoing adjustment became more plentiful. The works of
Addison and Demery (1985), Cornia, Jolly and Stewart (1987) and
Demery and Addison (1987) contributed greatly to raising the profile
of distributional issues in connection with adjustment programmes in
the academic sphere. After *Adjustment with a Human Face* (Cornia,
Jolly and Stewart, 1987), in particular, there was a considerable increase
in the attention paid to these issues, both at the Bank and elsewhere.
Heller *et al.* (1988), Cornia and Stewart (1990), Kanbur (1990), World
Bank (1990) and others provide early examples.

The *WDR 1990* on poverty marked a turning point in the Bank's
attention to poverty, both in general and as part of its structural adjustment lending. The focus on poverty did not come about overnight, but by
1990 the experience of SALs and SECALs in the 1980s had made it clear
that adjustment programmes could have significant negative short-run
effects on both poverty and income inequality in the adjusting countries.
Two important tasks of the 1990s have been to assemble further empirical
evidence on the impact of adjustment on poverty, and to understand the
mechanisms through which adjustment may affect different subgroups of
the poor differently.

Let us consider each of the three cases outlined above. Case (1) referred
to general adjustment failures. As we remarked in the previous subsec-

Table 6.7 *Average economic indicators of countries,*[a] *grouped according to whether OED performance rating is above or below the average success rate*

Average countries with greater/less than average rate of SAL and SECAL success

	Greater than	Less than	T-test of difference[b]
Change in GNP growth (1985–5) (per cent)	−0.09	−0.57	1.13 (44)
GNP *per capita* US$ (1995)	1,633.7	1,431.6	0.35 (50)
Gross domestic investment as per cent of GDP (1995)	21.44	17.95	1.06 (34)
Government current deficit/surplus as per cent of GDP (1995)	2.91	−1.29	1.34 (11)
Average per cent annual inflation (GDP deflator) (1985–95)	55.59	75.90	−0.36 (44)
Resource balance, per cent of GDP (1995)	−6.11	−5.05	−0.38 (30)
Gross international reserves (months of import coverage) (1995)	3.35	3.76	−0.49 (31)
Interest rate spread over LIBOR (per cent) (1996) (per cent)	18.55	23.04	−0.63 (32)
Poverty: per cent of people living on less than $1 a day (PPP) (1981–95)	24.10	35.47	−0.96 (27)
Life expectancy at birth (years) (1995)	60.6	57.5	0.51 (28)

Notes:
[a]Countries groups are greater/less than average success rates of each group. Average success rate is 62.8 per cent according to OED rating.
[b]Degrees of freedom in parentheses; all tests fail to reject the null hypothesis that the averages of the two groups are equal.
Sources: Jayarajah and Branson (1995); Jayarajah, Branson and Sen (1996); indicators from *WDR 1997* and World Bank (1998b).

tion, this is not entirely germane to this analysis, as it refers to the effects of the *absence* of adjustment, rather than of adjustment itself. Yet, there is some disturbing evidence that, if one defines completed adjustment in terms of having returned to satisfactory economic performance after a reasonable period of time, this case may actually be quite pervasive.

Consider the findings reported in table 6.7, constructed from data in Jayarajah and Branson (1995) and Jayarajah, Branson and Sen (1996). This table compares the average value of a number of economic performance indicators – from inflation rates to poverty ratios – for above-average and below-average adjusters (as measured by their OED ratings), in the mid-1990s (or roughly a decade after adjustment was taking place). While point estimates are generally better for the above-average performers, all differences across the two groups conspicuously fail to be statistically significant. This suggests that it is not statistically clear that having a better-than-average outcome rating for one's structural adjustment programme actually leads to sustained improvements in economic performance, bringing the usefulness of the OED rating as an indicator of success into question.

Case (2), as we noted earlier, seems to be more of a theoretical curiosity – albeit one which deserves pause for thought – than an empirical occurrence. Turning then to the short-run impact on the poor (case 3) once adjustment does take place, we note first that empirical assessments of the impact of adjustment on poverty or inequality (as indeed on anything else) are plagued by the essentially insurmountable 'counterfactual problem'. When a researcher concludes that adjustment led to greater poverty, does she mean greater than in what circumstances? Greater than prior to adjustment? But adjustment came about, as we have discussed, exactly because the situation prior to it was somehow unsustainable. The conceptually correct comparison is with the path the economy would have followed in the absence of the policies associated with the structural adjustment package being evaluated. This, however, is definitionally unobserved, and cannot be measured. The first-best option of measurement is not available.

Several second- (or third-) best options present themselves. One is to run counterfactual simulations to estimate what would have happened under different adjustment policies or no adjustment. This was done by Bourguignon, de Melo and Morrisson (1991) and Dorosh and Sahn (1993), for example. But as these authors themselves acknowledge, these counterfactual simulations are based on different computable general equilibrium (CGE) models, which have generally not been found to be particularly robust to small changes in the assumed functional forms or parameter values.

A second option is merely to look at whether poverty and inequality (however they are measured) improved or not over the period for a sample of adjusting countries. This was done for six African countries by Demery and Squire (1996). This alternative takes the counterfactual to be the situation prior to adjustment, and hence suffers from the caveat discussed above. In particular, given that that situation is likely to have been unsustainable, this method is likely to underestimate any benefits from the adjustment process.

A third option is to compare the changes in equity of a sample of adjusting countries with a sample of non-adjusting countries. An example of this type of analysis is Jayarajah, Branson and Sen (1996). This option implicitly assumes that differences across countries cancel out by taking a

Table 6.8 *Povery and inequality in rural Tanzania, 1983 and 1991*

Indicator			1983	1991
Poverty	Head-count	Poor ($1PPP per day)	0.646	0.505
		Hard core poor ($0.75 per day)	0.533	0.405
	Normalised poverty deficit	Poor ($1PPP per day)	0.358	0.342
		Hard core poor ($0.75 per cay)	0.273	0.272
Inequality	Gini (all population)		0.53	0.75
	Gini (positive income only)		0.52	0.72
	Theil		0.39	0.73
	Coefficient of variation		1.19	2.99

Source: Ferreira (1996).

sample but have the merit that only a simple calculation is necessary and that actual experiences rather than simulated ones are being compared.

Having acknowledged the shortcomings of these three options, the following stylised facts have been observed, and the details are documented in the references we cite. Poverty as measured by the head-count ratio, or indeed by its 'siblings' in the Foster–Greer–Thorbecke class, the poverty deficit and FGT(2), improved for most Asian countries during the 1980s, and indeed up until the mid-1990s, prior to the onset of the currency crises (Ahuja *et al.*, 1997). Experiences are considerably more mixed in Latin America (Lustig, 1995; Morley, 1995; Psacharopoulos *et al.*, 1997) and Africa (Husain and Faruqee, 1994; Demery and Squire, 1996). Even despite the counterfactual problem, and the caveats noted above about the likelihood that poverty might well have increased (or increased by more) in the absence of adjustment policies, these trends still suggest a potential neglect of poor subgroups of the population during adjustment (Demery and Squire, 1996; Jayarajah, Branson and Sen, 1996). Simulation analyses, on the other hand, generally find that adjustment is better than no adjustment and that more adjustment (e.g. devaluation and fiscal balance rather than just one of them) is better than less.[10]

Two examples for which at least two survey points are available, before and after the adjustment, are consistent with the facts outlined above. In the case of rural Tanzania, where adjustment policies were implemented with some success, poverty decreased but inequality rose between 1983 and 1991. In Brazil, during the 1980s, when adjustment policies repeatedly failed to take hold, both poverty and inequality increased between 1981 and 1990.[11] Tables 6.8 and 6.9 briefly summarise these results.

Table 6.9 *Povery and inequality in Brazil, 1981–1990*

Indicator		1981	1985	1990
Poverty	Head-count	0.445	0.457	0.450
	Normalised poverty deficit	0.187	0.195	0.199
	Foster–Greer–Thorbecke index ($a = 2$)	0.104	0.109	0.199
	Gini	0.574	0.589	0.606
	Theil	0.647	0.648	0.705
	Coefficient of variation	1.635	1.680	2.009

Source: Ferreira and Litchfield (1996).

There is also the highly policy-relevant point that distinct subgroups of the poor are impacted differently by adjustment. Contrasts include:

• the current poor and the future poor
• the urban poor and the rural poor (or agricultural net consumers and net producers)
• (poor) net sellers of tradeables and poor net sellers of non-tradeables
• different ethnic groups.

General prescriptions voiced in the literature regarding the treatments of these different subgroups are twofold. The first is that adjustment programmes must include the entire current population in productive economic activity. For example, agricultural sector reform, which is intended to reach the rural poor, should account for the effects on the urban poor of, say, price liberalisation. The second is that, although the future poor will presumably benefit from adjustment via growth, current *per capita* levels of social services and transfers should be maintained. This maintenance, coupled with increased efficiency and targeting in spending, can be consistent with a reduced fiscal deficit and will alleviate the poverty of the current poor.

In general, of course, adjustment policies are likely to give rise to winners and losers. When factor and goods prices are changing, and taxes and expenditures are being redesigned, the case of the pure Pareto-improving reform is the exception, rather than the rule. The distributional trade-offs to which this gives rise should not be neglected in designing even the essence of the programmes, for at least two reasons. The first is that the ultimate aim of the reforms must be, of course, to improve living standards, and that medium-run losses are important to people. The second is that, no matter how often the World Bank and other economists repeat that all will be well in the long run, once growth has made everyone better off, the short- and medium-run distributional impacts are certain to affect the political environment within which reform takes place. And, as Dollar and Svensson (1998) have shown, this may in turn make the difference between adjusting and failing to adjust altogether.

6 Conclusions

Structural adjustment does not, on balance, appear to have contributed in a statistically significant manner to the medium-term economic performance of most adjusting countries. Part of this failure to make a large impact may be attributable to the fact that the original design of adjustment loans did not focus enough on the microeconomic, supply-side reforms. Initial World Bank loan designs also neglected the impact of various policy components on the poor, particularly in the short run. However, the Bank's view of the purpose and composition of adjustment lending did change over the decade, to take increased account of both efficiency and equity considerations. While the Bank can reasonably claim to have exercised an important leadership role in emphasising the importance and supporting the design and implementation of microeconomic efficiency reforms as an integral part of adjustment programmes, it remains the case that the contribution of the lending programmes themselves to adjustment policy success seems to have been somewhat marginal. Recent empirical analysis suggests that the political economic conditions in the borrower country seem, instead, to have been the most important factor in determining the policy outcome. (Dollar and Svensson, 1998; Burnside and Dollar, 1999).

Our main findings are: (1) that individual policies associated with stabilisation and structural adjustment are – in themselves – likely to achieve their desired objectives (table 6.4); but (2) that improvements in overall economic performance (in the medium term) are statistically insignificantly related to a measure of successful implementation of the structural adjustment programmes financed (and often designed) by the World Bank during the 1980s (table 6.7); (3) that the World Bank's contribution to this process (through lending, preparation and supervision) also appears to have been of secondary importance (table 6.6); and (4) that the original design of most programmes paid insufficient attention to the short- and medium-term impacts on the poor.

Taken together, the evidence on which we draw suggests that there is nothing wrong with individual policies (such as fiscal contraction, devaluation, privatisation or institutional reform) well prescribed. Indeed, if a country finds itself in a predicament of the sort roughly stylised by figure 6.1, there is little option but to undertake them. There are two basic reasons for the poor historical record of structural adjustment which we have presented. First, the combination of different policies – macroeconomic, microeconomic and institutional in nature – raises complex issues of timing and sequencing, to which adequate attention was seldom paid. The same is likely to be true of the reforms now being discussed with various Asian countries, Russia and Brazil. In all of these countries, current account deficits led to large depreciations and required renewed fiscal efforts. In all, albeit to different degrees, these are to be accompanied by a strengthening of financial regulation, reforms of the labour market and of the pension system, and continued privatisation and enterprise reform. Once again, it would be surprising if the order and timing of these were not of the essence.

Second, the successful implementation of large policy packages seems to be determined largely by the willingness and ability of the national government to see them through. Governmental willingness and ability, in turn, depend partly on technical and administrative capacity, but the evidence suggests that the binding constraint is much more often nature of a country's political economy. This, in turn, needs to inform the optimal feasible design of the timing and sequence of reforms. Once again, the crises of the 1990s provide policy-makers with renewed opportunities to show that they have learned this lesson. What the Indonesian, Russian and Brazilian governments can achieve, in terms (say) of fiscal effort, depends crucially on the evolution of the political climate as the crisis and adjustment unfold. This, in turn, is influenced by the rate of unemployment, by changes in poverty, by the inflation rate, etc.

There is no universal blueprint to navigate these very diverse political and economic rapids. The 1980s taught us that (1) paying greater attention to timing and sequencing of reform policies; (2) protecting the welfare of the poor during adjustment; and (3) creating and maintaining political support for reforms are all crucial to improve the odds of a successful adjustment to a crisis. And that if a government is unable or unwilling to do these three things, lending to it – with any amount of associated conditionality – is unlikely to help much.

APPENDIX

Table 6A.1 *SAL and SECAL programmes, percentages of total, 1980–1990*

(Constant US$ million)		Africa (per cent)	Asia (per cent)	EMENA (per cent)	LAC (per cent)	Total (per cent)
Board date	1980	20.6	41.7	31.4	6.3	100.0
	1981	26.8	36.1	31.0	6.1	100.0
	1982	20.5	40.7	31.0	7.8	100.0
	1983	24.5	23.2	17.2	35.2	100.0
	1984	18.0	27.3	44.9	9.8	100.0
	1985	22.1	9.7	32.7	35.5	100.0
	1986	28.9	7.6	8.5	55.0	100.0
	1987	17.6	23.1	8.1	51.2	100.0
	1988	25.5	29.8	20.9	23.8	100.0
	1989	34.5	33.6	0.0	31.9	100.0
	1990	0.0	40.0	32.0	28.0	100.0
	Total	**23.0**	**23.8**	**18.5**	**34.7**	100.0

Table 6A.2 *Macroeconomic conditions of SAL and SECAL programmes, 1980–1992*

	Average number of conditions per operation: macro, fiscal and total					
	SAL			SECAL		
Region	Macro/fiscal	Per cent of total	Total	Macro/fiscal	Per cent of total	Total
Africa	13	30.2	43	5	23.8	21
Asia	8	32.0	25	8	28.6	28
EMENA	13	28.9	45	4	9.3	43
LAC	11	21.2	52	2	11.1	18
Total	**45**	**27.3**	**165**	**19**	**17.3**	**110**

Source: Jayarajah and Branson (1995).

NOTES

We are grateful to Chris Gilbert and Michael Walton for their very helpful comments. The usual disclaimer applies, and the views expressed are solely those of the authors. They do not represent those of the World Bank, its Executive Directors or the countries they represent.

1 The two main broad categories of lending instruments through which the Bank sought to support adjustment efforts by its clients were Structural Adjustment Loans (SALs) and Sectoral Adjustment Loans (SECALs). Both types are discussed in greater detail below.
2 This section draws heavily on Ferreira (1992) and Stern and Ferreira (1997).
3 By a 'distorted' economy, we simply mean one where the ruling price vector deviates from the shadow price vector (see Ahmad and Stern, 1989).

Table 6A.3 *OED SAL and SECAL rating results, per year, 1980–1990*

Board date	s	Per cent of total	u	Per cent of total	Total
1980	8	80	2	20	10
1981	6	67	3	33	9
1982	4	57	3	43	7
1983	13	59	9	41	22
1984	4	40	6	60	10
1985	10	71	4	29	14
1986	10	40	15	60	25
1987	20	77	6	23	26
1988	7	70	3	30	10
1089	6	75	2	25	8
1990	3	75	1	25	4
Total	**91**	**63**	**54**	**37**	**145**

Note: s = successful, u = unsuccessful; one project was not rated.
Sources: Jayarajah and Branson (1995); Jayarajah, Branson and Sen (1996); authors' calculations.

Table 6A.4 *SAL and SECAL OED ratings, overall and in combinations, 1980–1993*

Programme type	s	Per cent of total	u	Per cent of total	Total
SAL total	37	63	22	37	59
SECAL total	54	63	32	37	86
Grand total	91	63	54	37	145
SECAL without SAL	32	58	23	42	55
SAL during/after	16	76	5	24	21
SAL before	6	60	4	40	10
SECAL total	**54**	**63**	**32**	**37**	**86**

Note: s = successful, u = unsuccessful; one project was not rated.
Sources: Jayarajah and Branson (1995); Jayarajah, Branson and Sen (1996); authors' calculations.

4 Had the terms of trade shock been short-lived, and reversed rather than exacerbated by the second oil price shock of 1979, this policy might have been
successful. In the event, it left countries highly vulnerable to the second oil
shock and the subsequent deterioration in international financial conditions.
5 Although Wriston's remark is strictly correct, in the sense that sovereign
immunity prevents the cross-border seizure of assets, it does neglect the fact
that (most) sovereign borrowers cannot issue the currencies in which their
debts are denominated. The economics of sovereign borrowing has come a
long way since the 1970s. See Eaton and Gersovitz (1981) on the willingness-
to-pay approach, and Armendariz de Aghion and Ferreira (1995) on the
World Bank and the debt crisis.
6 The data presented in this section comes from Jayarajah and Branson (1995)
and Jayarajah, Branson and Sen (1996). To the extent possible, we have
matched our classification of programmes by region and by type (SAL and

Table 6A.5 *SAL sectoral conditions, by sector, 1980–1992*

Total SAL conditions	Africa (per cent)	Asia (per cent)	EMENA (per cent)	LAC (per cent)	Total (per cent)
Financial policy	6.5	8.6	13.2	15.9	9.1
Public enterprise	19.1	5.2	9.1	10.3	14.0
Public institutions	9.6	5.2	2.2	2.6	6.8
Industrial policy	2.9	8.3	0.9	2.1	3.4
Energy policy	1.1	4.0	16.1	5.6	4.6
Agricultural policy	17.2	13.9	10.7	11.2	14.8
Total conditions	**1,022**	**324**	**317**	**233**	**1,896**

Source: Jayarajah and Branson (1995), from ALCID database.

Table 6A.6 *SECAL sectoral conditions, by sector, 1980–1992*

Total SECAL	Africa (per cent)	Asia (per cent)	EMENA (per cent)	LAC (per cent)	Total (per cent)
Financial policy	7.8	11.0	6.9	20.4	10.9
Trade policy	16.3	32.9	16.1	54.6	27.0
Industrial policy	6.6	9.8	0.5	0.7	3.0
Agricultural policy	27.7	7.3	50.5	9.2	30.3
Public enterprise	10.8	2.4	13.2	1.8	5.0
Public institution	4.8	4.9	13.6	2.5	7.6
Energy policy	1.2	1.2	0.0	1.4	0.8
Total conditions	**322**	**82**	**434**	**284**	**1,132**

Source: Jayarajah and Branson (1995), from ALCID database.

SECAL) with those of the above studies, although slight differences persist. The conclusions reached in this chapter are robust to those small discrepancies.

7 Krueger's emphasis on reducing the distortions associated with trade quotas, tariffs, other taxes and subsidies and a myriad of regulatory and institutional features was summarised within the Bank through the slogan 'getting prices right', which quickly became a new institutional mantra.

8 However, this statistical significance disappears when instruments for Bank supervision and preparation are introduced.

9 This subsection draws heavily on Jayarajah and Branson (1995).

10 See, for example, Bourguignon, de Melo and Morrisson (1991); Fox and Morley (1991); Dorosh and Sahn (1993); and Jayarajah, Branson and Sen (1996).

11 For more details on these cases, including how poverty lines were constructed and poverty and inequality measured, see Ferreira (1996); and Ferreira and Litchfield (1996).

REFERENCES

Addison, T. and L. Demery (1985). 'Macro-economic Stabilisation, Income Distribution and Poverty: A Preliminary Survey', *ODI Working Paper*, **15**, London: Overseas Development Institute

Ahmad, E. and N. Stern (1989). 'Taxation for Developing Countries', chapter 20 in H. Chenery and T.N. Srinivasan (eds.), *Handbook of Development Economics, II*, Amsterdam: Elsevier Science

Ahuja, V., B. Bidani, F. Ferreira and M. Walton (1997). *Everyone's Miracle? Revisiting Poverty and Inequality in East Asia*, Washington, DC: World Bank

Armendariz de Aghion, B. and F.H.G. Ferreira (1995). 'The World Bank and the Analysis of the International Debt Crisis', chapter 13 in J. Harriss, J. Hunter and C. Lewis (eds.), *The New Institutional Economics and Third World Development*, London: Routledge

Bourguignon, F., W. Branson and J. de Melo (1992). 'Adjustment and Income Distribution: A Micro–Macro Model for Counterfactual Analysis', *Journal of Development Economics*, **38**: 17–39

Bourguignon, F., J. de Melo and C. Morrisson (1991). 'Poverty and Income Distribution during Adjustment: Issues and Evidence from the OECD Project', *World Development*, **19**: 1485–1508

Bruno, M. and J. Sachs (1985). *The Economics of Worldwide Stagflation*, Oxford: Basil Blackwell

Burnside, C. and D. Dollar (1999). 'Aid, Growth, the Incentive Regime and Poverty Reduction', chapter 8 in this volume

Cornia, G.A. and F. Stewart (1990). 'The Fiscal System, Adjustment and the Poor,' *Innocenti Occasional Paper*, **11**, Florence: UNICEF

Cornia, G.A., R. Jolly and F. Stewart (1987). *Adjustment with a Human Face*, Oxford: Clarendon Press

Deininger, K and L. Squire (1996). 'A New Data Set Measuring Income Inequality', *World Bank Economic Review*, **10**: 565–91

Demery L. and T. Addison (1987). 'The Alleviation of Poverty under Structural Adjustment', Washington, DC: World Bank

Demery, L. and L. Squire (1996). 'Macroeconomic Adjustment and Poverty in Africa: An Emerging Picture', *World Bank Research Observer*, **11**, February

Dollar, D. and J. Svensson (1998). 'What Explains the Success or Failure of Structural Adjustment Programs?', *World Bank PRWP*, **1938**

Dornbusch, R. and S. Fischer (1987). 'International Capital Flows and the World Debt Problem', chapter 6 in A. Razin and E. Sadka (eds.), *Economic Policy in Theory and Practice*, London: Macmillan

Dorosh, P.A. and D.E. Sahn (1993). 'A General Equilibrium Analysis of the Effect of Macroeconomic Adjustment on Poverty in Africa', *Cornell Food and Nutrition Policy Program Working Paper*, **39**

Drèze, J. and A. Sen (1989). *Hunger and Public Action*, Oxford: Clarendon Press

Eaton, J. and M. Gersovitz (1981). 'Debt with Potential Repudiation: Theoretical and Empirical Analysis', *Review of Economic Studies*, **48**: 289–309

Economic Report of the President (1997). Washington, DC: United States Government Printing Office

Ferreira, F.H.G. (1992). 'The World Bank and the Study of Stabilisation and Structural Adjustment in LDCs', *STICERD Development Economics Research Programme Working Paper*, **41**
　　(1995a). 'Structural Adjustment, Income Distribution and the Role of Government: Theory, and Evidence from Brazil', PhD dissertation, LSE
　　(1995b). 'Roads to Equality: Wealth Distribution Dynamics with Public–Private Capital Complementarity', *LSE–STICERD Discussion Paper*, **TE/95/286**

Ferreira, F.H.G. and J.A. Litchfield (1996). 'Growing Apart: Inequality and Poverty Trends in Brazil in the 1980s', *STICERDDARP Discussion Paper*, **23**
　　(1999). 'Educacion o Inflacion? Explicando la Desigualdad en Brasil en la Decada de los Ochenta', chapter 4 in C. Cardenas and N. Lustig (eds.), *Pobreza y Desigualdad en America Latina*, Bogota: Tercer Mundo Editores

Ferreira, M. L. (1996). 'Poverty and Inequality during Structural Adjustment in Rural Tanzania', *World Bank PRWP Working Paper*, **1641**

Fox, M. L. and S. Morley (1991). 'Who Paid the Bill? Adjustment and Poverty in Brazil, 1980–95', *Development Economics World Bank Working Paper*, **648**

Heller, P., A. Bovenberg, T. Catsambas, K. Chu and P. Shome (1988). 'The Implications of Fund-supported Adjustment Programs for Poverty: Experiences in Selected Countries', *Occasional Paper*, **58**, Washington, DC: IMF

Husain, I. and R. Faruqee (1994). *Adjustment in Africa: Lessons from Country Case Studies*, Washington, DC: World Bank

IMF (1981). *International Financial Statistics Yearbook*, Washington, DC: IMF
　　(1983). *Balance of Payments Statistics Yearbook*, **34**, Washington, DC: IMF
　　(1985). *International Financial Statistics*, December, Washington, DC: IMF

Jayarajah, C. and W. Branson (1995). *Structural and Sectoral Adjustment: World Bank Experience, 1980–92*, A World Bank Operations Evaluation Study, Washington, DC: World Bank

Jayarajah, C., W. Branson and B. Sen (1996). *Social Dimensions of Adjustment: World Bank Experience, 1980–93*, A World Bank Operations Evaluation Study, Washington, DC: World Bank

Kanbur, R. (1990). 'Poverty and the Social Dimensions of Structural Adjustment in Côte d'Ivoire', *World Bank SDA Working Paper*, **2**, Washington,DC: World Bank

Little, I.M.D. (1982). *Economic Development: Theory, Policy and International Relations,* New York: Basic Books

Lucas, R. (1988). 'On the Mechanics of Economic Development', *Journal of Monetary Economics*, **22**: 3–42

Lustig, N. (ed.) (1995). *Coping with Austerity: Poverty and Inequality in Latin America,* Washington, DC: Brookings Institution

Morley, S. (1995). *Poverty and Inequality in Latin America: The Impact of Adjustment and Recovery in the 1980s,* Baltimore: Johns Hopkins University Press

Psacharopoulos, G., S. Morley, A. Fiszbein, H. Lee and B. Wood (1997). 'Poverty and Income Distribution in Latin America: The Story of the 1980s', *World Bank Technical Paper,* **351**

Ravallion, M. and S. Chen (1997). 'What Can New Survey Data Tell Us about Recent Changes in Distribution and Poverty?', *World Bank Economic Review,* **11**: 357–82

Sachs, J. (ed.) (1989). *Developing Country Debt and the World Economy,* Chicago: The University of Chicago Press

Stern, N. and F.H.G. Ferreira (1997). 'The World Bank as "Intellectual Actor"', in D. Kapur, J.P. Lewis and R. Webb, *The World Bank: Its First Half Century, 2: Perspectives,* Washington, DC: Brookings Institution: 523–610

Summers, R. and A. Heston (1988). 'A New Set of International Comparisons of Real Product and Price Levels: Estimates for 130 Countries, 1950–1985', *Review of Income and Wealth,* **34**: 1–25

Uzawa, H. (1988). 'Optimal Technical Change in an Aggregative Model of Economic Growth', in *Preference, Production and Capital: Selected Papers of Hirofumi Uzawa,* Cambridge: Cambridge University Press: 112–26; previously published 1965

World Bank (1980, 1981, 1986, 1990, 1991, 1997) *World Development Report* (*WDR,* annual), New York: Oxford University Press for the World Bank
  (1986) 'Experience with Structural Adjustment Lending', February, draft
  (1990). *Making Adjustment Work for the Poor: A Framework for Policy Reform in Africa,* Washington, DC: World Bank
  (1997). 'OED Outcome Rating: What is it and Why are we Doing it?', World Bank Operations Evaluation Department, mimeo
  (1998a). *East Asia: The Road to Recovery,* Washington, DC: World Bank
  (1998b). *World Development Indicators,* Washington, DC: World Bank

7 The implications of foreign aid fungibility for development assistance

SHANTAYANAN DEVARAJAN AND
VINYA SWAROOP

1 Introduction

Since 1960 nearly $1.7 trillion (measured in 1995 dollars) in foreign aid has flown from rich to poor countries – much of it as project assistance.[1] As the leading project lending agency, the World Bank has, along with other donors, begun asking questions about whether this assistance is as effective as possible in promoting economic growth and reducing poverty. One source of concern has been whether aid projects actually finance what they are intended to, or whether development assistance earmarked for critical social and economic sectors directly or indirectly funds unproductive expenditures including those on defence.[2] What has aid financed in developing countries? What is the evidence on the 'fungibility' of aid? What are the implications of aid fungibility for donors in assessing the impact of their assistance programmes? These are the issues this chapter addresses. In section 2, we first define aid fungibility and then analyse its consequences. Section 3 provides a review of the literature on fungibility of foreign aid and reports some results. The review examines the evidence – both cross-country and country-specific – on the link between foreign aid and the recipient country's public spending. In section 4 we develop a link between fungibility and a donor agency's lending strategy. Moreover, in the light of the empirical findings on aid fungibility, we draw lessons for donor assistance and make recommendations for designing better lending instruments. In this section, we also provide a blueprint of a new lending instrument – a public expenditure reform loan (PERL) and discuss its strengths and potential shortfalls. Section 5 provides some concluding remarks.

196

2 Fungibility of economic assistance

By providing assistance, foreign governments and international donor agencies attempt to influence the public expenditure policies of recipient governments. Similarly, in a federal system of governance, subsidies and grants are used by governments to influence the budget of a subsidiary government. Aid may also be used to influence individual behavior (e.g. food stamps). The link between aid and the recipient's budgetary allocation, however, is not straightforward because some aid may be 'fungible'. For example, if a government would have undertaken a donor-financed project in the absence of that financing, then donor funds simply relax the government's budget constraint and finance, at the margin, something else. In a federal structure of governance, aid earmarked for a subsidiary government could end up replacing funds that the federal government would have given in the absence of that aid. Similarly, food stamps or rent subsidies to poor individuals may end up financing other consumption.

2.1 Aid fungibility: a definition

Suppose an aid donor gives money to build a primary school in a poor country. If the recipient government would have built the school anyway, then the consequence of the aid is to release resources for the government to spend on other items. Thus, while the primary school may still get built, the aid is financing some other expenditure (or tax reduction) by the government. In such a case, donor assistance is said to be fungible.

This concept of 'fungibility' could be illustrated a bit more rigorously. Suppose a country spends its total resources on a single private good, C_p, and two public goods, G_1 and G_2. All three goods are normal (non-inferior).[3] It pays for these goods by means of domestically generated resources. In addition to its own resources, the country receives earmarked assistance towards the purchase of good G_2 from a donor agency. For simplicity, we assume that there is no impact of aid on the relative price of the two goods. Figure 7.1 captures this scenario. BB' represents allocation choices that can be financed from domestic resources, and given the preferences of the recipient country, point A represents the preferred resource allocation. An amount F of earmarked foreign aid is given for G_2. The donor agency and the recipient country are assumed to have different preferences regarding how aid should be spent. (If they have identical preferences, then the distinction between earmarked aid or

Figure 7.1 *The concept of 'fungibility'*

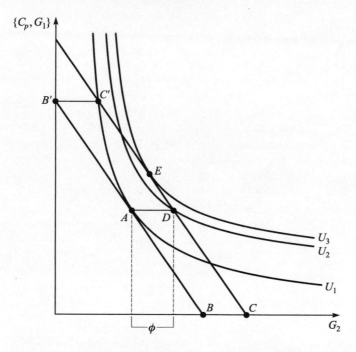

pure budgetary support has no meaning.) While the donor agency would like the aid funds to be spent on G_2 at the margin, for a variety of reasons, it is unable to monitor the intended pattern of public spending. Upon receiving aid, therefore, the recipient country is able to make it fungible by changing both the level and composition of its public expenditure programme.

If the recipient country can treat the entire aid amount as a pure supplement to its domestic resources, then aid is fully fungible.[4] As illustrated in figure 7.1, the post-aid resource constraint is $B'C'C$; the horizontal segment, $B'C'$, indicates that at least the aid amount has to be spent on G_2. The new optimal resource allocation is given by the point E. The latter indicates that in spending the acquired aid resources on good G_2, the country diverts some of its own resources from G_2 to G_1 and/or C_p. A diversion of funds to C_p implies a reduction in taxes. Suppose, on the other hand, the recipient country does not divert any of its resources away from the aided good while spending the earmarked aid on it. This could be owing to the donor agency's effective public expenditure monitoring process. In such a case, aid is fully non-fungible. The optimal allocation mix of the country's *own* resources is not influenced by the aid amount and point A (in figure 7.1) continues to be the country's preferred mix. Aid to G_2, however, increases overall utility. The post-aid consumption point, D, is on a higher indifference curve U_2.[5] This indicates that even if the aid were fully non-fungible, the recipient country would still benefit. Finally, if the country can treat a portion, $\phi(0 \leq \phi \leq 1)$, of the aid as a resource supplement, then aid is said to be 'partially fungible'and the fungible portion of the aid is given by ϕ. In such a case, the post-aid resource line (not drawn in figure 7.1) moves out by the fungible amount. In choosing the optimal resource mix, the country includes the fungible amount as an additional resource supplement to be spent but disregards the non-fungible portion, $1-\phi$. Depending on the value of ϕ, the final consumption point lies between points E ($\phi = 1$) and D ($\phi = 0$) in figure 7.1. This is the basic model that has been applied to data, when the fungibility coefficient ϕ is estimated (see Feyzioglu, Swaroop and Zhu, 1998, for an application).

2.2 Consequences of aid fungibility

Subsection 2.1 shows that if donor and recipient preferences differ, it is possible that the latter could convert aid into fungible resources. In granting aid, donors often require that proceeds be used for the purposes for which they are granted. The recipient could fulfil that conditionality by spending aid money for the purposes for which it was given. Yet, the earmarked funds may be releasing resources – that are already available to the recipient – for some other purpose. Is this a bad outcome? Not necessarily. Proponents of foreign aid argue that notwithstanding the diversion of local spending, aid money is intrinsically more effective than local spending as it comes packaged with technical assistance and superior management skills of donor agencies. Indeed, it is quite likely that donor involvement may increase the rate of return on the project. It may also lead to changes in policy, institutions and project design. Yet, if aid funds crowd-out domestic resources from that activity, they may end up financing, at the margin, very different and perhaps undesirable activities. In such a case, the developmental impact of external assistance may be quite different from that perceived from traditional measures of project success including the economic rate of return.

Precluding aid fungibility appears to be simple, at least on paper. All that is needed is conditionality on incremental spending. In practice, however, it is difficult to figure out what the recipient government would have done in the absence of that donor financing. Estimating the counterfactual is problematic. In most cases when they target aid to particular sectors, donor agencies use a proxy (e.g. the previous year's spending) of what the recipient government would have spent in the absence of aid. Treating past years'composition of spending as the pre-aid composition may not be very meaningful if the change in domestic resources is large relative to foreign aid. Moreover, the multiplicity of donors further complicates the analysis. The bottom line is that in most cases it is difficult to preclude switching of donor funds at the margin. Even if non-fungibility can be established, the recipient may not feel 'ownership' for the project if it was not planning to include it in its expenditure programme. The win–win situation results only if there is preference matching between the donor and the recipient and they both want to undertake a project which would not have been feasible in the absence of donor financing.

If most aid is fungible and it is difficult to search for non-fungible projects, what choices do the donors have to make aid more effective? In section 3, we argue that a solution to this fungibility problem is to tie assistance to an overall public expenditure programme (of the recipient country) that provides adequate resources to crucial sectors. To operationalise this reform programme, the section proposes a new lending instrument – a public expenditure reform loan (PERL). A PERL would tie an institution's lending strategy to the achievement of a set of mutually agreed development goals of the recipient country.

3 Aid fungibility: a research review

Past research has analysed aid fungibility along two main lines. Gramlich (1977), McGuire (1978), Mieszkowski and Oakland (1979) and Rosen (1988), among others, have studied the fiscal effects of inter-governmental grants and subsidy programmes. Recently, there have been several studies which have analysed whether foreign assistance provided for specific categories of expenditure is shifted by the recipient government, contrary to the wishes of donors. In a mix of cross-country and individual-country studies, Heller (1975), Cashel-Cordo and Craig (1990), Pack and Pack (1990, 1993, 1996), Gang and Khan (1991), Gupta (1993), Boone (1994), Khilji and Zampelli (1994), Devarajan, Squire and Suthiwart-Narueput (1999) and Feyzioglu, Swaroop and Zhu (1998), among others, have analysed whether foreign assistance provided for specific purposes is shifted by the recipient government. One study that synthesises the two approaches is Jha and Swaroop (1998) which, in tracing the fiscal effects of foreign aid in India, analyses the link between central and state governments.

The empirical literature on the effects of intergovernmental aid in federal systems has generally supported Gramlich's 'flypaper'theory. (Many of these studies are summarised in Inman, 1979.) According to this theory, an addition to resources through grants stimulates greater public expenditure than an additional dollar in local resources. In terms of the fungibility definition of section 2, there is little evidence that aid from higher- to lower-tier government is fully fungible. The presence of a 'flypaper' effect, however, does not preclude partial fungibility. Using data on US local government expenditure on education for the period 1964–71, McGuire (1978) found that restrictions placed by donors were largely ineffective and a large fraction of education grants were converted into fungible monies. McGuire analysed the impact of a grant into price- and income-changing components and devised a statistical method to estimate each component from data on the receiver's expenditure.

The literature on the effectiveness of foreign aid is replete with studies linking aid with macro economic variables – such as economic growth, consumption, investment (both public and private) and taxation – on the one hand and outcomes such as poverty, on the other.[6] Despite its importance to policy, there have been few studies which analyse economic fungibility of aid at the level of sectoral spending. One reason has been the difficulty in obtaining data on sector specific aid and spending. In a study of 46 developing countries, Cashel-Cordo and Craig (1990) analysed the impact of foreign aid (over the period 1975–80) on the size and composition of government expenditure. The expenditure components in their analysis were limited to defence and non-defence non-debt spending. Their main finding was that aid was quite stimulative of public spending and none of it was spilling over into the defence budget (table 7.1). Similarly, in examining the fungibility of US aid among eight major aid recipient countries, Khilji and Zampelli (1994) looked at defence and non-defence expenditures. They concluded that US aid was highly fungible with a major portion financing private sector consumption through some tax relief mechanism.

There has been a number of studies that have analysed, among other things, the fungibility of earmarked sectoral assistance (tables 7.1, 7.2). Several have relied on time-series data to analyse the question of aid fungibility across the sectoral classification of expenditures (McGuire, 1978, Pack and Pack, 1990, 1993, 1996; Gupta, 1993). Analysing the foreign aid experience of Indonesia over the period 1966–86, Pack and Pack (1990) did not find any evidence of fungibility across sectoral expenditures (table 7.2). On the other hand, in their analysis of the Dominican

Table 7.1 *Does foreign aid increase government spending?*

Sample	Estimates[a] ($)	Author/year	Foreign aid measure
46 non-European LDCs, 1975–80	1.60	Cashel-Cordo and Craig (1990)	ODA[b]
8 LDCs, 1972–87	0.26	Khilji and Zampelli (1994)	Annual disbursement of US aid
38 LDCs, 1971–90	0.33	Feyzioglu, Swaroop and Zhu (1998)	ODA
38 LDCs, 1971–90	0.63	Feyzioglu, Swaroop and Zhu (1998)	Concessionary loans only
18 Sub-Saharan African LDCs, 1971–95	0.89	Devarajan, Rajkumar and Swaroop (1999)	ODA
Dominican Republic, 1968–86	−0.27	Pack and Pack (1993)	Budgetary aid
Indonesia, 1966–86	1.58	Pack and Pack (1990)	Budgetary aid

Notes: [a]Change in government spending with respect to a dollar increase in foreign aid.
[b]ODA = Official Development Assistance.

Republic (Pack and Pack, 1993) they found major shifts from development expenditures to deficit reduction, debt service and tax relief. Based on data from 14 developing countries over 20 years Feyzioglu, Swaroop and Zhu (1998) found that roughly three-quarters of a dollar given in development assistance is spent on current expenditure and one-quarter on capital expenditure by the recipient countries. To test aid fungibility across public spending categories, they employed a newly constructed data series on the disbursement of sectoral concessionary loans. Their findings were that: concessionary loans given to agriculture, education and energy sectors are fungible; only loans to the transport and communication sector are non-fungible (table 7.2). Based on their findings, the authors argued that (a) the success of an aid programme should not be judged by the proportion of assistance going to capital expenditure and (b) because most aid is fungible, the rate of return on a specific donor-funded project tells little about the impact of that assistance.

Yet another paper on foreign aid fungibility is by Devarajan, Rajkumar and Swaroop (1999), which analyses the experience of Sub-Saharan Africa – the region with the largest GDP share of aid. Based on a data set of 18 Sub-Saharan countries from 1975 through 1995, the authors explore two issues: (1) the extent of aid fungibility in Sub-Saharan Africa; and (2) reasons why aid was fungible or not. In terms of the first question, they find that the broad pattern of aid fungibility observed in cross-country and country-specific studies is reflected in their analysis of African countries. Specifically, they find relatively little evi-

Table 7.2 *Does foreign project aid finance particular sectoral spending?*

Sample	Estimates[a] ($)	Author/year	Sector
8 LDCs, 1972–87	0.09	Khilji and Zampelli (1994)	Defence (US Aid)
14 LDCs, 1971–90	0.92	Feyzioglu, Swaroop and Zhu (1998)	Transport/ communication
14 LDCs, 1971–90	0.00[b]	Feyzioglu, Swaroop and Zhu (1998)	Agriculture, education/health
18 Sub-Saharan African LDCs, 1971–95	0.36	Devarajan, Rajkumar and Swaroop (1999)	Transport/ communication
Dominican Republic, 1968–86	0.92	Pack and Pack (1993)	Agriculture
Indonesia, 1966–86	1.00	Pack and Pack (1990)	Transportation/ tourism

Notes: [a]Change in government spending with respect to a dollar increase in earmarked sectoral aid.
[b]Statistically not different from zero.

dence that aid leads to greater tax relief in Africa; every dollar of aid leads to a 90-cent increase in government spending (table 7.1). The effect of aid on the composition of public spending between current and capital expenditures is also broadly consistent with international evidence: aid in Africa leads to an increase in current and capital spending in equal amounts. The result that appears as striking is that an almost equal amount of aid – equal to the amount going for current and capital spending – goes towards repaying the principal on past loans. The argument that the inability to meet debt-service payments would have threatened many African countries with a complete cutoff from foreign capital and, therefore, the use of aid resources to relax this constraint could have been quite rational. In their analysis of sectoral aid fungibility, Devarajan, Rajkumar and Swaroop find that sectoral aid in Africa is partially fungible: governments do not spend all sectoral aid in that sector, nor do they treat such aid as merely budget support.

In a federal structure of governance, foreign aid could also influence the inter-governmental fiscal transfer mechanism. Upon receiving aid on behalf of a subsidiary government, the federal government could make adjustments in its fiscal transfers to that lower level of government. An example of this comes from the practice of 'Budget Offset' in Ethiopia, a federal country. The federal government reduces the budget subsidy to states – which is based on a formula that includes weights for population, development indicators and states' own revenue efforts – by the full amount of expected external loans and grants that have been committed by donors towards projects in the respective states. While no such direct budgetary mechanism exists in India, concerns have been raised that states that procure externally aided projects are not able to reap the full benefits; central government transfers to states are reduced when foreign aid is secured for state projects. In India almost all external assistance (including funds earmarked for projects for the state governments) accrues to the central government, which is also liable for any repayments. Jha and Swaroop (1998) look at this issue. They find that external assistance intended for development purposes merely substitutes for spending that governments – central and states' – would have undertaken anyway; the funds freed by aid are spent on non-development activities in general and administrative services in particular. Moreover, in passing external assistance to states, the central government makes a reduction in other transfers to states.

4 Lending instruments and strategies: the implications of economic fungibility

At this point, a natural question to ask is: 'So what?' Fungibility may be a fact of life, and recent empirical evidence seems to support this notion, but are there any implications for development policy? We now argue that there are two, rather profound, implications for donor assistance. The first has to do with how donors evaluate the impact of development assistance. If funds are fungible, the traditional approach of calculating the project's rate of return will clearly not answer the question of the impact of the aid – since the aid is financing some other expenditure than the project (Devarajan, Squire and Suthiwart-Narueput, 1999). The second implication has to do with the instruments used by donors to deliver aid. If funds are fungible, and the recipient's public expenditure programme is not satisfactory, then project lending may not be a cost-effective instrument. If the country's public expenditure programme *is* satisfactory, the donor may also finance a portion of this programme, rather than concentrate on individual projects.

4.1 Evaluating development assistance

Consider the following problem. A country has a public expenditure programme of $100 million, consisting of $40 million in education expenditures, $40 million in agriculture, and $20 million in expenditures about which we know nothing. The rates of return on education and agriculture are 30 and 20 per cent, respectively. A donor is considering a $10 million primary-education project that has a rate of return of 35 per cent. What is the development impact of the $10 million?

Once we realise that aid may be fungible, the answer is not straightforward. Even though the primary-education project has a high rate of return, if it is a project the government would have undertaken anyway, the donor's $10 million is releasing resources for some other component of the public expenditure programme, possibly something in the 'unknown' category. The development impact of the $10 million could be the rate of return of one of these unknown expenditures. If we assume the rate of return on this unknown expenditure is zero, then the rate of return of the $10 million project could be zero. Even if we assume that the donor's $10 million is only 50 per cent fungible, and that free resources are spent in the same proportion as committed resources, the rate of return is only 28.5 per cent. In any event, the development impact is almost surely not 35 per cent.

Yet, donors spend enormous resources calculating the rate of return on their projects (or some other summary measure of the project's net benefit). As a first step, then, these resources could be better spent on appraising the recipient's overall public expenditure programme, so we have a better idea of where the marginal dollar is going. Second, donors and the development community in general should not read too much into the traditional rate of return calculations. For instance, it is not at all surprising that the correlation between World Bank project rates of return and the country's growth rate is around 0.3. The Bank's loans may have been financing projects with much lower rates of return than those in the appraisal document.

We should emphasise that calculating the rate of return to projects is still important for the recipient country. The calculations (if done properly) indicate whether the project is beneficial to the country. They could be used to guide the country's resource allocation process. But they should not be used by donors to evaluate the impact of external assistance, much less guide resource allocation within donor agencies.

4.2 Lending instruments

If a country's overall public expenditure programme (PEP) is satisfactory, then the donor could just as well finance a portion of that programme, rather than appraise and finance individual projects. If the

PEP is not satisfactory, then the donor should think twice before financing a project. The individual project may be a good one, but the financial assistance may be funding some other expenditure which, in the case of an unsatisfactory PEP, is likely to be unproductive. In either case, therefore, projects – the main mode of development assistance – may not be the best way to achieve development impact.

An alternative, which has been dubbed a public expenditure reform loan (PERL) at the World Bank, would involve replacing all project loans to a country with direct budgetary support, based on an agreement about the quality of the country's public expenditure programme. Such an instrument has several advantages:

- *Cost-efficiency*: The Bank would save on appraisal and preparation costs of the individual loans to the country. The additional cost of appraising the country's PEP – currently estimated at about $250,000 – is still substantially less than the administrative costs of projects.
- *Leverage*: At present, the donor can influence policies only in the sectors it is involved in. Yet if, owing to fungibility, the donor's money is going to other sectors, there could be significant gains if the donor could help improve the policy framework in those sectors. By financing a portion of the budget, a PERL provides that kind of leverage.
- *Donor coordination*: Everyone agrees that more coordination by donors is better. But this has been difficult to achieve, partly because individual donors have a preference for projects (usually with the national flag flying over them). By agreeing on a public expenditure programme and financing a portion of it, the Bank can credibly ask other donors to do the same. Some may fear that such a coordinated move towards programme finance might reduce the overall aid quantum. But if what is reduced is a set of uncoordinated (and possibly superfluous) projects, and what is increased is the government's overall management of public resources, the net impact is very likely positive.

There would still be a role for projects in the aid relationship, but now it will be concentrated on the transfer of know-how and policy advice, rather than on financing. Typically, these two are bundled together in a project, which means they are supplied in fixed coefficients. PERLs permit the two to be unbundled, and the scale of each tailored to the country's individual needs.

Despite their advantages, PERLs contain some risks as well. They are likely to elicit resistance from the recipient countries, especially those that are uncomfortable with having their whole public expenditure programme scrutinised. At the same time, PERLs may not find much support among traditional project specialists in donor institutions. But the point is whether converting all lending into a single instrument such as a PERL is an improvement over the status quo. In light of the evidence on fungibility, it certainly must be.

5 Conclusion

If foreign aid is fungible – and there seems to be a lot of empirical evidence supporting fungibility – then standard project appraisal techniques (such as the economic rate of return analysis) tell little about the development impact of that assistance. A donor project may actually have a very high rate of economic return, but at the margin it could be financing something very different, even undesirable expenditures. While increasing restrictions on donor assistance to reduce fungibility may have some impact, a better approach could be to tie aid resources to an overall public expenditure programme that provides adequate resources to crucial sectors.

The implications of this new mode of assistance for the World Bank are both minimal and significant. They are minimal because, in a sense, the Bank has been transferring assistance in this way all along. If – as the evidence shows – project assistance is fungible, the Bank has been financing the government's budget anyway. Furthermore, much of the Bank's project assistance involves providing advice to governments about policy and institutional reform – precisely the kind of dialogue that would continue under a PERL. But the implications are significant because moving to a PERL would make all these activities explicit. In addition, it would change the Bank's relationship with its client countries. Instead of imposing conditions on quick-disbursing loans, such as structural adjustment loans (SALs), or financing projects that are essentially enclaves in a country, the Bank would be supporting the client country's development programme through budgetary support, and assisting the country in managing all of its public resources. In short, a PERL provides a concrete means of achieving the new partnership between the Bank and its clients that the Bank's President, James Wolfenshohn, has made an integral part of the 'Comprehensive Development Framework' or CDF.

NOTES
The findings, interpretations and conclusions expressed in this chapter are entirely those of the authors. They do not necessarily represent the views of the World Bank, its Executive Directors, or the countries they represent. We thank Chris Gilbert for helpful comments.

1 Based on 36 years of data from 1960 to 1965 on Official Development Assistance (OECD, 1998).
2 See the UNDP's *Human Development Report* (UNDP, 1994) for an analysis of the human development cost of arms in developing countries
3 An implication of the neoclassical paradigm with normal preferences is that the government would never choose to spend any marginal increase in resources solely on one good.
4 In the literature on the effects of intergovernmental aid in federal systems, this is known as having no 'flypaper' effect (see Gramlich, 1977).
5 Point *D* could be optimal if supported by a policy which changes the relative price of the two goods.
6 For a comprehensive review of the foreign aid literature, see White and Luttick (1994).

REFERENCES

Boone, P. (1994). 'Politics and Effectiveness of Foreign Aid?', LSE Centre for Economic Performance, London, mimeo

Cashel-Cordo, P. and S. G. Craig (1990). 'The Public Sector Impact of International Resource Transfers', *Journal of Development Economics*, **32**

Devarajan, S., A. S. Rajkumar and V. Swaroop (1999). 'What Does Aid to Africa Finance?', Development Research Group, World Bank, mimeo

Devarajan, S., L. Squire and S. Suthiwart-Narueput (1999). 'Beyond Rate of Return: Re-orienting Project Analysis', *World Bank Research Observer*, **9**

Devarajan, S., V. Swaroop and H. F. Zou (1996). 'The Composition of Public Expenditure and Economic Growth', *Journal of Monetary Economics*, **37**

Feyzioglu, T., V. Swaroop and M. Zhu (1998). 'A Panel Data Analysis of the Fungibility of Foreign Aid', *World Bank Economic Review*, **12**

Gang, I. N. and H. A. Khan (1991). 'Foreign Aid, Taxes and Public Investment', *Journal of Development Economics*, **34**

Gramlich, E. (1977). 'Intergovernmental Grants: A Review of the Empirical Literature', in W. E. Oates (ed.), *The Political Economy of Fiscal Federalism*, Lexington, MA: Heath

Gupta, K. L. (1993). 'Sectoral Fungibility of Foreign Aid: Evidence from India', University of Alberta, mimeo

Heller, P. S. (1975). 'A Model of Public Fiscal Behavior in Developing Countries: Aid, Investment, and Taxation', *American Economic Review*, **65**

Inman, R. P. (1979). 'The Fiscal Performance of Local Governments: An Interpretative Review', in P. Mieszkowski and M. Straszheim (eds.), *Current Issues in Urban Economics,* Baltimore: Johns Hopkins University Press

Jha, S. and V. Swaroop (1998). 'Fiscal Effects of Foreign Aid: A Case Study of India', Development Research Group, World Bank, mimeo

Khilji, N. M. and E. M. Zampelli (1994). 'The Fungibility of US Military and Non-military Assistance and the Impacts on Expenditures of Major Aid Recipients', *Journal of Development Economics*, **43**

McGuire, M. C. (1978). 'A Method for Estimating the Effect of a Subsidy on the Receiver's Resource Constraint: With an Application to the US Local Governments 1964–1971', *Journal of Public Economics*, **10**

Mieszkowski, P. and W. Oakland (1979). *Fiscal Federalism and Grants-in-Aid*, Washington, DC: Urban Institute

Organisation for Economic Cooperation and Development (OECD) (1998). *Geographical Distribution of Financial Flows to Aid Recipients*, CD-ROM, Paris: OECD

Pack, H. and J. R. Pack (1990). 'Is Foreign Aid Fungible? The Case of Indonesia', *Economic Journal*, **100**

  (1993). 'Foreign Aid and the Question of Fungibility', *Review of Economics and Statistics*, **58**

  (1996) 'Foreign Aid and Fiscal Stress', The University of Pennsylvania, Philadelphia, mimeo

Rosen, H. (1988). *Fiscal Federalism: Quantitative Studies*, National Bureau of Economic Research, Chicago: University of Chicago Press.

UNDP (1994). *Human Development Report*, New York: Oxford University Press

White, H. and J. Luttik (1994). 'The Countrywide Effects of Aid', *Policy Research Working Paper*, **1337**, Policy Research Department, World Bank

8 Aid, growth, the incentive regime and poverty reduction

CRAIG BURNSIDE AND DAVID DOLLAR

I Introduction

Foreign aid has a strong positive effect on growth in low-income countries with good policies; it has no measurable effect in countries with severely distorted policy regimes (Burnside and Dollar, 1997). While that result is consistent with other econometric and case study work on aid,[1] it leaves open a number of important questions. How exactly does one measure 'policy'? Is the finding robust to different measures of policy? And does it hold for other outcomes of interest, such as poverty reduction or improvement in social indicators? Spurring growth in the developing world is one stated objective of foreign aid; but the most commonly cited objective is poverty reduction. In general, poverty reduction and growth go hand-in-hand, but it is still possible that foreign aid has been successful at mitigating poverty but not had much measurable effect on growth.

This chapter has several objectives. First, we revisit our basic results on aid, policies and growth – starting with our model and reviewing the empirical evidence. Second, in doing that we broaden our indicator of 'good policy' to include more micro or institutional dimensions. Third, we also examine the effect of foreign aid on infant mortality, an issue of interest for two reasons. First, infant mortality is an important social indicator in its own right. Second, changes in infant mortality provide indirect evidence about whether the benefits of development are reaching the broad mass of the population.

The main findings of the chapter are as follows. The impact of aid on growth is conditional on the quality of policies. We get stronger results using the broad measure of policy that includes institutional features. Furthermore, the impact of aid on infant mortality is similarly conditional on policy. In a poor incentive environment, there is no measurable effect of aid on the decline in infant mortality. These basic results are quite intuitive. There are institutions and policies that influence how efficiently resources in general are utilised in an economy. It should not be surprising that these same factors determine the effectiveness with which external resource are utilised. Thus, there is no basis from this additional work to change our recommendation that aid be more sharply targeted to low-income countries that have put good policies into place.

2 Aid and growth: theory and evidence

In this section we use a simple neoclassical growth model to motivate the form of our empirical growth equation. Our intention in doing this is to provide some examples, though there might be many more, of models in which the relationship between aid and growth is conditional on the quality of economic policies. The neoclassical model we discuss is one in which aid is viewed simply as a lump-sum transfer from abroad, and there are no strategic interactions between governments that need concern us.

A series of interesting experiments can be performed in the context of a perfect foresight, one-sector, neoclassical model. We assume that there is a single good over which households have isoelastic preferences, once they have satisfied a subsistence level of consumption.[2] Assuming households are infinitely lived, lifetime utility is given by

$$\sum_{t=0}^{\infty} \beta^t \frac{(C_t - \overline{C}^{1-\gamma}) - 1}{1 - \gamma}$$

where C_t represents time-t household consumption, $0 < \beta < 1$ is the discount factor, $\gamma > 0$ is the coefficient of relative risk aversion and $\overline{C}$ is a subsistence level of household consumption.

For simplicity we assume that each household operates its own technology using its beginning of period-t capital, K_t, and a single unit of labour which is supplied inelastically. The production function is assumed to be given by $Y_t = AK_t^{\theta}$, with $A > 0$ and $0 < \theta \leq 1$.

Net household income is taxed on the margin at the rate τ, and households receive lump-sum transfers from the government given by T_t. Given that we assume that there is no international private capital mobility, the household budget constraint is

$$C_t + I_t - \delta k_t \leq (1 - \tau)(Y_t - \delta k_t) + T_t$$

where I_t is time $-t$ investment.[3] Capital evolves according to

$$K_{t+1} = (1 - \delta)K_t + I_t,$$

where $0 < \delta < 1$.

The government is assumed to make consumption purchases, G_t. For simplicity we have assumed that these government purchases do not enter into the utility of private households. If we changed this assumption to allow government purchases to have a positive impact on utility, it would change some of our conclusions, though not necessarily those regarding the impact of foreign aid on growth. We assume that government purchases are financed by taxes net of transfers as well as by foreign aid. For the purposes of this section, we assume that time-t foreign aid is received in the form of a lump-sum transfer from abroad, F_t.[4] If we exclude the possibility of both domestic borrowing and printing money, the government's flow budget constraint is given by

$$G_t \le \tau(Y_t - \delta K_t) - T_t + F_t$$

The economy as a whole, therefore, has the resource constraint

$$C_t + I_t + G_t \le Y_t + F_t$$

It is worth noting that both in the model, and in the context of actual data, an injection of foreign aid does not show up instantly as an increase in GDP and, therefore, GDP growth. In both the model and actual economies, assuming that production takes place on the technological frontier, GDP depends only on domestic factors of production and the state of technology. Assuming labour supply is unaffected, aid impacts on GDP only when it is used to augment the stock of capital. If it is consumed, there is an increase in GNP inclusive of transfers, but not GDP. If some fraction of it is invested, then aid causes an increase in capital, and consequently domestic output.

We consider several special cases of the model. First, suppose that $\theta = 1$ and that $\tau = 0$, so that returns to capital are constant and subsistence consumption plays no role in the model. Under these circumstances it is straightforward to show that consumers will choose to have constant consumption growth given by

$$\frac{C_{t+1}}{C_t} = g = \left(\beta \tilde{R}\right)^{1/\gamma},$$

where $\tilde{R} = (1 - \tau)(A - \delta) + 1$.[5] The initial level of consumption is given by

$$C_0 = (R - g)K_0 + \frac{R - g}{R} \sum_{t=0}^{\infty} R^{-t}(F_t - G_t),$$

where $R = A - \delta + 1$.

So suppose we consider two economies, one in which $F_t = G_t = 0$, for all t, while in the other $G_t = 0$ for all t, $F_t = 0$ for $t > 0$ and $F_0 > 0$.[6] In the first economy, which receives no aid, $C_0 = (R - g)K_0$ while in the second economy, which receives aid at time 0, $C_0 = (R - g)K_0 + (R - g)F_0/R$. What this tells us is that when the inflow of aid takes place, part of it, $(R - g)F_0/R$, is consumed. The rest of it, gF_0/R, is additional investment.

We can also show that in the first economy the growth rate of GDP is constant and equal to g in every period. However, in the second economy, growth between period 0 and period 1 is given by $g + (gA/R)(F_0/Y_0)$, while growth after that returns instantly to the rate g.

It is interesting to note that the impact of aid on the growth rate of output depends not only on the size of the injection relative to GDP, F_0/Y_0, but also on the level of distortionary taxes through the gA/R term. The higher are distortionary taxes, the less effective will be the injection of aid, other things being held equal.

We think of the effect aid has on growth, in this example, as its *direct* effect through a one time increase in capital accumulation. Not surprisingly, the size of the direct effect depends on the incentives to accumulate capital.

If we maintain the same assumptions but allow the subsistence level of consumption to be non-zero we get other effects as well. We will now have the result that

$$\frac{C_{t+1} - \overline{C}}{C_t - \overline{C}} - g - \left(\beta\tilde{R}\right)^{1/\gamma}$$

which implies that the level of consumption beyond the subsistence level will grow at the constant rate. The model becomes somewhat more complicated to solve, but it turns out that if we repeat the experiment with the two economies described above, the one receiving aid will have a higher growth rate in period 1 by the amount of the direct effect: $(gA/R)(F_0/Y_0)$. This is because, as before, households will consume exactly of the injection of aid, while the rest, gF_0/R, is invested in capital. Capital stock grows and asymptotes to g. An injection of aid raises the capital stock, and by so doing not only raises output directly, but also moves the country onto a transition path with higher growth rates. This *indirect* effect which, in our two-economy experiment, is initially given by

$$\frac{\overline{K}}{K_0} \frac{R^{-1}F_0}{K_0 + R^{-1}F_0}(g - 1)$$

where $\overline{K} = \overline{C}/(R - 1)$, shrinks over time, and will be smaller the higher the country's capital stock is at the time of the aid injection (the further it is from the subsistence level of consumption). It will also be small if the injection of aid is small relative to the country's initial capital stock. The indirect effect also depends on the tax rate through g.

Different indirect effects occur in versions of the same model with diminishing returns to capital – i.e. $\theta < 1$. When there is no subsistence level of consumption, the model with $\theta < 1$ implies a monotonically declining growth rate of output as the capital stock grows. This is a case in which the indirect effect is negative. When we combine subsistence consumption with $\theta > 1$, for countries with low capital stocks the growth rate rises as the capital stock grows, peaks, and then declines along the transition path. In this case the indirect effect is positive or negative, depending on the size of the capital stock at the time of the aid injection. The indirect effects that arise from different parameterisations of the model are illustrated in figure 8.1.

To summarise this discussion, we have shown that injections of aid have two effects on economic growth within the context of simple neoclassical models. First, there is a direct effect that depends on how much of the injection of aid is transformed into additional investment. Second, there is an indirect effect, arising from the fact that when aid affects the capital stock, it also affects an economy's location along its transition path to some long-run steady state. Both of these effects are a function of the magnitude of distortions in the economy, which we have modelled here as taxes on household income. We have made the model very general to emphasise that in any model in which distortions affect accumulation – and hence growth – the same distortions will affect the impact of aid on growth. One gets this results with or without a subsistence constraint and with or without diminishing returns. In any case, aid effectiveness will be conditional on policy. With a subsistence constraint, the impact will generally be larger. And with diminishing returns, the impact will depend on where the economy is located on its transition path.

These models motivate our empirical specification that allows for the possibility that the impact of aid on growth depends on government policies that affect the size of distortions in the economy (and also allows for the possibility of diminishing returns). Specifically, the growth equation that emerges from our model can be stated as follows.

Per capita GDP growth depends on:

- initial income
- other initial conditions
- index of the incentive regime
- aid relative to GDP
- aid/GDP interacted with the incentive regime

Figure 8.1 *Indirect effects of aid on growth in the neoclassical model*
Note: Panel a–d show the growth of output, g_t, as a function of the level of capital, K_t, along the economy's transition path. An injection of aid, to the extent that it is invested, causes an increase in the capital stock that would not otherwise have occurred. Hence, the indirect effect of the injection of aid on growth is to move the economy onto a different part of the transition path.
Panel a uses a model with constant returns to capital, and no subsistence level of consumption, so there is no indirect effect.
Panel b uses a model with constant returns to capital, and a positive subsistence level of consumption, so the indirect effect is positive.
Panel c uses a model with diminishing returns to capital, and no subsistence level of consumption, so the indirect effect is negative.
Panel d uses a model with diminishing returns to capital, and a positive subsistence level of consumption, so the effect is ambiguous.

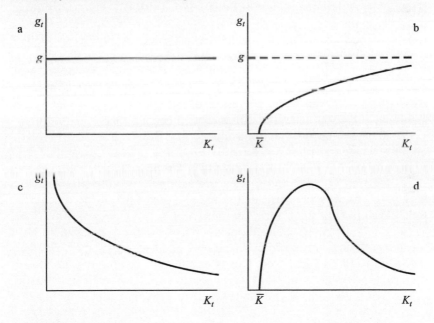

- aid/GDP squared interacted with the incentive regime (to allow for diminishing returns)
- error term.

To estimate this equation we need a measure of the incentive regime that incorporates important distortions. Some of the key distortions that have been identified in the literature on growth are closed trade regimes (Dollar, 1992; Sachs and Warner, 1995); high inflation (Fischer, 1993); and large fiscal deficits (Easterly and Rebelo, 1993). In our first paper (Burnside and Dollar, 1997), we formed an index of these three policies.

However, it is also the case that growth is affected by institutional issues such as poor protection of property rights or high levels of corruption (Knack and Keefer, 1995). For the present chapter we broadened the index of the incentive regime (which we call 'economic management') to include both the macro policies and the institutional dimension:

$$\text{Management} = -1.8 + 0.65 \times ICRGE + 5.4 \times$$
$$Fiscal - 1.4 \times Inflation + 2.1 \times Open$$

where *ICRGE* is a measure of strength of property rights, absence of corruption, and quality of the bureaucracy; *Open* is the Sachs–Warner measure of trade openness; *Inflation* is the rate of increase of the price level; and *Fiscal* is the budget surplus relative to GDP.[7] We have organised the data into a panel of 56 developing countries, averaged over four-year periods, beginning with 1970–3 and ending with 1990–3. Looking at the countries in the sample, Botswana or Thailand would be examples of very good incentive regimes. Indonesia fares pretty well, though its weak legal system and high level of corruption result in it scoring less well than Botswana, for example. Poor policy examples are Tanzania or Zambia. The difference in policy between Indonesia (1982–5) and Tanzania in the same period should have been 'worth' about 3 percentage points of growth.

Because the information has been organised into a panel, countries can shift over time. Bolivia and Ghana are examples of countries that had very poor policy in the early 1980s, and then reformed to become good-policy countries in the 1990s. The macro-policies included in this index are all ones that can be changed quickly if a society and government want to reform, and there are many examples of large policy improvements between the 1980s and 1990s. This is one of the encouraging findings of the new growth literature, that measures that are feasible for most countries have a significant impact on their growth rates. At the same time the more institutional aspects of good management – such as rule of law – take longer to improve.

Because we have put both policies and aid into the growth equation, we have to consider the possibility that policies are endogenous and in particular are influenced by aid. It is important to emphasise that the specific econometric issue is whether the *quantity* of aid received by a country affects the policies measured in our index. From the point of view of theory, there is no strong reason to expect a relationship in any particular direction. Conservatives have traditionally argued that large amounts of aid reduce the pressure on governments to perform (Bauer, 1971). On the other hand, some aid is specifically conditional on policy reform, though there is considerable scepticism about how effective conditionality actually is (Mosley, Harrigan and Toye, 1995; Collier, (1997). In our (1997) paper, we estimate an equation for policy, instrument for aid, and show that there is a very robust zero coefficient. That is, there is no evidence that the quantity of aid affects policies. The econometric evidence is consistent with casual empiricism as well. Among countries with large amounts of aid there is a wide spectrum of policies, as there is among countries with little or no aid. Some of the countries with the worst policies (Burma, Zaire) have been cut off from aid in recent years, and there has been no measurable progress toward good policy. Thus, in this chapter we take policies and the quantity of aid to be independent.

The estimation of the growth equation is shown in table 8.1.[8] The index of the incentive regime has a large amount of explanatory power (the individual elements could alternatively be used in lieu of the index). Aid receipts by themselves have no significant effect on growth in the OLS specification (Regression (1)). Our main finding is that aid interacted with the policy index has a strong positive association with growth, while aid squared interacted with the policy index has a negative coefficient (Regression (2)). In general, the results are stronger with this broader measure of policy, than we obtained initially by focusing only on macroeconomic policies.

There is an obvious simultaneity problem in these OLS regressions: aid may be deliberately allocated to countries in difficulty owing to exogenous shocks (drought, for example). We get around that by instrumenting for aid with variables that are correlated with aid but that have been shown not to belong in the growth regressions: population and measures of donor interests, such as memberships in the Franc Zone. In Regression (3) we instrument for aid, aid interacted with policy, and aid squared interacted with policy. The 2SLS regression has the same qualitative results as the OLS regression.

These results indicate that the effect of aid on growth depends on the quality of the incentive regime as well as on the volume of aid received. Specifically, from regression (3), the estimated derivative of growth with respect to aid is

$$-0.37 + 0.8 \times Policy - 0.16 \times Aid \times Policy$$

In table 8.2 we evaluate this derivative at nine different points, varying the policy index from zero to 1.1 (mean) to 2.7 (one standard deviation about the mean) and varying aid from zero to 1.7 per cent of real PPP GDP (mean) to 3.7 per cent (one standard deviation above the mean). The point estimate for the effect of even the first dollar of aid is negative in a poor policy environment. At the mean of policy the estimated impact

Table 8.1 *Panel growth regressions*

Time dimension: six four-year periods, 1970–3 to 1990–3
Countries: 56 aid recipients
Dependent variable: Growth rate of *per capita* GDP

Regression no.	(1)	(2)	(3)
Observations	272	272	272
Method	OLS	OLS	2SLS
Constant	3.43	2.42	7.33
	(0.76)	(0.53	(1.11)
Initial GDP *per capita*	−0.49	−0.36	−1.02
	(0.84)	(0.61)	(1.22)
Ethnic fractionalisation	−0.005	−0.004	−0.008
	(0.73)	(0.56)	(0.77)
Assassinations	−0.40	−0.38	−0.31
	(1.50)	(1.40)	(1.03)
Ethnic × assassin	0.007	0.006	.004
	(1.56)	(1.30)	(0.78)
M2/GDP (lagged)	0.02	0.03	0.03
	(1.64)	(1.77)	(1.58)
Sub-Saharan Africa	−1.40	−1.77	−1.86
	(1.91)	(2.40)	(2.22)
East Asia	0.91	1.28	1.67
	(1.62)	(2.07)	(2.40)
Policy index	1.02	0.79	0.38
	(7.01)	(4.32)	(1.38)
Govt consumption	−7.30	−7.51	2.08
	(1.57)	(1.65)	(1.38)
Aid/GDP	0.11	0.16	−0.37
	(0.86)	(1.18)	(0.82)
Aid Policy	–	0.26	0.80
		(3.07)	(2.37)
Aid^2 Policy	–	−0.03	−0.08
		(3.66)	(1.74)
R^2	0.40	0.41	
Adj. R^2	0.36	0.37	

Note: *t*-statistics (in parentheses) have been calculated with White's heteroscedasticity-consistent standard errors, for all regressions in the chapter.

of the first dollar is pretty high (with depreciation of, say, 10 per cent, a coefficient of 0.5 corresponds to a rate of return of about 40 per cent). However, because of diminishing returns, at the mean level of aid the estimated impact is much lower, and in fact not significantly different from zero. In a good policy environment, on the other hand, the estimated return is extraordinarily high for the first dollar and even for the mean level of aid. It is only at a high level of aid that the return diminishes toward zero.

Table 8.2 *Estimated impact of 1 per cent of GDP in aid on growth (from table 8.1, Regression (3))*

	Level of policy index		
	0 (Poor)	1.1 (Mean)	2.7 (Good)
Level of Aid (per cent of GDP)			
0	−0.37	0.51	1.79
1.7 (Mean)	−0.37	0.21	1.06
3.7 (High)	−0.37	−0.14	0.19

Aid thus has a strong effect on growth in countries with a good incentive regime. It should be emphasised that this effect is over and above what the good policy itself induces. The policy index is in the growth equation along with the interative term. In a weak environment the impact of aid on growth is not statistically different from zero. The negative coefficient on the quadratic terms means that there are diminishing marginal returns to aid: its marginal impact declines as the volume of aid grows, which makes sense. To the extent that the objective of aid is to promote growth in developing countries, these results imply that aid should be sharply targed to developing countries that have a sound incentive regime.

A final point about the growth regressions is that the interactive term, *Aid × Policy*, has a second – equally valid – interpretation. The positive coefficient on the interactive term means that the impact of policy reform on growth is conditional on the level of aid. Thus, a one-unit change in the policy index leads to higher growth of 0.4 percentage points with zero aid, and to higher growth of 1.5 percentage points with the mean level of aidd. Aid thus helps draw a supply response from policy reform.

3 Aid and infant mortality

If aid is not supporting productive investments in countries with poor policies, then it must be financing either unproductive investments or consumption. Supporting consumption in very poor countries is not necessarily a bad thing: the issue is, whose consumption? The central objective of development assistance is poverty reduction. It may be that aid is supporting the consumption of very poor households, which leads to reductions in infant mortality and improvements in other social indicators. These developments may support growth in the very long term, in a way not picked up by econometric studies.

There is quite a bit of evidence that the consumption that is being supported by aid is *government consumption*. 'Government consumption' is a broad category that includes recurrent spending on health and education (these might be considered investments, but the accounting tradition is to record them as government consumption). It also includes spending on social relief, defence and administration. Thus, large government consumption could reflect a big, corrupt bureaucracy, or it could reflect large expenditures on social welfare that are helping to reduce poverty. One cannot say *a priori* if it is good or bad for development.[9]

There are different estimates from different studies, but somewhere between one-half and three-quarters of bilateral aid finanaces additional government consumption (Burnside and Dollar, 1997; Feyzioglu, Swaroop and Zhu, 1998). Furthermore, the empirical growth literature finds that government consumption has no robust effect on growth. Some studies find a negative effect, others a zero relationship. The finding that aid largely finances government consumption, which in turn has no positive effect on growth, helps explain why aid is not fostering growth in many developing countries. It leaves open the question, however, of whether the consumption might be helping the poor through social expenditures.

Ideally, we would want to look directly at the effect of aid on consumption of the poor or on the incidence of poverty, but the number of countries for which such data are available over time is small. The approach that we take here is to look directly at the effect of aid on infant mortality. Infant mortality is itself an important social indicator for which data are widely available. Furthermore, if aid is particularly reaching the poor it should have an impact on infant mortality. Following earlier work, the model that we have in mind is as follows.

Decline in infant mortality depends on:

- initial conditions
- growth of *per capita* income
- government consumption
- aid/GDP
- error term.

Aid could potentially affect infant mortality indirectly through growth. But there may also be a direct effect if aid is particularly supporting poor groups.

Given our findings about growth, we can substitute for it and have the following reduced form equation:

Decline in infant mortality depends on:

- initial conditions
- incentive regime
- government consumption
- aid/GDP
- aid/GDP interacted with incentive regime
- error term.

It has been well established that growth leads to reductions in infant mortality (Pritchett and Summers, 1995), so it would be consistent with our earlier findings to see a positive coefficient on the interactive term.[10] An important additional question is whether government consumption and/or aid directly affects infant mortality, regardless of the incentive regime. Once again we have to be concerned about the correlation of aid with the error term (aid deliberately given to countries in distress) so that it is necessary to instrument for aid and for aid interacted with the incentive regime.

In the OLS regression ((1) in table 8.3) there is no significant relationship between aid and the decline in infant mortality. Actually, the model does only moderately well in explaining the decline in infant mortality over the relatively short period of time, four years. There is a kind of 'divergence' in that countries with high infant mortality to begin with show smaller declines, ceteris paribus. Countries with sound management have faster declines in infant mortality, but the statistical significance of the relationship is not strong. There is no effect of government consumption on infant mortality. Regression (2) is the same, except that we instrument for aid with population and donor interest variables. There are insignificant positive coefficients on both aid and government consumption. These results provide important information that supplements our earlier work. There is no evidence that the permanent component of aid – which is what is extracted by the instrumental variables technique – has any affect on this important social indicator within a four-year time period. Thus, in a poor policy environment, neither growth nor decline in infant mortality is supported by aid on average.

As with growth, there is, however, a relationship between decline in infant mortality and the interaction of aid and the incentive regime. The interaction term has a positive coefficient and the quadratic term a negative one (regression (3)). The statistical significance is weaker than in the growth regressions. It is interesting that the t-statistics rise if technical assistance is taken out of the measure of aid (regression (4)). This change could reflect the fact that the impact of technical assistance is not likely to be seen in a social indicator within a four-year time frame. Alternatively, it could be that technical assistance has less impact than capital assistance. Recall that the only impact at all here is in countries with sound management. It may be that financial assistance has a sharp impact in that case, but that technical assistance is less needed.

According to these estimates, the impact of aid on the decline in infant mortality depends on the quality of the incentive regime and on the volume of assistance. Based on regression (3), the derivative of the decline in infant mortality with respect to aid is

$$0.03 + 0.53 \times Management\ index - 0.12 \times Aid \times Management$$

The mean of aid is 1.7. (We measure aid relative to real PPP GDP, yielding smaller figures than those that result from deflating aid by nominal GDP.) Evaluating this derivative at the mean of aid, we find that the estimated decline in infant mortality resulting from an additional 1 per cent of GDP in assistance is zero in a poor-policy environment (index = 0); 0.4 per cent in an average environment (index = 1.1); and 0.9 per cent in a 'good-management' environment, defined as one standard deviation above the mean of the index (that is, a value of 2.7) (figure 8.2). Examples would be poor policy, Zambia or Zaire (1986–9); average policy (India in the 1980s); and good policy (Ghana, 1986–9 or Indonesia, 1982–5).

Figure 8.2 *Decline in infant mortality from 1 per cent of GDP in aid*

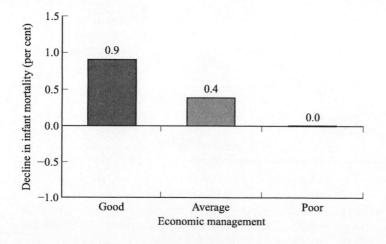

Table 8.3 *Panel regressions for decline in infant mortality*

Time dimensions: six four-year periods, 1970–3 to 1990–3
Countries: 56 aid recipients
Dependent variable: Percentage decline in infant mortality (annual rate)

Regression no.	(1)	(2)	(3)	(4)[a]
Observations	276	273	273	273
Method	OLS	2SLS	2SLS	2,SLS
Constant	7.5	7.8	6.3	6.5
	(4.56)	(4.01)	(3.16)	(3.20)
Initial infant mortality	−1.13	−1.2	−0.94	−1.01
	(3.31)	(2.91)	(2.24)	(2.33)
Ethnic fractionalisation	−0.01	−0.01	−0.01	−0.01
	(1.72)	(1.53)	(1.44)	(1.09)
Assassinations	0.05	0.05	0.04	0.03
	(0.77)	(0.74)	(0.45)	(0.32)
M2/GDP (lagged)	0.00	0.00	0.01	0.02
	(0.29)	(0.15)	(0.52)	(0.85)
Sub-Saharan Africa	−0.58	−0.67	−1.39	−1.44
	(1.46)	(1.66)	(2.95)	(3.08)
East Asia	−0.30	−0.32	0.15	0.04
	(0.72)	(0.75)	(0.25)	(0.07)
Policy index	0.19	0.19	−0.10	−0.09
	(1.37)	(1.35)	(0.32)	(0.29)
Govt consumption	1.96	1.62	4.53	3.08
	(0.56)	(0.37)	(0.84)	(0.51)
Aid/GDP	−0.03	0.02	0.04	0.11
	(0.52)	(0.16)	(0.23)	(0.50)
Aid × Policy	–	–	0.53	0.75
			(1.55)	(1.75)
Aid^2 × Policy	–	–	−0.06	−0.12
			(1.57)	(1.82)
R^2	0.21			
Adjusted R^2	0.17			

Notes:
t-statistics (in parentheses) have been calculated with White's heteroscedasticity-consistent standard errors, for all regressions in the chapter.
[a] The measure of aid in Regression (4) excludes technical assistance.

4 Conclusions

In developing countries with weak economic management – evidenced by poor property rights, high corruption, closed trade regimes and macro-economic instability – there is no relationship between aid and growth, or between aid and the change in infant mortality. In these distorted environments, development projects promoted by donors tend to fail (Isham, Kaufmann and Pritchett, 1997; Isham and Kaufmann, 2000).

Furthermore, aid resources are typically fungible, so that these projects are not in fact what is financed by aid (Feyzioglu, Swaroop and Zhu, 1998). Aid is financing the whole public sector at the margin, which is why the overall quality of management is key to effective assistance. A government that cannot put effective development policies into place is not likely to oversee effective use of foreign aid.

On the other hand, there is a relationship between aid and growth, and between aid and the change in infant mortality in cases in which a recipient has relatively good management. In this situation an additional 1 per cent of GDP is aid has a powerful effect, reducing infant mortality by 0.9 per cent. These results are consistent with what we found for growth in our (1997) work: aid spurs growth only in a good policy environment.

These new findings have implications for how aid should be allocated. Clearly it must be targeted to countries that are poor and have weak social indicators. It is here that there is the greatest potential for poverty reduction. Beyond that, aid should be targeted to countries with good policies. One potential criticism of our work is that low-income countries virtually by definition have poor institutions and policies. It is meanful, then, to talk about allocating aid on the basis of poverty and of 'good policy'? Yes it is meaningful, because the econometric results indicate a sharp positive impact of aid for 'relatively good policies' that are well within the range of the historic experience of low-income countries. India, Uganda, Ethiopia and Vietnam are all examples of low-income countries that have reformed to become 'good-policy countries' in the 1990s. There remain significant problems with their incentive regimes and none of these countries scores nearly as well as, say, Botswana or Thailand on the management index. Nevertheless, their policies are pretty good, and clearly better than many other low-income countries. The point is that the movement from very distorted regimes to relatively good regimes is necessary both for positive *per capita* growth and for effective use of aid.

There is much scope to improve the allocation of aid, focusing it more systematically on countries that are poor and have good policy. Looking at the historical record of bilateral aid, Alesina and Dollar (1998) find that there has been almost no relationship between the amount of aid that countries get and their economic policies. The allocation of aid instead depends on political–strategic factors such as UN voting patterns and colonial ties. Collier and Dollar (1999) show that this remains true in the later 1990s. In fact, after controlling for population and the level of poverty, aid actually has the 'wrong' relationship with policy. As one moves from countries with mediocre policies to ones with good policy, aid 'tapers out', when in fact it should 'taper in'. The same study also looks at the allocation of IDA, the World Bank's concessional assistance to the poorest countries and finds that here there is in fact the 'right' relationship with policy: after controlling for poverty, countries with good policies tend to get more assistance. There is quite a bit of dispersion around that tendency, however. Thus, the World Bank on average has the right allocations, but it could be more systematic about channeling assistance to the countries that are poor and that have made a lot of progress with policy reform.

NOTES

The finding, interpretations, and conclusions expressed in this chapter are entirely those of the authors. They do not necessarily represent the view of the World Bank, its Executive Directors, or the countries that they represent. We would like to thank Chris Gilbert and David Vines for helpful comments, and Mita Chakraborty and Charles Chang for excellent research assistance. Financial support from the World Bank's Research Support Budget (RPO 681–70) is gratefully acknowledged.

1 Krueger, Michalopoulos and Ruttan (1989); Killick (1991); Boone (1994); Van De Walle and Johnston (1996).
2 As Christiano (1989) and Rebelo (1992) have argued, including a subsistence level of consumption in the specification of preferences within a neoclassical model is a useful way of explaining the positive empirical relationship between income levels and savings rates.
3 Strictly speaking the budget constraint should allow for borrowing and lending between households. However, allowing for this does not change any implications of the model for aggregate behaviour, since we are assuming that all households are identical.
4 An alternative, but equivalent, assumption would be that the government can use international capital markets to convert the grant component of any loan into an immediate capital flow.
5 An appendix, available from the authors, provides the algebraic details of the models described in this section.
6 Both economies are ones in which taxes levied on income are rebated, in full, through lump-sum transfers to households.
7 The weights in this index reflect the relative importance of the different factors in a growth regression. The constant derives from the non-policy variables in the regression (initial conditions) evaluated at their means. The mean of this index, 1.1, is the same as the mean growth rate of *per capita* GDP for the sample. A one-unit increase corresponds to a policy improvement that should result in an increase in the growth rate of one percentage point, other things equal.
8 The measure of aid comes from Fernandez-Arias, Serven and Chang (1998); it combines grants with the grant component of concessional loans. The statistical results are the same if we use the more traditional OECD measure

of aid, which combines grants with net disbursements of concessional loans with at least a 25 per cent grant element.

9 Filmer and Pritchett (1997) find that there is little effect of health expenditure on infant or child mortality, concluding that the quality of government spending is more important than quantity.

10 Some insight into why growth typically leads to improvement in social indicators comes from Bruno, Ravallion and Squire (1998). They show that for the majority of developing countries there is no time trend in the distribution of income. Thus, increases in *per capita* income tend to benefit all segments of the income distribution and lead to broad-based gains in social indicators. Similarly, Ravallion and Chen (1997) find that growth and poverty reduction are highly correlated across countries.

REFERENCES

Alesina, A. and D. Dollar (1998). 'Who Gives Aid to Whom and Why?', *NBER Working Paper*, **6612**

Bauer, P.T. (1971), *Dissent on Development*, London: Weidenfeld & Nicolson

Boone, P. (1994). 'The Impact of Foreign Aid on Savings and Growth', London School of Economics, mimeo

Bruno, M., M. Ravallion and L. Squire (1998). 'Equity and Growth in Developing Countries: Old and New Perspectives on the Policy Issues', in V. Tanzi and K. Chu (eds.), *Income Distribution and High-quality Growth*, Cambridge, MA: MIT Press

Burnside, C. and D. Dollar (1997). 'Aid, Policies, and Growth', *Policy Research Working Paper*, **1977**, Washington, DC: World Bank

Christiano, C.J. (1989). 'Understanding Japan's Saving Rate: The Reconstruction Hypothesis', *Federal Reserve Bank of Minneapolis Quarterly Review*, **13**: 10–25

Collier, P. (1997). 'The Failure of Conditionality,' in C. Gwin and J. Nelson (eds.), *Perspectives on Aid and Development*, Washington, DC: Overseas Development Council

Collier, P. and D. Dollar (1999). 'Aid Allocation and Poverty Reduction', *Policy Research Working Paper*, **2041**, Washington, DC: World Bank

Dollar, D. (1992). 'Open Economies Really Do Grow More Rapidly', *Economic Development and Cultural Change*, **40**: 523–44

Easterly, W.R. and S.T. Rebelo (1993). 'Fiscal Policy and Economic Growth: An Empirical Investigation', *Journal of Monetary Economics*, **32**: 417–58

Fernandez-Arias, E., L. Serven and C. Chang (1998). 'Measuring Aid Flows: A New Approach', World Bank, mimeo

Feyzioglu, T., V. Swaroop and M. Zhu (1998). 'A Panel Data Analysis of the Fungibility of Foreign Aid', *World Bank Economic Review*, **12**: 29–58

Filmer, D. and L. Pritchett (1977). 'Child Mortality and Public Spending on Health: How Much Does Money Matter?', *World Bank Policy Research Working Paper*

Fischer, Stanley (1993). 'The Role of Macroeconomic Factors in Growth', *Journal of Monetary Economics*, **32**: 485–512

Isham, J. and D. Kaufmann (2000). 'The Forgotten Rationale for Policy Reform: The Impact on Projects', *Quarterly Journal of Economics*

Isham, J., D. Kaufmann and L. Pritchett (1997). 'Civil liberties, Democracy and the Performance of Government Projects', *World Bank Economic Review*, **11**: 219–42

Killick, T. (1991). 'The Developmental Effectiveness of Aid to Africa', *World Bank Working Paper*, **646**

Knack, S. and P. Keefer (1995). 'Institutions and Economic Performance: Cross-country Tests Using Alternative Institutional Measures', *Economics and Politics*, **7**: 207 27

Krueger, A. O., C. Michalopoulos and V. Ruttan (1989). *Aid and Development*, Baltimore and London: Johns Hopkins University Press

Mosley, P., J. Harrigan and J. Toye (1995). *Aid and Power*, London: Routledge

Pritchett, L. and L. Summers (1995). 'Wealthier Is Healthier', *Journal of Human Resources*, **31**: 841–68

Ravallion, M. and S. Chen (1977). 'What Can New Survey Data Tell Us about Recent Changes in Distribution and Poverty?', *World Bank Economic Review*, **11**: 357 82

Rebelo, S. (1992). 'Growth in Open Economies', *Carnegie–Rochester Conference on Public Policy*, **36**: 5–46

Sachs, J. D. and A. Warner (1995). 'Economic Reform and the Process of Global Integration', *Brookings Papers on Economic Activity*, **1**: 1–1

Van de Walle, N. and T. Johnston (1996). *Improving Aid to Africa* Washington, DC: Overseas Development Council

9 How policies and institutions affect project performance: microeconomic evidence on aid, policies and investment productivity

JONATHAN ISHAM AND DANIEL KAUFMANN

1 Introduction

Previous chapters have examined the conditions under which World Bank lending can positively affect economic growth and poverty alleviation. A key conclusion that emerges from these chapters, supported by macroeconomic evidence and country case studies, is that the policy and institutional frameworks are critical determinants of aggregate performance.

This chapter addresses the same set of issues at the microeconomic level: how do economic policies and national institutions affect investment productivity? We use data from a set of public and private investment projects financed by the World Bank to present evidence that both complements and extends the macroeconomic evidence from chapter 8. With a microeconomic unit of observation as the dependent variable – either a dichotomous investment project performance indicator or an economic rate of return (ERR) – these results on the determinants of project performance provide additional insights on how the policies and institutions that produce poor aggregate performance affect returns to investment at the microeconomic level.

Drawing from the in-depth empirical analysis of the productivity of investment projects financed by the World Bank, this chapter also sheds light on factors other than macroeconomic policies, including civil liberties. Assessing the importance of a participatory process and civil liberties for economic outcomes is important in the context of the debate about conditionality and aid, as it introduces an important dimension that can improve aid leverage without resorting solely to standard ('imposed') conditionality. In other words, if it is indeed the case that better policies and institutions are associated with improved socioeconomic welfare and with successful project outcomes, then it may be paramount to ascertain that aid flows are associated with improving the policy environment (and also because of the fiduciary responsibility of the lending financial institution). Yet this does not necessarily imply that standard conditionality may need to be the only mean to attain such objective. Instead, a participatory process in a country where consultations with stakeholders is encouraged, where IFIs such as the World Bank facilitate rather than dictate the reform programme, could serve as an alternative.

Are all types of investment projects financed by the World Bank likely to be negatively affected by an adverse economic and institutional environment, or is it the case that some projects can be better 'insulated' from poor policies than others? Answering this question empirically is also important in the debate about conditionality and aid, since a possible finding about sectors or types of projects that can be insulated from poor policy-making may suggest that some types of aid projects flowing to countries with poor policy prospects ought not be ruled out.

In order to identify a systematic linkage between country conditions and investment productivity, our empirical strategy is to match available project-level data with selected country-level policy and institutional variables. In particular, we test whether returns to these investments are significantly affected by the policy framework, levels of public investment and national institutions. We also test the magnitude of these effects relative to other country characteristics that affect productivity.[1]

Section 2 of this chapter presents and justifies a hypothesised framework for the mechanisms of this linkage. Section 3 presents evidence on the policy determinants of economic and social projects. Section 4 examines how the level and compositions of the public investment programme affects the performance of tradeable projects . Section 5 presents evidence on the institutional determinants of all public projects. Section 6 concludes with implications for World Bank policies and strategies, focusing on the coordination among the Bank's roles in policy-based lending, project lending, and information diffusion.

2 How policies and institutions affect project performance: a framework

In order to motivate the empirical evidence presented in this chapter, we begin by considering the investment decision that underlies World Bank financing of development projects. In particular, we consider why the Bank has financed projects in countries with poor economic polices, low levels of public infrastructure, or weak national institutions in contrast, say, to the likely investment decisions of a strictly private investor.

First, in building its investment portfolio, the World Bank has tried to pursue objectives consistent with socioeconomic development in its client countries, the emerging and transition economies. An economic justification of 'horizontal equity' has often been used to justify a modicum of lending to countries with a poor policy and institutional environment; in such cases, the value of a continued 'client relationship and dialogue' has also been emphasised when lending to a wide array of countries.

The evidence from chapter 1 suggests that in many cases, aid money to countries with poor policies and institutions was often used ineffectively (or misused by public officials). In this chapter, we consider the direct and indirect linkages between these country conditions and microeconomic performance: how the economy-wide policies, levels of public infrastructure and institutions that influence aggregate performance affect the performance of these investments during different stages of project execution from design until full operation. We hypothesise that these conditions affect performance through the distortion of output choice, underutilisation of capacity and misallocation or misappropriation of project resources by project officials.

During project identification and preparation, distorted price signals – for tradeable and non-tradeable goods and services – can lead to incorrect choices of output and scale and of types of inputs, including import and capital–labour intensities. This can be true for economic and social projects alike: a distorted pricing structure, including free tuition for universities, can create excess demand and hence distort investment decisions within an education project. Lack of transparency and participation in the decision-making process may lead to a mismatch between beneficiary demand and the selection of mechanisms for service delivery as well as outright diversion of funds by public officials.

During project implementation (when World Bank funds are disbursed) and the project's subsequent operational life, misaligned macroeconomic and exchange rate policies can lead to restricted access and higher costs of inputs and capital investments; lower than anticipated demand for output; as well as constrained access and higher costs of working capital and foreign exchange for inputs. Low levels of public investments often attributable to lack of institutional accountability for public sector officials can reduce the productivity of projects in tradeable sectors by increasing operating costs, reducing demand for their products and increasing downside risks. Poor accountability of the government officials who are charged with directing the project can discourage mid-project adjustments in response to consumer demand – as well as lead to further misappropriation of project resources.

These proposed linkages between selected country-level conditions and investment performance are consistent with many existing case studies. First, many *ex post* evaluation reports of unsuccessful projects suggest a link between poor policies and capacity underutilisation. For example, two projects in Jamaica in the mid-1970s – construction of rural infrastructure and rehabilitation of the main sugar-refining factories – performed poorly because an overvalued exchange rate and a restrictive trade regime led to critical shortages in imported inputs.[2] The reductions of output illustrated in many of these case studies are consistent with X-efficiency losses – i.e. an inward movement *within* the production possibilities frontier associated with underutilisation of project capacity. In such cases, distorted incentives and a weak public investment programme directly affect project performance by reducing output rather than by affecting output choice.[3]

Second, other cases show how incorrect levels and composition of public investment, often in conjunction with a poor policy framework, can further reduce performance. In the 1980s, a multi-million-dollar private meat production company in Sudan experienced lower than expected output because of an overvalued currency and domestic price controls. Output was further constrained because the state-owned electricity company was unable to meet production requirements.[4] By contrast, experience in other countries suggests that where the public sector overextends itself into lower-priority areas (where the public good component is non existent and/or the private sector can provide these services more effectively), productivity for individual investments may not be enhanced. Public investments in certain priority areas are complementary to the efficiency of individual investments; in other areas, they may supplant private investments.[5]

Third, myriad case studies illuminate how institutions that promote transparency and accountability affect project performance across many sectors. A community-based irrigation system in the Philippines has successfully improved production yields for over a decade through systematic, open collaboration with local beneficiaries; the responsible ministry offers financial incentives to the staff of provincial irrigation offices to treat local farmers as valued customers (World Bank, 1996). These case studies, along with emerging empirical evidence on the relative importance of accountability and participation, show that 'rules of the game' that improve the transparency and accountability of project-related transactions can significantly improve the overall returns to investment.[6]

Overall, this analytical framework, informed by diverse project case studies, suggests that the policy framework, the composition of public expenditures, and national institutions will critically determine investment productivity.[7] In sections 3–5, we test each of these hypothesised linkages in turn.

3 The policy determinants of project performance: evidence from economic projects

We begin this section with empirical tests of the hypothesised linkage between the policy framework and the performance of economic projects – as measured by re-estimated ERRs. From the World Bank's Operations Evaluation Department (OED) and the evaluation unit of the International Financial Corporation (IFC), we assembled a data set of public and private sector projects in 61 developing countries, implemented from the late 1960s into the early 1990s. The data include re-estimated ERRs as well as other project-specific information – from 1,163 investment projects financed by the Bank and implemented by public agencies in developing countries and from 113 private projects financed by the IFC. These are projects in tradeable sectors – agriculture, industry and tourism – and non-tradeable sectors – transport, infrastructure, energy, water and urban – for which such ERRs have been calculated and for which a minimum set of country-specific policy indices was available.

The re-estimated ERR of each project is measured via the World Bank's cost-benefit methodology, about two-to-three years after the completion of World Bank funding for project implementation. It makes use of actual data on costs incurred during project implementation; actual recurrent operating costs and benefits to date; and projections of future cost and benefit streams – all evaluated at shadow (or border) prices.

Table 9.1 presents the summary statistics used in this analysis, including the number of countries and periods covered for each variable. Indices of country characteristics and policy performance were gathered from independent sources.[8] Country characteristic data incorporated into this analysis include the capital–labour ratio, years of education and terms of trade changes.

Note that combining data on project performance with country characteristic data means that the data used in this analysis have an 'unbalanced' panel structure. Specifically, we are estimating the ERR of project i in country j in year t. Since the number and frequency of projects varies greatly by country (for example, many more projects in Indonesia and India than in Colombia), this means that a large proportion of the total matrix (country times year) does not contain observations. In addition,

Table 9.1 *Summary statistics*

	N	Mean	Std dev.	Min	Max	No. of countries
Dependent variable						
Ex post ERR	1625	15.9	15.1	−20	155	6
Policy performance data						
Black market premium[a]	1516	45.6	87.2	−7.8	508.2	6
Fiscal deficit	820	−5.30	4.99	25.28	8.40	3
Index of trade restrictiveness	531	1.66	0.86	1	5	3
Index of price distortions	1254	100.27	1.20	96.19	102.2	5
Real interest rate[b]	778	−1.96	15.25	−92.03	87.8	3
Standard independent variables						
Capital–labour ratio (log)	856	8.24	1.01	5.71	10.74	5
Education years of working age	856	4.39	2.08	0.39	11.22	5
Dummy for project complexity	1486	0.21	0.41	0	1	6
Change in terms of trade	1242	0.97	7.27	−24.24	54.18	6
GDP growth	1282	3.69	3.32	−16.61	21.96	5
Additional independent variables						
Total investment (per cent)	1243	9.3	4.4	0.9	34.5	6
Public investment/GDP investment (per cent)	1235	42.3	16.3	7.4	93.2	6
Black market premium at project approval	1577	22.3	14.5	1.0	161.0	6
World Bank presence (as percentage of overall investment)	1322	0.066	0.040	0.001	0.233	5

Notes: [a]See World Bank (1991b) for data descriptions and sources.
[b]Real interest rate dummy (= 1 if real interest rate > 0) used in analysis.
[c]One observation per country for time period.
Source: Isham and Kaufmann (2000).

there are less than two dozen cases where two projects from the same country are evaluated in the same year. As discussed below in the econometric analysis, possible biases from this structure – specifically, the potential for large fixed country or year effects – are tested and ruled out.

It is important to consider why these country characteristics are included in the econometric specifications below that test the determinants of project productivity. Begin by considering selected characteristics that are the cornerstones of myriad growth theories and of cross-country empirical studies: levels of physical capital, labour supply and human capital (Solow, 1956; Barro, 1991; Mankiw, Romer and Weil, 1992); and terms of trade shocks (Easterly *et al.*, 1994). First, because of decreasing marginal returns, one would expect these rates of return to investment projects to be negatively associated with the economy-wide capital–labour ratio. Second, controlling for the economy-wide capital–labour ratio, one might expect the rates of return to be increasing in levels of human capital. Third, external shocks might affect average investment productivity through terms of trade changes. Accordingly, in the econometric specifications that follow, we control for these country characteristics in testing for the effect of policies and institutions on project performance.[9]

The policy indices used in this analysis were: *black market premium* (the average annual mark-up of the parallel market rate for foreign exchange over the official exchange rate); *fiscal deficit of the central government as a share of GDP; index of trade restrictiveness* (based upon specific policy criteria such as tariffs and non-tariff barriers); *index of pricing distortions in tradeable goods* (measuring the deviation of the domestic price levels from international price equivalencies for final tradeable goods); and *real interest rate*. These indicators capture major policy distortions in each economy. For example, the black market premium reflects distortions in the trade, pricing and exchange rate regime, as well as macroeconomic instability and capital account restrictions (Barro and Sala-i-Martin, 1995; Kaufmann and O'Connell, 1997); the fiscal deficit is an indicator of macroeconomic instability.

We begin the analysis with a set of average ERRs, disaggregated by type of policy distortion and sector (within the larger public sector data set). As presented in table 9.2, the differences between investment efficiency in undistorted and distorted policy environments can be very large. In most cases, when classifying by a single policy distortion indicator, average ERRs of projects implemented under a distorted policy regime are at least five percentage points lower than those of projects implemented under an undistorted regime. In addition, each of the five policy distortion indices appears to be significantly associated with performance across the various sectors – although to different degrees. Further, the sensitivity of public sector projects to policy distortions is at least as significant as for private sector projects.[10] Note that the large reported differences in ERRs between distorted and undistorted policy regimes may even be underestimated when using these averages: the standard evaluation methodology at the World Bank and the IFC assigns any project with an ERR below −5 per cent a value of exactly −5 per cent. About 13 per cent of all observations in this data set have ERRs with this value, and they tend to be relatively more concentrated in settings with poor policies.

A country that mismanages its exchange rate is also likely to exhibit macroeconomic instability as well as trade and pricing distortions: it is therefore relevant to assess the *combined* effect of policy distortions on

Table 9.2 *Economic policies and the ERR of projects: single-policy distortions*[a]
Average ERR (per cent)

	All projects	Public projects	Agriculture	Industry	Non-tradeable sectors	Private projects
Overall average ERR	16.0	16.2	14.3	13.6	18.1	14.0
Policy distortion index						
1 *Trade restrictions*						
Highly restrictive	13.2	13.6	12.2	insf[b]	14.6	9.5
Somewhat restrictive	15.0	15.4	15.5	insf	16.0	10.7
Non-restrictive	19.0	19.3	14.3	insf	24.3	17.1
2 *Exchange rate overvaluation, black market premiums:*						
High (≥200 per cent)	8.0	7.2	4.0	insf	11.4	insf
Medium (20–200 per cent)	14.5	15.0	12.9	9.7	17.1	10.3
Low (<20 per cent)	17.5	12.7	16.2	15.9	19.2	15.2
3 *Real interest rate*						
Negative	15.0	15.4	12.7	12.7	17.9	11.0
Positive	17.3	17.5	17.0	17.8	17.9	15.6
4 *Fiscal deficit*						
High (>8 per cent of GDP)	13.4	13.7	11.7	10.3	16.6	10.7
Medium (4–8 per cent)	14.8	15.1	12.2	21.0	16.8	12.2
Low (<4 per cent)	17.8	18.1	18.6	14.1	18.2	14.3
5 *Price distortion index of tradeable goods*						
High distortions	15.6	15.9	13.1	14.0	18.4	11.0
Low distortions	17.5	17.5	17.0	16.5	18.1	17.2

Notes: [a]Average re-estimated economic rate of return of public and private projects, classified by single policy distortion.
[b]'insf' denotes insufficient number of observations (less than 10) to make inferences.
Source: Isham and Kaufmann (2000).

ERRs. Average ERRs, disaggregated by various combinations of policy distortions are presented in table 9.3.[11] Multiple policy distortions, when compared with an undistorted policy environment, can make a difference of over 10 percentage points. These large differences between investment efficiency in undistorted and distorted environments (measured through multiple indicators, as compared with the effect of single indicators) suggest independent contributions by different types of distortions.

In order to explore the relative importance of policies suggested by tables 9.2 and 9.3 – and to account for other potential determinants of investment productivity – a set of multivariate econometric specifications was estimated. Since the ERR data are censored at −5 per cent, so the Tobit procedure is required to generate consistent estimates.

We first tested 10 econometric specifications: a pair for each of the five policy variables. In addition to one of the five policy indicators, the first specification in each pair includes years of education and terms of trade changes and a dummy variable for the degree of institutional complexity

Table 9.3 *Economic policies and the ERR of projects: combined-policy distortions*[a]

	All projects	All public projects	Public agriculture	Public number of tradeable sectors
Overall average	16.0	16.2	14.3	18.1
Combined policy distortion indices				
1 *Trade restriction, black market premium and real interest rate*				
Highly distorted[b]	9.7	10.0	5.6	14.2
Somewhat distorted[c]	15.7	16.1	16.7	15.8
Non-distorted[d]	19.5	19.7	14.2	25.0
2 *Fiscal deficit and price distortion index of tradeable goods*				
Highly distorted	14.8	15.0	15.3	15.8
Somewhat distorted	16.2	16.2	14.7	17.4
Non-distorted	17.7	18.0	18.4	18.6
3 *Fiscal deficit and trade restrictions*				
Highly distorted	8.7	9.1	6.9	12.7
Somewhat distorted	15.0	15.3	15.2	15.7
Non-distorted	20.0	20.8	15.0	28.1

Notes: [a]Average re-estimated economic rates of return of public and private projects, classified by multiple policy distortions.
[b]'Highly distorted' categories include all observations with high distortions for each of the single policy indices.
[c]'Somewhat distorted' includes all remaining observations with non-missing observations for each of the single policy indices.
[d]'Non-distorted' includes all observations with low distortions for each of the single policy indices.
Source: Isham and Kaufmann (2000).

of the project (for subsectors regarded by evaluation units as more complex, such as integrated rural projects). The second specification in each pair adds the economy-wide capital–labour ratio and the average rate of GDP growth during the three years prior to project completion (to control for overall economy-wide dynamism). Since policies may affect capital intensity and overall GDP growth of an economy, the estimated policy coefficients in these specifications indicate the direct impact of policies on ERRs, net of the indirect impact of policies through capital intensity and GDP growth.[12]

The econometric results are presented in table 9.4. First, what is the effect of other country characteristics? Across specifications, the capital–labour intensity significantly affects ERRs in the expected direction. More complex projects are also significantly less productive. Neither years of education nor terms of trade changes have a significant, substantial impact.[13]

Table 9.4 *Determinants of ERRs: single-policy variable Tobit specifications*[a]

Independent variables	Parallel rate premium		Trade openness		Fiscal deficit		Distortion tradeable
Specification	(1)	(2)	(3)	(4)	(5)	(6)	(7)
Intercept	19.7	33.0	10.8	24.9	16.9	31.8	−207.0
Policy variable[c]	−0.055	−0.049	2.53	2.18	−0.33	−0.34	−2.26
	(6.1)***[b]	(5.1)***	(2.8)**	(2.4)**	(2.7)***	(2.9)***	(4.0)**
Capital labour ratio (log)	−	−2.04	−	−2.07	−	−2.37	−
		(3.0)***		(2.7)***		(3.4)***	
Years of education	0.30	0.18	−0.03	0.43	0.28	0.80	−0.66
	(1.0)	(0.6)	(0.1)	(1.3)	(0.9)	(2.4)**	(2.1)**
Project complexity	−2.74	−3.16	−3.50	3.80	−3.43	−3.68	3.54
	(2.0)**	(2.3)**	(2.6)***	(2.8)***	(2.5)***	(2.7)***	(2.6)***
Terms of trade improvement	0.02	0.00	0.00	−0.01	0.01	0.02	0.1
	(0.2)	(0.1)	(0.0)	(0.2)	(0.2)	(0.2)	(1.3)
GDP growth	−	0.34	−	0.49	−	0.64	
		(1.6)		(2.3)**		(3.1)***	
Log likelihood	2526	2410	2601	2520	2340	2328	−2522
No. of observations	656	656	656	656	656	656	656

Notes: [a]Dependent variable is re-estimated economic rate of return (ERR) for public and private projects.
[b]Numbers in parentheses are *t*-statistics.

When controlling for these other country characteristics, the results in table 9.4 suggest that policies are critical determinants of project performance. Relatively large changes in single policy indices are associated with statistically significant differences in ERRs from 3–7 percentage points. Based on the coefficients on each of the indices, specific policy changes are associated with increases of average ERRs as follows. Lowering the black market premiums from 120 per cent to 20 per cent is associated with an ERR increase of over 5 percentage points;[14] moving from a very restrictive trade regime (rated as a 1) to a fairly open one (4) is associated with an ERR increase of about 7 percentage points. A difference in the fiscal deficit (as a share of GDP) of 8 percentage points – for example, between 2 and 10 per cent of GDP – is associated with an ERR increase of almost 3 percentage points. A large difference in the index of distortion of tradeables is associated with an ERR increase of about 3 percentage points.[15] And a dummy variable for a positive versus negative real interest rate is associated with an ERR increase of 1.3–2.4 per centage points (significant in only the first specification of the pair).

If different economic policies have an independent contribution to investment productivity, the overall impact of policy distortions would be underestimated in the single-policy specifications. In table 9.5, we thus introduce a number of policy variables simultaneously into a multivariate policy specification; this can also suggest which policy indices dominate in their impact on ERRs. With the exception of the real interest rate dummy, policy indices appear to have a significant independent (and additive) effect. For example, in estimations including the capital–labour ratio and GDP growth as independent control variables, a 100-percentage point reduction in the black market premium coupled with a moderate opening up in the trade regime (e.g. from 1 to 3 or from 2 to 4) is associated with an improvement in ERRs of 9 percentage points, holding other factors constant. These estimated magnitudes are not altered when country fixed effects are included in the specification as additional controls (capturing other country-specific conditions, see column (2)). The combination of fiscal deficit and trade variables (columns (3) and (4)) also suggest significant and independent effects, although the implied effects of the changes in the policy parameters are not as large: ERRs of about 56 percentage points higher are associated with substantial policy changes in this combination.[16]

These seemingly strong results could potentially be undermined by
. sample selection bias related to the World Bank's unique investment objectives. This sample of projects is neither random nor necessarily representative of all investment projects in any given country. Sample selection bias – in an upward direction for the estimates of policy effects is possible if, in countries where the Bank's investment activities are low *and* which have better economic policies, the Bank can 'skim' the best possible projects.

To test for possible mis-specification owing to this bias, we constructed a World Bank 'project presence' variable: the Bank's accumulated project disbursements as a share of the total capital stock. This variable (a single observation for each country) was included as an additional independent variable in the primary set of Tobit estimations; the project presence variable was also used to truncate the sample for low and high values of World Bank presence. In all cases, the robustness of the policy coefficients was maintained.[17]

So far, this analysis indicates that the quality of the policy framework can make a large difference for project productivity. But these results do

Table 9.5 *Determinants of ERRs: combined-policy variable specifications*[a]

Specification	(1)	(2)	(3)	(4)
	Black market premiums, trade openness and interest rate	(1) and country fixed effects	Fiscal deficit and distortion in tradeable	Fiscal deficit and trade openness
Independent variables				
Intercept	30.2	67.7[a]	−134.2	27.9
Black market premium	−0.046	−0.038	−	−
	(4.9)***[b]	(2.1)**		
Trade openness	2.09	2.34	−	1.7
	(2.3)**	(1.9)*		(1.9)*
Real interest rate dummy	−0.41	−1.46		−
	(0.3)	(0.9)		
Distortion in tradeable	−	−	−1.71	−
			(2.9)***	
Fiscal deficit	−	−	−0.22	−0.32
			(1.8)*	(2.7)***
Capital–labour ratio (log)	−2.09	5.11	−2.46	−2.28
	(2.9)***	(1.6)	(3.6)***	(3.3)***
Years of education	0.07	−0.75	0.10	0.66
	(0.2)	(0.4)	(0.3)	(1.9)*
Institutional complexity	−3.1	−2.82	−3.79	−3.6
	(2.3)**	(2.4)**	(2.8)***	(2.6)***
Terms of trade improvement	0.02	−0.01	0.06	−0.04
	(0.2)	(0.2)	(0.7)	(0.5)
GDP growth	0.16	0.02	0.29	0.45
	(0.8)	(0.1)	(1.4)	(2.1)**
Country fixed effects	No	Yes***	No	No
Log likelihood	−2514	−2481	−2514	−2523
No. of observations	656	656	656	656

Notes: [a]Dependent variable is re-estimated economic rate of return (ERR) for public and private projects; intercept maintained by omitting one country dummy.
[b]Numbers in parentheses are *t*-statistics.
Significance levels: *** = 99 per cent; ** = 95 per cent; * = 90 per cent.
Source: Isham and Kaufmann (2000).

not necessarily imply that a major policy overhaul will immediately yield a vastly improved average ERR. Indeed, it is has often been argued that given the nature of project selection and implementation – and the cost and time of restructuring investments – many benefits of policy reform may not be apparent in the short term (in addition to economy-wide institutional deficiencies that take time to address).

In fact, summary statistics from these data suggest that within a few years significant payoffs to policy improvements are possible. On average countries which move from an inappropriate to an adequate policy environment are more likely to end up with much higher ERRs than countries in which policies do not improve. Projects whose preparation began when policies were distorted (i.e. the black market premium greater than 30 per cent) but completed the investment phase under a less distorted policy framework (the black market premium was very low) were found to have an average ERR of 17.8 per cent. By contrast, the evidence indicates that countries in which the policy framework deteriorates during project execution will experience a substantial drop in investment productivity. Projects that began preparation when policies were not distorted – black market premium less than 30 per cent – but were completed when the black market premium was higher, had an average ERR of only 13.2 per cent.[18]

To test econometrically the effects of a policy improvement during project implementation, we modified the basic multivariate analysis to control for initial conditions of the black market premium, as presented in table 9.6. Controlling for both fixed country effects and initial conditions, the statistical robustness of the relationship between policies and ERRs is maintained: economic reforms within a country seem to yield investment productivity payoffs within a few years.

This relationship between the ERRs and the black market premium – a good proxy of macroeconomic and trade distortions – obviously cannot capture the variety and complexity of policy reform measures that are required to improve investment productivity. Nevertheless, the results do suggest that when policies improve, high payoffs can be expected in the short-to-medium term. Conversely, deterioration in the policy framework can be very costly, even in the short term.

Overall, these results on the determinants of ERRs suggest that among economic projects, no sector can be isolated from the deleterious effects of poor policies. This raises the question of whether project investments in the social sectors – education and health – can still be justified in the face of poor policies. If so, this might lead to the claim that, given the Bank's special role in trying to promote poverty alleviation, significant

Table 9.6 *ERRs and policy reforms: controlling for initial conditions*[a]

	Not controlling for initial policy conditions	Black market premium change during project implementation
Intercept	87.5	82.4
Black market premium at project evaluation	−0.046	–
	(2.5)**[b]	
Black market premium at project appraisal	–	−0.031
		(1.0)
Premium change since project appraisal	–	−0.047
		(2.5)**
Capital–labour ratio	−6.8	−6.2
	(1.8)*	(1.6)
Education years	−1.6	−1.7
	(0.9)	(1.0)
Project complexity	−2.8	−2.7
	(2.0)**	(2.0)**
Terms of trade change	0.02	0.02
	(0.2)	(0.2)
GDP growth	0.06	0.07
	(0.2)	(0.5)
Country fixed effects	Yes***	Yes***
Log likelihood	−2368	−2369
No. of observations	624	624

Notes: [a]Dependent variable is re-estimated economic rate of return (ERR) for public and private projects (with black market premium data available at project appraisal and evaluation). The intercept was not suppressed in these specifications; a country dummy was omitted. Numbers in parentheses are *t*-statistics.

lending for schools and health clinics is appropriate even in the most distorted economies.

Project evaluation data from OED for 259 World Bank-financed social projects can be used to test the validity of this claim. These project data cover 84 countries for the period 1974–90, with 34 countries from Africa, 12 from Asia, 17 from Europe, the Mid-East and North Africa and 21 from Latin America and the Caribbean. For each project, information is available on the rating – given by OED regarding project performance – either satisfactory or unsatisfactory rating at the time of project evaluation, usually about 12–18 months after the completion of project implementation.

How are these project performance ratings to be interpreted? In general, unsatisfactory ratings are for those projects which truly performed very badly, whereas the satisfactory ratings include mediocre projects and those of uncertain performance quality. Among 259 social projects, 52 (20 per cent of the sample) are rated as unsatisfactory.

Table 9.7 presents summary statistics of the incidence of unsatisfactory social projects under different policy distortion categories. Cross-tabulations show that trade restrictiveness, currency overvaluation, fiscal deficits and price distortions are significantly associated with the performance of social projects; this is similar to the cross-tabulations for economic projects in table 9.2.[19] For example, no social project failed when trade barriers are low, as compared with a probability of failure of almost 30 per cent when trade restrictions are relatively high or very high. When the black market premium is high, 37 per cent of the projects failed, more than twice the likelihood of failure under a low premium; these probabilities are virtually the same than for economic projects (column (4) of table 9.7). Similarly, when the fiscal deficit is large or when relative prices are distorted, the likelihood of poor project performance is higher (and the magnitude and differences are similar than for economic projects, see table 9.7).

The first four results for all social projects (column (1)) are statistically significant, with Chi-squared statistics ranging from 2.9 to 8.5 (the critical value is 2.7 with 90 per cent confidence), suggesting strong statistical association between policy variables and the performance of projects. The impact of the real interest rate, while in the expected direction, is not significant at the 90 per cent level.

Only a limited multivariate test of the suggested relationship between policies and the performance of social projects is possible with the available data, since the country selection for these 259 projects is much broader than in the sample for economic projects, and many of the country-level variables that were used in the full specifications above are not available for these countries. The best that one can do in this case is to include the five policy variables and one non-policy variable (GDP growth) that do exist across most of these 84 countries, along with regional dummy variables.[20]

Table 9.8 presents the results of a Probit analysis with these selected determinants of social projects, where the dependent variable is the indicator of an unsatisfactory project. In specification 1, the black market premium has a significant positive effect on the probability of project failure. In specification 2, the fiscal deficit also has a significant positive effect on the probability of project failure, though in the case of these social projects, this occurs at the medium range of fiscal deficits and

Table 9.7 *Economic policies and the performance of social projects: single-policy distortions*[a]

| Economy-wide policy variables | Percentage of unsatisfactory projects | | | |
| | Social sector projects | | | Economic projects |
	All (1)	Education (2)	Health (3)	(4)
Number of projects	259	228	31	1488
Percentage unsatisfactory	20.1	17.5	38.7	21.6
Trade restrictiveness				
Low	0.0	0.0	insf[b]	16.3
High	28.1	23.9	insf	24.9
Black market premium				
Low	17.4	13.6	42.3	19.5
High	37.0	39.0	20.0	36.7
Fiscal deficit				
Low	11.3	11.1	12.5	14.3
High	29.2	22.6	58.3	25.4
Price distortions				
Low	48	11.9	28.6	18.1
High	25.7	22.9	62.5	25.3
Real interest rate				
Positive	17.5	13.7	33.3	16.4
Negative	29.4	23.3	75.0	17.4
Growth of GDP				
High	14.4	11.4	33.3	16.9
Low	23.8	21.3	60.0	28.3

Notes: [a]See the text for definitions of variables.
[b]'insf' stands for insufficient number of observations.
*Economic (not social) project/study for investment in industry, agriculture and, infrastructure (which do also have calculations for ERRS, as analysed in previous sections).
Source: Kaufmann and Wang (1995).

seems to have has no additional significant impact once the deficit exceeds about 4 per cent of GDP. This 'kinked' effect of fiscal balance is detected by the inclusion of two splined variables: 'low fiscal deficit' and 'high fiscal deficit'.[21] In the case of these social sector projects, when multi-policy models are estimated, the significant effects of the black market premium remains robust and dominates, while the fiscal balance variables become insignificant.

Overall, these results do not suggest that projects in the social sectors can be insulated from the policy environment, particularly where measured by the black market premium on foreign exchange. Indeed, the simple probability of failure or success *vis-à-vis* the quality of policies does not appear to differ significantly between economic and social projects. The quality of economy-wide policies appears to significantly affect

Table 9.8 *Determinants of performance of social projects: Probit estimations[a,b]*

	(1)	(2)
Intercept	−1.0860	−0.7188
Parallel rate premium	0.0034***	–
	(2.31)	
Low fiscal deficit	–	14.5*
		(1.74)
High fiscal deficit	–	−1.73
		(0.68)
GDP growth	−0.0553*	−8.08***
	(1.81)	(2.61)
Log likelihood	−119.23	−120.18

Notes: [a]Dependent variable is an indicator of unsatisfactory project. No. of observations = 259.
[b]Specifications included regional dummies and missing variable dummies (not shown) for independent variables.
Source: Kaufmann and Wang (1995).

economic and social projects alike; there is no evidence that particular types of (World Bank) conventional investment projects are subject to 'insulation' from inappropriate economic policies.

4 The effect of the overall public investment programme on investment returns

In underscoring the importance of undistorted economic policies in empirically explaining project investment failures, we note that such policies only partially account for the variation in performance of such investments.[22] As discussed in section 2, another likely determinant for projects in tradeable sectors is the nature of a country's public investment programme.

In the developing (and developed) world, governments have been responsible for the provision of basic infrastructure services – in transport, energy, and agriculture (World Bank, 1994). The economic justification for such public investments are familiar. These services enjoy a substantial public good component, their production and provision are often subject to externalities and/or large economies of scale, and commercial financing for such large-scale undertakings is often constrained. In developing countries, the private sector has been even less likely to provide these public investments, or has tended to do so in suboptimal amounts.

Data from agricultural and industrial projects demonstrate the importance of overall public investments for investment productivity in the tradeable sectors. The productivity of individual private and public tradeable projects increases significantly as the share of public investments in GDP grows – but only up to a point. Figure 9.1 depicts simple range averages from the raw data:[23] the average ERR for investment projects increases by about 5 percentage points as the share of overall public investment in GDP increases from 5 to almost 10 per cent. However, as the share of overall public investment in GDP increases beyond 10 per cent, the average ERR eventually declines.

The data plotted in figure 9.1 suggest that the relationship between overall public investment and the productivity of tradeable projects is particularly strong for projects implemented in a relatively undistorted policy framework. The ERR of projects implemented under an undistorted environment is on average about 13 per cent in countries where the share of public investment in GDP is 5 per cent or less, while the average ERR exceeds 19 per cent when the share of public investment in GDP is on average 9.5 per cent. But as the share of public investment in GDP

Figure 9.1 *Share of public investment in GDP and the productivity of tradeable projects*

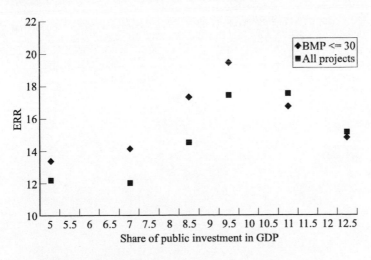

Notes: BMP   Black market premium.
◆ Indicates projects where BMP was 30 per cent or less.
■ Indicates all projects.

exceeds 10 per cent, investment productivity declines – to an average ERR of about 15 per cent.[24]

These data also suggest the importance of maintaining an appropriate balance between public and private investment shares (figure 9.2). In economies with undistorted policies, the average ERR of tradeable projects increases from 14 to 20 per cent as the share of public investment in total investment rises to about 40 per cent. Yet again, increasing the share of public investments in total above this range substantially reduces project productivity.

To test the statistical significance of these relationships, we conducted restricted Tobit analysis with spline functions (Greene, 1990) for the ratio of public investment in GDP and for the ratio of public investment in total investments. The results in table 9.9 indicate the statistical significance of the relationships depicted in figures 9.1 and 9.2.

The overall public investment programme of a country appears to affect strongly the productivity of individual projects, particularly so in settings where the economic policy environment is relatively undistorted. When the policy environment is distorted, the ERR of tradeable projects will be very low regardless of the relative size or shares of the public investment programme (columns (2) and (6)). By contrast, in an improved economic policy environment, increasing the size of public investment up to about 9.5 per cent of GDP has a statistically significant positive effect; but increasing the size further has a significant negative

Figure 9.2 *Share of public investment in total investment and the productivity of tradeable projects*

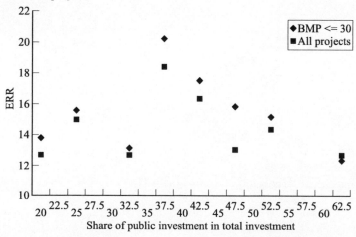

Notes: See figure 9.1.

Table 9.9 *Public investment and the ERR of tradeable projects*

| | Public investment/GDP | | | | Public investment/total investment | | | | |
| | All | | Low premium | | All | | Low premium | | High premium[c] |
	(1)	(2)	(3)	(4)	(5)	(6)	(7)	(8)	(9)
Intercept	4.6	12.6	6.9	11.1	7.0	9.1	5.5	11.4	7.3
Public investment[a]	1.22	0.65	1.23	1.12	0.26	0.28	0.35	0.31	−0.0?
	(2.7)***[d]	(3.1)***	(2.4)**	(2.2)**	(2.2)**	(2.4)**	(2.8)***	(2.4)**	(0.9)
High public investment[b]	−1.61	−0.76	−2.06	−1.95	0.60	−0.52	−0.69	−0.68	??
	(2.3)**	(1.1)	(2.4)**	(2.3)**	(3.5)***	(3.1)***	(3.5)***	(3.5)***	??
Black market premium	–	−0.059	–	–	–	0.057	–	–	–
		(5.4)***				(5.2)***			
Terms of trade change	–	0.06	–	0.02	–	0.06	–	0.03	0.26
		(0.5)		(0.2)		(0.6)		(0.2)	(1.1)
Project complexity	–	−2.47	–	−2.34	–	−2.54	–	−2.73	−0.80
		(1.7)*		(1.4)		(1.7)*		(1.6)	(0.3)
Years of education	–	−0.09	–	−0.50	–	−0.09	–	−0.66	1.43
		(0.2)		(1.2)		(0.2)		(1.5)	(1.9)
Log likelihood	−1607	−1588	−1255	1253	−1601	−1584	−1252	−1249	−336
No. of observations	411	411	321	321	422	422	321	321	101

Notes: [a]For public investment/GDP, the segment up to 9.5 per cent of GDP; for public investment/total investment, the segment up to 40 per cent of total investment.
[b]For public investment/GDP, the segment exceeding 9.5 per cent of GDP; for public investment/total investment, the segment exceeding 40 per cent of total investment.
[c]This specification (in column (9)) is linear, not kinked, since there were no significant breaks in the relationship between public investment and ERRs in regimes with high black market premium sample.
[d]Numbers in parentheses are *t*-statistics.
Significance levels: *** = 99 per cent; ** = 95 per cent; * = 90 per cent.
Source: Isham and Kaufmann (2000).

effect (columns (3) and (4)). Likewise, increasing the share of public investments in total investment up to about 40 per cent has a statistically significant positive effect; but increasing the share further has a significant negative effect (columns (7) and (8)). When the private sector is crowded out by a bloated public investment programme, the productivity of marginal public investments can be very low indeed.[25]

Overall, these results – as well as illustrative case studies such as the Jamaican sugar processing projects and the Sudan meat processing factory – suggest two complementary and powerful aspects of policy reform.

The best public investment programme or 'balance' cannot compensate for poor macroeconomic, trade and pricing policies. Indeed, undistorted policies are necessary for high productivity of projects in the tradeable sectors. Yet in themselves they may not always be sufficient: they need to be complemented by an adequate public investment programme (see also *WDR 1994* on Infrastructure, World Bank, 1994).

5 The effect of institutions on investment returns

As discussed in section 2, another likely determinant of project performance is the set of institutions that affects decision-making by public officials who are charged with directing the project. Specifically, involvement of potential beneficiaries in project decision-making, and the degree to which the public sector officials are held accountable for their performance, are two keys to the success of public investment projects.[26]

Since micro-level data on project participation and public sector accountability are not available for the available public projects, our empirical strategy is to use cross-country indicators of civil liberties to test for this relationship. Both greater beneficiary involvement and greater accountability of public sector officials are facilitated by an environment in which basic civil liberties – such as the freedom to speak out and the ability of groups to organise to protect and advance their interests – are recognised.

We use data from three cross-country efforts that have attempted to rank countries by degree of civil liberties:

- *Freedom House* (1994 and previous years) has constructed a ranking of civil liberties for 165 countries from 1972 to 1994. This ranking – on a seven-point scale – is based upon a 14-item checklist of civil liberties.[27]
- *Humana* (1986) constructed an index of human rights achievement in 89 countries for the year 1985. This index, on a scale of zero to 100 (actual range is 13 to 98) was based upon the definition of human rights adopted by the General Assembly of the United Nations in 1966 under the International Covenant on Civil and Political Rights.
- *Coppedge and Reinicke* (1990) constructed two series – 'media pluralism' and 'freedom to organise' – to capture institutional arrangements that permit public opposition in 170 countries for the year 1985.

These indicators are likely to capture the institutions that promote open and transparent decision-making by public officials and which may in turn affect project performance.[28] At least six of the 14 elements of the Freedom House civil rights index, for example, are directly compatible with beneficiary participation in projects: media free of censorship, open public discussion, freedom of assembly and demonstration, free trade unions, peasant organisations, businesses or cooperatives, free professional or other private organisations and freedom from gross government indifference or corruption.

The estimation strategy in this section builds on the previous results on the policy determinants of projects. While we focus on the relation between civil liberties and performance, we must still account for country structural and policy characteristics which have been shown to be determinants of project success. Accordingly, for each civil liberties variable tested, we estimate four specifications which include various degrees of control variables: (A) country and structural characteristics only; (B) these variables plus regional dummies; (C) country and structural characteristics with selected policy variables; and (D) these variables plus regional dummies. By estimating and reporting each of these specifications, we are able to explore possible endogeneity of policies and civil liberties.

The independent variables in this section are classified as follows:

- Exogenous and/or structural variables (denoted Xs), including the country capital–labour ratio, terms of trade changes, and the dummy for project complexity.
- Possibly endogenous policy and economic variables (denoted Zs) that could be correlated with each other and/or with the governance variables, including the black market premium, the fiscal deficit and GDP growth.
- Regional dummies for South Asia, East Asia, Sub-Saharan Africa, Latin America and Europe and the Mid East.

When only structural variables are included (specifications A and B) the estimate of the partial impact of better governance on project performance could be overstated because of omitted-variables bias. Conversely, when policy variables are included (specifications C and D), this estimate could understate the true total impact of civil liberties if part of the impact of better civil liberties is through better policies – through the same mechanisms of open decision-making public sector accountability.

The inclusion of the regional dummies, which are obviously exogenous, is simply a robustness test. In order to be persuasive, the results should survive the introduction of regional fixed effects; otherwise, the results may simply be capturing some other unmeasured historical, cultural or ideological effect that covaries across regions and is perhaps correlated with both project returns and civil liberties.

Since we focus on the impact of civil liberties variables in this section, we (as a presentational matter) report only the coefficients of the various civil liberties indicators when added to these four base specifications, rather than repeat all the results for each control variable in each regression. None of the coefficients on any of the variables above including the black market premium and the fiscal deficit – changes dramatically with the inclusion of any civil liberties indicator.

Table 9.10 shows the results of including each of the measures of civil liberties in basic performance regressions with ERRs. There is a consistent, statistically significant and empirically large effect of civil liberties on the return to projects.[29] Taking the estimates from specification D, if the Freedom House civil liberties index were to improve from the worst (1) to the best (7, as in Costa Rica for all evaluated years), the ERR is predicted to increase by 7.5 percentage points. Similarly, with the estimates using the Humana index, improving from the worst civil liberties (13) to one of the best (91, as in Costa Rica) would improve the ERR by 22.5 percentage points.

Since these civil liberties indices are on a different scale, a more standard method for comparison is to calculate how much the ERR is predicted to increase if each index were improved by one standard deviation (column (5)).[30] An increase of this magnitude in the Freedom House index would raise the predicted ERR by 1.6 points; a similar increase in the Humana index would raise the ERR by 50.2 points; a standard deviation increase in 'media pluralism' would improve the predicted ERR by 3.1 points.

This finding of a positive relationship between civil liberties and ERRs is the central positive finding of this section.[31] The results are qualitatively similar to the project performance rating for the larger sample of economic *and* social projects. Table 9.11 reports the estimates of a Probit regression for specifications C and D (results for A and B were similar). Naturally, since the binary indicator discards a great deal of statistical information, these results are less precise: the *p*-levels are lower, and the estimates for the Humana ranking are insignificant. For the other variables, the estimates show large increases in the likelihood of a good project when implemented under higher civil liberties. For instance, at the mean of the Freedom House variable, a one standard deviation increase in civil liberties would lower the probability of an unsatisfactory project by 30.2 percentage points, which reduces the predicted failure rate by 16 per cent (from the mean of 20 per cent). Similarly, a one standard deviation improvement in media pluralism would reduce the failure rate by almost 5 percentage points, or 25 per cent from the mean.

Table 9.10 *Impact of civil liberties on rates of return*[a]

	Specification				Effect of 1 std dev. increase on ERR
	A Exogenous	B With regional dummies	C With policy variables	D With regional dummies and policy variables	
	(1)	(2)	(3)	(4)	(5)
Freedom House Civil (1978–87)[c] (N = 649)[b]	1.81 (0.0005)	10.16 (0.079)	1.71 (0.002)	10.07 (0.114)	1.57
Humana (1982–5) (N = 236)	0.290 (0.03)	0.299 (0.007)	0.296 (0.002)	0.289 (0.013)	50.19
Media pluralism (1983–7) (N = 448)	4.61 (0.0001)	4.45 (0.002)	3.66 (0.001)	3.43 (0.026)	30.12
Freedom to organise (1983–7) (N = 448)	30.17 (0.0001)	10.81 (0.184)	2.41 (0.006)	−00.26 (0.854)	2.70

Notes: [a]See the text for description of the four specifications and the calculations in column (5).
[b]P levels in parenthesis.
[c]Annual values from 1978–87. The other three indices are single values extrapolated to cover the listed time period.
Source: Isham, Kaufmann and Pritchett (1997).

The strong empirical relationship between performance of economic and social projects and civil liberties is striking.[32] Yet the interpretation of this partial correlation is problematic: it may well be that some country conditions cause both greater civil liberties and better projects, so that the implied relationship above is not causal. While we can not totally eliminate the possibility that human rights and civil liberties are jointly determined with economic performance, we argue in the analysis below that the statistical relationship between manifestations of civil strife and project success suggest a causal chain from better civil liberties to better project performance.

In table 9.12, we sort countries into groups based in their average ERR: for example, countries in the 'high ERR' category had average rates of return twice as high as those countries in the 'low ERR' category. The table shows that high ERR countries have, on average, much higher

Table 9.11 *Impact of civil liberties on satisfactory performance of economic and social projects: Probit estimations*[a]

	Specification	
	C	D
Freedom House Civil (1978–90)[b]	0.018	0.022
$N = 1155$	(.056)	(.060)
Humana (1982–6)	−0.00067	00012
$N = 604$	(.589)	(.388)
Media pluralism (1983–90)	0.022	0.054
$N = 740$	(0.296)	(0.045)
Freedom to organise (1983–90)	0.042	0.040
$N = 740$	(.009)	(.085)

Notes: [a]See the text for the description of the specifications. The values reported in table 9.11 are the marginal change in the probability of a successful project as the variable changes, evaluated as the means of the independent variables. *P*-levels of the test that the Probit coefficient is zero in parenthesis.
[b]Annual values from 1978–87 while for the other three indices are single values for the listed time period.
Source: Isham, Kaufmann and Pritchett (1997).

Table 9.12 *Indicators of civil strife, by average ERR, by country*[a]

ERR category	Average ERR	No. of countries	Regional distribution	No. of projects	Indicators of political unrest, averages per year by country (deviations from population-adjusted means)		
					Riots	Demon-strations	Strikes
High	220.2	6	South Asia: 3 East Asia: 3	181	2.48	0.30	3.19
Medium	17	11	LAC: 5[b] SSA: 2[b] EMENA: 3[b] South Asia: 1	253	0.00	0.16	−0.02
Low	110.2	12	SSA: 9 LAC: 2 South Asia: 1	209	−0.19	−0.04	−0.23

Notes: [a]ERR categories are determined by average rates of return classified by country for all countries with at least 10 projects over the period from 1974 to 1987.
[b]LAC is Latin America; SSA is Sub-Saharan Africa; EMENA is Europe and the Mid East.
Source: Isham, Kaufman and Pritchett (1997).

levels of civil unrest than low ERR countries: this includes more riots, demonstrations and strikes *per capita* (adjusted for population effects).[33]

The finding that higher indicators of civil strife are *positively* associated with project performance might at first seem paradoxical: how is this finding consistent with our analytical framework? All of the projects in this analysis are financed by governments (partly with World Bank financing). While markets for private goods rely on information from consumers (expressed in the form of the aggregation of individual purchase decisions made in the market), governments must rely on other channels for expressions of citizen's preferences and for the monitoring of the performance of government agents in carrying out their functions It seems likely that in countries with more open channels, all forms of expression of popular will – including civil unrest – are greater. The statistical relationship between the indices of civil liberties and riots, strikes, and demonstrations supports this perspective: for all the indicators except for Humana, greater civil liberties are strongly correlated with greater degrees of civil unrest.[34]

Table 9.13, using the same regression base specification as above, shows that there is a modest positive effect of various indicators of civil unrest on project returns. In both of the specifications without regional dummies, the number of riots, protest demonstrations and political strikes are *positively* and significantly related to the rate of return. Projects apparently do better in environments with greater civil strife when civil liberties are not included as a determinant (e.g. a coefficient of 0.56 in specification A for riots). However, with the addition of any of the indicators of the degree of civil liberties,[35] the impact of political manifestations is reduced in magnitude. For instance the coefficient on riots falls from 0.56 to 0.32 in specification A. For any given level of civil liberties, neither riots nor strikes are associated with better performance at a statistically significant level; protests still seem to still have an independent effect.

The results support a chain of causation that runs from greater civil liberties to higher levels of the citizen's involvement – including as one dimension civil manifestations – to better projects. Environments that allow civil strife or unrest to occur also allow other mechanisms for expression of popular (dis)content with government performance. The availability and effectiveness of those mechanisms improves government efficacy.[36]

Table 9.13 *Indicators of civil strife and project returns, without and with controls for civil liberties*[a]

| | Specification[c] | | | | |
| | A | | C | | D |
	Without Freedom House	With Freedom House	Without Freedom House	With Freedom House	With Freedom House
Adding just riots					
Riots	0.56	0.32	0.42	0.21	−0.34
	(0.062)[b]	(0.148)	(0.040)	(0.34)	(0.245)
Freedom	–	1.48	–	1.51	1.19
House Civil		(0.090)		(0.093)	(0.083)
Adding just protest demonstrations					
Protest	1.04	0.88	0.81	0.68	0.17
demon-	(0.0001)	(0.014)	(0.003)	(0.013)	(0.607)
strations					
Freedom	–	1.46	–	1.48	1.08
House Civil		(0.053)		(0.006)	(0.112)
Adding just political strikes					
Political	1.58	0.201	1.67	0.45	−0.81
strikes	(0.127)	(0.857)	(0.097)	(0.683)	(0.520)
Freedom	–	1.77	–	1.61	1.09
House Civil		(0.002)		(0.006)	(.109)
Adding all three civil strife variables					
F-test[c] for all	4.39	3.66	2.69	2.30	1.09
three	(0.004)	(0.012)	(0.045)	(0.076)	(0.352)
indicators					
without and					
with civil					
liberties					

Notes: [a]See the text for descriptions of the four specifications.
[b]*P*-levels in parenthesis.
[c]*F*-tests calculated with and without all three indicators, sample size = 649.
Source: Isham, Kaufmann and Pritchett (1997).

6 Implications for World Bank policies and strategies

The results in this chapter build a powerful case for coordinating the Bank's interventions in policy and project lending. When a country has an undistorted economic policy framework and supportive public investments, and when institutions promote open and transparent decision-making, the tangible payoff will be felt at the microeconomic level: in the aggregate performance of publicly and privately financed investment projects – along with the performance of firms, farms, and private entrepreneurs – that over the long-term determine a country's growth rate.

Based on the analysis and findings laid out in this chapter, a number of implications emanate for the World Bank. They refer to the importance of: (1) supporting an undistorted policy framework; (2) supporting the building and maintenance of a supportive public infrastructure; (3) promotion of an institutional framework within public agencies that builds openness and transparent decision-making; (4) assuring that, under the aegis of project lending, decision-making by project officials is consultative, participatory and transparent; (5) refraining from lending to countries with distorted and ineffective policies or public institutions, unwilling to embark on economic and institutional reforms (in which case, knowledge diffusion, participatory non-lending services, etc. would be more appropriate).

The evidence presented here elucidates the much-debated and ambiguous empirical evidence on the link between policies and institutions and aggregate performance. We establish a very strong statistical association between a country's policy environment and investment project performance. All types of projects – in the tradeable and non-tradeable sectors, economic and social, with public or private financing – are adversely affected by distortions in the macroeconomic, trade, pricing and institutional regimes. Jointly such policies, when distorted, can lower the economic returns on investments by about 10 percentage points. That difference in investment productivity, if economy-wide, can add up to a very significant difference in the aggregate growth rate of the country.

We find that within a country, improvements in the policy framework do result in improved productivity; conversely, policy reversals lower investment productivity rapidly. The sizeable effects of the quality of economy-wide policies on investment project performance is not affected by inclusion of a host of control variables. We also find evidence that some institutional variable at the project level, such as the level of complexity of the investment project, does matter. Importantly, we also find evidence that civil liberties matter significantly.

The performance of projects in the tradeable sectors is related to the size of public investment in a non-linear fashion. A balanced public investment programme complementing the requirements of individual project investments enhance project-level productivity significantly where macroeconomic and trade policies are undistorted. Yet where economic distortions prevail, economic rates of return are likely to be low irrespective of the size and nature of the overall public investment programme.[37]

The implications for investors are straightforward: selectivity. They would generally fare better by staying away from settings with poor economic and institutional policies, even if it is an underinvested setting: the negative effects of poor policies are likely to dwarf the positive benefit of (apparent) higher marginal productivity of 'first-advantage' movers in a setting with low capital–labour ratio. However, if improved economic and institutional policies are evident (and likely to be sustained) the pay-offs from investing in new projects can be rather large. Furthermore, a country with an appropriately balanced public investment programme complementing entrepreneurial growth will be more attractive to investors, as long as such a country exhibits undistorted macroeconomic policies.

While the adverse impact of poor economic policies on investment performance is not a major new insight (private investors world-wide have known this for a long time), the magnitude and significance of these new empirical results needs underscoring. Studying the World Bank's own expected rate of returns to planned investments prior to project implementation suggest that in the past there was *some* limited sensitivity towards the effect of policies; on average it was expected that a project implemented in a setting with undistorted policies may end up with an ERR of about 1–3 percentage points higher (than in a distorted policy setting). Yet we find that this pales in comparison with the *actual* differentials attributable to economic policies after project execution is completed – estimated at about 6–10 percentage points. Part of this difference is accounted for by unanticipated policy deterioration during project execution, which tended to occur on more than one-third of the settings where the project was prepared under initially auspicious policy conditions. Still, in the majority of the cases the prevailing policy environment prior to the project start would have constituted a fairly reliable predictor of the future quality of policies during project implementation. Thus, in hindsight, the likelihood and incidence of poor economic policies may have been insufficiently accounted for when appraising projects prior to their execution. Furthermore, in the past there was little *ex ante* consideration of institutional factors, particularly outside the project realm, such as the quality of the public investment programme and civil liberties and participatory factors.

Thus, investors from institutions like the World Bank and other similar developmental agencies, where some non-financial considerations may also play a role, should recognise that lending in settings with poor policies and institutions and unwillingness to reform are likely to result in significantly lower socioeconomic returns. Conversely, the findings suggest room for hope: donor financing in countries where the policy, institutional and civil liberties record is improving is likely to pay off. Supporting broad-based economic and institutional reforms raise the productivity of public and private socioeconomic investments.

In concluding, we emphasise the need for an integrated and more comprehensive approach in providing a climate for investment project success. The view that emerged from the 'macroeconomic fundamentalism' of the 1980s is not sufficient. First, we found that economic policies other than purely aggregate macroeconomic measures matter significantly, too. Second, economic *institutions*, such as the budget and the nature of public investment programmes, matter significantly as well. Third, increasing attention needs to be paid to non-economic variables in explaining economic development outcomes, even when coldly analysing the economic and financial success of investment projects: we find that civil liberties and participatory factors are also key. And fourth, one ought to focus not only on the quality 'level' of policies and institutions when making decisions about aid, but also on the actual and prospective rate of change of such policies and institutional factors: where there is a reform programme underway and a serious commitment for sustained change, the fact that the country's point of departure in terms of policies and institutions is low ought not signify an undue penalty in terms of aid flows.

The case for a more holistic approach in development, where economic, institutional and social-participatory variables are all inter-linked determinants, is supported by the evidence at the project-level. At the same time, we find that the case of a more *comprehensive* approach *vis-à-vis* 'inputs' to success also needs to be more *selective* with respect to aid support to particular country choice: aid funding to projects in countries without the will to address the important economic and institutional preconditions do show disappointing returns. Indeed, the case for a strong link between aid and improved policy-making and institutional development is backstopped by the micro-economic evidence. Yet there are alternatives to standard donor-driven conditionality to attain progress on the policy environment and sustained commitment to institutional reforms likely to prove superior in terms of country ownership of their reforms as suggested by the empirical evidence on the importance of participatory processes and civil liberties for project-level success, and as currently being operationalised in the World Bank through the pilot countries undertaken by the Comprehensive Development Framework (CDF).[38]

APPENDIX: A VERY SIMPLE THEORETICAL MODEL

Using a simplified version of the standard cost-benefit formula, we derive a basic model to show how the internal rate of return of a project may depend on the policy and institutional environment.

Let the net present value (NPV) of a project be defined as:

$$NPV = \sum_{t=1}^{\infty} \frac{(B-C)_t}{(I-r)^t} - I_0 \tag{1}$$

where

$(B-C)_t$ = gross benefits − recurrent costs = net benefits
r = discount rate;
I_0 = initial capital investment

Setting $NPV = 0$ and assuming a constant net recurrent benefit $(B-C)$ yields

$$r = \frac{B-C}{I} \tag{2}$$

Differentiating (2) yields

$$r_b > 0; r_i < 0; r_i < 0. \tag{3}$$

Assume that the quality of economic and institutional (including quality of public expenditures framework) policies can be indexed in a meaningful fashion and that gross benefits, recurrent costs, and the initial capital investment are affected by policies through a set of specific channels (see section 7) such that:

$$B_p > 0; C_p < 0; I_p < 0 \tag{4}$$

where

p = policy and institutional quality index (higher values associated with better policies and institutions)

Using (3) and (4) to totally differentiate (2) yields

$$r_p > 0. \tag{5}$$

Thus, this simple model predicts that project returns are positively associated with better economic and institutional policies as captured by the policy and institutional index.

NOTES

1 The empirical results presented in this chapter are based on material found in the *World Development Report 1991*, 'The Challenge of Development' (World

Bank, 1991a, 1991b), to which the authors contributed; Kaufmann and Wang (1995); Isham, Kaufmann and Pritchett (1997); and Isham and Kaufmann (2000).

2 Additional details from this and the subsequent case study are found in Isham and Kaufmann (2000).

3 Thus, even if correct shadow prices had been used in the *ex ante* calculation of ERRs via the standard World Bank cost-benefit methodology, the likelihood of underutilisation of capacity in project execution would have underplayed.

4 See Lee and Anas (1995) for documentation of the costs of underprovision of public infrastructure services on manufacturing enterprises in Nigeria.

5 Additional evidence on the supportive role of public infrastructure – and the underlying institutional determinants of infrastructure effectiveness   is found in World Bank (1994).

6 While empirical studies of accountability and participation are rare, Wade (1994) and Paul (1996) suggest that the degree to which public sector employ- · ees are responsible is an important dimension to performance. Isham, Narayan and Pritchett (1995) use composite data from 121 water projects financed by different donors to present empirical evidence that greater parti- cipation by potential beneficiaries directly caused better project performance.

7 For a simple exposition of an analytical model, see the appendix (p. 257).

8 Descriptions of these data and their sources are listed in World Bank (1991b).

9 In addition, GDP growth and the degree of project complexity   as discussed below – are also incorporated into our econometric framework.

10 We conducted an analysis of possible measurement bias with the available subsample of 70 public projects with true *ex post* evaluations, which had been undertaken five–eight years after project completion. The re-estimated ERR and the *ex post* ERR were found to be very highly correlated ($r = 0.9$), yet the average *ex post* ERR (11–12 per cent) was 3–4 percentage points below the average reestimated ERR. Since the *ex post* ERR is a better approximation of the true economic value of the project, this suggests that, on average, a project implemented in a distorted policy framework will have a true ERR lower than 10 per cent.

11 Recognising that different distortion measures do reflect partly overlapping policy distortions, the types of policy variable combinations was circum- scribed to those where indices measured different types of distortions – thus, for instance, indices of trade openness and of distortions in the price of tradeable are not introduced simultaneously, and neither is the fiscal deficit and the real interest rate. Note that these reestimated ERRs are not a true *ex post* rate of return: the stream of project benefits has been flowing for only a few years by the time the calculation of a reestimated rate of return is per- formed.

12 When policies affect both the capital–labour ratio and GDP growth, the estimates on policy variables will tend to be overestimated in the first of each pair of specifications in table 9.4 and underestimated in the second. More precisely, let the set of equations for determining ERRs be:

$$ERR_i = \beta' P_i + \delta' X_i + \alpha' Z_i + \varepsilon_i;$$
$$Z_i = \Gamma' P_i + \nu_i$$

where P = policy variables, X = exogenous country- and project-specific inputs, and Z = capital–labour ratio and GDP growth. The estimate of the direct impact of policies (β) will be overestimated when Z is omitted; the direct and indirect impact of policies when Z is included is $\beta + \Gamma\alpha$.

13 We find the same results on education using the *World Development Report 1991* data (see the appendix, p. 257) and the education series developed by Barro and Lee (1993). But a sample selection bias may be at play, since Bank/ IFC projects in countries with lower skill levels may tend to compensate by allocating additional World Bank staff and external consultants in sectoral analysis (World Bank, 1996) and in project design and supervision.

14 Three econometric notes. *First*, unless otherwise noted, all continuous independent variables in these and subsequent specifications are three-year averages, including the ERR evaluation year and the two previous years. Alternative specifications with evaluation-year data do not alter the results. *Second*, the parallel rate premia variable in all specifications is linear up to a premia of 500 per cent. To prevent outliers from driving the results, higher values are equated to 500 per cent plus a logarithmic transformation of the difference between the real value and 500 per cent. Equally robust results were estimated from alternative specifications with different transformations of the black market premia, including: (1) any value above 200 per cent equalled to 200 per cent; (2) truncating sample for values higher than 200 per cent; and (3) any value above 500 per cent equalled to 500 per cent. *Third*, in order to maintain the same sample size across specifications, we imputed the variable means for missing values of trade openness and tradeable price distortions and then included a 'missing variable' dummy for each of these series. This procedure produces consistent estimates for these variables without throwing away observations.

15 In the case of the black market premium and other indicators of policy distortions, it is possible that there may be a form of 'asymmetry' in upward and downward effects. It is possible that a large policy distortion – say, an increase of the black market premium from 20 per cent to 120 per cent – may not be completely offset by a subsequent restoration to the original level. While the possibility of asymmetry cannot be totally ruled out with a statistical test, the underlying question of interest – whether policy changes affect performance – is addressed below.

16 Specifications including country fixed effects are estimated only for the policy indices that vary from year to year: the black market premia, the trade openness variables and the fiscal deficit variable. Segmented samples and specifications including year fixed effects – not presented here – were also tried to test whether year effects or structural breaks between time periods were apparent. They reveal no significant difference in the behaviour of the policy variables over different time periods.

17 See Isham and Kaufmann (2000) for these supplementary regressions and results from a second statistical test for possible selection bias, using expected rates of return calculated before project implementation.

18 A cross-tabulation with these results is presented in Isham and Kaufmann (2000).

19 Kaufmann and Wang (1995), using the performance evaluation indicators for all projects, use an F-test to show that the null hypothesis (that the impact of policies on the likelihood of project failure is the same for social and economic projects) cannot be rejected.

20 In addition, in order not to sacrifice any observations of this small sample, the mean value for an independent variable was imputed when the variable was missing. This imputed value was then included in the estimation, along with a missing variable dummy. At least in the case where the independent variables are uncorrelated, this procedure produces consistent estimates and potentially improves the efficiency of estimation by not throwing out any observations.

21 The 'low fiscal deficit' variable = the fiscal deficit when the fiscal deficit ≥ -4; = 0 otherwise. The 'high fiscal deficit' variable = the fiscal deficit when the fiscal deficit < -4; = 0 otherwise.

22 Even after incorporating a number of policy variables into the econometric analysis of economic projects, much of the variability in ERRs remains unexplained: the adjusted R-squares in ordinary least squares specifications equivalent to these Tobit specifications do not exceed 15 per cent with country fixed effects excluded. The adjusted R-squared increased to 0.65 when country dummies are included, suggesting that unidentified country characteristics (which may also include unmeasured policy distortions) are important. See Isham and Kaufmann (1999) for summary tables on the relative importance of policy distortions.

23 For figures 9.1 and 9.2, the points represent ERR averages for each segment.

24 This (average) turning point should not be interpreted, however, as a precise benchmark for policy in an individual country setting; they suggest only that beyond a certain point public investment expenditures do not increase the ERR of individual tradeable investment projects.

25 Statistical tests of estimated spline models are conditional on the choice of the 'knot' locations (9.5 per cent for public investment/GDP and 40 per cent for public investment/total investment). As presented here, the choice of these knots is based on the changes in the trends of ERRs depicted in figures 9.1 and 9.2. Robustness experiments were performed to establish that one can achieve similar results with knots that are in a narrow range around 9.5 per cent and 40 per cent, respectively.

26 Open decision-making and accountability arise through different mechanisms in private projects. In competitive markets, profit-maximising shareholders can oversee investment decisions, and discriminating buyers can choose alternative shareholders. By contrast, shareholders and consumers cannot pressure public officials through these channels. Accordingly, the private projects funded by the IFC are not included in the analysis below.

27 The 14 items are: media free of censorship; open public discussion; freedom of assembly and demonstration; freedom of political organisation; non-discriminatory rule of law in politically relevant cases; free from unjustified political terror; free trade unions and peasant organisations; free businesses and cooperatives; free professional and other private organisations; free religious institutions; personal social rights (e.g. property, internal and external travel); socioeconomic rights; freedom from gross socioeconomic inequality; and freedom from gross government indifference or corruption.

28 The correlations of these indices of civil liberties are reasonably high, which creates some confidence that they measure the same thing and do so reasonably well. The correlation of the Freedom House index (averaged over 1979–86) with the Humana index is 0.83, with freedom to organise, 0.78 and with media pluralism, 0.81. The correlation of the Humana index with freedom to organise is 0.68 and with media pluralism, 0.79. The correlation of freedom to organise with media pluralism is 0.82. (Coppedge and Reinicke's use of the information in the Freedom House and Humana studies in their own ranking procedure may account for part of the high correlation between the latter two and former two series.)

29 For the Freedom House and the Coppedge and Reinicke indicators, we have reversed the scales for comparability. Thus, for all indices, a higher value represents more liberties.

30 The standard deviations of the four civil liberties indicators are 1.47, 17.97, 0.91 and 1.12, respectively. The magnitude calculations in the text use the coefficient estimates from column C in table 9.11.

31 One possible concern with these econometric results is that they are driven by a few outlying observations, as some projects have very high estimated rates of return. We have dealt with that problem in two ways. First, in addition to a Tobit specification accounting for the lower truncation, we truncated the ERRs above at the more or less arbitrary level of a 50 per cent rate of return. This truncation did not affect the results. Second, in addition to OLS, we estimated specification D using quintile (median) regression, a technique that is more robust to extreme observations. Again, all the civil liberties variables that were significant in specification D in table 9.3 were statistically significant using median regression estimates.

32 Note that among the data on human rights and civil liberties, only the Freedom House ranking of civil liberties is time-varying, but as in the case of Costa Rica it is often the same (or very similar) through time. Accordingly, in addition to testing for regional fixed effects, it is not possible to test this model with country fixed effects. Given the inclusion of many other country-level regressors in these specifications, it is unlikely that they are capturing some other unmeasured country characteristic. In addition, Isham, Kaufmann and Pritchett (1997) list other possible country-level determinants, such as ethnolinguistic fractionalisation. that were also tested in these specifications. Further, we also ran estimations with other institutional variables (such as

BERI's institutional quality index); none added to the explained variance (nor did affect the policy coefficients).

33 The civil unrest variables (riots, protest demonstrations and strikes) came as number of incidents per country per year (Banks 1979, updates). This meant that countries with larger populations had a greater absolute number of incidents. However, it did not seem right to simply normalise to *per capita*, as there is plausibly some increasing returns to scale in civil unrest. Consequently, for each of the three variables, we regressed the absolute number of incidents on population*ln(population) (which is equivalent to adjusting the *per capita* level for the total population in semi-log form) and report the residual of this regression as 'excess' civil unrest over the amount expected for a given level of population. The population adjustment was also very significant and the R-squared varied from 0.02 (strikes) to 0.18 (riots). The results reported below were unchanged by using other concave functional forms in place of this semi-log form.

34 For example, the respective correlations of the Freedom House civil liberties index with population-adjusted levels of riots, strikes and demonstrations are 0.27, 0.34 and 0.17, all at significance levels better than 0.99 per cent.

35 Only the Freedom House civil indicator is shown in table 9.13, but the results for the other three are similar.

36 Isham, Kaufmann and Pritchett (1997) use indicators of levels of democracy to show that the finding of an association between more civil liberties and better ERRs does not imply an association between different types of political regimes and better performance.

37 We indicated that the mechanisms whereby bad policies affect investment performance have not been accorded sufficient emphasis and suggested two mechanisms that lower returns: inappropriate output choice and underutilised capacity. We noted that insufficient account is often taken of the likelihood of shortfalls in the 'quantity' axis. While we lack direct data to indicate the relative importance of each dimension in the link between distorted policies and economic returns of projects, one piece of data is suggestive: those few projects for which a financial rate of return was also calculated (alongside the ERR) tell us that the linkage between economic policies and financial returns are no different than the relationship between policies and economic returns. There is thus little evidence that shadow price adjustments are driving these results, providing a hint about the possible importance of adjustments along the quantity axis instead. Undoubtedly, more research is needed to explore analytically and empirically these complex mechanisms whereby the quality of economy-wide policies affect project performance.

38 An example of a different way of doing business (as in the CDF) is now being piloted with seven African countries. It does not start with any loan preparation (with concomitant conditions), but instead as a (participatory) learning sharing activity organised by the World Bank Institute (WBI). Each country sent to Washington a delegation representing stakeholders from the executive, civil society, media, private sector, etc. After the first phase of their work

together on initiating a preparation of a Governance action programme, with facilitation and transfer of rigorous tools and techniques by (WBI) experts, they returned to their countries, and the seven country groups continued to work with Headquarters through simultaneous distance learning (including Video-Conferencing). Two months later each country had prepared an action programme, presented it at a major conference, and in the next stage this approach would call for identification of the actions and strategies that would be subject to financial support by the donor community. For details, see Durban conference volume at < http://www.worldbank.org/wbi/gac >.

REFERENCES

Banks, A. S. (1979) (and subsequent updates). 'Cross-national Time Series Data Archive', Center for Social Analysis, State University of New York at Binghamton

Barro, R. (1991). 'Economic Growth in a Cross-section of Countries', *Quarterly Journal of Economics*, **106**: 407–43

Barro, R. and J.-W. Lee (1993). 'International Comparison of Educational Attainment', *Journal of Monetary Economics*, **32**: 363–94

Barro, R. and X. Sala-i-Martin (1995). *Economic Growth*, New York: McGraw-Hill

Burnside, C. and D. Dollar (1997). 'Aid, Policies, and Growth', *Working Paper*, Policy Research Department, The World Bank, June

Coppedge, M. and W.H. Reinicke (1990). 'Measuring Polyarchy', *Studies in Comparative International Development*, **25**: 51–72

Easterly, W., M. Kremer, L. Pritchett and L. H. Summers (1994). 'Good Policy or Good Luck? Country Growth Performance and Temporary Shocks', *Journal of Monetary Economics*, **32**: 459–84

Freedom House (1994 and previous years). *Freedom in the World: Political Rights and Civil Liberties*, New York: Greenwood Press

Greene, W. (1990). *Econometric Analysis*, New York: Macmillan

Humana (1986). *World Human Rights Guide*, London: Hodder & Stoughton

Isham, J. and D. Kaufmann (2000). 'The Forgotten Rationale for Policy Reform: The Productivity of Investment Projects', *The Quarterly Journal of Economics*, **114**: 149–84

Isham, J., D. Kaufmann and L. H. Pritchett (1997). 'Civil Liberties, Democracy, and the Performance of Government Projects', *World Bank Economic Review*, **11**: 219–42

Isham, J., D. Narayan and L. H. Pritchett (1995). 'Does Participation Improve Performance?: Establishing Causality with Subjective Data', *World Bank Economic Review*, **9**: 175–200

Kaufmann, D., A. Kraay and P. Zoido-Lobatón (1999a). 'Governance Matters', *Policy Research Working Paper Series*, 2196, World Bank < www.worldbank.org/wbi/gac >

(1999b). 'Aggregating Governance Indicators', *Policy Research Working Paper Series*, **2195**, World Bank < www.worldbank.org/wbi/gac >

Kaufmann, D. and S. A. O'Connell (1997). 'The Macroeconomics of Delayed Exchange Rate Unification', in M. A. Kiguel, J. S. Lizondo and S. A. O'Connell (eds.), *Parallel Exchange Rates in Developing Countries*, New York: St Martin's Press

Kaufmann, D. and Y. Wang (1995). 'Macroeconomic Policies and Project Performance in the Social Sectors', *World Development*, **23**, 751–65

Lee, K. S. and A. Anas (1995). 'The Costs of Infrastructural Deficiencies in Nigeria', Infrastructure and Urban Development Department, Washington, DC, World Bank

Mankiw, N. G., D. Romer and D. N. Weil (1992). 'A Contribution to the Empirics of Economic Growth', *Quarterly Journal of Economics*, **107**, 407–37

Paul, S. (1992). 'Accountability in Public Services: Exit, Voice, and Control', *World Development*, July

(1996). 'A Citizen Report Card on Public Services: Exit, Voice, and Control', mimeo

Solow, R. (1956). 'A Contribution to the Theory of Economic Growth', *Quarterly Journal of Economics*, **70**, 65–94.

Wade, R. (1994). 'Public Bureaucracy and the Incentive Problem', Background Paper for *World Development Report 1994*

World Bank (1991a). *World Development Report*, New York: Oxford University Press

(1991b). 'World Development Report 1991: Supplementary Data', Office of the Vice President, Development Economics, Washington, DC, mimeo

(1994). *World Development Report*, New York, NY: Oxford University Press

(1996). *The World Bank Participation Sourcebook*, Washington, DC: World Bank

10 Increasing aid effectiveness in Africa? The World Bank and sector investment programmes

STEPHEN JONES

1 Introduction

Recent literature, much of it deriving from World Bank research, has reached strong conclusions about the conditions under which official development assistance (ODA) can make a positive contribution to poverty reduction and other development objectives. These conclusions, if correct and broadly accepted, would have a profound impact on development assistance practice, especially when combined with effective commitment by donors to the DAC target of halving absolute poverty by 2015.

This chapter examines, in the light of this literature. experience with one specific instrument, the Sector Investment Programme[1] (SIP), that the World Bank has taken the lead in promoting as a way of increasing aid effectiveness, especially in Africa. This initiative, coordinated with other bilateral and multilateral agencies through the UN Special Programme for Africa (SPA), has been part of a broader interest in the concept of what are now generally termed Sector-Wide Approaches (SWAps). Several bilateral agencies, notably in the Nordic countries (see for instance DANIDA, 1996; SIDA, 1995), have explicitly incorporated the principles of the sector-wide approach into their development assistance policies.

Section 2 briefly reviews the findings of recent analyses of aid effectiveness, focusing on five issues: policy environment, ownership, fungibility, conditionality and institutional capacity. Section 3 discusses the SIP instrument and the broader SWAp concept and examines how SIPs were intended to improve aid effectiveness. Section 4 summarises experience with application of the SIP concept in practice, focusing on the agriculture sector in Africa. In the light of the discussion in section 2, section 5 draws conclusions about why the record with SIPs has been disappointing and what should be the place of sector programmes in a broader strategy to improve aid effectiveness.

2 Key issues for aid effectiveness

Recent literature has drawn attention to five central issues in the effectiveness of aid. These lessons derive in particular from reviewing the World Bank's chequered experience with adjustment lending since the early 1980s.

The first issue is the *policy environment*. World Bank (1998) presents evidence that while there is no general positive relationship between the level of aid receipts and the rate of economic growth in general, there is a positive relationship in countries with sound economic management.[2] Burnside and Dollar (chapter 8 in this volume) present evidence that a similar relationship holds between aid and infant mortality (which can be used as a proxy for poverty).

The second issue is *ownership*. Killick, Gunatilaka and Marr (1998: 87) provides a 'general ideal-case' definition of this concept in the context of policy reform:

Government ownership is at its strongest when the political leadership and its advisers, with broad support among agencies of state and civil society, decide of their own volition that policy changes are desirable, choose what these changes should be and when they should be introduced, and where these changes become built into parameters of policy and administration which are generally accepted as desirable.

This is contrasted with a situation where 'reforms are donor-initiated and designed, with little domestic support and few local roots'. Johnson and Wasty (1993) present empirical evidence that likelihood of success of adjustment programmes is strongly related to the extent of 'ownership'.[3]

The third issue is *fungibility*. Devarajan and Swaroop (chapter 7 in this volume) report empirical findings that suggest that ODA is in general highly fungible, in the sense that the effect of aid earmarked to specific projects or sectors is to release recipient government resources to fund the government's priorities at the margin. Aid, regardless of the specific project it is tied to, therefore functions as an increment to total government resources. Fungibility is linked to the question of ownership and objectives – fungibility is a problem only if the objectives of donors and recipients differ.

The fourth issue is *conditionality*. Killick, Gunatilaka and Marr (1998) and Collier (chapter 12 in this volume) argue that the imposition by donors of conditionality on adjustment lending generally fails to bring about policy change because it cannot be made 'incentive-compatible'. Recipient governments who are not committed to the policy change have incentives to renege on commitments, and donors are not able effectively to enforce the sanction of suspending access to aid (because of a combination of incentive problems within the agency and wider political economy considerations). Collier suggests that aid should therefore be provided to countries with a track record of appropriate policies, rather than offered as an incentive to bring about policy reform.

The fifth issue is *institutional capacity*. Recent literature stresses the importance of institutional factors in aid effectiveness, but also the (at best) patchy record of aid in achieving sustainable institutional capacity improvements. The 1998 World Bank *Annual Review of Development Effectiveness* (Buckley, 1999) focuses on the role of institutional performance, especially in the light of the Asian Crisis. It reports (1999: 4) that World Bank projects are almost twice as likely to fail in low-income countries with low institutional quality than in low-income countries with high institutional quality[4] and that strong institutions more than double the likelihood that a country undergoing adjustment can sustain policy reform (1999). On the other hand, it also reports that World Bank projects that are specifically aimed at achieving improved institutional capacity through civil service reform have been 'among the weakest-performing interventions in the Bank's portfolio' (1999: 30).[5]

The discussion of institutional issues in the *Assessing Aid* study (World Bank, 1998, chapter 3) focuses heavily on the composition and quality of public expenditure as a whole as a key determinant of aid effectiveness (given the view that fungibility is high). However, the 1998 *Annual Review* also quotes further evaluation study results that show that Public Expenditure Review exercises had achieved little impact on government expenditure policies, and had paid little attention to issues of cost efficiency or quality of public services.

3 Sector investment programmes[6]

The sector-wide approach attempts to bring all donor support to a sector (however defined) within a common management and planning framework around a government expenditure programme. The objectives of the sector-wide approach can in principle be pursued in different ways.

Sometimes, the term 'SIP' has been used to apply to any programme of aid to a sector that has these characteristics. An important confusion has been a tendency to use the successes of a number of cases where such arrangements have successfully been developed[7] to justify what has become in effect a particular methodology for the preparation of a World Bank operation. This methodology has typically involved the following elements: a systematic and formal stakeholder consultation process, preparation of a strategy document and a process of joint donor appraisal of the strategy, expenditure plans and management framework.[8]

Three main factors can be seen as influencing the development of the SIP concept by the World Bank. The first was consideration of the far-reaching criticisms of the Bank's project lending policies and practices that were set out in the 'Wapenhans Report' (World Bank, 1992). The second was the implementation during the first half of the 1990s of a large element of the World Bank's adjustment agenda in Africa (World Bank, 1994). As a result, by the mid-1990s, most countries in the region had achieved a substantial liberalisation of the foreign exchange regime, removed most quantitative controls on trade and sharply reduced the direct role of the state in production, marketing and price-setting (especially in agriculture). The third element was some significant project successes, notably in relation to the Road Maintenance Initiative (RMI). This sought to coordinate donor support to road-building, improve planning for the recurrent costs of road maintenance, establish secure funding mechanisms for road maintenance and involve a broader range of sector stakeholders in decision-making about the roads sector. One particularly influential operation was the Tanzania Integrated Road Project (TIRP) (Jones, 1997).

The underlying logic of the approach was therefore to take advantage of the improved post-adjustment policy environment in many African countries to increase project-based lending, while seeking to overcome a series of problems that had led to low project effectiveness in the past. Lessons derived from the success of the RMI were used to develop the model set out in Harrold and Associates (1995). The objective of a SIP was to bring all donor and government capital and recurrent funding of a sector within a single planning and implementation framework, in support of an agreed sector strategy. The SIP would replace the proliferation of poorly coordinated and separately managed donor projects that existed in most countries and sectors with a single financing and management framework. Donors would commit resources into a common pool managed by government, rather than using separate and parallel project implementation units.

A genuine SIP was defined as exhibiting six 'essential features'[9] (Harrold and Associates, 1995: xixii):

- *The programme is 'sector-wide' in scope and covers both current and capital expenditures.* The appropriate scope for a SIP was defined (Harrold and Associates, 1995: 8) as covering 'all expenditure programs and policies in an area where fragmentation of planning and implementation would seriously reduce efficiency or output'. The key issues are whether the coverage of the strategy is appropriate, and whether the coverage of government and donor expenditure included in the programme was sufficient to prevent intrasectoral fungibility[10] and to allow effective joint planning of recurrent costs and capital expenditures.
- *The programme is based on a clear sector strategy and policy framework.* Appropriate sector policies are required to ensure effective development impact of donor and government expenditures, while the strategy provided the basis for the specific expenditure plans into which donors were buying, and ensured that expenditures were allocated to agreed priorities.
- *Local stakeholders (meaning government, direct beneficiaries and private sector representatives) are fully in charge of the SIP process.* This feature encompassed two objectives. First, that local ownership of and commitment to the programme was strong. Second, that this commitment extended beyond government to encompass a broader range of sector stakeholders.
- *All main donors sign on to the approach and participate in financing the programme ideally in a process led by government.* Signing on required that donors endorse the strategy for all new activities, and begin to phase out or adapt activities that are not consistent with it, while moving to establish common implementation arrangements. This was required to achieve effective integration of planning for donor and government activities.
- *So far as possible, common implementation arrangements are established for all donors participating in the programme.* This principle sought as an ultimate objective to establish a common pool or basket of funding, and the phasing out of separate projects (other than as accounting devices). The objective was to simplify management processes and bring them back under the control of government. The key areas in which common arrangements were to be sought included: planning and budgeting, financial management, performance monitoring and progress reporting, procurement, and the management of technical assistance.

- *Local capacity, rather than long-term technical assistance, should be relied upon as much as possible to design, manage and implement the programme.* The SIP approach was based on a very negative view of the role of long-term technical assistance, which was seen as a contributory factor to undermining government capacity and ownership of programmes. Reliance on government and locally contracted consultants was intended to improve ownership and build national capacity.

Two sets of preconditions for a SIP were identified. First, at the macroeconomic level there needed to be both broad stability (in terms of the level of inflation, budgetary and balance of payments and an absence of exchange or interest rate distortions) and an adequate revenue effort and intersectoral allocation of expenditures. Second, sufficient government capacity was required in three areas: willingness and ability to take a leadership role, adequate capacity in project management and 'reasonably well developed and articulated strategies for the sector' (Harrold and Associates, 1995: 22).

The role envisaged for the World Bank in sector programmes was twofold. First, in some cases it might take a lead in supporting and financing the preparation of a SIP, preferably along with other lead donors. Second, it could play a special role as a 'lender of last resort' to ensure that the agreed expenditure programme as a whole was financed. This reflected, first, that it would be preferable to use grant financing if available rather than a Bank loan or IDA credit to fund government expenditures, and second that the Bank might have greater funding flexibility than bilateral donors in cases where full pooling was not yet feasible. For example, if an agreed health sector programme included both primary health care and the costs of hospitals, it might be easier on policy grounds for some bilateral donors to earmark funds against the primary health component.

The loans supporting SIPs were designed to be traditional project loans in form, designed to disburse regularly (for instance, quarterly) over five years, nominally against specific items of government expenditure within the agreed programme. It was recognised that the approach poses major problems for traditional methods of project evaluation, since 'it is the sector itself that is the project, not the goods and services that the Bank [or any other donor] finances' (Harrold and Associates, 1995: xiv).

The approach embodied in the SIP instrument addresses the five issues discussed in section 2 in the following ways:

- *Policy environment.* Application of the SIP concept presupposed that a broadly adequate macroeconomic and sectoral policy framework had been achieved. The process of developing a sector strategy would identify outstanding policy issues that needed to be addressed during the programme.

- *Ownership*. Ownership was to be ensured through two of the features of a SIP. First, by ensuring that a broad range of local stakeholders (going beyond government) is in charge of the process. Second, by minimising the role of external technical assistance and removing separate project implementation units, both of which were regarded as compromising local ownership.
- *Fungibility*. The prior existence of agreement at the level of broad intersectoral expenditure allocations was the main route for ensuring that there was not a problem resulting from the fungibility of the assistance provided. The agreed sector-wide strategy ensured there is no problem of intrasectoral fungibility.
- *Conditionality*. Harrold and Associates (1995) does not discuss in detail the issue of conditionality. The logic of the approach set out is that explicit conditionality is not required because the approach is based on a prior consensus between donors and the recipient government. However, Harrold and Associates (1995: 20) states that this consensus is required because the sector approach 'puts the entire sector support on the line', implying that breakdown of consensus would lead to the suspension of aid at the sector level. Whether such a threat would in practice be credible was not discussed.
- *Institutional capacity*. The SIP model assumes, first, that sufficient institutional capacity to manage the programme exists before the programme begins (or at least that the move to common implementation arrangements is sequenced with capacity improvement). Second, the integration of separate projects into a common framework is expected to release government management capacity that has been tied up in project management. The SIP should reduce the transactions costs associated with managing aid (Disch, 1999).

The implementation of the SIP concept was expected to be rapid across a range of sectors and countries largely in Africa and notably in health, education, agriculture, transport, energy and environment. The Bank identified a large number of projects that had the potential to be designed as, or converted to, SIPs (Harrold and Associates, 1995, table 5). The following section reviews the main features of experience with the implementation of sector programmes to date.

4 Sector investment programmes in practice: examples from Africa[11]

A first observation is that the degree of success in developing SIPs has varied by country and by sector. Most progress has been made in the health and (to a lesser extent) education sectors, and in the roads sector through continuation of the approaches pioneered through the RMI.[12] Despite heavy investment in programme preparation processes across a range of countries, progress in moving to 'fully fledged SIPs' in the agricultural sector has been slow.[13] The countries where most substantial progress has been made with the approach (though significant problems have been encountered in all four) are Ethiopia, Ghana, Mozambique, Uganda and Zambia. Although experience is limited, it is possible to make some observations about emerging achievements and problems in relation to each of the issues identified above:

- *Policy environment.* A feature of those sector programmes that have generally been regarded as most successful has been the development of a consensus on major sector policy issues between senior local officials and donors.[14] This has usually been the result of many years of joint work and discussion it has not been created by the sector programme preparation process itself. One of the reasons for the failures to make significant progress in agriculture has been the absence of a consensus on the role of the state in the sector – for instance, in the provision of agricultural extension.

  In Zambia, a major problem for the implementation of the sector programmes was the weak macroeconomic environment that made it difficult for government to meet financing commitments (Chiwele, 1998; Jones, 1997). Broader concerns about governance have also caused difficulties in government donor relations. In both Ethiopia and Uganda, the escalation of regional tensions has recently created difficulties in government–donor relations, including pressures for increased military expenditure, though this has not yet compromised the sector programmes that are being developed. The main point here is that even if an adequate macroeconomic and sectoral policy environment is achieved, this situation is likely to be fragile and vulnerable to change, often for reasons that are external to the sector.

- *Ownership.* In several cases, especially in the agriculture sector, the SIP approach has been driven by the World Bank. In particular, timetables have been influenced by the lifecycle of the World Bank's existing project portfolio. There has been a tendency to promote formulaic processes of stakeholder consultation (such as the establishment of Task Forces involving the private sector to manage the programme).

These approaches have suffered from several weaknesses. They have led to confusion about the appropriate roles and responsibilities of government and non-government actors.[15] They have also failed to distinguish two distinct (and potentially conflicting) objectives from stakeholder consultation. First, that of winning over powerful interests, whose support is needed for the programme to work.[16] Second, ensuring the representation of the interests of those, such as the poor, who may otherwise be marginalised in decision-making. (Jones, 1997).

A further problem has been that even in cases where local ownership has been perceived as strong it has not always been sufficiently broad to prevent policy reversals. For instance in the health sector, policy consensus has operated at the level of health sector professionals and has not commanded wider political support – so the conditions identified in Killick's definition above have not held. For example, in the Zambian health programme, the primary health care approach has been perceived by politicians and the wider community to have failed to deliver visible results (or measurable improvements in health outcomes). This has led to policy backtracking in the face of severe political pressure – including reallocating resources away from primary health cares towards hospital facilities.

The approach to the issue of ownership set out in Harrold and Associates (1995) and implemented in practice has proved to be superficial. It paid too much attention to the role of technical assistance (whose negative role may be better seen as a symptom than a cause of poor ownership) and stakeholder consultation mechanisms, and too little to the wider political environment. By not seeking potentially observable tests of ownership (such as the criteria proposed by Johnson and Wasty, 1999) it failed to provide practical guidance for assessing ownership.

A further issue is that the drive towards sector programmes is taking place at a time when there are also important donor and government initiatives under way to encourage decentralisation of decision-making and expenditure management. To the extent that the sector approach requires coordinated planning of sector expenditures, there is a potential conflict with decentralisation where the latter implies that intersectoral resource allocation decisions will be made at lower levels of government.[17]

- *Fungibility and conditionality.* These two issues are closely linked. A persistent feature is that even relatively successful sector programmes have not been firmly embedded within a broader overall expenditure framework. There has also been little progress in establishing a clearly articulated framework of the respective responsibilities of government and donors. This partly reflects the lack of progress in moving towards common funding mechanisms or wider partnership arrangements. Instead there has been at best agreement at the level of particular mechanisms (like the district health services basket-funding arrangement established in Zambia).

Three problems have emerged. First, the appropriate sector-level response by donors to macroeconomic difficulties has not been defined whether sector-level assistance should increase, be reduced, or be unaffected by the government's ability to deliver on its expected level of sector expenditure.[18] In the absence of a framework defining the overall pattern of public expenditure, the fungibility of funds is likely to be high

Second, a particular implementation difficulty relates to the use of cash budgets (as in Zambia). The imposition of this form of expenditure discipline (restricting expenditure to the level of funds received and not allowing recourse to central bank borrowing to smooth revenue fluctuations) has reduced inflationary pressures at the cost of militating against effective management of public expenditure.

Third, line ministries have indeed frequently seen the SIP approach as a way of breaking out of budget constraints imposed by Ministries of Finance, rather than as a way of bringing donor resources into the budget.[19] This reflects how sector programmes have tended to derive from sector-level initiatives (whether led by donors or sector ministries), rather than as a sector-level response to broader government-wide attempts to improve the effectiveness of public expenditure management.

- *Institutional capacity.* Attempts to implement the SIP model have largely foundered on weak implementation and management capability within government. First, there has been an observable and systematic tendency by donors to overestimate the implementation and absorption capacity of government – a point that the 'Wapenhans Report' had made earlier in relation to the Bank's project lending. The SIP model has therefore sometimes in its application fallen into the trap of assuming away the main problem that has been at the root of poor project implementation. Second, the processes of SIP preparation that have been advocated have often tended to increase, rather than reduce, the demands on government management and planning capacity. In almost all cases in the agricultural sector, for instance, the preparation process has involved setting up parallel systems (such as 'ASIP Secretariats'), linked to but operating largely outside the normal government planning and budgeting system. Sector programme initiatives have not been based on a coherent strategy to reduce the transactions costs involved in aid management. Third, the process often created unrealistic expectations about how quickly it would be possible to move to common implementation arrangements. This has sometimes led to premature attempts to establish such arrangements that may (at worst) have proved counterproductive (for example, see Chiwele, 1998).

5 The role of the sector approach in increasing aid effectiveness

Many of the initial problems encountered by attempts to implement the sector approach therefore reflect an overoptimism born from a failure fully to take on board the lessons from project and adjustment programme experience. Organisational imperatives within the World Bank and other donors to keep the flow of funds moving are also likely to have played a part. The difficulties (in particular, the issue of the stringent institutional capacity requirements for effective operation of common implementation arrangements) have increasingly been recognised. As a result, the initial expectation of a rapid move to the full SIP model (based on common implementation arrangements) has become more modest. The SIP model is now seen more realistically as a long-term ideal.

It is therefore recognised that in most countries and most sectors in Africa the conditions for an effective sector programme do not yet exist (and even where they do exist, they are likely to be fragile and subject to change). Movement towards this model requires the strengthening of management and policy capacity within government, a broadened policy dialogue aimed at consensus-building, and more sustained attention to the issue of financial sustainability in the context of an overview of the level and effectiveness of public expenditure as a whole.[20]

Two significant questions may be raised. First, if the conditions for full sector programmes typically do not exist, what does this imply for the traditional project model for donor financing? Second, if the conditions for a sector programme (based on pooled funding) can eventually be created, what role should there be for sector-based aid, given the strong emphasis in the recent aid effectiveness literature on intersectoral fungibility? If intersectoral fungibility is irreducibly high, then the most transparent way of providing support is to channel it explicitly to the government's public expenditure programme (PEP) as a whole (through for instance the Bank's public expenditure reform loan instrument, or PERL), rather than to individual sectors.

Figure 10.1 sets out a possible framework for understanding sector programmes in relation to other methods of managing the provision of aid. The framework has two dimensions. The first is a measure of financial management capacity (broadly understood). The second is a measure of the degree of consensus between donors and government on the effectiveness of public expenditure this measure encompasses policy, ownership and delivery issues.

Four basic cases can be identified (though the framework is better understood as a continuum):

- *High consensus, high capacity.* Under these conditions, broad support to a national PEP is in principle the preferred approach. Sector programmes (based on pooled funding arrangements) would be broadly equivalent in effect, but would be likely to have higher transactions costs. On the other hand, for donors who face constraints on the sectors to which they can formally provide funds, sector programmes may be feasible while broad expenditure support is not. Likewise, high government capacity may mean that separate donor projects can be effectively managed despite potentially high transactions costs, if administrative or political constraints dictate a project approach.

- *Low consensus, high capacity.* In this situation, there is no case for aid to be provided, and the focus of donors should be on policy dialogue and other measures to build consensus and improve expenditure effectiveness. To the extent that fungibility can be controlled (for instance, through conditionality on the share of public expenditure between sectors) there would be a case for sector programmes in those sectors on which there was consensus.

- *High consensus, low capacity.* In this case, project-based models or parallel funding at sector level may be appropriate. However, the

Figure 10.1 *A framework for understanding sector programmes*

	High capacity	Low capacity
High consensus	A	C
Low consensus	B	D

high transactions costs involved in project-based approaches run the risk of weakening still further the limited management capacity of government. Effective measures to build capacity (so that transactions costs arc reduced) and to reduce the capacity intensity of projects are therefore required. Parallel financed sector programmes may reduce capacity intensity provided they are well designed, with this objective explicitly built into them.

• *Low consensus, low capacity*. Under these conditions it is unlikely that any form of financial aid through government will be effective. Donor efforts would need to focus on policy dialogue (at sector and broader levels). Project-based support in this scenario is likely to be ineffective because of problems of fungibility and lack of ownership, and to lead at best to the creation of project enclaves.

A critical strategic question for donors is where in this framework particular African countries are located. Sector approaches may provide a framework for a productive policy dialogue if there is low consensus (and may help reduce transactions costs), but it will not be possible to move money effectively unless consensus can be achieved at sector level and the problem of fungibility can be contained. This would require solutions to the problems of incentive-compatibility that have made much programme-level conditionality ineffective in the past. The effective use of aid also requires greater success in 'capacity-building' within government than has to date been achieved in Africa. In the absence of progress in these areas, the conclusion is not that sector approaches may not have a role in improving aid effectiveness, but rather that there are in many countries probably only limited opportunities for financial aid delivered in any form to be used effectively.

NOTES

The chapter is derived from the experience of the author and his colleagues working as consultants on the preparation and implementation of sector programmes in a number of countries. This work has been supported by several agencies, especially in the UK Department for International Development. A version of this chapter was presented at a NORAD seminar on Sector-Wide Approaches (Oslo, February 1999). The author wishes to thank participants at the seminar, and the editors of this volume, for helpful comments.

1 A note on terminology is required. The concept of a 'Sector Investment Programme' is set out in Harrold and Associates (1995). More recently, the World Bank has preferred the more general term 'Sector Programme' (e.g. Okidegbe, 1998) since the focus on 'Investment' is misleading given that the approach aims to support the whole of the public expenditure programme in a sector, and not just to provide investment resources. The term is particularly

misleading in social sectors where the 'SWAp' terminology has been generally used by bilateral and UN agencies such as WHO. In this chapter, a SIP is regarded as particular instrument for implementing the broader concept of a Sector-Wide Approach (see section 3, p. 268).

2 This is defined based on an index which is a weighted sum of the inflation rate, budget surplus, trade openness and institutional quality (World Bank, 1998: 122).

3 The performance measurement criteria Johnson and Wasty use are: (a) whether the initiative for formulating and implementing the adjustment plan was the borrower's; (b) whether there is observable consensus among key ministries and decision-makers on the nature of the crisis and the necessary actions; (c) whether specific up-front actions were initiated before the programme and (d) whether there has been participation by broader civil society in decision making (see Buckley, 1999. 24).

4 The institutional quality index used is based on variables indicating the extent of corruption, the rule of law and bureaucratic quality based on the International Country Risk Guide.

5 Only 16 per cent of completed civil service reform operations were rated as achieving 'substantial' institutional development impact.

6 This section draws heavily on Jones (1997). See also Akroyd and Duncan (1998).

7 See in particular the discussion of the Zambia and Mozambique Health sec tors in Jones (1997).

8 See Okidegbe (1998).

9 Jones (1997) discusses the conceptual and practical aspects of these six features in the light of initial experience with the sector programmes in roads in Tanzania, health in Mozambique and health and agriculture in Zambia.

10 For instance to prevent resources intended for financing primary education being used at the margin to finance tertiary education.

11 This section draws in part on the four case studies in Jones (1997) and on subsequent direct OPM involvement with sector programme initiatives especially in agriculture (in Ghana, Kenya, Lesotho, Malawi, Uganda, Zambia and Zimbabwe). Other significant examples from which examples are drawn include agriculture in Mozambique (PROAGRI), and Health and Education in Ghana, Ethiopia (Stridsman, 1998; Oksanen, 1999) and Uganda.

12 The TIRP, however, has encountered difficulties resulting from mismanagement of contracts and corruption within the Ministry responsible for road construction and from macroeconomic difficulties that have prevented the release of funds earmarked for road maintenance (Jones, 1997).

13 Apart from the Zambia Agricultural Sector Investment Programme (ASIP) against which disbursement began in 1996, only PROAGRI in Mozambique has reached the stage of implementation following joint appraisal.

14 See the discussion of the Mozambique and Zambia health sector programmes in Jones (1997). A very similar process took place in the Ghana health sector.

This consensus has involved a focus on strengthening the role of the state in primary health care and a redirection of expenditures towards this level.
15 This was identified as one of the main reasons for the breakdown of both the national and district level management systems established as part of the Zambia ASIP (see Chiwele, 1998).
16 A particular problem in agriculture has been that a need for substantial down-sizing and rationalisation of agriculture ministry activities has usually emerged from sector review process. This has obviously been seen as a threat to the civil servants implementing the programme. The poor management of a radical reform of the Ministry of Agriculture was one of the main causes of the difficulties encountered with the Zambia ASIP (Chiwele, 1998).
17 See Akroyd and Duncan (1998).
18 Jones (1997) suggests that the level of donor resources provided under sector programmes should be conditional on government meeting agreed expenditure targets. This approach would be incentive compatible, but would face practical implementation difficulties.
19 In the case of Ethiopia, the initial proposals for the Health, Education and Roads sector programmes exceeded the total of all government spending. In Mozambique and Kenya agriculture, expenditure programmes were developed that were initially rejected by the Ministry of Finance as far exceeding the budget ceilings envisaged for the sector.
20 The Adaptable Programme Loan has been advocated as an appropriately flexible instrument for supporting the process of sector programme development.

REFERENCES

Akroyd, S. and A. Duncan (1998). 'The Sector Approach and Sustainable Rural Livelihoods', in D. Carney (ed.), *Sustainable Rural Livelihoods: What Contribution Can We Make?*, London: Department for International Development
Buckley, R. (1999). *1998 Annual Review of Development Effectiveness*, World Bank Operations Evaluation Department, Washington DC: World Bank
Chiwele, D.K. (1998). 'The Zambia Agricultural Sector Investment Program: Design and Implementation Experience', Lusaka: Institute of Economic and Social Research, University of Zambia, mimeo
DANIDA (1996). *Guidelines for Sector Programme Support (Including Project Support)*, Copenhagen: Ministry of Foreign Affairs
Disch, A. (1999). 'Developing Sector Budget Support: A Transactions Costs Perspective', paper presented to the NORAD Seminar on Sector-Wide Approaches, Oslo
Harrold, P. and Associates (1995). 'The Broad Sector Approach to Investment Lending: Sector Investment Programs', *World Bank Discussion Paper*, **302**
Johnson, J.H. and S.S. Wasty (1999). 'Borrower Ownership of Adjustment Programs and the Political Economy of Reform', *World Bank Discussion Paper*, **199**

Jones, S. (1997). 'Sector Investment Programs in Africa: Issues and Experience', *World Bank Technical Paper*, **374**

Killick, T. with R. Gunatilaka and A. Marr (1998). *Aid and the Political Economy of Policy Change*, London and New York: Routledge

Okidegbe, N. (1998). 'Agriculture Sector Program Sourcebook', *World Bank Technical Paper*, **418**

Oksanen, R. (1999). 'Preparation of ESDP in Ethiopia Reflections by Participants', paper presented to the NORAD Seminar on Sector-Wide Approaches, Oslo

SIDA (1995). 'Sector Programme Support – Background Document to SIDA Policy', Stockholm: Department of Legal and Policy Affairs

Stridsman, M. (1998). 'Report from the Seminar on Practical Planning and Implications of Sector-Wide Approaches for Education and Health Development', Stockholm: Swedish International Development Cooperation Agency

World Bank (1992). 'Effective Implementation: Key to Development Impact', *Report of the World Bank's Portfolio Management Task Force*, Washington DC: World Bank

(1994). *Adjustment in Africa: Reforms, Results and the Road Ahead*, New York: Oxford University Press for the World Bank

(1998). *Assessing Aid: What Works, What Doesn't, and Why*, New York: Oxford University Press for the World Bank

11　The World Bank, conditionality and the Comprehensive Development Framework

RAUL HOPKINS, ANDREW POWELL, AMLAN ROY
AND CHRISTOPHER L. GILBERT

1 Introduction

Almost all commentators note the multiplicity of the World Bank's functions and objectives. Oliver's (1971, 1975) accounts of the Bretton Woods and subsequent negotiations demonstrate differences of opinion, both between the Americans and the British, and also within the US administration itself, about *what* the World Bank should do, going back to the very origins of the organisation. Gavin and Rodrik (1995: 329) state that the debate surrounding its creation was about what it should do, not just how it should do it. Naïm (1994) accuses the current structure of generating goal congestion. We argue that the World Bank's strength arises from complementarity among these functions, and that conditionality is the cement that generates this complementarity. We see the World Bank's objectives as being closely aligned with the interests of borrowing countries, and view Bank conditionality, which we interpret in a broad sense, as a mechanism for helping governments realise some of these objectives. We suggest that this view of conditionality meshes well with the 'Comprehensive Development Framework' or CDF approach to development assistance which the Bank is now promoting.

2 The World Bank: a functional analysis

The World Bank is a large and complex organisation comprising a set of imprecisely focused institutions with overlapping responsibilities. It may be analysed in terms of these institutions or alternatively in terms of the economic functions it fulfils. In this chapter, we focus on the Bank's functions and ignore the institutional embodiments of these functions that we have discussed in Gilbert *et al.* (1996).

We distinguish three economic functions exercised by the Bank:

(1) the World Bank as a *bank*
(2) the World Bank as a *development agency* and
(3) the World Bank as a *development research institution.*

The *banking* role played by the Bank is that of direct intermediation. The Bank has AAA status and is able to borrow on the finest terms while its client governments either have very limited access to international capital markets or can borrow only on less advantageous terms. By intermediating, the Bank is able to substantially reduce the cost of capital to borrowers. The viability of this function relies on the Bank's ability to mitigate the effects of capital market failures, of which the most important are those associated with sovereign risk. Lessard (1986) argues that the Bank's ability to bear these risks stems from a comparative advantage in enforcement.

The *development agency* role of the Bank is the monitoring and supervision of government and other public sector decisions with the objective of promoting 'good development practice'. Monitoring generates the substantial information flows from permanent and regular visiting missions that relate, not only to specific Bank investment projects, but also to the overall economic and political climate in the borrowing country. This function also includes the provision of technical assistance, but more generally involves the Bank's activities in development training. Governments, whether in developing or in developed economies, often fail to adopt economic policies that will clearly benefit the majority of their citizens. As Bates and Krueger (1993: 2) note, 'it is very often political factors which inhibit or prevent the authorities from adopting programs which, on economic grounds, appear to offer the soundest prospect for resumption of growth and increasing living standards'. World Bank conditionality and programme lending are instruments that may assist governments in moving in this direction – see sections 4 and 5.

The Bank's role as a *development research institution* in part reflects the activities of the Research Department, and also those of the economists working in operational divisions. It is these research activities which inform the development agency function. This role is emphasised by Stern and Ferreira (1993) and Gavin and Rodrik (1995). Gavin and Rodrik justify this role by the claim (1995: 332) that borrowing countries sorely lacked the technical expertise required to prepare project applications. We would have substituted acceptable project applications, the implied premise being that Bank staff have a comparative advantage in identifying profitable projects and/or projects that will contribute substantially to the development process. More generally, Bank staff have developed practical experience in good development practice, which allows them to advise on policy.

We argue that the three functions we have identified are complementary. In particular, the promotion of development-oriented reform improves the prospects for contractual debt service, and by the intermediation of funds, information provision is enhanced. In these ways, the banking and development agency functions become mutually reinforcing. If this view is correct, it is wrong to see the Bank as facing a general conflict between the banking objective of improving the quality of the loan portfolio and general developmental objectives. This is not to argue that the Bank should undertake low-return projects, but rather that by simultaneously pursuing profitable lending and best development practice, the Bank will do better on both counts than if it gives priority to one or the other.

Recognition of this multiplicity of function[1] is important because simple discussions of World Bank reform tend to isolate only the one or two functions that fit the solutions the authors wish to advance. Walters (1994), for example, argues that because no dividends are paid, all Bank lending is subsidised. He thereby implicitly dismisses the Bank's banking function. At the same time, he regards conditionality as merely window-dressing (1994: 13). He concedes that the Bank does give good policy advice (the development research institute function), but suggests that perhaps this function might be privatised, leaving open the question of whether client countries would be willing to pay commercial fees for this advice. He suggests that, more radically, 'A case can be ... made for abolishing the Bank' (1994: 18) but it is not clear whether this case rests on the unimportance of Bank lending or because the Bank could advise on what projects should be undertaken without actually lending the funds to do this (1994: 19), an argument which appears to conflict with the alleged concessional nature of all Bank lending. By contrast, Gavin and Rodrik (1995) saw no need for Bank reform, but failed to address the conditionality issues which have dominated the Bank's development over the past 15 years.

3 How to understand the World Bank

Does it make sense to bundle together the banking and the development agency functions which, we argue, are the World Bank's core? One simple argument for bundling these two roles is that similar skills are required to identify and assess potential investment projects as those required to analyse the more general development needs of a borrowing country. This implies the existence of economies of scope in the provision of these two functions. But although this argument may have some validity, it is insufficiently strong by itself to act as an explanation for the Bank's structure. In what follows, we stress additional – and, we suggest, more important – sources of complementarity.

We argue that the success of the banking function derives, first, from the enforcement powers of the Bank in ensuring contractual lending terms are met and, second, from the conditionality that the Bank is able to apply, although we acknowledge that some countries have a modest record in conditionality compliance.[2] We will argue that the application of conditionality aids enforcement. In turn, the development agency function benefits from the banking function in at least two ways. First, countries may be more willing to provide accurate information where potential financing is an issue; and, second, reform may face fewer impediments when undertaken as part of a lending programme. The link between the banking and development agency functions may therefore be seen as stemming from their complementarity in the Bank's production function.

Considering the banking function alone, the rationale for the existence of the World Bank rests on a claimed comparative advantage in enforcement and not on any general argument for public sector banking. Enforcement of debt service may be analysed within a game-theoretic framework – see, for example, Eaton and Gersowitz (1981), Eaton, Gersowitz and Stiglitz (1986) and Anderson, Gilbert and Powell (1989, 1991, hereafter AGP). The penalty (negative payoff) to a country which fails to comply with agreed debt service may arise from the denial of future access to international capital markets, from the expropriation of the country's overseas assets, or from the curtailment of access to the normal instruments of international trade.

This is illustrated in figure 11.1, which is taken from AGP (1991). The borrowing country is scheduled to make a payment, R, to the lender, but alternatively may threaten default. In that case, the lender may declare default, resulting in the borrowing country making some cash payment, P, as a penalty. In addition, the borrowing country will lose future access

Figure 11.1 *Enforcement of debt service: a game-theoretic framework*
Source: AGP (1991).

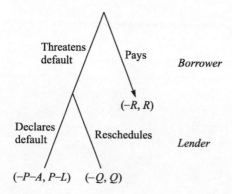

to capital markets. Thus, if A is the value of this access, the net payoff to the defaulting country is $-P-A$. The lender receives the amount $P-L$, where L is the deadweight loss associated with declaring default. On the other hand, if the lender faced with non-performance does not declare default, a negotiation will take place to determine a payment, Q, on the now rescheduled loan. AGP show that the Nash equilibrium of this bargaining process will be

$$Q = P + \lambda A - (1 - \lambda)L$$

. where λ is the World Bank's bargaining power. Consider two states of the world across which R and L are constant. With probability $1 - \pi$, the country's income will be high and in this circumstance, the lender will be able to extract a high penalty, P^+, in the event of default. The cost to the borrowing country of subsequent loss of access to capital markets will also be high at A^+. On the other hand, with probability π the country's income will be low, implying a lower penalty, $P^- < P^{+,}$ and access cost, $A^- < A^+$. Assume

$$P^+ + \lambda A^+ - (1 - \lambda)L > R$$
$$P^- + \lambda A^- - (1 - \lambda)L < R$$

so that the borrowing country repays on schedule in the good state but not in the bad state. Then the expected repayment, prior to revelation of the state of the world, is

$$(1 - \pi)R + \pi[P^- + \lambda A^- - (1 - \lambda)L]$$

A claimed comparative advantage in enforcement translates into higher expected repayments as the consequence of (a) a higher threatened penalty, P^-, in the event of a possible default and/or (b) the imposition of greater access costs, A^-, subsequent to default.

Now suppose the lender is able to impose policy conditionality at the time the loan is negotiated. The objective of conditionality is to advance reforms which should, over time, raise the country's income. In the willingness-to-pay framework reflected in models of the sort considered here, higher income levels can affect expected repayments only by altering the penalty level, P^-, or the cost of future access, A^-, in the poor state. Suppose that P is rising in income, which is likely to be the case if asset expropriation or trade inhibition are the penalties envisaged. The consequence is then that conditionality, if complied with, will raise expected repayments. In this model, conditionality therefore strengthens enforcement.[3] This argument is independent of the form conditionality takes and the way that it is applied, although certain forms of conditionality and modes of application may be more effective than others.

In this framework, conditionality raises expected repayments both to the World Bank, as the enforcer of conditionality, but also to private sector banks. It therefore generates an externality. The World Bank's comparative advantage in enforcement arises through internalising this externality, both because it values development *per se* and because it values governments servicing private sector borrowing in order to maintain future access to credit markets. Private sector banks will be concerned only about their own repayments, and indeed may even try to obtain these at the expense of repayments to other banks (through assertion of seniority). Paradoxically, therefore, by asserting a development objective in addition to a profit objective, the Bank's lending activities may result in the selection of the cooperative equilibrium. If this does happen, both private banks and the Bank itself may enjoy a higher level of income than that which would have resulted if the Bank had been concerned solely with profits.

This raises the question of whether a market comprising purely private banks could also attain the cooperative equilibrium. This is a possible reformulation of Rodrik's (1995) question, 'Why is there multilateral lending?' However, the World Bank, as the IBRD, lends against its capital by borrowing from financial markets rather than lending the capital directly so the defining feature of multilateral lending is the enforcement of repayment rather than the source of funds. Multilateral lending is 'multilateral' in the sense that borrowing and lending governments both accord it preferred status. Could preferred status ever describe an equilibrium in a market of purely private sector institutions?

Any individual profit-maximising bank will have an incentive to defect in bad states by placing repayment on its own loans ahead of the general development objective which would generate a higher overall level of repayment. The cooperative equilibrium can be sustained only if banks can credibly commit not to seek repayment on a unilateral basis. Only multilateral institutions can make such commitments, which are effectively guaranteed by their charters and by their ownership structures. It matters that the Bank's shareholders are governments and not investors, and that, furthermore, a proportion of the voting equity is held by borrowing governments.

These conceptual discussions are important because different views of the fundamental economic functions which the World Bank performs will have different implications for current policy debates. We draw two lessons from the foregoing discussion:

(1) Because of its ability to apply policy conditionality, the World Bank is complementary with private sector development lending. Better policy will enhance lending opportunities and potential rates of return and result in superior debt service.
(2) This externality would not be available in the absence of a strong public sector institution which combines banking and development functions.[4]

4 The conditionality debate

There has been significant recent research on the role and effectiveness of conditionality (summarised in World Bank 1998; see also Killick, 1998 and Deverajan and Swaroop and Burnside and Dollar, chapters 7 and 8 in this volume). Much of this work has been conducted considering conditionality with respect to aid flows or highly subsidised lending. However, while we recognise that conditionality may take various forms (and in particular there has been a marked difference in IMF-style versus World Bank-style conditionality), we consider this analysis as highly relevant not only for highly subsidised lending, but also for IBRD-type flows. The prevalent view from this literature is that aid is effective but only in conjunction with 'good' policy.

As a result there is a movement towards favouring 'policy-level conditionality' and away from 'policy-change conditionality'.[5] The implication is that, to obtain good value for each dollar spent, donors should be much more selective as to which countries they provide aid to.

Governments that persist in pursuing poor or weakly implemented economic policies will benefit instead from the Bank's development advice. This approach emphasises the importance of policy ownership, and of dialogue and partnership between donors and recipients.

Another useful distinction has been proposed by Killick (1998), between *hard core* conditionality and *pro forma* conditionality. The former refers to 'a requirement for involuntary action of some sort on the part of the recipient government without which assistance would not be granted or continued' (Killick, 1998: 27). We prefer the terms 'imposed' and 'agreed' conditionality, on the basis that Killick's nomenclature may be thought pejorative, and, in particular, because the term 'pro forma' might give the incorrect impression that these conditions are not serious. Agreed conditionality relates to policy commitments included in aid agreements for the convenience of both parties (Killick, 1998: 188). They are measures laying down what could be done and in what sequence, serving as a kind of institutional memory against the possibility of changes among key officials. In general, Killick refers to 'conditionality' as the imposed, hard core component of it, although it admits that there is a grey area between the two types.

Although the debate is far from over, a number of conclusions have been reached. Perhaps the most important one is that conditionality, at least in the form that has been implemented, has had very limited results. The explanations for this are various: (1) the overriding importance of domestic political factors as determinants of long-run policy changes; (2) the difficulties of international organisations to put in place a consistent and credible set of rewards and penalties; (3) serious problems of implementation; and (4) the influence of external shocks, making it difficult for governments to keep to their original commitments.

Perhaps the most interesting aspect in the debate on conditionality relates to the search for an alternative. For Collier (chapter 12 in this volume) there are a number of factors that create an opportunity to redesign conditionality (the end of the Cold War, the concerted efforts to reduce indebtedness, the improvement in economic policies in many developing countries and the results of recent research on aid effectiveness). Collier argues that, aside from exceptional circumstances, the relationship between aid recipients and donors should be viewed as a partnership between a government with satisfactory policies and aid providers. In this approach, conditionality is not abandoned but redesigned: 'I am thus suggesting that donor conditionality should, to be effective, take a different form ... donors should condition their financial resource transfers not upon policy *change* but upon policy *levels*.' To other authors, the new role for conditionality is not so clear.

Killick (1998) suggests continuing using agreed conditionality but rejects the imposed variety. He is willing to accept the use of imposed conditionality only under exceptional circumstances (e.g. where there are specific grounds for believing that levying policy conditions will tip the political balance in favour of change, 1998: 190). He proposes, instead, an alternative model of donor–recipient relations, based upon four principles: ownership, selectivity, support and dialogue. The contribution of Killick is in this respect particularly important as it is based on a rich body of evidence and years of direct experience advising governments of developing countries and international organisations.

There is little to disagree with regarding these principles: they are a healthy reaction to an overuse of conditionality, neglecting essential aspects of the donor–recipient relationship (ownership, in particular). The question, however, is to what extent these principles imply a move away from conditionality.

The principle of 'selectivity' deserves a close scrutiny. It states that programme aid should be reserved for countries that have adopted for themselves efficient pro-development policies. The implementation of higher selectivity would increase the effectiveness of aid and the credibility of the programmes with which it is associated. In this view, donors take on responsibility only for something they can deliver. This principle implies, however, a partial reinstatement of conditionality, in that for a government to receive aid it must deliver sound policies. It has the additional complication of requiring a clear definition of a good-policy environment, and the identification of objective indicators of ownership, a problem of which Killick is aware (1998: 180, 183–6). Selectivity therefore appears to be a form of policy level or *ex ante* conditionality.

Non-governmental organisations (NGOs) have been quick to recognise the weakness in the argument and have raised their concern about this new form of conditionality, 'rather than withdrawing from conditionality, selectivity could in reality imply more up-front conditionality' (Wood and Lockwood, 1999: 1). Recent events suggest that this is indeed not only a relevant conceptual discussion but also that it has implications for the allocation of aid.[6]

5 Conditionality trade-offs

At least in a weak form, conditionality is inevitable, as lenders will wish to ensure repayment. World Bank lending has always involved an element of conditionality in recognition of the fact that there is little merit in lending to finance a project if the potential benefits arising from the project are dissipated through upstream or downstream inefficiencies. However, the major shift that resulted from the debt crisis of the 1980s was away from project-based aid to programme-based aid. In its first 25 years, the Bank used conditionality in order to ensure the success of projects and to guarantee that their potential benefits were captured. Since the mid-1980s, lending has often been justified in terms of the benefits of the policies adopted as the result of conditionality clauses. The policies have become the projects, with investment in economic infrastructure replacing investment in physical infrastructure. Loans are justified by policy changes, instead of vice versa.

If conditionality cannot be avoided, at least as one ingredient of development programmes, it is worth exploring the advantages and disadvantages of its various forms and the trade-offs involved. Table 11.1 illustrates the advantages and disadvantages of the three forms of conditionality contrasted above. Policy-change conditionality is applicable to any country but has apparently been only modestly effective, as the consequence of time-consistency problems, high monitoring costs and lack of reform ownership. It is suggested that policy-level conditionality has the potential to be much more effective, but its coverage is limited to those countries with 'good' policy environments. It therefore implies a cut in the resources flowing to those countries whose governments fail to satisfy these conditions. It may also create a vicious circle in which negative policy environments are reinforced (particularly in those countries that are far from the minimum policy levels required for receiving aid). In the absence of the aid 'bribe', governments in such countries may perceive little incentive towards implementing reforms which impose high costs in the short to medium term.

The implications of altered allocation criteria for poverty alleviation are unclear. Advocates of policy-level conditionality argue that aid is fungible (Devarajan and Swaroop, chapter 7 in this volume) and, by implication, targeting aid at poverty reduction is effective only where governments embrace this objective. Against this view, it may be argued that if good policy is positively correlated with economic success (and one must expect this to be the case eventually), a decision to direct aid away from countries where governments have poor policies entails a lower priority for poverty, at least over the short to medium term.

Table 11.1 emphasises that, in modifying aid allocation criteria, the Bank faces a potentially acute choice between aid effectiveness and wide aid coverage, and that the difficulties in making this choice may be exacerbated by poverty considerations. But, in any case, the Bank may be politically constrained. Its structure ensures that all member countries are

Table 11.1 *Forms of conditionality*

	Scope	Effectiveness	Monitoring costs	Poverty alleviation
a Policy-change conditionality	High (applicable to any country)	Low	High	Low
b Policy-level conditionality	Low (restricted to countries with 'good-policy environments')	High	Low	Uncertain
c Agreed conditionality	Uncertain (depends on the donor–recipient relationship)	High	Uncertain	High

represented at Board level, although weighted voting may imply that a borrowing country's voice is associated with relatively little power. This at least partially representative structure may make it difficult for the Bank to fully implement a shift towards policy-level conditionality.

Agreed conditionality constitutes a third alternative. As explained above, this type of conditionality refers to consensual policy measures agreed between donors and recipient governments. It has a great potential in terms of effectiveness and poverty alleviation (as it is correlated with ownership, Killick 1998: 11) but its scope is uncertain. It will depend on the compatibility of objectives between donors and recipient governments and on the possibility of reaching genuine consensual agreements.

Both the conditionality debate, and table 11.1 that attempts to outline some of the trade-offs involved, oversimplify the practical decisions which the Bank will face in attempting to move towards a policy-level conception of conditionality. This oversimplification is reminiscent of Sellars and Yates' famous pastiche of English history, *1066 and All That*, in which every monarch was either a 'good king' or a 'bad thing'. Most developing country governments will defy this easy classification.

One alternative might be to relate the degree of 'policy-level' conditionality to the type of 'product' offered by the Bank. The current Bank's policy spectrum ranges from (1) highly subsidised lending (IDA), (2) lending to governments through the standard loan products of the IBRD, (3) lending to the private sector with government guarantees, (4) lowering the cost of finance through the use of guarantees either to the public or private sector, (5) lending or taking equity stakes in private sector enterprises through the IFC and to (6) providing trade and political risk guarantees through MIGA.

One possibility might be to apply different types of conditionality to different products. For example, it might be argued that policy-level conditionality might be applied more to the more advanced 'products' in the World Bank product spectrum, while more traditional conditionality might still apply to the more traditional lending operations. However, the Bank Group faces greater competition in selling its more advanced (and less subsidised) products and so has less scope to put conditions on purchase of these products, and it may also be argued that it is the traditional subsidised products where increased selectivity is most important.

Actual aid decisions will, more often that not, involve judgements about countries where policies are a mixture of good and less good, and implementation is a mixture of more and less effective. In these instances, it will be difficult to avoid augmenting level judgements with views about the direction and velocity of change, and of conditioning upon such changes.

It is common to all sides in this debate that the Bank should encourage the development of good policy. In countries with 'middling' policy, the Bank should aim to become a partner in working to improve policy. Aid and advice are both elements in the partnership package that the Bank can offer. However, the terms on which these are available need to be clearly understood by both sides. It will not help to pretend there is no policy-change conditionality if in fact there is an element of it in aid decisions see Eade (1997), who argues that any 'fudging' of the nature of the relationship between two partners undermines the basis for honest negotiation.

6 Conditionality and the CDF

The 'Comprehensive Development Framework' (CDF) concept was a significant development in Bank thinking during 1999 (Wolfensohn, 1999). The CDF approach to development attempts to be comprehensive in two respects: across different aspects of development, and across participants in the development process. Governments are expected, in conjunction with donors, NGOs, the private sector and 'civil society', to construct a tabular CDF matrix, the cells of which indicate the required actions for each development objective (across columns) by each organisation (down rows). It is intended that construction of this matrix will ensure both that development planning is comprehensive and that leadership and implementation responsibilities are clear.

Bank country programmes presumably aimed for comprehensiveness across development objectives even before the CDF. However, the Bank cannot do everything, so increased coordination among donors can ensure complementarity in the development effort within an overall balanced approach. Comprehensiveness across participants is more important in that government, the private sector and 'civil society' are among the intended participants.[7] This implies that ownership, free markets and democracy are central to the CDF concept.

The CDF has important implications for the conditionality debate which has hitherto largely been conducted among academic and Research Department economists. The CDF concept looks to substitute a cooperative and comprehensive view of development for the approach in which development objectives were imposed by donors. From the CDF standpoint, the continuing debate about the form of conditionality appears as a throwback to the previous confrontational style of donor operation. Mutually agreed targets replace unilaterally imposed conditions, and, in that sense, the CDF may be thought of as adopting Killick's concept of agreed conditionality. The comprehensive, democratic and consultative elements of the CDF process are seen as giving the targets increased legitimacy and as delivering national ownership. Increased ownership may be seen as justifying greater flexibility on the Bank's part – if there is consensus about objectives, there is less requirement to impose a rigid view on means.

Many of the same problems which have arisen in relation to conditionality will reappear with the CDF framework. We see two broad areas of difficulty. First, the Bank has acknowledged that the CDF approach should result in greater selectivity in Bank funding within countries, as the consequence of increased donor coordination. Implicitly, there will also be selectivity between countries, and in this regard, priorities imposed by the CDF framework may conflict with selectivity based on policy quality. Will a well formulated CDF be a (or even the) criterion of satisfactory *ex ante* policy? Will the absence of a CDF imply that policy is unsatisfactory even if traditional indicators (openness, low inflation, etc.) imply sound policy? The root of this problem is that CDF targets translate into Killick's 'agreed conditionality', but this may run counter to the 'value for development dollars' approach which emphasises current policy quality.

The second potential problem is that agreed targets can be missed just as, hitherto, conditions have failed to be met. The overall CDF philosophy is that development is a management problem. The CDF is a management tool to ensure that everyone is 'on board' with agreed development objectives. There are no conflicts of interest and no principal–agent problems. This contrasts with economists' views of development which emphasise the requirement for incentives to be correctly aligned, for clearly defined and enforced property rights and for measures to ameliorate malfunctioning markets. Neither the economists' nor the management view is entirely correct, and it is probably right that the balance be redressed towards better management, but exclusive reliance on better management to achieve development is likely to result in disappointment.

7 Conclusions

The World Bank has evolved over its 50 years of operation so that it simultaneously exercises a number of different functions. Its core functions are those of bank and development agency. We argue that the role of conditionality is important to understanding the World Bank's operations. The Bank applies conditionality as part of its development mission – structural adjustment has resulted in policy reforms taking priority over projects as a justification for lending. But the ability to apply conditionality gives the Bank a comparative advantage in enforcement of debt service. This generates a complementarity between the Bank's development agency and banking functions. However because successful conditionality will also result in improved service of private debt, there is an externality. The Bank is concerned with development and not simply with profits, and is therefore willing to allow the gains from conditionality to be shared with private sector banks. This results in a superior lending equilibrium than would exist in the absence of a strong multilateral institution.

This view of the World Bank sees its comparative advantage over other financial and developmental agencies as arising from the complementarity of the banking and development agency functions, which, through the application of policy conditionality, allows the internalisation of what would otherwise be a positive externality. But this view neither requires an imposed definition of conditionality nor that the Bank confine itself to this form of lending. Furthermore, there may be ample scope for improvements in implementation, or for alteration of the content of conditionality requirements to put greater emphasis on poverty alleviation or environmental concerns. In the spirit of the Comprehensive Development Framework initiative, conditionality should be seen as part of the dialogue between the World Bank and recipient governments and not as an alternative to dialogue.

NOTES

This is an expanded and revised version of Hopkins *et al.* (1997) which was itself a modified version of Gilbert *et al.* (1996) prepared for the American Economic Association 1996 meeting in San Francisco. We are grateful to Mark Baird, Kalyan Banerji, Bejoy Das Gupta, Ron Duncan, Huw Evans, Richard Frank, Andrew Hughes Hallett, Ravi Kanbur, Tony Killick, John Mitchell, Paul Mosley, Guy Pfeffermann, Brian Pinto, Lex Rieffel, David Vines and Gerald West for useful comments on one or more of this sequence of papers. However, the views expressed are entirely our own and do not necessarily represent any of the institutions or persons listed above. Financial support comes from the Global Economic Institutions programme of the ESRC to whom we express our thanks.

1   Naim (1994) also emphasises the multiplicity of the Bank's functions but adopts a slightly different classification: the 'Bank-as-bank', the Bank as an instrument for 'promotion of values not readily accepted by the traditional power structures within developing countries', the Bank as development consultant and the Bank as a resource-transfer mechanism. One might also see the Bank as also possessing a *credit-rating* function.

2   Gilbert, Powell and Vines (chapter 2 in this volume) summarises the empirical evidence. Any move towards more effective conditionality, either by making it more appropriate or even just simpler (Mosley, Harrigan and Toye, 1995), or by revising the manner in which it is applied (Collier, chapter 12 in this volume), will increase the Bank's enforcement powers.

3   Rodrik (1995) makes a similar argument that multilateral lending is justified by conditionality. However, he does not go on to note that this creates a public good. Mosley (1987) and Mosley, Harrigan and Toye (1995) argue that Bank conditionality should be seen as a bargaining process between the Bank and the borrowing government, and this adds a further strand to the standard debt game. That view is developed in Fafchamps (1996), who sees conditionality as a partial substitute for the inability of sovereign borrowers to commit on repayment. However, his model, which focuses on the balance between production of traded and non-traded goods, is better seen as a model of bargaining over the extent of exchange rate overvaluation than over reform. The simple model we have used suffers from the usual limitations of one-shot models. In principle, these might be overcome in a repeated-game framework.

4   In Gilbert *et al.* (1996), we extended these arguments to demonstrate why then topical proposals to privatise the World Bank were misconceived (Walters, 1994; Eberstadt and Lewis, 1995).

5   Note that this discussion has also been prominent in the IMF regarding the Contingent Credit Line (CCL), albeit with different language. The now approved CCL explicitly includes 'policy-level' conditionality or *ex ante* preconditions in the language of the Fund. The idea is that this more automati-

cally disbursing credit line, which is designed to limit contagion from one emerging country with economic problems to another with sound fundamentals, will be available only to countries that satisfy certain policy conditions.
6 A note in the March 1999 Bretton Woods Update, entitled 'Selectivity: conditionality by any other name', summarises the meeting between government officials and the World Bank discussing new criteria for allocating its IDA resources among countries. Participants made a number of critical comments on the 20 criteria describing a 'good-policy environment', asserting, among other things that the selectivity criteria are tantamount to upfront conditionality and not compatible with Bank initiatives to foster ownership (Bretton Woods Project, 1999).
7 The CDF also seeks to bring NGOs on board into Bank programmes prior to Wolfensohn's Presidency, many NGOs tended to see themselves as in opposition to Bank programmes.

REFERENCES

Anderson, R.W., C.L Gilbert and A. Powell (1989). 'Securitisation and Commodity Contingency in International Lending', *American Journal of Agricultural Economics*, 71 (Supp): 523–30
(1991). 'Securitising Development Finance: The Role of Partial Guarantees and Commodity Contingency', in T. Priovolos and R. C. Duncan (eds.), *Commodity Risk Management and Finance*, Oxford: Oxford University Press
Bates, R.H. and A. O. Krueger (1993). *Political and Economic Interactions in Economic Policy Reform*, Oxford: Blackwell
Bretton Woods Project (1999). Bretton Woods Update', London, March
Eade, D. (1997). *Capacity-Building, an Approach to People-Centred Development*, Oxford: Oxfam
Eaton, J. and M. Gersowitz (1981). 'Debt with Potential Repudiation: Theoretical and Empirical Analysis', *Review of Economic Studies*, 48: 289–309
Eaton, J., M. Gersowitz and J. E. Stiglitz (1986). 'The Pure Theory of Country Risk', *European Economic Review*, 30: 481–513
Eberstadt, N. and C. M. Lewis (1995). 'Privatising the World Bank', *The National Interest* (Summer): 14–18
Fafchamps, M. (1996). 'Sovereign Debt, Structural Adjustment and Conditionality', *Journal of Development Economics*, 50: 313–35
Gavin, M. and D. Rodrik (1995). 'The World Bank in Historical Perspective', *American Economic Review, Papers and Proceedings*, 85: 329–34
Gilbert, C.L., R. Hopkins, A. Powell and A. Roy (1996). 'The World Bank: Its Functions and its Future', ESRC, *Global Economic Institutions Working Paper*, 15
Hopkins, R., A. Powell, A. Roy and C. L. Gilbert (1997). 'The World Bank and Conditionality', *Journal of International Development*, 9: 507–16
Killick, T. (1998). *Aid and the Political Economy of Policy Change*, London: Overseas Development Institute

Lessard, D.R. (1986). 'The Management of International Trade Risks', *Geneva Papers on Risk and Insurance*, **11**: 255–64

Mosley, P. (1987). 'Conditionality as Bargaining Process: Structural Adjustment Lending, 1980–86', *Princeton Studies in International Finance*, **168**

Mosley, P., J. Harrigan and J. Toye (1995). *Aid and Power: The World Bank and Policy-Based Lending*, 2nd edn., London: Routledge

Naim, M. (1994). 'The World Bank: Its Role, Governance and Organisational Culture', in Bretton Woods Committee, *Looking to the Future*, **C273-86**, Washington, DC

Oliver, R.W. (1971). 'Early Plans for a World Bank', *Princeton Studies in International Finance*, **29**
    (1975). *International Economic Co-operation and the World Bank*, London: Macmillan

Rodrik, D. (1995). 'Why is there Multilateral Lending?', in M. Bruno and B. Pleskovic (eds.), *Annual World Bank Conference on Economic Development*, Washington, DC: World Bank: 167–93

Stern N. F. and Ferreira (1993). 'The World Bank as an 'Intellectual Actor'', STICERD, *Development Economics Paper*, **50**, London School of Economics

Walters, A. (1994). 'Do We Need the IMF and the World Bank?', *Current Controversies*, **10**, London: Institute of Economic Affairs

Wolfensohn, J. (1999). 'A Proposal for a Comprehensive Development Framework – A Discussion Draft', available at < http://www.worldbank.org/cdf/cd-text.htm >

Wood A. and M. Lockwood (1999). 'The 'Perestroika of Aid'?', in *New Perspectives on Conditionality*, London: Bretton Woods Project and Christian Aid

World Bank (1998). *Assessing Aid: What Works, What Doesn't and Why?*, Washington, DC: World Bank

12 Conditionality, dependence and coordination: three current debates in aid policy

PAUL COLLIER

1 Introduction

In this chapter I distinguish between aid *transfers* and aid *relationships*. The traditional literature on the economics of aid focused on the resource transfer. Aid relaxed constraints on economic performance, either by increasing savings or by increasing foreign exchange. There was no *relationship* between donor agencies and recipient governments. Aid, in this analysis, was indistinguishable from a government-owned oil well.

I consider three aid debates in which the central issue is the relationship between the donor and the recipient. The first of these is policy-based lending, or 'conditionality'. This relationship has been criticised both as intrusive and ineffective (although these two criticisms sit together uncomfortably). The second debate is on 'aid dependency'. This criticism is that the aid relationship is intrinsically undermining of national capacities, analogous to the weakening of household capacities in the syndrome of welfare dependency. The third debate is around the suggestion that aid is missing an opportunity for a coordinating relationship. By focusing upon individual nations aid has, it is argued, missed its comparative advantage in the financing of coordinated development at the supra-national level, such as region-wide transport systems.

I discuss these three debates in turn.

2 Policy conditionality

Although policy conditionality became established only during the 1980s, the idea that international public resources should be used to induce policy reform has a long history. Its origin lies in Fund crisis programmes. For example, in one of the largest IMF programmes ever undertaken, in 1976, the British government was provided with finance on condition that it changed economic policies. There is a continuum from the imposition of conditions on credit expansion in return for an IMF loan at a time of crisis, through to the imposition of conditions on detailed distributional and development policies in return for aid in normal circumstances of growth. However, although policy conditionality started with the former, by the 1990s it had advanced to the latter.

In principle this might have succeeded. Indeed, chapter 11 in this volume, by Hopkins *et al.*, assumes that World Bank conditionality is effective, and argues that the resulting complementarity between its development and banking functions provides a rationale for the Bank. In practice conditionality did not succeed. I first discuss why it failed. I then draw a distinction between appropriate and inappropriate circumstances for conditionalities intended to change policy. Finally, I consider a different rationale for conditioning aid allocations on policy – namely that aid is more effective in some policy environments than in others.

2.1 Why policy conditionality was introduced, and why it failed

During the 1980s three factors led donors to introduce policy-based lending. First, donors correctly perceived that in the poor policy environments which had built up during the previous decade, project aid was ineffective. By conditioning aid upon policy change they were attempting to rehabilitate the policy environment. The analytic literature developed formal principal–agent models to characterise this new relationship in which differences between donor and government preferences were central. The decision problem was how the donor could set incentives so as to induce policy change from the government.

Secondly, because of a combination of poor policy and negative external shocks, some countries were facing difficulties servicing their debts. Some creditors were willing to contemplate defensive lending, but this faced a further difficulty. In some countries, the government administration was unable to cope with the bureaucratic burden of increased project aid. Much project aid could simply not be disbursed. Hence, defensive lending through increased project aid would be ineffective. An important motive for the Special Program of Assistance to Africa was that lending based upon the promise of policy change could disburse large sums at minimal administrative burden.

Thirdly, some countries descended into crisis and needed IMF programmes to extricate them. As in all IMF crisis programmes, there was a reasonable presumption that the government had made serious mistakes so that it should be required to make policy changes in return for the finance that it was seeking. Since donor finance was typically part of the rescue package, the development conditionalities with which donors were concerned could simply be tagged on to this existing medium of policy conditionality.

The first two factors inducing the introduction of policy-based lending, the inducement of policy change and defensive lending, were incompatible. If governments did not adhere to their promises of policy change then the donors would be faced with a choice between discontinuing lending and thereby causing loan default, or forgiving the conditions. Since donors valued two outcomes which were incompatible, even had they been able to make this choice in their own best interests, it is unclear what the decision would have been. Quite possibly, the desire to avoid default would have been given more weight that the desire to induce policy change. However, the actual decision structure in the International Financial Institutions (IFIs) and the donor agencies produced a bias in favour of forgiveness.

In each particular instance of a breach of conditions enforcement is time-inconsistent: the decision by a donor not to disburse will not directly produce any improvement in government policy, but it will directly lead to default. Enforcement has public good properties: each time a condition is forgiven, expectations of enforcement are reduced and so breaches of conditions become more likely. Usually, the time-consistency problem is presented as a two-agent relationship. However, in the case of donor–government relations, it is in reality a matter of the behaviour of a system. Forgiveness of a government by one agent increases the likelihood of breaches in conditions not only by that government, but also by other governments against other agents. Hence, whether the time-inconsistency problem is overcome depends upon whether each donor agency can internalise the externalities of each particular decision so as to defend the integrity of the system. In practice, much of the power of decision on whether conditions are waived must be decentralised to the country team within the donor agencies, because the country team has an informational advantage over higher managerial levels. This has the consequence that any behavioural change which the decision might induce in other borrowing governments is external to the decision process. Further, because the staffing of country teams typically changes every three years, the team has little incentive to take into account any behavioural change which the decision might induce in the government itself. Because the remaining incentive for the country team is to avoid default, there is an unresolved time-consistency problem. This is compounded because staff have tended to be rewarded for getting loan agreements approved.

At the apex of the IFIs are the governing boards, which can take a system-wide view. However, during the 1980s Cold War politics meant that the system-wide view which those delegates with the most votes took reflected strategic considerations rather then the effectiveness of conditionality as a means of changing policies. The Cold War supported an aid game in which the leading protagonists competed for allegiance, and in which adept players such as President Nyerere of Tanzania were able to attract large uncritical aid inflows from a wide political spectrum.

There is considerable evidence for such lending behaviour. For example, the World Bank appears to have financed the same Kenyan agricultural pricing reform five times in 15 years.[1] More generally, Svensson (1998) demonstrates that during the 1980s heavy indebtedness was far more important in determining further lending than was the policy environment.

Even without conditionality most governments would have gradually been reforming their economic policies. Partly, reform was induced by the simple experience of economic failure. For example, the African countries which were the strongest reformers from 1987 onwards had policy ratings which were much worse than average just prior to reform (Collier and Pattillo, 1999). Partly, reform was induced by the increasing examples of market-assisted growth and the collapse of the socialist model. Partly, as democratisation spread, governments were forced to become more responsive to their populations so that the political costs of economic failure were increasing. Hence, the background to conditionality was of other forces for policy improvement.

Given the evident concerns of donors for matters other than policy change, it would not have been unreasonable for governments to regard compliance with conditions as optional. In a context in which some reforms were happening anyway, and there was in any case plenty of noise in the system owing to external shocks, governments could expect to be able to gain forgiveness from donors because they had done some reform, even if not as much as had been envisaged, and because there had been unforeseen circumstances.

Because the other forces inducing policy change coincided with conditionality, the era of conditionality was one of considerable policy reform. However, the test of how much conditionality contributed to this process is the country-by-country relationship from aid flows and policy change. Burnside and Dollar (1997) find that there has been no overall relationship from aid flows onto policy change: aid did not succeed in buying reform.

Recall that the impetus for conditionality had been the correct perception that projects failed in the poor policy environments prevalent by the beginning of the 1980s. Two phases of aid failure can therefore be distinguished, the pre-conditionality phase in which aid supported projects which failed because of the policy environment, and the conditionality phase, in which aid was targeted on buying policy reform in poor environments, but failed to do so. As a result of these two failures, overall, it is not surprising that aid should have had no significant effect on growth (Burnside and Dollar, 1997).

2.2 The opportunity to rethink conditionality

Four factors have radically changed the potential for aid to be effective. Between them, they have created an opportunity for conditionality to be redesigned.

First, with the end of the Cold War it has become more feasible for developed country governments to rebase their aid policies on considerations of long-term poverty from considerations of political allegiance. Of course, there is continuing pressure on bilateral donors to favour their own commercial interests, but there is a constituency to oppose such pressure. For example, the current British government has rebased its aid policy on the UN agreed goals, explicitly severing the previous link with commercial interests.

Secondly, there have been concerted efforts to reduce indebtedness, currently through the Heavily Indebted Poor Countries (HIPC) initiative. As this proceeds, it will considerably reduce pressures for defensive lending, since it is designed to reduce debt service to manageable levels.

Thirdly, the gradual improvement in economic policies in many developing countries has brought some countries to the stage at which the policy environment is now satisfactory (though certainly capable of further improvement). In low-income sub-Saharan Africa, around 25 per cent of the population lives in such environments. The average growth in *per capita* GDP for this group during the most recent two years for which data are available (1995 and 1996) was 4.2 per cent p.a. Hence, reform has brought in a phase of quite rapid growth in some, though not all countries. Because the reforming countries started from the worst investor risk ratings, private investment has yet to rise to levels which could sustain these growth rates. Growth is currently high owing to a bounce-back from poor policies. This creates a role for aid in sustaining growth in these newly post-stabilisation economies until private investment rises.

Fourthly, as a result of research, we now know much more than we did on aid effectiveness. Burnside and Dollar (1997 and chapter 8 in this volume) show that to be effective in raising growth and reducing infant mortality, financial transfers should be conditioned not upon the *change* in the policy environment, promised or achieved, but in its level. Below a certain level of policy aid simply fails to achieve growth. The current area of research uncertainty is as to which policies are most important. Burnside and Dollar used a composite of only three aspects of macroeconomic policy: economic openness, fiscal order and the containment of inflation. However, they recognised that because many policies are quite highly correlated, this narrow range of macroeconomic policies might itself proxy a wider, but less measurable range. The World Bank has recently constructed standardised and comparable numerical measures for 20 aspects of policy, across the entire spectrum of government for all its client countries. These measures are confidential, but some research has already been done on their properties. First, they are indeed highly correlated, so that a simple unweighted average of the 20 measures is virtually identical to the first principal component. Secondly, replicating the Burnside and Dollar study on growth performance during the 1990s but replacing their narrow measure of policy with the simple average of the 20 policies yields qualitatively the same results (see Collier and Dollar, 1999).[2] Policy and aid interact, so that the better is the policy environment the more effective is aid. In the best policy conditions aid powerfully raises the growth rate.

Having been ineffective for so long, the above four changes provide a choice between two aid strategies, either of which could be effective.

One option is to build on the opportunity provided by debt forgiveness and the end of the Cold War to make the previous form of conditionality work. This time, breaches would not be forgiven, because the impetus for forgiveness is much reduced, so that the Boards of the IFIs could focus on development performance. However, there are four factors counting against this option.

The first is that probably the main reason why conditionality failed was that it under-estimated the importance of the domestic political forces which determine policies in the long-term. There has been a tendency to overestimate donor power over governments. Governments and the 'left' has exaggerated donor power in order to raise the spectre of neo-colonialism, and the IFIs have been reluctant to admit that they have considerably less power than such accusations imply. Major economic policies (those which have powerful distributional consequences) are in the long term determined by a domestic political process in which the calculus of aid is often marginal.

Recent work on modelling aid bargaining between the donor and the government explicitly allows for a political equilibrium between pro-reform and anti-reform forces within the society (Coate and Morris, 1996; Adam and O'Connell, 1997). The new analytic approach is to search for donor interventions which irreversibly strengthen the pro-reform lobby – for example, by inducing irreversible investment in the export sector. However, while this is analytically correct, its main operational message is surely that *sustainable* reform in the context in which a government is opposed to it, is radically more difficult than temporary reform. A non-democratic government is likely to have a longer time horizon than the country team of an aid agency. Country teams seldom last for more than three or four years, and this limits the scope for credible long-term threats on the part of the donor, although potentially management systems might enable the continuity of aid agency policy to outlast the country team.

The second factor counting against the rehabilitation of conditionality is that the record of donor and IFI behaviour has made it much harder for conditionality to be credible. The aid industry lacks any institutions which are capable of credibly binding themselves to new behaviour. For years, donors have complained about non compliance and made menacing noises about getting tougher. In practice, were donors now to announce that henceforth they would enforce conditions, there would be a phase during which their resolve would be tested by continued non-compliance. A phase of non-compliance which triggered reductions in aid would be costly.

The third factor is that the reform agenda has largely moved on from macroeconomic policies to sectoral policies, such as civil service reform and privatisation. These policies are intrinsically more complex, both politically and administratively, and so less suited to timetabled conditions than the earlier generation of reforms.

The fourth factor is that using aid to buy policy reform has an opportunity cost in that it precludes both other uses of the resources and other styles of donor–government relationship.

2.3 IFI relations with governments: IMF relations during crisis management compared with development agency relations

Recall that one impetus for donor conditionality was the easy link with IMF crisis programmes. However, the IMF is in something of a unique position in its relationship with governments. The IMF is invited in only once a government is in a crisis, and this is usually fairly clearly at least partly of the government's own making. Immediate policy change is inevitable, and it is reasonable for the Fund to treat the government as part of the problem which needs to be overcome. Hence, money for policy change is a sensible stance. The time-consistency problem is considerably less severe in the context of financial crisis. Governments do not choose to enter financial crises, they stumble into them through incompetence, and invariably pay a high political price with or without IMF financial support. The government may at some future date again lapse into crisis, but this will reflect not the Machiavellian cunning implied by the time-consistency problem, in which a government rationally chooses to break its promise, but rather the persistence of incompetence.

The IMF is not a development finance institution, in contrast to the World Bank, the European Union, the UN and the bilateral donors. While development finance institutions must necessarily take a view on appropriate development policies, their goals are long-term and their relations with governments are not primarily concerned with crisis management. The scope of pertinent policy is much more wide-ranging. As a result, the scope for the time-consistency problem is much more severe than during fiscal crises.

A non-democratic government may quite rationally pursue policies which sacrifice both growth and poverty reduction for elite interests, and enhance resources available for the elite by reneging on promises. Faced with such a government the true implication of the time-consistency games is that outside the context of crisis there is little which aid can do to induce a government to undertake sustained policy change.

In democratic societies there are unlikely to be substantial sustained conflicts between the *objectives* of the government and the objectives of the donors because the overriding goal of donors is that governments should be responsive to their own electorates. Donors may occasionally lay claim to ethical superiority over democratic governments – for example, with respect to the treatment of minorities or the environment – but such cases are exceptional. Substantial disagreements between the two are then more likely to arise because of differences in information or ideology. In many respects governments are likely to know best because they are closer to the concerns of their citizens, and because they know their economy better than external agencies. In some respects, however, external agencies have an informational advantage. The IFIs are able to recruit better qualified staff, and these staff have access to comparative material as to what has worked elsewhere. Since neither party has an absolute overall informational advantage, while both parties have similar overall objectives, the appropriate model for donor–government relations is not that of a game played between an altruistic donor and a recalcitrant government. Rather, it is one of partnership between two agents who gain from cooperation. In such a partnership, threat–promise negotiations are quite dysfunctional since they signal that the donor either has different objectives from the government, or that the donor considers itself to have informational dominance, with nothing to learn from the government.

The appropriate stance for donors in democratic societies is thus to convince and to listen rather than to cajole. This will obviously not always be successful. There is a market place in ideas, and sometimes dysfunctional populist economic policies will gain the ear of democratic governments and of democratic societies. Donors should not, in such circumstances, lapse into the mode of offers and threats unless the economy collapses into crisis. Rather, they should improve their knowledge-dissemination and bide their time. This, of course, cannot be the approach of the IMF during the onset of a crisis, but most of the time developing countries are not in crisis.

By abandoning the notion of aid as a 'reward' for policy improvement, donors move to a model of partnership. However, with those governments which adopt really poor policies, partnerships are not beneficial. Engagement with those governments and with their societies in the battle of ideas is the means by which donors can best hope to influence policy. Where governments have reasonable policies donors need to engage both financially and through knowledge. The presumption must be that there will be continuous differences in opinion, reflecting the fact that each party has very different knowledge, with neither party having full knowledge. A relationship of trust, in the sense that each side is confident that the goals are shared, is more likely to be conducive to mutual learning. The threat–promise mode of negotiation is destructive of trust because it presupposes that the donor believes that it has difference preferences or globally superior knowledge.

I am thus suggesting that donor conditionality should, to be effective, take a very different form from IMF crisis management conditionality. In the latter, the Fund can reasonably be supposed to know better than the government and, government incompetence having been demonstrated, can reasonably coerce the government until the economy is stabilised with as little hardship to the poor as is possible. In the former, donors should condition their financial resource transfers not upon policy *change* but upon policy *levels.* Their engagement in policy debate should, however, be at its most vigorous where policy is worst, so that aid and knowledge can be sequenced.

2.4 The crisis-management role of the donors

The Fund cannot stay out of economies in crisis – that is, after all, its core rationale. By contrast, the development finance institutions should find crisis environments unattractive for financial resources intended to secure growth and poverty alleviation through growth. There are, however, two rationales for donor financing of crisis management.

First, there will sometimes be a case for emergency assistance which directly alleviates poverty by mitigating the decline in the consumption of the poor even though it does not achieve sustainable growth. This is closely analogous to humanitarian assistance in response to natural disasters.

Secondly, the success of a Fund stabilisation programme may be dependent upon larger resources than the Fund has at its disposal. This is not inevitable: beyond a certain level of resources additional money may simply reduce the need for the government to take corrective action. The appropriate aggregate level of funding at which the chances of stabilisation are maximised is a complicated judgement. Once the Fund has determined the right level of financing, if the amount is beyond its resources, it should attempt to broker assistance. Such assistance might well come from the same institutions which are involved in development financing, just as humanitarian emergency assistance will often come from aid agencies. However, just as humanitarian assistance has to be negotiated in a different mode from development assistance, so stabilisation funding may need to be treated as a distinct entity from development assistance.

2.5 The post-stabilisation role of the Fund

Until recently, the proposed different specialisations of the Bank and the Fund would have been unproblematic since Fund engagement was confined to crisis situations. However, recently, the Fund has extended its involvement to post-stabilisation environments – for example, Uganda, which came out of economic crisis in early 1992, still has an ESAF programme in 1998. The Fund can play a very useful role in such post-stabilisation environments, but it is not the same as its role in crisis management. Instead of being there to cajole a recalcitrant government, the main function of the Fund is to assess government macroeconomic policies, freely chosen and, where appropriate, reassure the domestic and international investment community that policies are sound, thus accelerating the recovery of reputation and investment. The role of the Fund thus evolves from that of coercing policy change to accreditation of policy levels.

The role of accreditation is particularly important in post-stabilisation low-income economies. Investor confidence is often at a low level. Policy reform can achieve rapid growth even with low levels of investment for a few years, but in order for growth to be maintained investment must recover. The government needs to establish a reputation as a competent economic manager, demonstrating that it has learnt its lesson from crisis. In order to establish its reputation, a government needs gradually to be given the overt power to initiate policy reform, while maintaining macro economic order. For this, it needs to be released from the coercion mode in which its good actions are seen as being the result of *force majeur*. At some point, the Fund might thus usefully signal that its role has changed from that of crisis manager to that of post-stabilisation evaluator.

Obviously, the passage from crisis management to post-stabilisation is a continuum. However, in many circumstances it is useful to convert continua into discrete phenomena even though the dividing line will be arbitrary. The advantage gained is in reducing the costs of information. For example, the European Union converted the continuum of a fiscal deficit measured as a proportion of GDP to the target of 3 per cent. This created an identifiable hurdle which could thereby be readily monitored by electorates: the target solved the coordination problem as to what level of deficit was unsatisfactory. Analogously, the Fund could usefully create a hurdle between crisis and post-stabilisation environments. The passage to post-stabilisation would signal to investors that the environment should be taken seriously, and to donors that stabilisation-mode funding should taper out, while development assistance funding should taper in.

2.6 *Tapering-in of development assistance*

Assuming that development aid should avoid crisis economies, and those economies in which government policies are so poor as to be heading for crisis, at what stage in policy reform post-crisis should donors come in?

Suppose, for the moment, that whether reforms persist is independent of aid flows. In this case the calculation for donors is simple. The Burnside and Dollar results show that there are diminishing returns to aid, as might be expected, and that for a given level of aid returns are higher the better is macroeconomic policy. A reasonable objective for the donor would be to have as high a return on aid money in terms of poverty reduction as possible, and for this the impact of the marginal dollar would need to be equated across aid-receiving countries. The level of aid relative to GDP would thus rise as the policy environment improved. Aid would thus gradually taper in with reform. Donor resources would be provided on the basis of partnership described above, and so would not be implicated in Fund conditionality. Donor resources would start to flow only when the need for Fund conditionality ceased as the economy emerged from crisis. Figure 12.1 shows the relationship between aid and

Figure 12.1 *The relationship between aid and policy for the median developing country*
Source: Collier and Dollar (1999: figure 3).

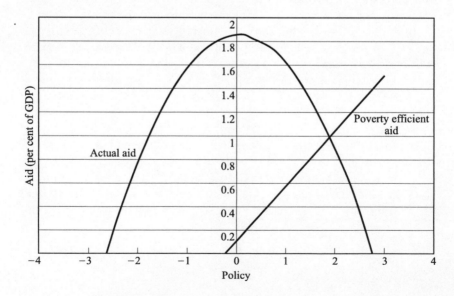

policy for the median developing country during the 1990s. The efficient 'tapering in' relationship keeps the marginal impact of aid on growth constant: hence as policy improves, more aid can be productively absorbed. The actual relationship, estimated from global aid flows, is very different. Aid typically comes in too early in the reform process to be used effectively, and is then withdrawn, or tapered out, over precisely the range of policy in which it is effective.

Now suppose that aid at the right time increases the chance that reforms will be maintained. At present there is little formal research on this question. However, an important recent discovery is that in satisfactory macroeconomic policy environments aid leads in private investment: an extra dollar of aid increases private investment by $1.90 (World Bank, 1998). A potential point of fragility in reform programmes is if growth rates decelerate as the initial direct contribution of reform to raising economic activity fades before private investment has risen sufficiently to maintain growth at this level.

In the early post-stabilisation years private investment is too low because of high risk. Once private investment has risen to levels at which rapid growth is sustainable the investment is itself liable to be sustained. In the process of investing, agents acquire further information which enables them to reassess risk. Hence, just as risk discourages investment, so investment would improve the risk ratings. The World Bank now emphasises that it has a dual function both as a provider of finance and as a provider of knowledge. In the case of newly stabilised economies it has a considerable informational advantage over private agents, and so has a rationale for using finance to raise private investment to rates which will become self-sustaining but which would otherwise not take place prior to a growth deceleration. To give orders of magnitude, in the African good policy group investment is currently only 18.2 per cent of GDP. To sustain rapid growth it needs to be increased by around 10 per cent of GDP. Public investment in Africa is similar as a share of GDP to that in other continents, so the task is to raise private investment by this amount. Using the implied coefficient from Burnside and Dollar (1997), this would require an increase in aid of around 5.3 per cent of GDP. This would be temporary, until investor confidence recovered, endogenously.

Because aid both raises growth and private investment, there are two relationships which determine its trajectory. The long-term growth relationship links growth to the share of aid in GDP, subject to diminishing returns. Because of diminishing returns, efficient use of aid would imply a fairly constant share of aid in GDP, subject only to tapering in as policy improved, and tapering out as income rose. The short-term growth relationship links investment to aid. In economies in which investment starts well below target levels for sustainable rapid growth, aid would need temporarily to be higher than long-term levels. Hence, aid would taper in much more rapidly than implied by the long-term growth relationship, being reduced back to its long-term path once investment had reached its target.

3 'Aid-dependency'

While conditionality sought to use aid transfers as the basis for a relationship which would augment growth over and above the direct effect of the resource transfer, so that conditional aid would be more valuable than an oil well, the aid-dependency argument is that the aid relationship is dysfunctional, so that aid is less valuable than an oil well, and indeed may have overall negative effects. The aid-dependency argument is partly institutional, partly microeconomic and partly macroeconomic.

At the institutional level the critique mainly focuses on project aid rather than policy lending. It is that the activities of government become swamped with the requirements of negotiating and administering donor-determined projects. Each donor has its own particular negotiating and reporting requirements, and since much bilateral aid is tied to the use of the consulting and contracting services of the donor country, even within a sector there will be a multiplicity of project designs and makes of equipment. Hence, precisely where the local civil service is in any case too weak to impose its own agenda on donors, it will acquire a portfolio of projects which is so complex that it would challenge even a strong bureaucracy (Kanbur, 1998).

At the microeconomic level, the critique focuses on the negative incentives of transfers analogous to welfare dependency at the level of the household. The argument is partly that crises force change and that aid, by averting crisis, enables poor policies to be maintained. Note that this runs counter to the rationale for conditionality, which presupposed that by being linked to policy change, aid would increase the incentives for good policies. The two opposing views can be reconciled analytically by thinking of them as income and substitution effects. The notion that necessity forces reform is that the income elasticity of demand for reform is negative: a reduction in income increases reform. Conditional aid raises income, and so its income effect is to reduce the incentive for reform, but if the conditionality is credible it also has a relative price effect which increases the payoff to reform, so that there is a substitution effect inducing policy change. Which of these two effects predominates can be settled only empirically.

A related argument is that because aid reduces tax 'effort' it weakens domestic political pressure on government. Taxation has historically been important both in achieving democratic government ('no taxation without representation') and in increasing the incentive of electorates to hold governments to account. While even the government is spending aid money, the electorate is less concerned about corruption and a failure to deliver public services.

At the macroeconomic level the argument is partly that aid appreciates the exchange rate and so implicitly taxes the export sector. Since the export sector is an important engine of growth, aid could thereby reduce growth. A further argument is that aid is volatile: donors are fickle, with aid flows interrupted for political reasons, so that an aid-dependent country is subject to more shocks, especially to government resources. Since governments are particularly bad at managing their own income volatility, aid shocks can destabilise the economy.

3.1 At what point does a country start to drown in aid?

Aid, like most other things, is subject to diminishing returns. Hence, the hypothesis of the aid-dependency arguments is not that 'aid is harmful' but rather, that 'big aid is harmful', with the implicit question hanging, 'at what point does aid switch from being useful to being harmful?' Of course, part of the aid-dependency argument is that this depends upon how aid is delivered. As Kanbur argues, aid delivered as budget support has many fewer institutional problems than aid delivered as projects. Since to date project aid has been much more important than budget support, there is considerable potential for defusing the institutional critique by changing the composition of aid, instead of reducing its overall volume.

Collier and Dollar (1999) estimate diminishing returns to aid on a panel of observations for 1970–93, introducing aid/GDP as a quadratic. They find that, while aid is indeed subject to significant diminishing returns, the point at which returns reach zero depends upon the policy environment. In poor-policy environments aid soon becomes ineffective. In good-policy environments, however, quite large amounts of aid can be productively absorbed. Typically, with good policies, a country starts to 'drown' in aid only when the share of net aid inflows to GDP exceeds around 12 per cent, which is a very high figure.

Hence, in good-policy environments 'big aid' is effective. Further, 'big aid' interacts favourably with policy improvement. A new study (World Bank, 1998) compares a country with an average amount of aid with one which has double the average. In both cases it investigates the effect of a given improvement in policy. The country with 'big aid' gets a 50 per cent larger increase in its growth rate from the policy reform than the country with average aid. Hence, on this evidence, if anything 'big aid' appears to help a government to manage change rather than distract it. Recall, however, that Burnside and Dollar (1997) find no link from aid flows to policy reform itself: aid does not induce reform, although it does increase the payoff to reform.

Thus, within the range of aid flows which is pertinent, the evidence suggests that, subject to a satisfactory policy environment, the more aid which is provided the faster will an economy grow.

3.2 Is aid-dependency like welfare-dependency?

If aid really had the sort of disincentive effects on poor countries that welfare payments have on poor households, aid should reduce growth irrespective of the policy environment. Indeed, we might expect that the better the policy environment, and so the higher the potential growth rate in the absence of aid, the more damage aid would do. However, the analogy with welfare-dependency is not just empirically questionable, it is more fundamentally mistaken.

First, the scale of aid relative to income is tiny by comparison with welfare payments. The 'poverty trap' of welfare-recipient households commonly involves households for whom welfare payments constitute a large majority of total income and who thereby face implicit marginal tax rates of 80 per cent or more. By contrast, gross aid flows to Africa peaked at around 12 per cent and implicit marginal tax rates are correspondingly radically lower. Alesina and Dollar (1998) analyse the patterns of donor aid allocation. The donors who most sharply reduce aid in response to rising incomes are the Nordic group. Their aid flows start to fall once *per capita* incomes rise above $600 and are largely eliminated once incomes rise above $1,600. However, since the loss of aid involved in this policy is only around $3 *per capita*, the marginal tax rate implied by Nordic policy is well under 1 per cent. Similarly, USAID tapers out its, historically, much larger aid budget but it does so much more gradually. The implicit tax rate imposed by USAID is less than one-half of 1 per cent. Other donors currently are less responsive to changes in income.

Hence, the aggregate marginal tax rate implied by donor reductions in aid as income rises is probably in single digits. Any disincentive effect at the aggregate level is therefore trivial. Further, incentive effects can operate only at the level of individual decision-takers, rather than the national aggregate. Suppose for the moment that, implausibly, it was indeed the case that for each extra dollar of (say) Zambian national income, aid declined by a dollar. At the aggregate level there would therefore be a 100 per cent marginal tax rate and so no incentive whatsoever to work. Nevertheless, this would not create a poverty trap for Zambians. This is because Zambians do not decide their income collectively. Each individual Zambian household, if it earned an extra dollar, would lose only its infinitesimal share (less than a millionth) of the dollar of aid which Zambia in aggregate would lose. The loss of aid would therefore take the form of negative externalities to individual household decisions. In effect, Zambians would be locked in a 'work trap': households would work even though in aggregate it made them no better off.

The one exception to the absence of an incentive effect of aid is with respect to the behaviour of governments. Directly, aid accrues to the government and so it indeed faces an incentive problem *vis-à-vis* taxation. In the absence of aid a government has to balance the political unpopularity of taxation against the political popularity of public expenditure. At the margin, a dollar of tax revenue has as many political costs as a dollar of expenditure has political benefits. The receipt of aid by the government does not change this fundamental balancing requirement of political economy, but it necessarily changes the levels of taxation and expenditure at which balance is achieved. Figure 12.2 depicts the rising political costs of taxation by the T-T schedule, and the diminishing political benefits of public expenditure along the E-E schedule. The intersection of the two schedules at E_0 is the equilibrium without aid. The with-aid equilibrium, Ea, involves both higher expenditure and lower taxation than without aid.

If the political process broadly encapsulates the economic costs and benefits of taxation and expenditure, then this response is optimal. The first inference from this is that aid will indeed induce governments to have lower taxation than without aid. In effect, the population is choosing that some of the benefits of aid accrue to households most efficiently by passing the money on to them to spend, by means of reducing taxation, while some of the benefits of aid accrue to households most efficiently through increased public expenditure. It is hard to see this as an incentive *problem* since it is the solution to a household welfare-maximising problem which is identical to that which faces the donors. *A priori*, donors have no particular reason to prefer aid to accrue directly or indirectly to

Figure 12.2 *The fiscal effects of aid*

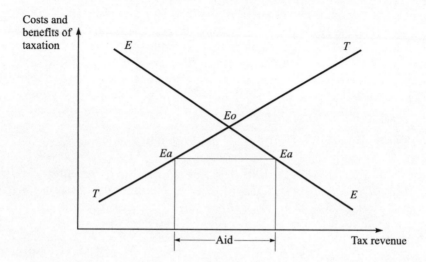

households. However, the reduction in taxation has favourable incentive effects at the household level. The marginal costs of taxation are often quite high in developing countries because there are few efficient tax handles. Hence, reduced tax effort can free households and firms from powerful disincentive effects of taxation. Thus, precisely counter to the welfare-dependency analogy, aid actually improves the incentive environment at the level of the individual agent. A simple extension of this argument is the more familiar 'debt-overhang' effect. Debt, which is simply future negative aid, discourages investment because it constitutes a future tax liability. Hence, it is increased debt rather than increased aid which gives rise to an incentive problem: the counterparts to welfare households trapped into idleness are firms trapped into disinvestment.

3.3 Is aid a source of fiscal instability?

I now turn to the macroeconomic arguments on aid dependence. The effect of aid on the appreciation of the real exchange rate, though obviously correct, does not imply anything about the net effect of aid on growth. Rather it points out one negative channel. The empirical resolution has already been discussed above: in good policy environments the net effect of aid is to raise the growth rate until very high levels of aid are reached.

The second macroeconomic effect of aid is more contentious, namely that it destabilises the budget. This is indeed the reason given by the IMF for treating aid receipts as an exceptional financing item to meet a budget deficit, rather than as a core component of non-tax receipts. The fiscal deficit is reported *excluding* aid because aid cannot be relied upon.

There are two main reasons why aid receipts might be unreliable. One is that donors may use aid to advance a political agenda driven by the political concerns of their domestic electorates. Secondly, donor procedures for disbursement may be so cumbersome that, even when funds are committed, there may be long and unpredictable lags before governments are able to utilise them. There are good grounds for both of these concerns. For example, the aid cutoff to Pakistan when it matched India's testing of nuclear weapons constitutes a major fiscal shock which could not reasonably have been anticipated in budgetary planning. Similarly, both Côte d'Ivoire and Uganda received entitlements to Stabex funds from the EU as a consequence of the fall in world coffee prices in 1989. However, Côte d'Ivoire was able to gain access to these funds in a reasonably timely fashion, whereas disbursement to Uganda was so delayed that much of the money was received during the boom in world coffee prices five years later. However, while such stories demonstrate that there is some basis for concern, similar stories could be told about the unreliability of tax revenues. African governments are highly dependent upon trade taxes for their revenue, typically accounting for half of overall receipts. Yet trade taxes are dependent upon the capacity of the economy to export and import. African exports are highly concentrated in a narrow range of commodities the prices of which are volatile. Hence, exports are much more volatile than GDP as a whole. The capacity to import is dependent partly upon exports, and partly upon aid. Hence, *a priori*, it is not clear that aid would be significantly less reliable than government revenue.

Even if aid is less reliable than government revenue, it might nevertheless reduce the overall unreliability of the resource flow to the government if it moves inversely with revenue. That is, as with any portfolio, an important consideration is not just the variance of each component, but whether the risks are co-variant. Hence, in measuring the reliability of aid both its variance and its covariance must be taken into account.

I measure the relative reliability of aid and government revenue for 36 African countries which are IDA recipients over the period 1970–95. I standardise by measuring both aid and revenue year-by-year in 1995 US$

per capita. The weighted average for these countries over the period was that aid amounted to $72.4 while government revenue was $279.7.

In assessing the reliability of aid and revenue we need some measure of unpredictability. In principle, unpredictability is very different from variability: for example, if either aid or revenue has a regular cycle it could be highly variable yet highly predictable. One approach would therefore be to model both aid and revenue as time series, determining how well they could be predicted econometrically, and taking the regression errors as the measure of 'unreliability'. However, this is not the approach followed here. In practice, both governments and the IFI teams that assist them do not make such predictions, often for the good reason that the results would lack robustness. Hence, I rely upon a much more straightforward measure of unpredictability namely, variance. The measure of variance which scales for the mean level of receipts is the coefficient of variation (standard deviation/mean). I thus calculate the coefficient of variation of aid receipts and revenue both for each country and for the weighted average of all 36 countries. The results are reported in table 12.1. The final column of the table reports the normalised covariance of aid and revenue (covariance/the product of the means).

The results are, of course, country-specific. However, in assessing the future riskiness of aid policy-makers may well regard the information from the entire group of African countries a better guide than the historical experience of just their own country. After all, the move from a single country to the full sample represents the move from 25 observations to 900. The best guide to the full sample is the weighted average.

The coefficient of variation of aid is lower than that of revenue. Aid is *more* reliable than revenue, not *less* reliable as the aid-dependency school believes. Secondly, the normalised covariance of aid and revenue is *negative* (although not significantly different from zero). This implies that there is a further benefit from aid: it acts as a buffer to revenue shocks – if anything, tending to increase when revenue is low. More importantly, being essentially uncorrelated with revenue, dependence upon aid provides benefits of diversification and so is stabilising. Hence, on the aggregate evidence, a budget with a large component of aid would be more reliable than one with a small component of aid, because the aid component is more certain than revenue, because it tends to offset revenue shocks, and primarily because government funding is more diversified.

In some countries the contribution of aid to the overall stability of government resources is striking. For example, in Uganda the coefficient of variation of aid is only one-tenth that of revenue. In such a case, if reliability was the criterion for inclusion in the budget the fiscal deficit

Table 12.1 *The coefficient of variation of revenue and aid in 36 African countries, 1970–1995*

Country	Aid ($ per capita)		Revenue ($ per capita)		Covariance/ Product of means
	Mean	Coeff. of variation	Mean	Coeff. of variation	Aid with revenue
Burundi	42.7	0.29	39.8	0.27	0.0156
Benin	44.7	0.18	86.1	0.08	0.0101
Burkina Faso	44.6	0.22	36.4	0.21	0.0330
Botswana	150.7	0.31	853.1	0.64	−0.0729
Cameroon	47.0	0.29	198.2	0.34	−0.0515
Congo	82.9	0.33	324.9	0.65	0.1173
Comoros	167.6	0.05	69.5	0.18	−0.0024
Ethiopia	18.7	0.32	33.3	0.31	−0.0279
Gabon	169.9	0.30	2493.1	0.39	−0.0258
Ghana	35.2	0.51	65.8	0.37	−0.0124
Guinea	77.0	0.12	80.6	0.10	−0.0080
Gambia	104.2	0.44	86.4	0.34	0.0288
Guinea-Bissau	123.6	0.23	0.4	0.20	0.0159
Kenya	39.3	0.34	105.4	0.29	0.0083
Liberia	67.3	0.35	175.5	0.23	0.0028
Lesotho	76.7	0.26	121.1	0.39	0.0624
Madagascar	37.2	0.28	66.5	0.85	−0.0417
Mali	60.1	0.21	42.3	0.21	0.0102
Mauritania	265.9	0.34	193.7	0.08	0.0199
Mauritius	79.1	0.20	170.1	0.33	0.0040
Malawi	39.8	0.39	50.6	0.17	0.0214
Niger	65.1	0.23	88.8	0.28	0.0121
Nigeria	2.6	0.65	216.6	0.51	0.0333
Rwanda	48.2	0.22	39.4	0.30	0.0294
Sudan	43.1	0.52	107.4	0.20	0.0199
Senegal	75.9	0.31	152.0	0.24	0.0290
Somalia	50.2	0.43	38.9	0.23	−0.0314
Swaziland	103.2	0.38	358.2	0.33	0.0806
Seychelles	399.3	0.30	2718.7	0.27	−0.0562
Chad	49.2	0.21	28.3	0.40	−0.0370
Togo	67.7	0.30	158.2	0.34	0.0231
Tanzania	46.0	0.46	74.7	0.20	0.0465
Uganda	18.0	0.07	19.3	0.70	0.0011
Zaire	19.9	0.38	53.5	0.68	0.1249
Zambia	82.5	0.57	206.4	0.69	−0.2150
Zimbabwe	37.2	0.59	273.1	0.25	−0.0390
Weighted average	**72.4**	**0.35**	**279.7**	**0.37**	**−0.0007**

should be reported excluding revenue, rather than excluding aid. More generally, this particular proposition of aid-dependency has little empirical basis.

4 The aid relationship as an instrument for regional coordination

Aid has some potential to increase the incentives for governments to coordinate their behaviour. This is at its most important in regions which are Balkanised into many small states. The region most characterised by this is Sub-Saharan Africa, where a population less than half that of India is divided up into more than 40 countries. This has two important consequences.

First, the average economic size of a country is very small. As a result there are potentially large-scale economies from market integration with neighbours. Similarly, some government projects are subject to problems of small scale, and so would gain from being amalgamated at the regional level.

Secondly, the average geographic size of a country is small. One consequence is that an unusually high proportion of a country's population is proximate to neighbouring countries, so that both populations and diseases can readily move across borders. A crisis in one country becomes a refugee problem in its neighbour, and an epidemic in one country becomes an epidemic in its neighbour. A second consequence is that many countries are landlocked. As a result the provision of the transport infrastructure on which the country depends for its link to the sea is determined by its coastal neighbour, which also has the power to interrupt transport links for political reasons (for example, in 1977 Kenya cut off oil supplies to Uganda).

These two considerations of small economic size and small geographic size suggest that there would be atypically high returns from regional cooperation. Presumably because of this insight, African governments have a long history of attempts at such cooperation, mainly for trade, on which there are around 30 agreements, but also for transport such as East African Railways and East African Airlines, and for currency, notably the Franc Zone. However, few of these attempts have yielded sustained success. Partly, this is because regional trade agreements have encountered the problem that, in the presence of high external trade barriers, preferential agreements produce powerful transfers, with the less industrialised countries subsidising the industries of the more industrialised. Partly, it is because, given this history of failed cooperation in trade agreements, the same expectations carry over into other areas where cooperation would be more fruitful. In effect, African governments are in a 'low-trust' equilibrium in their relations with each other, expecting that agreements will be broken, and so having little incentive not to break them or to free-ride. Partly, it is because (until the emergence of South Africa) Africa has lacked any obvious countries which know that they are too important to free-ride, and therefore take on a leadership role.

There are several ways out from such a lack of cooperation. One is for a lead country within the continent to act as the catalyst and coordinator. In Southern Africa this role is now being played by South Africa, and possibly a democratic Nigeria may assume such a role in West Africa. A second approach is to reduce coordination problems by reducing the number of cooperators: bilateral cooperation is usually easier than cooperation among large groups. However, in some of the important areas for cooperation, notably relations between landlocked countries and their coastal neighbour, bilateral bargaining leaves the negotiating range too wide. The landlocked country has an interest in the coastal government providing a good road. At one extreme, the landlocked economy simply free-rides on the transport investment of the coastal economy. At the other extreme the coastal economy extracts from the landlocked economy the full economic rent associated with international trade, levying road tolls at the revenue-maximising rate. In between, the coastal economy may under-invest in the road, while the landlocked economy may be unwilling to finance the road because it faces its own time-consistency problem: once the road has been financed by the landlocked economy, the coastal economy may still extract the full rent for using it.

This gives a potential dual role for the international development agencies as catalysts of cooperation and as enhancing the incentives for cooperation. The agencies can provide the leadership role which is missing when several similar countries face a free-rider problem. They can also increase the incentives for cooperation by providing aid financing for regional endeavours. For example, donor agencies could finance coastal road links conditional upon certain rules of operation of the road, protecting both the landlocked and the coastal economy from a time-consistency problem. Such a use of aid would depend in part upon it having an effective enforcement effect. This is to an extent analogous to policy conditionality where aid has evidently failed to have such an effect. However, conditionality to enforce regional agreements would be on firmer ground. It would have greater moral authority, which could be sanctioned by international consortia of developing countries such as the

UN or the OAU. It would focus on a narrow and precisely monitorable aspect of behaviour.

5 Conclusion

In this chapter I have considered three aspects of the aid relationship: conditionality, aid-dependence and inter-government coordination. The first of these has been the predominant relationship of the past decade, while the second has been the predominant criticism. I have argued for a new basis to the aid relationship. Outside the context of crisis, the relationship between governments and aid providers is more productively viewed as a partnership than as a principal–agent problem. I have shown that a partnership between a government with satisfactory policies and 'big' aid providers would significantly raise growth, and so would not be subject to the dependency critique. I have suggested that there is also a role for aid as the catalyst and enforcer of regional cooperation.

I have attempted to draw a distinction between crisis lending and development assistance. To date, the mode of using aid directly to increase the incentive for policy change, which is appropriate for crisis management, has also been adopted for development assistance. This may well be because the development assistance agencies got into policy-based lending at a time of crisis in the early 1980s. The development assistance agencies came in on Fund stabilisation programmes, but added a development policy agenda. Hence, conditionality spread across a wide array of policies which have little bearing on crisis management. Not only were development assistance institutions functioning in the same mode as the crisis management institution, but also the mode continued post-crisis. As argued by the external evaluation of Fund operations in low income countries, (IMF, 1998) the Fund evolved into a quasi-development assistance agency. It negotiated development policy in post-stabilisation environments across a range outside its traditional area of expertise, but in its traditional mode of relations with governments. Its power in such an environment derived not from its own lending, which was typically only a small proportion of international public transfers, but from the cross-conditionality clauses which the World Bank and the other development assistance agencies kept in their own agreements with the government. Without Fund approval, there would be no aid.

The mentality of crisis management has contaminated the much wider process of development assistance in two respects. First, it has contaminated the *relationship*: as a result, development assistance agencies have been drawn into the attempt to use their resources as an incentive for policy change. Outside the context of crisis it has proved largely ineffective in achieving generalised policy reform, and it precludes the trust-based partnership which would be more appropriate for development assistance agencies. Secondly, it has contaminated the *resource flows*. The financing of crises is quite properly temporary: stabilisation finance should indeed taper out as stabilisation succeeds. By contrast, development assistance should, to be efficient in reducing poverty on a sustainable basis, taper in as stabilisation succeeds. To date, as demonstrated in figure 12.1, donor flows have followed the short trajectory appropriate for crises, rather than the path appropriate for growth and development.

In the post-stabilisation environments which will increasingly be the norm in the developing world, the range of potential policy change is necessarily wide and the mode of relationship is more effective if it is based on partnership rather than coercion. The World Bank has reassessed its role in the development process and has determined a new departure, termed the 'Comprehensive Development Framework' or CDF (World Bank, 1999). The CDF is a major attempt to change lending practices to come to terms with these realities and its approach will be piloted in a sample of countries during 1999. It provides for a comprehensive review of the development challenges facing a society, and so explicitly accepts that the range of potential policy change is extremely wide. However, its main innovation is its emphasis upon partnership, both between donors and the government, and between the government and civil society. The CDF is thus a clear departure from the narrow and coercive conditionality appropriate for crisis management and re-establishes the distinctive role of the Bank as a development agency.

NOTES

The findings, interpretations and conclusions expressed in this chapter are entirely those of the authors. They do not necessarily represent the views of the World Bank, its Executive Directors or the countries they represent.

1 See Collier (1997).
2 Although the first principal component is close to a weighted average, this does not necessarily imply that this average is necessarily the best policy measure in explaining growth. In Collier and Dollar (1999) we also use a simple average of the 10 policy measures which are each individually significant in the growth process. However, the correlation between this measure and the simple average of the 20 policies is 0.97.

REFERENCES

Adam, C. and S. O'Connell (1997). 'Aid, Taxation and Development: Analytical Perspectives on Aid Effectiveness in Sub-Saharan Africa', Centre for the Study of African Economies, University of Oxford, mimeo

Alesina, A. and D. Dollar (1998). 'Who Gives Aid to Whom and Why?', Washington, DC: World Bank, mimeo

Burnside, C. and D. Dollar (1997). 'Aid, Policies and Growth', *Policy Research Working Paper*, 1777, Washington, DC: World Bank

Coate, S. and S. Morris (1996). 'Policy Conditionality', Department of Economics, University of Pennsylvania, mimeo

Collier, P. (1997). 'The Failure of Conditionality', in C. Gwin and J.M. Nelson (eds.), *Perspectives on Aid and Development*, Washington, DC: Overseas Development Council

Collier, P. and D. Dollar (1999). 'Aid Allocation and Poverty Reduction', *Policy Research Working Paper*, 2041, Washington, DC: World Bank

Collier, P. and C. Pattillo (1999). *Investment and Risk in Africa*, London: Macmillan

International Monetary Fund (1998). *External Evaluation of the ESAF: Report by a Group of Independent Experts*, Washington, DC: IMF

Kanbur, R. (1998). 'Aid, Conditionality and Debt in Africa', Cornell University, mimeo

Svensson, J. (1998). 'Aid Tournaments', Development Research Group, Washington, DC: World Bank, mimeo

World Bank (1998). Assessing Aid: What Works, What Doesn't and Why', *Policy Research Report*, Development Research Group, Washington, DC: World Bank

(1999). 'A Proposal for a Comprehensive Development Framework', Discussion Draft < http://www.worldbank.org/cdf >

Index